W9-DEE-472

Environmental Politics in Canada

Managing the Commons into the Twenty-First Century

JUDITH I. MCKENZIE

OXFORD
UNIVERSITY PRESS

HE
790
.C2
M45
2002

OXFORD

UNIVERSITY PRESS

70 Wynford Drive, Don Mills, Ontario M3C 1J9
www.oup/ca

Oxford University Press is a department of the University of Oxford.
It furthers the University's objective of excellence in research, scholarship,
and education by publishing worldwide in

Oxford   New York

Athens   Auckland   Bangkok   Bogotá   Buenos Aires   Cape Town
Chennai   Dar es Salaam   Delhi   Florence   Hong Kong   Istanbul   Karachi
Kolkata   Kuala Lumpur   Madrid   Melbourne   Mexico City   Mumbai   Nairobi
Paris   São Paulo   Shanghai   Singapore   Taipei   Tokyo   Toronto   Warsaw

with associated companies in Berlin   Ibadan

Oxford is a trade mark of Oxford University Press
in the UK and in certain other countries

Published in Canada by Oxford University Press

Copyright © Oxford University Press Canada 2002

The moral rights of the author have been asserted

Database right Oxford University Press (maker)

First published 2002

All rights reserved. No part of this publication may be reproduced,
stored in a retrieval system, or transmitted, in any form or by any means,
without the prior permission in writing of Oxford University Press,
or as expressly permitted by law, or under terms agreed with the appropriate
reprographics rights organization. Enquiries concerning reproduction
outside the scope of the above should be sent to the Rights Department,
Oxford University Press, at the address above.

You must not circulate this book in any other binding or cover
and you must impose this same condition on any acquirer.

National Library of Canada Cataloguing in Publication Data

McKenzie, Judith, 1951–
Environmental politics in Canada : managing the commons
into the twenty-first century

Includes index.
ISBN 0-19-541508-6

1. Environmental policy – Canada. I. Title.

GE190.C3M38 2001   333.70971   C2001-902289-1

1 2 3 4 – 05 04 03 02

Cover design by Joan Dempsey

This book is printed on permanent (acid-free) paper ∞.

Printed in Canada

4778659

Contents

List of Tables, Figures, and Boxes

Tables

Figures

Boxes

Preface

Between the mid-1980s and the early 1990s, a number of ambitious environmental initiatives were introduced by the federal government; they included the Canadian Environmental Protection Act, the Canadian Environmental Assessment Act, and the Green Plan. In addition, there was an expansion of policy capacity at both levels of government that was largely supported by the public's interest in environmental issues. By 1993, however, environmental issues seemed to have fallen off the agendas of the federal and provincial governments alike in this country. Moreover, in three subsequent federal election campaigns (1993, 1997, and 2000) and numerous provincial campaigns, environmental issues were generally not considered by the electorate to be issues of much consequence. Indeed, since the mid-1990s, most non-economic issues have been marginalized by government preoccupation with fiscal deficits, tax relief, job creation, productivity, and the quest to expand markets. For the most part, environmental issues have lain dormant in the shadow cast by continued government inaction and public apathy. In the past, this indifference has characterized attitudes about the environment until an accident, tragedy, or catastrophic event rekindled public interest and provoked a government response. The residents of Walkerton, Ontario were made all too aware of this in May 2000, when seven people lost their lives and hundreds of others became seriously ill by the *E. coli* bacterium that had contaminated the town's water. This event has reignited interest in the environment and has raised serious questions about the responsibility of citizens, governments, corporations, and environmental non-governmental organizations (ENGOs) to ensure that our shared resources are managed properly. Although the exact causes of the Walkerton tragedy will not be known for months or even years, pointed questions have been asked about the status of water as a public good and the responsibility of governments to ensure that safe drinking water is available to everyone. Rather than the scarcity of a resource—which has long been the focus of government policy makers—Walkerton clearly raised another important side of the environmental problem—the management and sustainability of our resources. In the days following Walkerton, attention became focused on the continued de-staffing of government environmental agencies, ineffectual enforcement, the weakening of environmental regulations, privatization of water testing, and the roles that these played in this tragedy. In a broader sense, the Walkerton story made many Canadians realize that we all may be vulnerable to similar environmental catastrophes.

Another event that took place in the summer of 2000 revolved around the issue of Aboriginal rights to fish in areas where quotas have been imposed by the

Department of Fisheries and Oceans. As a result of a Supreme Court decision in September 1999 (the Marshall decision), which was qualified in November of the same year, there is an intense dispute about whether Aboriginal rights to fish supersede federal regulations relating to acceptable catches. The situation has become violent in some places, including Burnt Church, New Brunswick, and that has complicated the search for a compromise. Moreover, it has fuelled a dispute between Native and non-Native fishers that has divided communities along racial and ethnic lines. A third critical issue that has captured the attention of Canadians relates to the warning, issued by the Intergovernmental Panel on Climate Change in January 2001, that climate change will be more radical than originally thought and, if unstopped, could be as catastrophic as the last Ice Age.

This book will not revolve around the themes of doom and gloom that surround the state of the environment in Canada or about the growing frustration and disillusionment among environmental activists in this country. Moreover, it recognizes that the environmental problems of the past continue to exist and that new ones will present themselves. In this sense, any book about the environment will be immediately outdated. What this book does attempt to do is provide an analytical framework within which environmental issues of the past, present, and future may be studied. It is not concerned primarily with government, nor does it take a strong institutional approach. Rather, the book takes a much broader perspective on the factors that influence the way the environment and natural resources are viewed and managed. The issues examined range from our domestic fisheries, mining, and forest industries to health issues related to the air we breathe, the water we drink, and the food we eat. Although scarcity of a resource has been experienced mainly by the fisheries on both coasts, effective management of our shared resources has been an increasingly important objective of governments, industry groups, and interest groups in other environmental areas.

For an environmentalist, it is difficult not to despair of government ambivalence and corporate arrogance towards our most important resources—our air, water, nature, wildlife, and the health of present and future generations. This book will examine the reasons *why* governments have become reluctant to legislate in the environmental area. *Why* have some groups and individuals been listened to at the expense of others? *Why* is the environment as a criterion for economic growth and development seemingly last on the list? And *why* do governments believe that the environmental health and welfare of its citizens, both human and non-human, come second to fighting the deficit, creating jobs, cutting taxes, and raising productivity? This book will try to answer these questions in a straightforward and balanced manner, albeit from an environmentalist's point of view.

This book is a compilation of the themes and approaches that I have used in attempting to make environmental politics an informative and relevant area of study for my students over the past five years. Although environmental issues will change in the future, the ways in which we study and understand them will not. Those who know me and have studied with me are well aware of both my passion for, and admiration of, the work and life of Rachel Carson and will not be surprised that this book is dedicated to her memory. To me, she is the quintessential symbol of the power and influence that one voice can have. Single-handedly, Rachel Carson took on a powerful and influential multinational chemical industry and forced the world to question things as they were.

I would like to thank Laura Macleod and Phyllis Wilson of Oxford University Press for their commitment to this project and their guidance in moving it towards completion. In addition, I owe a large debt to the three anonymous reviewers of this manuscript whose suggestions and constructive criticism improved the quality of this book. My thanks also go to Freya Godard for her thorough and sympathetic editing of the manuscript. Of course, all errors of fact and judgement remain mine alone.

Introduction: Managing the Commons into the Twenty-First Century

In 1968, Garrett Hardin wrote a thought-provoking article entitled 'The Tragedy of the Commons' that was published in the journal *Science*. He used the example of a common rangeland on which a number of herdsmen grazed their livestock as a metaphor for the world's natural resources. There will always be a tendency, according to Hardin, for a herdsman to add an extra animal to his herd in order to increase his profit. The other herdsmen follow suit. What results is the tragedy of the commons:

> Each man is locked into a system that compels him to increase his herd without limit—in a world that is limited. Ruin is the destination toward which all men rush, each pursuing his own best interest in a society that believes in the freedom of the commons. Freedom in the commons brings ruin to all.[1]

In the three decades since his article was published, Hardin's metaphor has become the most widely accepted explanation of what happens to resources when they are overexploited. The main idea was that resources held in common, including oceans, wilderness areas, and air, were subject to massive degradation because of overconsumption caused by individual greed. His conclusion about the commons has been accorded by some the status of scientific law.[2]

Hardin's use of the term 'commons' provoked a heated debate on a number of fronts. First, because he failed to define the term 'commons', there were some who believed that Hardin was advocating state ownership of property and limited access to it. Not only was state control unnecessary in areas with low population densities, it was argued, but the lack of local control by communities over their forests and arable land would likely lead to corruption and policies that would render the resource unsustainable.[3] State control of property was viewed as a clear threat to private property rights and an assault on liberal democracy. A second contentious point was the pessimistic tone of the article, in which the destruction seemed to be the inevitable result of capitalism run amok. Hardin painted a bleak and cynical vision: a war of all against all, where each person follows his or her own self-interest down the road to social and environmental chaos. In many respects, his work was viewed as an indictment of humankind whose short-sightedness and profit-taking superseded a long-term vision of communal sharing and reduced consumption. His pessimism about people's ability to work and live together co-operatively and in harmony with one another had a similar tone to Thomas Hobbes's *Leviathan*. Given the variety and diversity of his detractors, it is hard to believe that Hardin's ideas have been so influential.

At the time it was published, 'The Tragedy of the Commons' was criticized for its superficial approach to such diverse themes as overpopulation, natural resources, and human behaviour. As a biologist, Hardin was not particularly interested in the politics or economics underlying these themes. Rather, his principal concern was the world's physical capacity to absorb ever increasing numbers of people. In addressing this issue, he prescribed a number of controversial measures, including population control that was to be imposed on poorer countries. A more controversial 'solution' called for a moratorium on foreign aid to the developing world. In this sense, many of his remedies had an eerie Malthusian ring to them, not to mention racist overtones. Many in the American Left portrayed his work as a manifesto authorizing the developed world to continue exploiting and oppressing undeveloped and developing nations. They dismissed the article as a fascist, authoritarian 'rant' that trampled on the rights and freedoms of the less prosperous. Moreover, Hardin's position that the problems of our diminishing natural resources had no technical solution provoked the wrath of liberals and other 'cornucopians' who saw the potential of new technologies as unlimited.

In the ecology movement, some hailed his article as a visionary warning of the impending dangers of greed, unbridled capitalism and excessive consumption in the industrialized world, but others believed that the inevitable tragedy that Hardin foresaw was not only overly pessimistic but premised on a false myth. Although there is a widely held impression that the tragedy that Hardin described was a regular occurrence on the common lands and villages in medieval and post-medieval England, the truth of the matter is that it was not.[4] Indeed, for hundreds of years, the commons were managed successfully. Rather than being destroyed by greed, the system of the commons failed to survive 'the industrial revolution, agrarian reform, and transfigured farming practices'.[5] This historical inaccuracy is important because it fails to recognize that 'commoning' was a successful practice for many years. Because of this, it is important to 'search for the ideas and practices which led to successful commoning for centuries and to try to find lessons and applications for our own time.'[6] Elinor Ostrom, among others, has extensively studied shared open-access areas—what she refers to as 'common pool resources' (CPRs). CPRs have two important characteristics—excludability (or controlled access) and subtractability (or rivalry). It is very difficult to control access to many resources because of cost and the migratory nature of many of them, such as fish, wildlife, and groundwater. As for subtractability, the level of exploitation by one user adversely affects the ability of another user to exploit the resource.[7] Despite these characteristics, there are numerous examples of successful CPRs today, and that, Ostrom argues, is reason to believe that 'tragedy' is not an inevitable outcome. More important, she considers that the pursuit of one solution for all commons problems is short-sighted and that easily designed and optimal institutional solutions will remain elusive—through not impossible. Indeed, Ostrom is far more optimistic than Hardin about the potential of individuals to be rational:

Instead of presuming that the individuals sharing a commons are inevitably caught in a trap from which they cannot escape, I argue that the capacity of individuals to extricate themselves from various types of dilemma situations *varies* from situation to situation. . . . Why have some efforts to solve commons problems failed, while others have succeeded? What can we learn from experience that will help to stimulate the development and use of a better theory of collective action—one that will identify the key variables that can enhance or detract from the capabilities of individuals to solve problems?[8]

There are also other theorists who question Hardin's assumptions about the irrationality of human behaviour in the commons. As evidence, they claim that if his thesis about human behaviour were valid, the human race would have died out centuries ago. According to a British livestock expert, 'rational men do not pursue collective doom, they organize to avoid it.'[9] Similarly, Paul Harrison has argued that 'the tragedy of the commons arises [only] when institutions of ownership or control fail to move in step with the prevailing level of population density.'[10]

Other criticisms, including those by David Feeny and his collaborators, were directed at Hardin's methodological approach to the question. In their view, his model was incomplete because it was based on a number of assumptions that did not exist in the real world. For example, in Hardin's metaphor, access to the commons was open and the herdsmen appeared to be incapable of altering the rules. These critics claimed that after a few years of declining productivity, the herdsmen would probably get together to '(1) control access to the pasture, and (2) agree upon a set of rules of conduct, perhaps including stinting, that effectively limits exploitation.'[11]

Hardin's article prompted considerable debate at the time: in the ensuing years, however, his concerns about the management of the commons have acquired a new currency and been given new meanings. It is the premise of this book that Hardin's passionate conviction that 'something had to be done' has been largely misunderstood by those who have interpreted his thesis through the lenses of liberal democracy, individual behaviour, market economics, and property ownership. When it is viewed from the environmental perspective, other meanings have emerged. The interpretation of the term 'commons' that will be used in this book pertains to natural resources, including collective and communal ownership, private ownership, or public ownership. Moreover, access to the commons may be open or limited. This book recognizes that the effective management of these resources has no one solution and may take the form of government regulation, voluntary regulation, or communal regulation. Where appropriate, the book will highlight some successes and failures of various environmental groups, management regimes, and other policy instruments, including regulations, new institutions and agencies, and laws, among others. The 'commons' then, as it is used in this book, will be an inclusive term that refers to Canada's natural resources. It will examine how these have been managed in the past and suggest how they might be managed better in order to sustain them for the betterment of all humans and non-humans now and in the future.

In Canada, our natural resources have always been an important part of our history, our economy, and our national identity. Historians have shown that Canada's abundant natural resources—our forests, fish and wildlife, vast mineral wealth, and rich, fertile soil—were the reasons for colonization by the French and British. Until recently, Canada's economy continued to be based largely on the cultivation and sale of these resources. Over time, our economic base has become more industrialized and diversified; however, many Canadians continue to rely, both directly and indirectly, on resource-based industries for their livelihoods.

In the last two decades of the twentieth century, it became clear that the endless abundance of many of these resources is no longer certain. The cod and other groundfish have all but disappeared from the east coast. The salmon stocks off the west coast have declined at alarming rates. Temperate forests are disappearing everywhere across the land. The growing scarcity of certain resources and the policies and other factors that have contributed to the crisis will be one of the main themes of this book, as will the efforts made by governments, industries, and environmental groups to counteract these scarcity problems. Scarcity, however, is only one part of the environmental problem in Canada. The other important side of this issue is the effective and sustainable management of our resources. Environmental questions related to agriculture, for example, highlight the more complex side of the environmental imperative. While many of Canada's agricultural commodities are in great demand on world markets and will be for the foreseeable future, new challenges have emerged in terms of their management. Over and above the abandonment of farms, low commodity prices, and the difficulties confronting traditional family farms, there are a series of trends in the agriculture sector that have profound implications for the environment. While the debate in the agricultural sector over the use of chemicals and pesticides continues, a new debate has emerged over the use of biotechnology in our agricultural industry. Over the past two years, consumers and groups representing their interests have expressed concern over the environmental and health implications of these technologies. Furthermore, questions have been raised about both the desirability of industrial or factory farms and the management of animal wastes emanating from them. Therefore, the environmental problem in this country goes far beyond the issue of scarcity. It must necessarily include a closer look at *how* our resources are managed.

Over and above the loss and degradation of our natural resources, there are other reasons for considering the manner in which we treat our environment. The renowned biologist Rachel Carson, a victim of breast cancer herself, issued a warning in her insightful book *Silent Spring* about our obligation, as citizens, to ask questions and to take responsibility for ensuring that we pass on a safe, healthy, and natural world to succeeding generations. A number of studies by epidemiologists and other scientists have demonstrated environmental links to various forms of cancer as well as a host of respiratory illnesses and congenital birth defects. In addition, certain multilateral trade agreements have raised questions about differing standards related to the foods we import, the products we make, and the wastes we discharge. As was evident in the protests of the meetings of the World Trade Organization in December 1999 in Seattle, public attention is being drawn to the implications of international trade agreements both for the environment and for human rights.

On the international-security front, experts have predicted that acute conflicts may ensue over food and water, which Canadians assume will be everlasting. What is Canada, as a country of plenty, prepared to do to avert these new threats to international peace and security? The management, use, and sustainability of the commons in Canada cannot be studied in a vacuum. While there is much that governments in this country can do to preserve our natural resources, the international dimension to environmental problems cannot be overlooked.

This book is organized as follows

Chapter One examines the evolution of environmental thought through the lenses of the liberal democratic tradition in North America, particularly the ways that nature has been viewed in political theory. Although musings about nature can be traced as far back as Plato and Aristotle, this theoretical discussion will begin with the ideas of John Locke. Departing somewhat from the Lockean tradition, transcendentalist thinkers, including Henry David Thoreau and Ralph Waldo Emerson, saw nature in a more spiritual way, and they influenced a new generation about the intrinsic value of nature in and of itself. The discussion of the classical period concludes with a visit to Thomas Malthus's writing—a largely fearful account of the incapacity of the earth to sustain itself with continued—or what he termed exponential—population growth. The three themes captured by classical theorists—man in nature, the value of nature, and sustainability—continue to be the primary focus of contemporary writers in the field of environmental thought. The works and contributions of modern-day environmental thinkers, including Paul and Anne Ehrlich, the Club of Rome, Barry Commoner, James Lovelock, Donella and Dennis Meadows et al., and Arne Naess will be briefly examined in relation to these three themes.

There is little question that a 'green' world may involve limitations on individual liberties, may threaten a number of the elements of a free-market economy, and may require national or supra-national governments to act as environmental policemen. Such measures may have an authoritarian cast to them which challenges a number of the fundamental tenets of liberal democracies. Although many of the central ideas of green political thought borrow from social democracy, liberalism, and conservatism, they have also been influenced by Marxism, feminism, and utopianism, among others. These influences will be briefly touched on in Chapter One, as will the influence of the Aboriginal view of nature and the land, and religions outside the Judeo-Christian tradition.

Chapter Two examines the environmental movement in North America and Canada, in particular, as a social movement. There have been two distinct waves of environmentalism largely spearheaded by environmental issues or accidents and guided by classic written works. For the second wave, the publication and popularity of Rachel Carson's *Silent Spring* was a defining moment, as was the first Earth Day, which took place on 22 April 1970. Some greens and groups that work on their behalf have been mobilized by a profound change in values and the development of a green consciousness. From this perspective, environmentalism is best understood as a social movement associated with the rise in post-materialist values. As part of this analysis, this section of the book will investigate how the attitudes of Canadians towards the environment have changed. These attitudes have been measured, in an on-going way, through public opinion surveys and, since 1974, in National Election Studies. Chapter 2 also examines the environmental lobby in Canada and describes the myriad groups and organizations that advocate for environmental causes. This chapter presents the view that there are five broad categories of green organizations—Canadian ENGOs, international green groups, local and grass roots organizations, advisory green groups, and green political parties. A brief case study of one organization (and in some cases two) in each of these groups is undertaken in order to illustrate certain variables, including organization, financing, tactics, and strategies.

Chapter Three examines both the federal and provincial roles in environmental policy and regulation and presents an overview of three distinctive eras and the various policy instruments that were used in them. This chapter concludes with a brief case study of the Species at Risk Act, which like its predecessor, the Endangered Species Act, died on the order paper when the Chrétien government called a federal election in the fall of 2000.

Chapter Four provides an overview of the state of Canada's renewable and non-renewable natural resources, including the east and west coast fisheries, the forest industry, agricultural land, minerals, and water resources. Historically, Canadian natural resources have been viewed as staples of a resource-based economy; however, more recently these resources have been viewed through the lenses of scarce commodities and sustainability. Current problems and issues as well as public policies will be examined in this section.

Chapter Five discusses two emerging imperatives that have contributed to the growing importance of the environment—the health imperative, and domestic and international security. Recently, a number of studies have pointed to a strong correlation between toxins in the environment and cancer. Other illnesses and alarming increases in respiratory disorders, such as asthma, have also been linked to environmental agents. Congenital birth defects similar to those discovered in children living in the Love Canal area have raised questions about the long-lasting effects of environmental toxins. This chapter will discuss international agreements such as the Montreal and Kyoto Protocols and the UN Framework Convention on Climate Change and Canadian responses to them for a variety of environmental issues including acid rain, persistent organic pollutants, pesticides, ozone-depleting substances, climate change, and municipal solid waste management. Water pollution is treated briefly, but the limitations of space and time have not permitted an examination of pollution in Canada's North.

Chapter Six examines Canada's role as a participant in the movement towards international initiatives on issues such as ocean pollution and biodiversity. The functions performed by a variety of international organizations are summarized and Canada's participation in them is identified. In addition, the relationship between multilateral trade agreements and the environment will be discussed. As part of this discussion, the chapter examines GATT, the World Trade Organization, and the North American Free Trade Agreement in terms of how trade-related decisions have affected the environment.

The Epilogue will return to Hardin's metaphor relating to the future of the commons. Is Canada on the right track in moving towards the sustainability of the commons and the prudent management of our natural resources?

Chapter One

Green Political Theory

At the core of the environment-democracy debate lies the question of whether they can co-exist. The two passages below illustrate the divergent points of view on this question.

> To continue to support liberal democratic values and institutions is to undercut the positive understanding of citizenship necessary to address the global ecological crisis. But to reject liberal democracy is to cut ourselves off from the most successful democratic tradition in the world today, and its precious inheritance of human rights, reason, and government under law.[1]
>
> *J. Ronald Engel*

> By failing to understand the inverse relationship between population size and the quantity of democracy, some societies may be pushed into totalitarianism. Other societies may become intelligent enough to ignore the Pollyannas of population. I hope that ours is one of the second group. Survival depends on taking Cassandra seriously.[2]
>
> *Garrett Hardin*

The Liberal Democratic Tradition in Canada

Although many streams of environmentalism have developed over the years, this discussion will attempt to combine them into two broad green visions. The first—which I call light or shallow green—is generally considered the mainstream approach to environmental politics in Canada. It is incremental and moderate, and its ideas can be accommodated within our existing liberal democratic and capitalistic traditions. The second stream—which I term dark green environmentalism or ecologism—is much more radical. It proposes a new world view where liberalism, capitalism, and democracy are no longer the organizing principles. Some ecologists take a pessimistic look at democracy and believe it cannot survive in a world with fewer and fewer resources, reduced food-growing capacity, population growth, and increased energy consumption. For these doomsday theorists, it is just a matter of time before democracy will be replaced by severe political control, economic restraint, enforced discipline, and social unity—all characteristics that are not associated with liberal democratic regimes.[3] The third section of this chapter examines a number of classic works that express the deep-ecology political theory. Given the significance of Aboriginal involvement in Canada's natural resources, section four will examine their view of nature and its relationship to both the land and animal life. The last section of the chapter examines the influences on green political thought of a number of other socio-political theories, including Marxism, utopianism, anarchism, ecofeminism, and animal rights theory as well as religion.

In order to evaluate and distinguish among the various currents that exist within the environmental movement in Canada, it is useful to begin with a brief discussion of the ideas that form the basis of a democracy. This is an important starting point because some green groups have been summarily dismissed by governments, industry, and media as anti-democratic. Similarly, some green groups have described governments as undemocratic because they believe that their voices, as citizens, have not been heard or acknowledged by their elected representatives and the bureaucrats who are responsible for environmental policy. It will become evident in the discussion of the two broad visions of green political thought that while some green ideas are very compatible with democratic ideals, others may not be.

In both Canada and the United States, there is general agreement that our democracies are best described as liberal. Regardless of whether the governing parties are conservative or socialist, the basic elements of this democratic government remain intact. Although modifications may take place that shift the ideological framework of liberalism—including the primacy of individualism, a focus on individual freedom, a belief in the limited (as opposed to activist) government, and a belief in the value of science and technology—for the most part, the Canadian nation state characteristically has been described as a liberal democracy that blends the principal ideals of representative democracy with the values and beliefs of liberal ideology.

In spite of the many variations of both these concepts that exist, it can be argued that there are five main components of representative democracy. It must be kept in mind that these components are ideal types. As such, they rarely exist in a pure and uncontested way, in nation-states. These ideals are as follows:

Ideals of Representative Democracy

Popular Sovereignty

Popular sovereignty means that the people should have the final say, which, in large nation-states, takes the form of *regular, free,* and *competitive* elections. In Canada, it was always understood that elections would be held regularly, but this requirement was only formalized when it was entrenched in the Charter of

Rights and Freedoms in 1982. No government can hold power for longer than five years, and the government of the day must sit at least once a year. In Canada, elections are not held on fixed dates because our system of government—the Westminster system (i.e., cabinet parliamentary government)—is premised on the notion of responsible government. According to this principle, the government of the day can hold power only with the confidence (i.e., support) of the elected legislature.

'Free' means this vote should be cast freely without coercion or force. 'Competitive' means that citizens must have a choice of candidates and political parties. Most Canadians accept the results of elections as being legitimate and acknowledge them as an expression of the popular will. This principle is more deeply ingrained in the United States, where power is seen as flowing from the people to the governors. In Canada (and in other parliamentary systems), we subscribe more closely to the principle of parliamentary sovereignty. This principle suggests that the laws of parliament are supreme. In Canada, this doctrine has been limited because of our federal system in which powers are shared with provinces. Moreover, our constitution authorizes the Supreme Court to rule on contested cases where constitutionality is challenged.

Political equality
This ideal embodies the notion that everyone is equal on election day. Every citizen has one vote and one vote only. Suffrage has not always been universal and at one time or another certain groups in Canada have been excluded from the vote, including women, Aboriginal Canadians, certain ethnic groups, and those not owning property. Currently, all Canadian citizens 18 years of age and older have the right to vote in municipal, provincial, and federal elections. Similarly, all eligible voters have the right to seek elected office, although there are numerous practical barriers (institutional and economic, among others) that serve to reduce this opportunity.

Political freedom
Although most Canadians have enjoyed political freedoms for many years, these were entrenched in the Charter of Rights and Freedoms. Specifically, section 2 of the Charter reads as follows:
Everyone has the following fundamental freedoms:
(a) freedom of conscience and religion;
(b) freedom of thought, belief, opinion, and expression, including freedom of the press and other media of communication;
(c) freedom of peaceful assembly; and
(d) freedom of association.
Although there have been some violations of these political freedoms in our nation's history,[4] generally speaking it is believed that these rights are now enjoyed by most Canadians.

Majority Rule
Most Canadians believe that democracy incorporates the idea of majority rule—that is, when there is a dispute, the majority position should prevail. This principle is the basis on which election results are accepted. From time to time in Canada, governments have seen fit to protect certain minority rights—Protestant and Roman Catholic minority education rights, Aboriginal rights, equality rights for women (although women actually constitute a majority), and have prohibited federal or provincial discrimination against minorities.

The Rule of Law
The rule of law is the doctrine that states that every person, even the Prime Minister, is subject to the same laws of the state. According to this doctrine, no citizen is above the law.

In the Canadian democratic tradition, democracy is delivered and provided through the nation-state, although the provinces and territories are assigned certain powers and authority. The federal and provincial governments each have exclusive jurisdiction in a number of areas, which are enumerated in sections 91 and 92 of the Constitution.

Liberalism

As in the case of representative democracy, there are numerous interpretations of the political ideology of liberalism. In the Canadian case, many theorists have distinguished among many strands of liberalism—classical liberalism (also referred to as business or conservative liberalism), reform liberalism, and even neo-liberalism. Nevertheless, a number of beliefs hold constant throughout liberal thought as it has evolved in Canada:

The Primacy of Individualism
The ideology of liberalism embraces the idea that individuals are rational and self-interested. Most liberals hold a fairly optimistic view of human nature, referred to as a Lockean view. Liberals have a great faith in the rationality of humankind and believe that reason will prevail over emotion. A liberal also believes that humans are naturally competitive and acquisitive. In a world where resources are finite, individuals must compete in order to acquire property (or wealth). Liberal optimism about the individual leads to meliorism—the belief that society can change for the better and evolve through human endeavour.

A Focus on Liberty
Liberals argue that, because they are naturally driven to compete, they should have the freedom to compete and to look after their own interests. Although governments may be necessary to protect an individual's liberties from the coercion of other people, most liberals hold that the ideal form of governance is limited government that is accountable to the people. In the United States, civic

republicanism held that virtuous Americans would rise above self-interest and were capable of balancing liberty with the public good.[5] However, many American theorists believe that this principle was eventually sublimated by individual self-interest. The emphasis on liberty also explains liberal attitudes about property. The ultimate distribution of goods in a perfect world 'depends upon the efforts of the individual: she who works hard will acquire a great deal of property; she who is lazy will acquire little.'[6] A system that rewards people according to their efforts is known as a 'meritocracy' and liberals believe that this kind of system provides the best motivation for individuals.

Limited Government
As mentioned in the discussion about liberty, liberals believe that the ideal form of governance is limited government in which government and individuals form a two-way contract that each is obliged to uphold. Citizens agree to obey the government and its laws or pay a penalty. Governments consent to uphold and protect the individual rights and liberties of the citizens. In addition to protecting the freedoms of individuals, the state is also necessary to resolve the problem of collective goods. A collective good is 'something that all people have access to and benefit from, and for which one person's consumption does not limit another's.'[7] For example, clean water is a collective good. While all individuals benefit from clean water, no one individual has the personal incentive to provide or contribute to this collective good; in fact, it is much easier to be a *'free-rider'*—to benefit from the collective good but not contribute to the good's creation. A government is necessary, therefore, to ensure that collective goods can be provided.

A Belief in Capitalism and the Primacy of Science and Technology
Liberals view capitalism as the best economic system. The necessary components of a capitalist economy—private property, economic liberty, competitive self-interest, and minimal government—are all key ideas in liberal political ideology. Capitalism also supports the notion of meritocracy, and liberals believe that capitalism fosters progress and change. According to liberals, the free market allows humans to progress and improve their abilities and circumstances. On occasion, liberals may support government intervention in the market economy in order to ensure that individual rights and freedoms are protected and that collective goods are provided.

In Canada, our liberal democracy continues to evolve. Individual rights and freedoms have always been assumed to exist, although these were not constitutionally entrenched until 1982 with the Constitution Act, 1982 and the Charter of Rights and Freedoms. Our constitution also contains certain collective rights in the form of language guarantees and Aboriginal rights. With the exception of treaty rights granted to First Nations, property rights are not protected by the constitution. In Canada, the liberal democratic tradition has been upheld by the Westminster system and all the various conventions associated with it. The Canadian democratic tradition has blended many of the traditions of the British Westminster system with the American traditions of a formal constitution and the federal principle.

The two broad green visions that are summarized in this chapter both enrich and challenge the Canadian system of liberal democracy. The shallow-ecology or light green 'vision' perceives itself to be consistent with the ideals described above. According to its proponents, it does not undermine or challenge these central tenets. Indeed, within a liberal democracy individuals are free to join green groups, join political parties, create new ones, and have considerable scope to attempt to influence government policy. On the other hand, the deep ecology or dark green 'vision' challenges a number of the postulates of liberal democracy, namely, the liberal values of the primacy of the individual, limited government, and the capitalist economic system. The emphasis on providing a stable environment for individual rights has consistently overshadowed group claims on resource management. For that reason it has been argued that the notion of communal rights is missing, for all intents and purposes, from the ideology of liberalism. Moreover, the expansionary ethic of capitalism has, in the view of dark greens, contributed to the overuse of limited resources and the degradation of the physical environment.[8] Therefore, a dark green world view demands considerable revision to the liberal underpinnings of this model. Furthermore, some radical greens believe that ecologism may not be possible in a democracy. In the dark green world view, green politics requires a rethinking of politics. This helps explain why dark green political theory is more controversial and threatening to existing political and economic interests.

The Two Perspectives of Green Political Theory: An Overview

Green political theory has been approached in a variety of ways and has been studied in compelling detail by many contemporary theorists. Key ideas from this rich literature will be surveyed with a view to simplifying the main issues and debates within the growing body of literature that has been devoted to the study and analysis of green political theory. Because green political theory is composed of many shades ranging from radical environmentalism (dark green or ecologism) to moderate environmentalism (light or shallow green), this body of literature is diverse and is distinguished by complex and, at times, contrasting theoretical underpinnings. In some of the theoretical works, there is an emphasis on ethics, religion, or spirituality rather than the *political* dimensions of environmentalism. In the literature that emphasizes the political nature of green theory, there are two broad schools of thought. On the one hand, there are political purists who believe that contemporary political discourse continues to be best understood through the traditional left-right spectrum. These theorists argue that green values can simply be added or grafted on to each of the 'big three' 'isms'—conservatism, liberalism, and social democracy—making them richer and more relevant to modern political times. In this world view, green values are thought of as new variables to be added to the collection of principles, ideals, and values that characterize Canada's liberal democratic system. From this perspective, green ideals do *not* challenge the fundamental tenets of liberal democracies in North America and elsewhere. Proponents of this stream of environmentalism are inclined to consider it to be as a social movement in much the same way that they view liberal feminism, civil rights, and the gay and lesbian liberation movements. Rather than constituting new world views, they claim that green values can be accommodated within our current democratic model. This is the mainstream approach to environmentalism, or what Arne Naess referred to as *shallow ecology*, in which the central objective is to maintain the status quo, try to be more environmentally friendly, and work for the health and affluence of human beings.[9] Others have described this current of environmental thought as human welfare ecology because its central focus and beneficiary is humankind. Furthermore, they are optimistic about the ability of individuals to find technological solutions to environmental problems.

For other green theorists, the values and political ideals implicit in green political theory constitute a radical departure from the ideals of our liberal democratic system. Most of the disagreement revolves around the principles of liberalism and not the ideals of democracy; therefore it is argued that the need exists for an entirely new 'ideological axis' that has a green or ecocentric world view at one pole and a non-green or anthropocentric view of the world at the opposite pole. In other words, rather than a liberal democratic model, dark greens propose a green democratic model. This would replace the current liberal democratic regime—also referred to by dark greens as an anthropocentric or grey world view. Marcel Wissenburg posits that sentientism, zoocentrism, and biocentrism would constitute other 'isms' on this new ideological spectrum (see Table 1.1).

Sentientism (also known as pathocentrism) attributes moral value to all sentient creatures, zoocentrism attributes value to all animals, sentient or not, and biocentrism gives value to all of nature.[10]

This new spectrum has little in common with the traditional left-right categorization of life in the civil society. Naess refers to this vision of a green world view as *deep ecology* because it 'concerns itself with whole-system values and with the well-being of people in the poorer and developing countries.'[11] By whole-system, he is including the welfare of humans, animals, and other organisms in

Table 1.1 The Green Spectrum—Version 1

green world view (ecocentrism)			grey world view
biocentrism	zoocentrism	sentientism	anthropocentrism

the environment. Clearly, this is a much broader spectrum than the shallow ecology current within green political thought.

The debate about the relationship between natural-resource scarcity, population growth, and economic prosperity has gone on for generations. A number of critics have dismissed the deep ecology movement as theoretically undeveloped since it has failed to define new values and has become 'befuddled by mysticism.'[12] To counter the label 'Pollyannas'—given by dark greens to naive, optimistic, moderate environmentalists—the adherents of deep ecology have been depicted by their opponents as 'Cassandras':

> The name 'Cassandra,' often used interchangeably with 'prophet of doom,' is interpreted by many people in a pejorative way: they think that the term refers to someone whose warnings about the future will turn out to be wrong. But the Cassandra of Greek mythology was right in her warnings. The tragedy was that she was not believed; if her warnings had been heeded, the disasters she foresaw could have been averted.[13]

In order to be seen as a viable alternative to existing ideologies, Robert Paehlke, among others, argues that green ideology must develop a theoretical framework within which clear positions can be formulated on an entire range of social and political issues including unemployment, feminism, social programs, defence, and the economy.[14] Other radical environmentalists disagree, suggesting that this politicization may undermine important environmental objectives.

Complicating this discussion about spectrums and levels of politicization are the works of Robin Eckersley, among others, who argues that there are many different kinds of environmentalism along the green continuum, many of which overlap. In her groundbreaking book *Environmentalism and Political Theory* she identifies these streams of environmentalism as resource conservation, human welfare ecology, preservationism, animal liberation, and ecocentrism (see Table 1.2).[15]

Each of these environmentalisms has had varying success in countries around the world. As Eckersley notes, human-welfare ecology has been more prominent in Europe, whereas the preservationist current has been more pronounced in the New World countries in North America and Australasia.[16] Each of these streams varies in which pole it lies closer to; for example, resource conservation and human welfare ecology are more anthropocentric than the others. However, this

Table 1.2 The Green Spectrum—Version 2

ecocentrism				anthropocentrism
ecocentrism	animal liberation	preservation	human welfare	resource conservation

Source: Robin Eckersley, *Environmentalism and Political Theory* (New York: State University of New York Press, 1992), Chap. 2.

categorization is problematic in certain applications. For example, the essence of the resource conservation stream is the wise use of natural resources and the conservation of nature for development. Preservationism, on the other hand, can best be described as reverence for nature, 'in the sense of the aesthetic and spiritual appreciation of wilderness'.[17] Rather than advocating development—sustainable or not—preservationists argue that the goal should be to preserve nature from development. Human-welfare ecology emphasizes improving environmental quality for the benefit of humankind. The fourth stream, animal liberation, has developed relatively independently of the others. Although its supporters would likely be predisposed to supporting some of the other currents of environmentalism, their central focus is on the protection of and respect for animals.

In a similar effort to provide a framework for environmentalism, Doyle and McEachern identify four environmental streams—deep ecology, social ecology, eco-socialism, and ecological post-modernism (see Table 1.3).

According to their classification system, social ecology emerged as a critique of deep ecology, primarily in its proposed use of the state to solve environmental problems. This stream, which has been heavily influenced by the work of Murray Bookchin, espouses the view that nation-states should be abolished and replaced with autonomous, decentralized local communities. Added to the mixture are heavy doses of anarchism and grassroots democratic ideals:

> If the foregoing attempts to mesh ecological and anarchist principles are ever achieved in practice, social life would yield a sensitive development of human and natural diversity, falling together into a well-balanced, harmonious unity. . . . Freed from an oppressive routine, from paralyzing repressions and insecurities, from the burdens of toil and false needs, from the trammels of authority and irrational compulsion, the individual would finally be in the position, for the first time in history, to fully realize his potentialities as a member of the human community and the natural world.[18]

Like social ecologists, eco-socialists are also critical of the deep-ecology position. In their view, resource scarcity is a 'consequence of bourgeois exploitation and capitalist overconsumption rather than of natural limits coupled with over

Table 1.3 The Green Spectrum—Version 3

local decentralized communities	Regulatory state		local decentralized communities
ecocentrism			anthropocentric
deep ecology	social ecology	eco-socialism	ecological post-modernism

Source: Timothy Doyle and Doug McEachern, *Environment and Politics* (London: Routledge, 1998).

population.'[19] Lastly, postmodernists 'tend to emphasize the importance of locality and difference as against centralisation and the notion of an homogenized sameness. Nature itself would be seen as a social construct and the relations between humans and nature would be capable of almost infinite variety.'[20]

The existence of these various streams within green political theory enriches the literature but also complicates it. While acknowledging the diversity and contradictions found in this theoretical literature, the discussion in this chapter simplifies the assumptions of green political theory and provides an overview of its compatibility with contemporary political thought. This chapter will highlight the two broad visions of green thought—environmentalism as ideals and beliefs that can be accommodated within the traditional liberal democratic tradition and environmentalism as new ideology, commonly referred to in the literature as ecologism, ecocentrism, or deep ecology. These visions are an important theoretical starting point because they have guided the policies and strategies of domestic green groups and organizations, liberal democratic environmental policy regimes, green political parties, as well as international organizations, including the World Bank, the United Nations, the World Trade Organization, and the International Monetary Fund. Gaining insights into these two competing views helps to elucidate our understanding of the polarized views of the myriad members of the green movement itself. Although this factionalism is often depicted as power struggles within green organizations, it can be argued that the polarization of the green movement is rooted in two very different visions of environmental politics, which date back to John Locke and before.

For the purposes of this discussion of the two visions of green political thought, the organizational framework will be based on the ideals and values of liberal democracy. These dominant values and ideals and beliefs of the liberal democratic paradigm are compared with their counterparts of ecologism (deep ecology) in Table 1.4.

Table 1.4 Green Thought and the Liberal Democratic Tradition

Liberal Democratic Tradition	Ecologism/Deep Ecology/Ecocentrism
• anthropocentrism (domination over nature)	• ecocentrism (harmony with nature)
• individual self-interest/competitive lifestyle	• communalism/co-operative lifestyle
• capitalism and the primacy of science and technology	• sustainability
• representative democracy	• grass-roots/direct democracy
• the nation-state centralization	• bioregions decentralization

Vision One—Green Thought within the Liberal Democratic Tradition

Anthropocentrism (Domination of Nature by Humankind)

Anthropocentrism refers to the philosophy that 'intrinsic value is generally taken to reside exclusively, or at least preeminently, in humans.'[21] Because the English philosopher John Locke talked about 'natural rights' in his *Second Treatise on Government* (written in 1690), it is often mistakenly assumed that he was one of the early classic thinkers who had something important to say about nature. In fact, his work has been criticized more for its eco-unfriendliness than for his concern about the environment. In fairness to Locke, it is more accurate to suggest that the environment, in his times, presented neither moral nor factual problems and did not really exist as a thing in its own right.[22] His term 'natural rights' pertained to the right of human self-preservation and the right not to be interfered with.[23] Humans, according to Locke, also had a natural right to possessions as well as the right to enjoy the fruits of their labour. Nature had two roles to play in liberal thought: 'Physically, it was an inexhaustible source of resources; intellectually, it was the incarnation of the laws of nature over which humankind had triumphed, which it had transcended.'[24] In other words, according to the light green vision, nature is viewed as a resource and its intrinsic value is only to humans.

Green theorists have argued that Locke mistakenly based his ideas related to laissez-faire economics on false cornucopian (that is, optimistic) assumptions. The fruits, so to speak, were—in Locke's mind it appears—limitless:

> Lockean thought legitimated virtually endless accumulation of material goods; helped equate the process of accumulation with liberty and the pursuit of happiness; helped transplant the idea that with ingenuity man can go beyond the fixed law of nature, adhering only to whatever temporary laws he establishes for himself in the process of pursuing happiness; and helped instill the notion that the 'commons' is served best through each man's pursuit of private gain, because there will also be enough for those who are willing to work.[25]

This prevailing liberal view that humankind's interests were superior to and transcendent over those of everything else—including animals and plants—was shared by the early colonialists. The first Europeans who came to North America had a dark view of wilderness, which was a 'place of fear and loathing, of chaos and disorder, inhabited by fierce and dangerous animals'.[26] Thus, they were driven to impose order on chaos by cutting down trees, dividing the land into planted fields and rural communities, and turning 'the native inhabitants on the continent into Christian farmers and artisans like themselves.'[27] The predominant view, then, was that the relationship between man and nature was one of opposition and struggle. In this sense, 'Man' was set apart from nature and 'his destiny was to become its master and possessor.'[28] By the late eighteenth century, this view of wilderness had undergone a partial metamorphosis in intellectual circles with the publication of the Romantic poets, such as Byron, and the American

Transcendentalists, including Emerson and Thoreau. This Romantic view saw wilderness as a refuge from the stress of urban life, a place that brought people into closer contact with their inner selves and the wonders of the universe. Rather than being at the centre of the universe in a position of dominance over nature, humankind was simply one organism, among many, that lived in nature. This view was a major intellectual shift. It is important to note, however, that this was a view that was found largely in 'the classic salons of Europe and not the log cabins of the frontier'.[29] Although this alternative view of nature had considerable support, it can more accurately be described as a countermovement that, while challenging the mainstream view of man's place in nature, never replaced it.

In modern times, citizens of liberal democracies have began to realize that the quality of the land, water, and air is deteriorating. However, economic development, job creation, and continued industrialization continue to be dominant policy objectives pursued by most western democratic polities. Nature continues to have only the value that humans place on it.

The Canadian Experience

Although a considerable amount of land in this country was deemed Crown land, something that never existed in the United States, the conservation movement was not only slower to develop in Canada but was much more modest as well. A series of early measures were undertaken to manage our considerable natural resources, including the creation of federal and provincial parks, such as Banff in 1887 and Algonquin Park in 1893.[30] Far from being created for altruistic reasons or the desire to preserve large wilderness areas for the common good, most of these parks were intended to promote the burgeoning tourism industry and to protect forestry resources.[31] There is considerable evidence that this anthropocentrism remains strongly ingrained in Canada. Numerous interest groups have been formed in British Columbia and elsewhere to protest the clearcutting of forests and to demand that ancient rainforests be protected. In addition, the government of Canada has been slow to introduce endangered species legislation and regulations prohibiting the sale and trade of animal parts for consumer goods such as aphrodisiacs. Much of the environmental activism in Canada can be explained as a reaction to the continued dominance of anthropocentrism within our liberal democratic tradition.

Individualism

Some theorists suggest that Locke's conception of property has been misinterpreted and that his concern with property 'was a function of survival, not greed. One's property would ensure self-preservation, and ultimately liberty.'[32] Lockean liberalism, which guided liberal democracy in the United States, for example, posed several difficult problems for early environmental thinkers. Governments, Locke argued, were only necessary to protect individual rights. Because these natural rights were inalienable—that is, they could not be limited by the state—

the concept of communal good became both irrelevant and theoretically impossible. In other words, the Lockean view of liberal democracy did not embody the notion of the common good nor did it recognize obligations that arose by virtue of our membership in both the human and natural community.[33]

According to Cahn, 'civic virtue has been defined variously as altruism, self-control, sobriety, productivity, and love of country.'[34] In the United States, this notion of civic virtue was originally conceived to have a tempering influence on self-interest. Over time, however, this notion of communal interest was largely supplanted by individual self-interest, leaving 'the scope of public policy choices severely limited'.[35] The rise to modernity in the United States was premised on a number of the cornerstones of the Enlightenment where the path to human prosperity was 'through scientific discovery, technological innovation, capitalism, factory production, and the *efficient* use of nature.'[36] Modern liberalism continues to value the sanctity of individual self-interest and human ingenuity.

Capitalism and the Value of Science and Technology

Traditionally, economic theory and practice has taken an instrumental view of nature: 'The dominant development paradigm sees the planet merely in terms of resources, "raw materials", to be exploited, "developed", thereby "adding value", and exchanged for money on the world market. This approach aims at the maximization of production, and disregards the destruction and degradation which attend it.'[37] Locke and other eighteenth- and nineteenth-century philosophers, including Jeremy Bentham and Adam Smith, saw privatization of the commons as desirable. On this basis, Americans sold off their public domain between 1785 and 1935,[38] leaving no constitutional grounds for allowing governments to limit the pursuit of individual wealth and profit taking and protect the common natural resources. As an economic system for the supply and distribution of goods, capitalism was 'largely inconsistent with the collective good of maintaining environmental quality.'[39] Moreover, the success of the capitalist system has historically been measured and defined by economic growth.[40] From the outset, industrialization and commerce were paramount and nature was worthless unless it was reshaped. Intellectuals like Franklin and Jefferson believed that new knowledge, new scientific discoveries, and new inventions would all result in a better standard of living and quality of life for all humanity.[41]

Most dark greens believe that there is an inherent contradiction between capitalism and a greener society. There is no doubt that large numbers of moderate environmentalists are sympathetic to this view. And many other moderate environmentalists, though supporting the basic premises of capitalism and the free market, believe that the state should regulate more, enforce better, and be more prescriptive in addressing some environmental problems.

The natural result of a capitalist economic system has been the growth of a consumer culture. This culture translates wants into needs, stresses material-intensive forms of social gratification, and overwhelms older, more ecologically sustaining traditions that stand in its way. As consumerism spreads through increasingly sophisticated advertising, popular culture, and the global media, more and more regions of the planet adopt the aspirations of the consumer society.[42] For capitalists, this means more markets and an increased demand for their products.

Some postmodernists suggest that a new social system will result from the growing international flow of capital, on both a global and local level. David Harvey, among others, posits that this new type of capital will lead to the disintegration of the Fordist regime of industrial production, capital accumulation, and state intervention that existed from the 1930s through the 1970s in national welfare states.[43] In their place will be regimes of 'flexible accumulation, productive specialization, and state deregulation in loosely coupled transnational alliances of market centres, factory concentrations, technology generators, capital suppliers, and public administrators.'[44] In combination, these will result in a greening of capitalism.

Science and technology are seen by many citizens as tools available to humankind for taming and controlling the environment. Indeed, theorists such as Neil Postman believe that the primacy of science and technology in the human experience has supplanted traditional human values such as family, religion, and community. Many liberals believe that new scientific technologies have unlimited potential to make the world a greener place. However, in the event that technological solutions are unable to solve environmental problems, it appears that some modern-day liberals may be prepared to entertain limitations on individual freedom as it pertains to consumption and property.

Among liberals, there is a heated philosophical debate about capitalism and economic growth. Economic growth, according to some, is necessary because we must have growth to be rich enough to clean up the environment and cure poverty. Liberals point to voluntary efforts by corporations to become more green in order to satisfy a growing public demand that capitalism intrude less on the environment. Examples of this volunteerism include reforestation by multinational forestry companies and rehabilitation of land by mining companies. However, critics of this voluntary 'greening' claim that there is more and more evidence that growth actually makes us poorer by increasing costs faster than it increases benefits. This is the dilemma of growth and economic development: is it the cause of environmental degradation or is it the potential solution for a greener world?

The Nation-State and Centralization

In modern liberal democratic states, the responsibility of the state has evolved from the protection of property to the safeguarding and promoting of individual rights and freedoms, including the freedom of individuals and corporations to pursue wealth. In the Canadian case, it can also be argued that the state has, from its very beginning, been involved in the protection of certain collective rights (including denominational education rights and Aboriginal rights), although with varying degrees of success. Canada's constitution is silent on the rights of non-human forms of life.

Because of Canada's size and diverse regions, the nation's founders adopted a federal system that gives the lion's share of jurisdictions to the federal government. Over time, a number of areas have been either forcefully (through constitutional interpretation) or voluntarily delegated to the provincial level. Early in Canada's history, several nation-building enterprises, including the railway as well as other endeavours related to the transportation and telecommunications industries, resulted in the development of a mixed economy in which the state played an important role in equalizing services across the country. Since the mid-1980s, a number of these mixed enterprises have been privatized, which has led to a freer, market economy driven by the private sector.

With the establishment of capitalism as the dominant economic system in many parts of Europe, coupled with the Industrial Revolution, the trend towards centralization began. In the case of Canada, economic historians, including Harold Innis, argued that Canada's staple-based economy contributed to a pattern of economic development characterized by a metropolitan central core and a resource hinterland. For most of Canada's history, this metropolitan central core comprised the Montreal-Toronto corridor, which dominated not only the country's economic development but its political life as well. Innis's *staples theory of development* helped to explain why regional identification was strong in Canada and why nationalism and social cohesion were comparatively weak. For most of the twentieth century, Canada's federal system was characterized by a strong federal government and relatively subordinate provincial governments. In the post-war period, there has been a slow and continued devolution of authority and power from the federal level to the provinces. In part, this has happened because Quebec has opted out of various federal social programs and has assumed new powers in other areas, including immigration and employment training. In addition, a series of decisions by the Judicial Committee of the Privy Council and the Supreme Court of Canada, also granted the provinces more authority in trade and commerce and in property and civil rights. The fact that many areas of jurisdiction in the public sphere are now shared by the federal and provincial governments has led to disputes in a number of policy fields, including natural resources and the environment. Another factor contributing to the devolution of power has been the development of capable and competent provincial bureaucracies.

Representative Democracy

Before the days of universal suffrage, which had been achieved by the second decade of the twentieth century in North America and much of western Europe, voting in popular elections was restricted, more or less, to propertied white men. Elected representatives largely reflected the ideals and beliefs of those voters.

Although the barriers to suffrage were slowly dismantled in Canada, other cultural and institutional impediments delayed the entry into the legislative arena of under-represented groups. Although the election of more women and people of more varied ethnic origins has made legislatures more representative than they used to be, some groups continue to be under-represented in elected legislatures. Nevertheless, liberals believe that in a representative democracy, citizens are free to create new parties—which may include green parties—to represent changing interests. They are free to join interest groups and to make their views known through such legal means as protests, boycotts, and petitions. Moreover, they have the ability to vote their representatives out of office in periodic elections. All of these factors are pointed to as evidence that green views can be accommodated within a liberal democracy.

Summary of Green Thought within the Liberal Democratic Tradition

For the most part, contemporary liberal and mainstream environmentalism is concerned about the effects that (for example) pollution and resource depletion may have on human life—the human-welfare ecology stream, as Eckersley describes it. For liberals, environmental problems are considered to have resulted from overly rapid cultivation and exploitation of natural resources and the failure to regulate pesticides and other environmental pollutants adequately. The solution to these problems, liberals argue, is better science, conservation, and laws. Many of these values and ideals associated with liberal democracy have undergone a gradual evolution since classical times. Occasionally they have been challenged by progressive intellectuals and groups. Some believe that liberal democracy has been good for the environment: 'In spite of the contradictions involved, the economic wealth generated under the aegis of a free market economy has liberated countless persons from oppressive toil and scarcity, created leisure to enjoy nature, and in many cases generated the means necessary to protect the environment.'[45] Present-day cornucopians believe that there are many indicators that the world's environmental tide may be about to turn. It has been suggested, for example, that by the late twenty-first century, global population is likely to level off, ending 200 years of dramatic growth.[46] Moreover, some scientists claim that greenhouse gases are growing much more slowly than twenty years ago.[47] Greg Easterbrook claims that the solutions to every environmental problem are available and all that is now required is a commitment to become better managers.[48]

While some greens argue that there are simply too many contradictions between liberalism and environmentalism, others claim that liberalism has come a long way in accepting the need to address environmental issues though they recognize that it has a long way to go. Part of liberalism's problem with becoming 'greener' is that liberal democracy and economic liberalism are often treated as one and the same:

Capitalism is not a necessary condition for the existence of the political structure and liberties associated with liberal democracy, the free market existed before liberal democracy evolved, political liberalism is not predestined to a laissez-faire attitude towards the market, nor does it hold that life is all about making profits or the satisfaction of material self-interest; it sees trade and commerce as one way of life, one means to the realization of a plan of life, among others. The critique of economic liberalism must therefore be judged on its own merits and cannot reflect on political liberalism.[49]

Despite these optimistic claims, many greens have expressed disillusionment with liberal democracy and its capacity to respond to the challenges of post-industrialism, including environmental problems such as global warming, desertification, deforestation, and widespread poverty in the developing world. Moreover, a deepening critique of liberal democracy charges that it is a myth that rights and freedoms are enjoyed by all. In addition, it is said to be a system that perpetuates continued economic growth, consumerism, and resource exploitation. Many environmentalists believe that a green world view is impossible under this model of governance. Although the ideals and values of liberal democracies were attacked in the past for their social and economic limitations, they are now under siege for their alleged weakness in addressing environmental problems. This critique of the ability of liberal democracies to be green is known as deep ecology.

Vision Two—Deep Ecology

Ecocentrism

A world view described as 'ecocentric' is essentially the converse of the anthropocentric view of man in nature. An ecocentric view sees the world as 'an intrinsically dynamic, interconnected web of relations in which there are no absolute discrete entities and no absolute dividing lines between the living and the nonliving, the animate and the inanimate, or the human and the nonhuman.'[50] In other words, all beings—human and non-human—possess intrinsic value. In this sense, ecocentrism challenges what has been an axiom of western liberal democratic thought—that nature is a resource to be used by humankind. Ecocentrism also challenges the anthropocentric view that there are higher and lower life forms in nature. In doing so, it challenges the view that rights are strictly human categories.[51] Another important idea in ecocentrism is the notion that the Earth is finite in its carrying capacity and that there are too many people on the planet: 'The flourishing of human life and cultures is compatible with a substantial decrease in the human population. The flourishing of non-life requires such a decrease.'[52] Human beings, therefore, are not the sole purpose of evolutionary progress but are simply another species, according to the dark green perspective.

Over the years, ecocentrism has been severely criticized by liberals and others as absurd and naive. Anthropocentrism assumes that the distinctiveness of humans makes them more worthy than the distinctive features of other life forms. Furthermore, it believes that humankind is the only or principal source of value and meaning in the world, and that the only purpose of non-human nature is to serve people:[53] 'There is a sense in which we cannot know the Other (whether it be other species, other cultures, the other sex or even each other); however, we must remind ourselves that other meanings exist, even if we may be severely limited in our understanding of them.'[54] Although humankind will never truly understand what it means to be nonhuman, humans are capable of developing a non-anthropocentric consciousness. Dark greens advocate that decision making must take into account both the human and non-human world. Ecocentrism, therefore, necessitates an entirely different emphasis in the way we think about our natural resources and their use.

Communalism

In a society that espoused green values and ideology, the needs of individuals would not come first. Moreover, individual self-interest is not encouraged in the green world. Instead, the needs and betterment of the communities in which the individuals live would have priority. In many respects, the ideal of communalism bears some similarity to the conservative notion of the organic society in which individuals make contributions on the basis of their own skills and talents to the community. The result, according to this theory, will be a harmonious group or community if it is organized on the basis of this overarching principle. In part, this ideal can be viewed as a classical conservative one, except that the green view does not see social stratification in the communal society. It is more collectivist and egalitarian and is aligned more closely with democratic socialist dogma. In this view, individual self-interest must be subordinated to the needs of the broader community. This emphasis represents a major departure from the liberalism that underpins our current democratic systems.

The Sustainable Society

The term 'sustainable society' has been fraught with internal inconsistencies and multiple contradictions. Indeed, many theorists believe that it is a term that 'defies definition'.[55] A neoclassical economist, for example, would define sustainable development as development that will allow his or her company to stay in business forever. For the deep ecologist, sustainability means no development at all as we know it.[56] For the deep ecologist, sustainable society is both an economic system and a new way of life. Both capitalism and technology and the cultures associated with them are rejected by the deep-ecology notion of sustainable society. This spectrum of sustainability is shown in Table 1.5.

Sustainable communities in and of themselves are not new ideas, as tribal villages, medieval towns, and intentional communities were viewed in this manner. What is new, however, is the term 'sustainable development', which entered contemporary environmental discourse in 1987 with the publication of *Our Common Future* after a meeting of the World Commission on Environment

Table 1.5 The Sustainability Spectrum

ecocentrism	anthropocentrism
sustainable society	sustainable development

and Development (WCED) in 1986. By sustainable development, the report's authors were referring to 'development that meets the needs of the present without compromising the ability of future generations to meet their own needs.'[57] Although this study had a definite slant towards economics, including analyses of the character and quality of economic growth and development, the reorientation of science and technology, and the conservation of the resource base,[58] it was applauded by environmentalists all over the world when it was published. For the first time, a report by a respected international body revealed how interlocking world economies and current industrial development were creating a greater polarization of the world's wealth, which prevented large numbers of people from meeting the most basic needs. At the same time, this development was destroying nature's ability to replenish its own resources.[59] By recognizing that industrial development had a negative side, the report called into question the desirability of continuing western-style development in the developing world. In this sense, it was considered quite revolutionary. In the years since it was published, however, the so-called Brundtland Report has been severely criticized for its contradictions. For example, in order to reduce poverty, it called for the world economy to grow by a factor of five to ten while at the same time respecting ecological limits. Critics argued that growth of this magnitude was impossible if ecological limits were respected. Indeed, several studies have made compelling cases that this scale of economic growth will overshoot the ecosystem's regenerative and sink capacities.[60] In reply, advocates of sustainable development claim that economic growth as it has been traditionally been measured is misleading. As evidence, they point to the primary indicator used—GNP. It has been argued that if a broader set of indicators, including those related to quality of life, were used to measure economic well-being, the idea of sustainable development would be achievable. This argument has, for the most part, been rejected by dark greens, who claim that the term sustainable development has been co-opted by business to mean sustainable profit. They point to the use of the term 'sustainability' by both the Klein government in Alberta and the Harris government in Ontario as meaning fiscally responsible. Under the banner of 'sustainability', both these governments have cut financial assistance to most municipalities, which are then expected to sustain their own services and employment under current tax regimes. In other words, the term has become a catch-all for sustaining the status quo, which is a far cry from the meaning it was given in *Our Common Future*.

Many theorists argue that sustainable development is an 'impossibility theorem', simply put, it is 'impossible for the world economy to grow its way out of poverty and environmental degradation. . . . Sustainable growth is impossible.'[61]

In the spirit of *Our Common Future*, sustainable development is not just about consumption, supply, underdevelopment in poor regions, and overexploitation in the developed world. The move to a *sustainable society* requires a fundamental shift in belief systems: a shift from expansionary capitalism to an economic system that brings consumption and waste into equilibrium with the resource capacity of the ecosystem.[62] As Dobson notes, there are two underlying tenets of the sustainable society—that the consumption of material goods by individuals in 'advanced industrial countries' should be reduced and that human needs are *not* best satisfied by continual economic growth.[63] In other words, sustainability, as it is conceived in the ideology of ecologism, involves radical changes in consumption and materialism. Such changes, deep ecologists posit, will have a positive spiritual effect since less consumption will be seen as an attractive choice. Moreover, as sustainability is conceived, it challenges the foundations of the modern capitalist system. Therefore, sustainability is not simply about consumption; it falls clearly within the realm of significant value change.

Sustainability also presupposes a significant change in economic practices. For example, greens advocate significant changes to agricultural methods. In a sustainable society, there would be less production by giant agribusiness and biotechnology firms and more local agricultural production. And the taxes, subsidies, and farm credits that discriminate against small producers would be done away with. In a green society, there would also be movement from chemical-dependent to organic farming: 'Organic agriculture is devoted to restoring and enhancing natural soil fertility, which is severely depleted by long-term use of chemical additives. Large field monocultures, which are highly susceptible to disease, are replaced by crop rotation practices that respect the need for soil nourishment and biological diversity.'[64] The winners in an organic farming system are both the consumers, who will benefit from more healthful and nutritious foods, and farm operators, who will enjoy a chemical-free workplace. The disadvantage of organic farming is that food will probably become more expensive, at least for a time, although if foods are produced locally, transportation costs will be lessened.

In a sustainable society, an alternative to the economics of growth must be pursued. Unchecked industrial expansion is viewed as the culprit that has brought the modern world to the brink of ecological collapse. New technologies, rather than enriching the human experience, are believed to be feeding a relentless militarism that is hastening the destruction of the biosphere while at the same time virtually enslaving people to machines.[65] Other groups besides deep ecologists are wary of the worship of technology, and there is a large body of critical literature on post-industrialism and the information society.[66] However, deep ecologists, in particular, have often been dismissed as Luddites (see Box 1.1), which many believe is an unfair accusation:

Neo-Luddites are twentieth-century citizens who question the predominant modern world view, which preaches that unbridled technology represents progress. Neo-Luddites have the courage to gaze at the full catastrophe of our century. . . . Western societies are out of control and desecrating the fragile fabric of life on Earth. Like the early Luddites, we too are seeking to protect the livelihoods, communities and families we love. . . . Stopping the destruction requires not more regulating or eliminating individual items like pesticides or military weapons. It requires new ways of relating to life. It requires a new worldview.[67]

Box 1.1 The Luddites

The origin of the term, Luddite, is not known for certain. Some believe that it refers to the actions of an English youth named Ludlum. Others believe that a mythical hero, named Ned Ludd, was created to enrich the narrative. As the story goes, after being told by his father to repair a weaving machine, he proceeded to destroy it. Whatever the origin of the term, between 1811 and 1816, there arose widespread support in Britain for workers who bitterly resented what they saw as a deterioration in their living standards as a result of industrialization. Machines were taking their jobs and destroying their families and communities. Among other changes, they witnessed a cut in their wages, the introduction of child labour, and the elimination of laws and customs that had once protected them. Most of the discontent of the times was turned on the garment and fabric industry, and many machines were destroyed. This action has contributed to the notion that Luddism has a violent component. Defenders of Luddism argue, however, that nothing could be farther from the truth. According to the *Rue Cottage Books for Luddites, Greens and Like-Minded Readers*, 'it is a respect for and a confidence in those things that make us human, with a related rejection of the mechanistic approach to being that devalues humanity.'[1] Luddites were simply trying to defend the rights, privileges, and laws that had protected them in earlier times. They were not against new machines *per se* but were against the changed social relations which were brought into being and of which mechanization was a part.

The relationship between Luddism and the environment is examined in the following passage:

Environmentalism has its roots in resistance to this same ruthless domination of the machine and those who use it to conquer and subdue nature, a sentiment that has its roots in the writings of John Muir and Aldo Leopold and evolves into the deep ecology of Arne Naess. Behind the modern Luddite movement is a solid body of philosophical writing. Jacques Ellul and Lewis Mumford construct a base upon which present-day eco-philosophers such as Edward Goldsmith build. And carrying forth this thinking are contemporary writers and thinkers such as Jerry Mander, Stephanie Mills, Kirkpatrick Sale and many others, who with clear arguments and passionate voices articulate valid concerns that technology may undo more than we bargained for, leaving behind a wake of damage from which it may be difficult to recover.[2]

Modern-day Luddites (sometimes referred to as neo-Luddites) insist that their protests involve an attempt to introduce alternative priorities to those being imposed by industrial capitalism. In recent times, 'Luddite' has come to mean a naive opposition to technology and is considered a derogatory term by those who oppose the growing penetration of technology into our day-to-day lives.

The term has been applied to groups opposing biotechnology, the growth in information technologies, and post-industrialism generally. Some journalists, by attaching the term to Ted Kaczynski (the Unabomber), have helped to perpetuate its violent connotations. Most recently, *Time Magazine* described the protesters at Seattle as the new Luddites.[3]

Notes

1. *Rue Cottage Books for Luddites, Greens and Like-Minded Readers*, http://www.ruecottage.com/about.htm/
2. Ibid.
3. Richard Lacayo, 'Rage against the Machine', *Time*, Canadian edn, 13 Dec. 1999.

Further Reading on Neo-Ludditism

E. Etzioni-Halevy, *The Knowledge Elite and the Failure of Prophecy* (London: George Allen and Unwin, 1985).

R. Haynes, ed., *High Tech: High Co$t. Technology, Society and the Environment* (Chippendale, New South Wales: Pan Books, 1991).

L. Siegel and J. Markoff, *The High Cost of High Tech: The Dark Side of the Chip* (New York: Harper and Row, 1985).

F. Webster and K. Robins, *Information Technology: A Luddite Analysis* (Northwood, N.J.: Ablex, 1986).

Though it is likely that dark greens would support environmentally friendly technologies, they do not consider most of the new technologies to be green.

Therefore, whereas light greens support sustainable development, dark greens see the term as simply a buzz phrase that has been appropriated by liberals and others espousing an anthropocentric view of nature and the environment. The sustainable society, as dark greens view it, calls for a retreat from capitalism, economic growth, non-green technology, and the consumer society. Before the sustainable society can be realized, fundamental changes in behaviour and values will be necessary, which will require considerable revision to our liberal democratic tradition.

Bioregions and Decentralization

A bioregion can be defined as 'an area of land defined, not by political boundaries—cities, states, countries—but by the natural, biological and geological features that cast the real identity of a place.'[68] In a society dominated by the ideology of ecologism, citizens are no longer bound together by ethnicity, religion, language, or any other particularism. In fact, a person who embraces ecologism would likely argue that in recent times these particularisms have been divisive rather than unifying. In a green world order that is composed of bioregions rather than nation-states, 'it becomes possible to more readily determine the most ecologically-sound and sustainable ways for people to live in a particular place.'[69] Bioregionalism embodies the idea of dwelling in mixed communities, which include people, animals, and plants. Animals and plants would no longer be viewed as economic resources, 'but also—perhaps instead—as neighbours'.[70]

The bioregions of North America would include the Great Lakes area, the Maritimes, the Pacific Northwest, and the plains and prairies, to name just a few. Of course, there are many practical reasons why bioregions will be a contested concept in North America, not the least of which is American, Canadian, Quebec, and Aboriginal nationalisms, among countless other cultural identities. For a green, however, the advantages of bioregions far outweigh the practical difficulties:

> Bioregionalists advocate a 'breakdown of nations' into self-sustaining, co-operatively-relating, ecologically-scaled entities which would become models of ecological diversity at the level of the human community. One would hope to be able to travel across a mosaic of bioregional communities the way the earliest explorers traveled across Indian villages years ago—freely and with no apparent fixed borders.[71]

Although bioregionalism has been described as a hopelessly romantic notion, in some small ways, there has been co-operation between Canada and the United States over such issues as acid rain, the Great Lakes, and more recently the west coast salmon fishery; however, national identities and agendas have commonly been obstacles to international co-operation. Once communities were restructured along such biologically rational lines, bioregionalists believe that societies would naturally evolve toward decentralization and political decisions would be made according to the health of the biotic region.[72]

Decentralization is often referred to in connection with government services, but for the deep ecologist it is a far broader concept:

> The decentralization of social and political life is fundamental to the Green vision of a sustainable society. Face-to-face communities encourage a sense of social responsibility which is lacking in the anonymity of large-scale industrial and city life. In small communities, it is more likely that consensus can be achieved and societal stability could be achieved; that local production for local use with less trade and travel reduces a community's impact on its environment; that 'human-scale' forms of living are more congenial than their modern counterparts; and that decentralized

forms of production and exchange satisfy a human demand for improvements in the quality of life rather than catering for the modern—and misplaced—emphasis on quantity.[73]

In political terms, individuals in small communities will be masters of their own destinies and 'will enjoy the rewards of the small community, of knowing and being known.'[74] In addition to the political and social advantages of decentralization, deep ecologists also contend that there are economic benefits. For example, the need for costly highways and sewage treatment plants will be reduced.

Two years after 'Blueprint for Survival' was published in *Ecologist*, E.F. Schumacher wrote *Small Is Beautiful: A Study of Economics As If People Mattered*. His collection of essays put forward the view that the only solution to the world's ecological and economic crises was a complete reversal of the developed world's development strategies. Hope for humanity lay in the development of small-scale, non-violent technologies, decentralization, and local control. He implored people to rethink the goals of market economics:

> Therefore we must learn to think in terms of an articulated structure that can cope with a multiplicity of small-scale units. If economic thinking cannot grasp this it is useless. If it cannot get beyond its vast abstractions, the national income, the rate of growth, capital/output ratio, input-output analysis, labour mobility, capital accumulation; if it cannot get beyond all this and make contact with the human realities of poverty, frustration, alienation, despair, breakdown, crime, escapism, stress, congestion, ugliness, and spiritual death, then let us scrap economics and start afresh.[75]

The idea of decentralization has also been espoused by a number of green socialists, such as William Morris, G.D.H. Cole, Robert Owen, and the French utopian socialists, among others. Diametrically opposed to the liberal democratic view of the nation-state and centralization, it requires a rethinking of the value of nationalism, the nation-state, and the economic idea that bigger is better. This value of deep ecology is likely the most altruistic of all its tenets, for it requires a rethinking of the modern notions of the nation-state. An additional benefit of bioregions and decentralization is that the value given to non-human life is enhanced.

One of the main features of bioregions would be that all species, human and non-human, would be equal. In a biocentric approach 'the rights of nature are defended first and foremost on the grounds of the intrinsic value of animals, plants, rivers, mountains, and ecosystems rather than simply on the basis of their utilitarian value or benefit to humans.'[76] Furthermore, rights granted to humans would be extended to other life forms including the right to life, freedom from human oppression, and a habitat that offers them opportunity for well-being.[77]

Direct Democracy

From a green perspective, democracy does not consist of going to the ballot box every few years to elect representatives. Rather, it consists of making decisions at the local level, where choices can be discussed openly and face to face by the people who will be affected by them.[78] In the ideal world view advanced by deep ecologists, small, efficient, sustainable, and biotic regions are essentially self-governed entities. Collectively, they will result in a greener world. They are democratic communities but are underpinned by communal values, not liberal-individual ones.

Summary of Deep Ecological Thought

Deep ecological thought represents a radical departure from environmental thought within the liberal democratic tradition in almost every way. Socially, it represents a world view that values all life forms equally—human and non-human—and places more value on the needs of the community than on those of the individual. In political terms, it sees a world organized into decentralized bioregions rather than centralized nation-states. It denounces capitalism and its attendant consumer culture and technologies, which would be replaced by a sustainable society. Deep ecological thought, therefore, does not believe that a green world is possible within the dominant liberal democratic tradition of the western world. Although some ecological critiques of liberal democracy are decidedly authoritarian, many of the ideals and values of deep ecological thought do not abandon democratic principles; rather, they promote a more direct form of democracy.

Currents within Ecological (Dark Green) Political Thought
Limits to Growth and Malthusianism

Thomas Malthus's controversial work, *An Essay on the Principle of Population; or a View of its Past and Present Effects on Human Happiness: with an inquiry into prospects respecting the future removal or mitigation of the evils which it occasions* was published in 1798. (In 1803 he published a revised version, which had a more liberal slant. However, he is most often associated with his original piece.) Malthus came from a position of relative privilege and he wrote this essay some nine years after the French Revolution had broken out. Thus his work can be best understood as a critique of liberalism. In 1795, in an attempt to address widespread poverty in England, the Speenhamland system[79] was introduced. Although this system was created to redistribute income, it was criticized 'as encouraging idleness, dissipation, and overproduction of children.'[80] Malthus believed that inequality was inevitable and that poor people allowed the wealthy to 'practise charity'.[81] Malthus's essay, which marked a departure from other writings of the time, issued two warnings: natural resources were finite and uncontrolled population growth was quickly leading to their depletion. Of particular concern to Malthus was the production of food. Human population, he argued, would always tend to increase in geometrical (exponential) ratio (1, 2, 4, 8, 16, and so on). However, food production, he argued, could only increase in arithmetic ratio (1, 2, 3, 4, 5 and so forth). Historically, plagues and disease had worked to limit population growth to a point that more or less approached the growth in the food supply. He was not convinced that technological improvements would result in increased agricultural production, and he made a compelling case for the need for birth control. In doing so, he challenged the dominant Christian belief that children are sent by God.

In the 1960s, there was a rebirth of Malthusianism with the publication of a number of studies that warned of impending doom. The apocalyptic or doomsday tone that characterized this current of green political thought placed it squarely within the realm of Malthusianism. A number of green theorists have argued that without population control and major changes in the use of resources, the survival of the planet is in jeopardy. This stream of thought varies in how it sees technology and its efficient use, particularly in energy production and use. Survivalism was a theme that was prevalent in the works of a number of theorists who have been described both as neo-Malthusians and radicals. Included in this current are the works of US ecologists, Paul and Ann Ehrlich, whose 1967 book, *The Population Bomb*, gave a second life to the ideas of Thomas Malthus. James Lovelock, the US team led by the economist Dennis Meadows, and the Club of Rome, among others, have also borrowed from Malthus.

The Population Bomb (1969)

The world's population will continue to grow as long as the birth rate exceeds the death rate; it's as simple as that. When it stops growing or starts to shrink, it will mean that either the birth rate has gone down or the death rate has gone up or a combination of the two. Basically, then, there are only two kinds of solutions to the population problem. One is a 'birth rate solution', in which we find ways to lower the birth rate. The other is a 'death rate solution', in which ways to raise the death rate—war, famine, pestilence—find us. The problem could have been avoided by population control, in which mankind consciously adjusted the birth rate so that a 'death rate solution' did not have to occur.[82]

Like Malthus, Paul and Anne Ehrlich believed that the biggest threat to humanity was overpopulation. They predicted that sometime between 1970 and 1985 there would be catastrophic famines and that hundreds of millions would die.[83] Among their controversial proposals was the termination of foreign aid to the developing world, particularly for health programs. One tool they advocated was 'triage', the method used by doctors during wartime to prioritize medical care for injured soldiers; similarly the Ehrlichs argued that food aid should be given not necessarily to the poorest nations but only to those who embarked on aggressive population control.[84] Building on this idea, a theorist in the 1980s urged that the United States cease food shipments to India, where 'dispassionate analysis indicates that the imbalance between food and population is hopeless.'[85]

As one would imagine, the Ehrlichs came under attack from liberals in the United States and elsewhere who thought these proposals were tantamount to endorsing genocide in parts of the developing world. Others, who are often labelled as cornucopians, believed that the problem was not overpopulation but the distribution of wealth and that there was plenty for everyone. American economist Julian Simon advanced a counterargument to Malthus's contention that the problem was overpopulation. Indeed, Simon argued that increased population growth has led to *increased* wealth. That is to say, 'more people mean bigger markets and easier communications. Economies of scale become possible. Productivity improves as larger numbers of factories with higher output learn by each other's mistakes. Above all more people bring more brains to dream up more technical solutions to problems.'[86]

In 1988, Garrett Hardin's article, 'Cassandra's Role in the Population Wrangle', summarized the population problem as follows:

> What we call *the* population problem is, then, the problem of finding an acceptable way of giving up what has been a widespread, though not universal, freedom in the past, namely, the freedom to breed. In the past we could cling to this freedom because of the providential presence of crowd diseases, which acted as a deus ex machina to keep human populations from breeding themselves into misery (not that disease and death are all that pleasant). This god, this deus, is dead now, and we must learn to live without it. Exactly *how* we will control breeding is open to debate. Controls need not be brutally direct; many indirect incentives and disincentives are available. The problem is one of social engineering. This is a problem for the future—the *near* future.[87]

The Malthusian tradition continues to be alive and well. Although advances in medicine and scientific advances in the ability to give advance warnings of natural disasters have counteracted Malthus's idea of natural checks, there remain areas in the world where these natural checks still play a role. The rampant spread of AIDS in parts of Africa and disastrous natural disasters such as droughts, earthquakes, and floods continue to ravage a number of overpopulated areas of the world.

The Gaia Hypothesis

In 1975, the British scientist James E. Lovelock put forward the idea that the earth (Gaia) is a 'living being of immense complexity that ought to be the object of our wondrous contemplation, rather than the source of satisfaction for our rapacious material greed. The message is that Gaia needs protection.'[88]

> Working in a new intellectual environment, I was able to forget Mars and to concentrate on the Earth and the nature of its atmosphere. The result of this more single-minded approach was the development of the hypothesis that the entire range of living matter on Earth, from whales to viruses, and from oaks to algae, could be regarded as constituting a single living entity, capable of manipulating Earth's

atmosphere to suit its overall needs and endowed with faculties and powers far beyond those of its constituent parts.[89]

For Lovelock, humanity is considered but one organism among the rest of nature. In other words, this hypothesis displaces human beings from the centre of creation. Lovelock suggests that 'we might be signing our own suicide note by continuing our industrial practices, in that the "perturbations" that we, as a species, occasion in the atmosphere might trigger some compensatory change, perhaps in the climate, which would be good for the biosphere as a whole but bad for man as a species.'[90] The Gaia concept of Earth as a single, self-regulating organism called for a fundamental change of thinking about the nature of earth. Unless this shift of thinking occurred, it was argued, any attempts to implement green initiatives were destined to fall short. Without this sea change in attitude, 'we will have difficulty moving beyond the shallowist levels of ecology.'[91] Lovelock's work was an important contribution to the green ideal of ecocentrism and the green critique of industrial capitalism.

The Limits-to-Growth Thesis (1972)
In 1971, Professor Jay W. Forrester of the Massachusetts Institute of Technology developed a prototype model that formed the basis of *Limits to Growth*, written by Donella H. Meadows and Dennis L. Meadows et al. one year later. The authors posited that technological progress and capital expansion did not address the essential problem which was exponential growth in a finite and complex system. Their conclusion was stark: 'Our attempts to use even the most optimistic estimates of the benefits of technology in the model did not prevent the ultimate decline of population and industry, and in fact did not in any case postpone the collapse beyond the year 2100.'[92]

Despite the pessimism of their predictions about the limits to growth, the authors did offer a ray of hope, which involved the pursuit of a strategy for global equilibrium:

> Man possesses, for a small moment in history, the most powerful combination of knowledge, tools, and resources the world has ever known. He has all that is physically necessary to create a totally new form of human society—one that would be built to last for generations. The two missing ingredients are a realistic, long-term goal that can guide mankind to the equilibrium society and the human will to achieve that goal. Without such a goal and a commitment to it, short-term concerns will generate the exponential growth that drives the world system toward the limits of the earth and ultimate collapse.[93]

In 1974, the Club of Rome (a name given to an informal group of researchers, intellectuals, and scientists) published the findings of a computer modelling experiment that equated certain variables with five trends of global concern as listed below.

Trends of Global Concern	*Associated Variables*
accelerating industrialization	industrial output per capital
rapid population growth	population
widespread malnutrition	food per capita
depletion of non-renewable resources	resources
deteriorating environment	pollution

When combined in various applications, several scenarios emerged. The 'status quo' scenario posited that the limits to growth were reached because of the depletion of non-renewable resources. Scenario 2 assumed the solution of resource depletion and the limits to growth in this case were reached as a result of increased pollution because of industrial expansion. The next computer run involved 'not only a doubling of resources but also a series of technological strategies to reduce the level of pollution to one-quarter of its pre-1970 level. This time the limits to growth were reached because of a food shortage produced by pressure on arable land owing to its being taken out of agricultural production for urban-industrial use.'[94] Although *Limits to Growth* was attacked for alleged methodological shortcomings and flawed assumptions, its findings sounded alarm bells. Deep greens, who criticized the report for its optimistic vision that technological solutions could be found for these environmental problems, argued that the research pointed to the necessity of changing social and economic practices to avert the impending ecological disaster.

A second important finding in this report pertained to the notion of exponential growth. For example, a 3 per cent growth rate in resource extraction each year would double the rate of production and consumption every twenty-five years, not to mention the waste and pollution caused by this growth. A third finding was the interconnectedness of these variables. Changes in one of the variables might have profound and unintended implications for other variables. For example, new chemical fertilizers might increase food production but might kill fish and wildlife if they contaminate the water.

Although the limits-to-growth approach was viewed by many as a doomsday prediction, one of its scenarios did avoid cataclysm. That was the one that massively reduced resource use and pollution per unit of gross national product; developed new energy sources, namely solar energy; reoriented economies from manufacturing to services; introduced soil conservation; undertook recycling of all wastes, including sewage; and stabilized population at 1970 levels.[95]

American Transcendentalism

American Transcendentalism was a nineteenth-century philosophic and literary movement centred in the Boston area—a liberal spinoff from Puritanism.[96] Primarily associated with the writings of American essayist Ralph Waldo Emerson and his student, Henry David Thoreau, the transcendentalists expressed doubts about the value of Enlightenment empiricism. Emerson wanted 'nature and nature's God to enfold him in a mystical union.'[97]

> This is a delicious evening, when the whole body is one sense, and imbibes delight through every pore. I go and come with a strange liberty in Nature, a part of herself. As I walk along the stony shore of the pond in my shirt-sleeves, though it is cool as well as cloudy and windy, and I see nothing special to attract me, all the elements are unusually congenial to me. The bullfrogs trump to usher in the night, and the note of the whip-poor-will is borne on the rippling wind from over the water. Sympathy with the fluttering alder and poplar leaves almost takes away my breath; yet, like the lake, my serenity is rippled but not ruffled.[98]

Transcendentalists believed that human values did not spring from man's conquest of nature; rather they emanated from wild nature itself. They implored their political leaders to rethink the ideal of industrial progress and to follow a different path.[99] Although those who embraced American Transcendentalism were often dismissed as oddballs who were wildly out of touch with mainstream thinking, many of their works were embraced by the modern environmental movement a century later. Thoreau, in particular, became a counterculture hero. (Indeed, Skinner's *Walden Two* was widely considered the counterculture manifesto of the Woodstock generation. Written after the Second World War, the book chronicled a fictional experimental community that was premised on co-operation and sustainability rather than individualism, competitiveness, and the pursuit of wealth. Walden Two produced its own food and governed itself through its own form of direct democracy.) The movement's ideals of a holistic and natural world, a fundamental human need to remain in contact with nature, and a naturalistic ethic struck a chord with modern environmentalists in the 1960s and 1970s. Although this current of thought did not predict the ruin or breakdown of society, it did raise serious questions about blind trust in science and the unfettered profit-taking of capitalism.[100] Thoreau's musings about agriculture are credited with laying the groundwork for organic farming and his recommendation that each New England town should preserve a primitive forest of no less than 500 acres made him a visionary for modern timber conservation.[101] In addition to the naturalist writings of Emerson and Thoreau, among others, American landscape painters, such as Thomas Cole (1801–48), revered the American landscape and 'rooted nationalism in the physical reality of the republic—purple mountain majesty, amber waves of grain, the fruited plain.'[102]

Transcendentalism enjoyed a renaissance in the mid-1980s. Sometimes referred to as the emancipationist school of green political theory, it contains a number of ideas that have parallels with the Transcendentalist movement of the nineteenth century. In 1987, Thomas Berry wrote that the emphasis in common law on personal rights and the assumption that the natural world exists for human use provides strong support for the entrepreneur. This has led to what he terms a 'spiritual and psychic degradation'.[103] He states further: 'Our main experience of the divine, the world of the sacred, has been diminished as money and utility values have taken precedence over spiritual, aesthetic, emotional, and religious values in our attitude toward the natural world. Any recovery of the natural world will require not only extensive financial funding but a conversion experience deep in the psychic structure of the human.'[104]

Aboriginal Perspective on Nature

At One with Nature

Rod Preece points out that there are significant differences among Aboriginal societies: 'Aboriginal societies *qua* Aboriginal societies do not possess a single type of relationship to nature. Some are decidedly *not* "at one with nature," others are very much so—though even here we must make such statements with some significant reservations. Much depends upon the type of Aboriginal society under discussion.'[105] It is also important to acknowledge that many contemporary Aboriginal cultures have undergone considerable westernization. Fewer and fewer Aboriginal people are fishers, hunters, and gatherers, who are widely considered to be more consistently custodial and conservationist toward nature and non-human animals than non-Aboriginals.[106]

Although Preece's main hypothesis that western and oriental traditions have been unfairly criticized as being anti-nature and anti-animal and that Aboriginal traditions have been overly glorified as environmentally friendly is both compelling and controversial, much of the literature does speak to the 'at one with nature' ideal among Aboriginal peoples. In certain respects, it has become fashionable in mainstream Western society to embrace elements of traditional Native knowledge about nature,

> as long as they are suitably couched in sentimental, romantic, or culturally subordinate terms. . . . But the instant that Native visions of the natural world—and the intellectual capacities of the generations of Native minds that helped shaped them—challenge dominant Western ideas, . . . our cultural and racial biases often become more apparent.[107]

Scholars of Aboriginal culture claim that the Native mind reveals a profound sense of empathy and kinship with other forms of life, rather than a sense of separateness from them or superiority over them. This view regards each species as being as richly endowed with its own singular array of gifts and powers as are human beings.[108] Knudtson and Sukuki argue that although there is diversity within the Aboriginal community itself, there is consensus on the ecological order and the integrity of nature. In many respects, this world view might be described as 'a "sacred ecology" in the most expansive, rather than in the scientifically restrictive, sense of the word "ecology"'.[109] According to J. Donald Hughes, Aboriginal people view Nature as a larger whole of which humankind is only a part. 'People stand within the natural world, not separate from it; and are dependent on it, not dominant over it. All living things are one, and people are joined with birds and trees, predators and prey, rocks and rain in a vast, powerful interrelationship.'[110]

> And they did all this without destroying, without polluting, without using up the living resources of the natural world. Somehow they had learned a secret that Europe had already lost, and which we seem to have lost now in America—the secret of how to live in harmony with Mother Earth, to use what she offers without hurting her; the secret of receiving gratefully the gifts of the Great Spirit.[111]

Aboriginal people lived in careful balance with the natural environment because they had to in order to survive. It has been said that the unmistakable Indian attitude toward nature is appreciation, which varies 'from calm enjoyment to awestruck wonder'.[112] Although the accuracy of the translation of Chief Seattle's famous speech by Dr Henry Smith before the governor of Washington Territory in 1853 has been challenged by several scholars (see Box 1.2), there is little question that Indians saw nature as sacred:

> Every part of this soil is sacred in the estimation of my people. Every hillside, every valley, every plain and grove, has been hallowed by some sad or happy event in days long vanished. Even the rocks, which seem to be dumb and dead as they swelter in the sun along the silent shore, thrill with memories of stirring events connected with the lives of my people.[113]

Because the earth herself was conceived of as being alive in Aboriginal culture, it was important to refrain from harming her. For this reason, Indians often objected to frontier miners who dug holes in the ground, or farmers who plowed, thus tearing the breast of Mother Earth. In contrast to their non-Aboriginal counterparts, 'Indian farmers used a digging stick, an implement that symbolized the natural process of fertilizer.'[114]

For many of Canada's Aboriginal peoples who now live in cities and have become assimilated by the secular, western industrialized society, the bond with nature continues to resonate. Ohiyesa, a celebrated Aboriginal writer states: 'As a child I understood how to give; I have forgotten this grace since I became civilized. I lived the natural life, whereas I now live the artificial. Any pretty pebble was valuable to me then; every growing tree an object of reverence.'[115]

The Land

Land has emerged as a critical component in Native versus non-Native relations in North America. In part, this tension has an unquestionable economic foundation. However, land also has important non-economic meanings to Native peoples. Many Aboriginal religious practices, for example, are land-based theologies whose effectiveness is dependent upon access to specific sacred sites. In other words, sacred geography is an essential feature of the land dilemma.[116] In 1912 a Crow said: 'The soil you see is not ordinary soil, it is the dust of the blood, the flesh and the bones of our ancestors. . . . The land as it is, is my blood and my dead; it is consecrated; and I do not want to give up any portion of it.'[117]

Box 1.2 'All things are connected.' (Chief Seattle)

Chief Seattle almost certainly made an environmentalist speech, somewhere on or near the west coast of the United States sometime between 1853 and 1855. We cannot be more precise than that. A Dr Henry Smith witnessed the oration and it is said he made copious notes on it. However, Smith probably did not understand Seattle's native tongue. Presumably his notes were a derivative rendering. Smith did not write up the speech probably based on a translation until more than thirty years after the speech was delivered. Indeed, he no longer knew in what year it had been delivered. It was published in the *Seattle Star* in 1887.

Given that the article was rendered from notes, which were probably based on a translation (Chief Seattle's native Lushotseed language was probably first translated into Chinook, then English), that more than three decades had elapsed before the notes were revisited, and that the whole was written to impress an American audience, we may have some doubts about the faithfulness of his 1887 article to the 1850s original.

Yet even if the article were Chief Seattle's words verbatim, what we are now offered as Chief Seattle is emphatically not Chief Seattle. Moreover, if the subsequent history of the article reflects anything of the preparation of Smith's article, we would have grounds for doubting its authenticity too. When the speech was republished in the *Washington Historical Quarterly* in 1931, a few mysterious new ecologically impressive sentences were added without any acknowledgment or justification. In the 1960s and 1970s, the piece underwent several further 'refinements', each a rephrasing to meet changing environmental emphasis. Whatever the latest orientation, by a few deft strokes Chief Seattle was presented as its embodiment.

The piece most frequently cited today as the speech of Chief Seattle is a fictional re-interpretation written in 1970 by an American university instructor and screenwriter. The piece was written as an elaboration of Seattle's theme with no intent to misrepresent. Nonetheless, what is now reiterated time and again as Chief Seattle is 1970s Western environmentalism.

Source: Rod Preece, *Animals and Nature: Cultural Myths, Cultural Realities* (Vancouver: University of British Columbia Press, 2000), 18-19.

As discussed in the previous section, Mother Earth herself is seen as sacred. The Aboriginal tribal tradition is that each member and the tribe itself have

a moral, an ethical, relationship with the land. The land is the Mother. The grass is her hair. She is fertile and generous with her gifts, yielding life and beauty in abundance. She provides nourishment for the living and a welcoming embrace for the dead. She is not prejudiced, for she treasures the so-called weeds as readily as the more resplendent flowers. Not only do Indians love the land because it mingles with the dust of the dead, but because it is vital and alive, and is part of the life of each person.'[118]

The most significant difference between Canada's Aboriginal peoples and their European colonial masters, at least in environmental terms, was the way in which they envisioned the land. The Western view of nature sees land as an inert commodity that can be surveyed, subdivided, and zoned. As a commodity, it may be valuable, but it is 'no more "sacred" than a stack of cedar logs, a heap of coal, or any other economic resource. It is a financial investment to be bought, "developed", and resold (hopefully at a handsome profit) by shuffling official titles and deeds.'[119] However, it cannot be said that the Western view has monolithically been without regard for the land. Indeed, the American conservation movement in the late eighteenth century displayed a willingness to protect geographic spaces that were judged to be important natural sanctuaries for wildlife. It can be argued that in lobbying for the perpetual protection of vast, pristine tracts of land as wilderness areas or national parks, they were calling for a collective sanctification of nature.[120] In most important respects, however, the Aboriginal view of land is fundamentally different. To Canada's First Peoples, the land belonged to all; it was sacred and was inscribed with meaning regarding the origins and unity of life. The ownership of land and its legal partitioning into commercial real estate holdings was a foreign concept to them.[121]

Animals and Nature

E.O. Wilson, the distinguished Harvard entomologist and evolutionary zoologist, referred to a profound human affinity for other life forms as 'biophilia'.[122] Many advocates of animal liberation come from the non-Native community. The motivations behind this biophilia among Natives and non-Natives are different. Many non-Natives see animal liberation in ethical terms. For Native peoples, however, the motivations are more spiritual: 'Adequate land and wildlife were fundamental to Indian cultures. More than most other cultures, theirs were founded on a practical and spiritual relationship to the land and wildlife.'[123] Unquestionably, the need to hunt for food appears, at first blush, to be a betrayal of this relationship. However, Native hunters are expected 'not simply to slay [their] prey but to try, within the context of spiritual values and practices of [their] culture, to come to terms psychologically with a number of potentially disturbing moral contradictions.'[124]

Other Theoretical Influences On Green Political Thought

Religion

There are those within the green movement who object to bringing religion into the debate for fear that religious ideals may threaten 'objectivity, scientific investigation, professionalism, or democratic values'.[125] Others believe that religion may strengthen green political thought by making human beings aware that there are limits to their control over the animate and inanimate world. Religion instils the recognition 'that human life cannot be measured by material possessions and that the ends of life go beyond conspicuous consumption.'[126]

Christian scholars claim that many teachings of the Bible reinforced the idea that the world was created primarily, if not exclusively, for humankind. Thus the biblical tradition generated anthropocentric, dualistic, hierarchical, and patriarchal ideas and attitudes that are problematic from an ecological as well as a democratic perspective.[127] In Genesis 1:28, human beings are created in the image of God, and they are consequently given the charge to 'subdue' the earth and 'have dominion' over it.[128] Because the biblical tradition preaches that 'non-human life forms and the rest of nature exist in a realm separated from God, they possess instrumental but not intrinsic value. Consequently they are not part of the moral community.'[129]

In 1967, the historian, Lynn White, Jr., wrote an article in *Science* on the historical roots of the ecological crisis. According to White, the exploitative view that has generated much of the environmental crisis, 'particularly in Europe and North America, is a result of the teachings of late medieval Latin Christianity, which conceived of humankind as superior to the rest of God's creation and everything else as created for human use and enjoyment.'[130] White argues that 'Christianity is the most anthropocentric religion the world has seen.'[131] This belief that humankind has dominion over the earth has led to an arrogance and a careless use of the land. Moreover, 'our science and technology have grown out of Christian attitudes towards man's relation to nature which are almost universally held not only by Christians and neo-Christians but also by those who fondly regard themselves as post-Christians.'[132]

But religions outside the Judeo-Christian tradition have been viewed more favourably. Buddhism has great respect for and gratitude toward nature, which is seen as the mother that gives rise to all the joyful things in life.[133] The Buddha is said to have taught his disciples 'to communicate to animals their wishes for peace and happiness. This was only possible when they did not eat the animals' flesh, and harbored no thoughts of harming them.'[134] The Fourteenth Dalai Lama of Tibet, a prominent Buddhist leader, has said: 'Our ancestors viewed the Earth as rich, bountiful and sustainable. . . . We know this is the case, but only if we take care of it.'[135]

Hinduism is also viewed as a religion that sees nature in a spiritual way. In particular, it has a deep respect of animal life that is credited to the Hindu theological belief that the Supreme Being was himself incarnated in the form of various species. Additionally, the Hindu belief in the 'cycle of birth and rebirth where a person may come back as an animal or a bird gives these species not only respect, but also reverence. This provides a solid foundation for the doctrine of *ahimsa*—nonviolence against animals and human beings alike. Hindus have a deep faith in the doctrine of non-violence.'[136] The Hindu religion teaches a

renunciation of worldly goods and preaches against materialism and consumerism.'[137] Of course, not all countries with a Buddhist and Hindu tradition are
necessarily 'at one with nature'. In some countries, including India, the ancient
educational system that taught respect for nature has been replaced by more Western secular systems that have been imported from Europe, primarily Britain.[138]

Ethics and Morality

As an academic and intellectual discipline, 'ethics' is the philosophical study of
morality which provides a guide to proper human conduct. Within this broad
philosophical discipline has emerged the sub-area of eco-ethics. This relatively
new field 'attempts to create a conceptual framework for human interaction with
the environment, a framework that can assist us in holding our own lives
together and enable us to act with discipline, understanding, and reverence
toward the natural world.'[139] Eco-ethics has developed out of increasing public
alarm about the state of the environment and has led to a broader and deeper
understanding of ethics that transcends the concern we have for our fellow
human beings.[140] Eco-ethicists argue that any viable modern ethic must also
include our moral responsibility and connectedness to the natural world.

Steven Rockefeller suggests that there are two basic approaches in developing
a moral argument about environmental degradation. The first suggests that 'protecting the environment and nonhuman creatures is a matter of enlightened
human self-interest and intergenerational responsibility.'[141] In other words, it is
morally irresponsible to deny future generations the benefits of a clean environment. This appeal to the sense of responsibility of citizens is not a novel idea and
was very much evident in Rachel Carson's *Silent Spring*, and in particular, her
argument that it was humankind's obligation to endure.

Eco-ethicism owes a debt to Aldo Leopold, who was one of the first thinkers to
develop the ethical implications of ecology. In his well-known essay 'The Land
Ethic', which appeared in *A Sand County Almanac* in 1949, he suggested that 'all
ethics so far evolved rest upon a single premise: that the individual is a member of
a community of independent parts. His instincts prompt him to compete for his
place in that community, but his ethics prompt him also to cooperate.'[142] In the
development of the notion of the land ethic, the idea of community was widened
to include soils, waters, plants, and animals.[143] Although the development of a
land ethic would not necessarily result in the prudent management and conservation of resources, Leopold does suggest that it would 'affirm their right to continued existence, and, at least in spots, their continued existence in a natural state.'[144]

According to eco-ethicism, as a citizen of this biotic community, a human
being has an obligation to the land and the non-human members of the biotic
community that goes beyond those dictated by economic self-interest. From this
obligation, Leopold argued, a new 'ecological conscience' will emerge that views
land uses as an ethical rather than merely an economic question.[145]

Marxism

Like Locke, Karl Marx formed his ideas at a time when the extent of global ecological degradation could not be foreseen. Therefore, the contributions of Marxist thought to the environmental debate have been given an interpretation by scholars who believe that Marxist thought has an important contribution to make to green political theory. As to which of his ideas—political economy, social life, or culture—are most important, there is no consensus. One of the more contentious notions of Marxist thought is his characterization of nature. This concept was one of the most important categories in all stages of Marx's work. For Marx and his adherents, the interaction between man and nature through labour was the key to the understanding of history; the natural science and industry of the nineteenth century represented the most highly developed, to date, of the ongoing 'theoretical and practical relation of men to nature'.[146] In one sense, man is presented as a natural being, and his capacity for labour is only a form of nature's energy. However, man also seeks to transform nature so that his growing needs may be satisfied:

> He opposes himself to Nature as one of her own forces, setting in motion arms and legs, heads and hands, the natural forces of his body, in order to appropriate Nature's productions in a form adapted to his own wants. By thus acting on the external world and changing it, he at the same time changes his own nature. He develops his slumbering powers and compels them to act in obedience to his sway.[147]

Marx presents here in outline the dialectic of man and nature. 'Nature is the "field of employment" for all human activity, the universal ground of the labor-process that is common to every form of social organization. In his activity, man changes the natural world, but also is himself changed; his creative abilities unfold, opening up new possibilities for utilizing nature's resources, and the process continues indefinitely.'[148] In Marx's concept of alienation experienced by people under capitalism, one facet is humankind's alienation from nature. In capitalist systems, nature is transformed into something 'other' to be exploited and valued for its utility and exchange values or as a property, possession, or commodity. Overcoming alienation involves restoring our relationship to nature and rediscovering it as something of value in itself.[149] In terms of political economy, long-term co-ordination in the common interest, as opposed to competitive self-interest in pursuit of private gain, would require collective ownership.[150] Adherents to this political-economy approach argue that the collective ownership of the means of production is better able to solve environmental problems than private capitalist ownership.

Not all theorists see Marx as a defender of the environment. Indeed, some critics believe that his concept of the human-nature relationship was based on the goal of human betterment and not the well-being of non-human entities or of nature itself. Other critics have argued that Marxist thought was silent on the issues of natural limits and obligations to the non-human world. The theory that nature is our inorganic body is not set up to provide a basis for care for nature but to show how transformation of it is part of the furtherance of human development.[151] Indeed, some green theorists, including Eckersley, believe that an ecocentric perspective cannot be wrested out of Marxism 'without seriously distorting Marx's own theoretical concepts'.[152] Rather, they have chosen to develop an ecocentric view from other traditions, such as utopianism, anarchy, and feminism.

Utopianism and Anarchism

One of the fierce critiques of deep ecology came from social ecologists, who rejected the use of the state to solve environmental problems and the lack of social perspective in deep ecology.[153] The adherents of deep ecology believed that marrying ecology and anarchism would deliver humanity and 'other nature' to some higher plain of existence. Eco-anarchism believes in the abolition of nation-states and the granting of political and economic autonomy to decentralized local communities. In addition, it is a strong defender of the non-institutional grassroots politics of social movements.[154] Both the utopian and anarchist ideas that are advanced in deep ecology emphasize the benefits of decentralization and direct democracy. The best-known advocates of these ideals are Murray Bookchin, author of numerous books, including *Our Synthetic Environment, Toward an Ecological Society*, and *The Ecology of Freedom*; Ivan Illich; and E.F. Schumacher. Bookchin claims that our ecological problems are social problems requiring fundamental change:

> All this loose talk of 'we' masks the reality of social power and social institutions. It masks the fact that the social forces that are tearing down the planet are the same forces which threaten to degrade women, people of color, workers, and ordinary citizens. It masks the fact that there is an historical connection between the way people deal with each other as social beings and the way they treat nature. . . . It makes a big difference how societies relate to the natural world whether people live in co-operative, non-hierarchical, and decentralized communities or in hierarchical, class-ridden, and authoritarian mass societies. Similarly, the ecological impact of human reason, science, and technology depends enormously on the type of society in which these forces are shaped and employed.[155]

Bookchin favours the creation of new communities and technologies associated with direct action: 'Direct action becomes the practical means for local communities to recover individual control from bureaucratic agencies of the nation-state and corporate firm. . . . The direct action of social ecology could overturn, bit by bit, the administrative regime of centralized welfare states and transnational firms used in megatechnics.'[156] Together, ecocommunities and ecotechnologies, Bookchin maintains, 'would open a new era in face-to-face relationships in direct democracy, providing the free time that would make it possible in Hellenic fashion for people to manage the affairs of society without the mediation of bureaucracies and professional political functionaries.'[157]

A fundamental idea of both utopianism and anarchism is voluntary simplicity, which, its advocates claim, has the potential to solve many of the problems related with consumer society, including social passivity and alienation: 'Living simply, as a rule for the conduct of everyday life in advanced industrial society, allows many others to simply live.'[158] Recognizing that capitalism will continue to predominate, social ecologists have attempted to promote the idea of voluntary simplicity as a middle way between the extremes of poverty and self-indulgence:

> In practice, a voluntarily simplified mode of living implies moving toward less consumption of consumer goods, more self-production of personal goods and services, greater use of energy-frugal appropriate technologies, less dependence on corporate and state services, and cultivation of new kinds of personal growth by devoting time to enlivening local institutions such as co-ops, extended families, collectives, churches, neighbourhood organizations, and community schools. It is essentially an alternative vision of modernity waiting to be put into practice.[159]

Utopianism and anarchism make important contributions to the deep-ecology political theory, particularly its ideas of decentralization, conservation, and voluntary simplicity. Their key contributions lie in their position that environmental degradation can best be understood as a social problem because all forms of domination are caused by hierarchies in human societies and the subordination of non-humans. The principles of social ecology allow for their hierarchies to be dismantled.

Ecofeminism

The term 'ecoféminisme' was first coined in 1974 by the French writer Françoise d'Eaubonne, who called upon women to save the planet through an ecological revolution.[160] Some theorists view ecofeminism as a new kind of environmental ethics, while others believe that it can best be understood as a new stream within feminist theory. Each of the streams of feminist thought—liberal, cultural, and socialist—has made contributions to ecofeminist thinking. In the case of liberal feminism, the views are consistent with those of moderate environmentalism that call for the alteration of human relations with nature from within existing structures of governance.[161] Cultural feminism is described by Carolyn Merchant:

> For cultural feminists, human nature is grounded in human biology. Humans are biologically sexed and socially gendered. Sex/gender relations give men and women different power bases. Hence the personal is political. Their perceived connection between women and biological reproduction turned upside down becomes the source of women's empowerment and ecological activism. Women's biology and Nature are celebrated as sources of female power. This form of ecofeminism has largely focused on the sphere of consciousness in relation to nature—spirituality, goddess worship, witchcraft—and the celebration of women's bodies, often accompanied by such social actions as anti-nuclear or anti-pornography protests.[162]

Socialist feminism, on the other hand, seeks 'the total restructuring of the market economy's use of both women and nature as resources.'[163] However one chooses to categorize it, ecofeminism establishes the connection between the oppression of women and the oppression of nature. Ecofeminism believes that the historical and symbolic association of women with nature demonstrates a special convergence of interests between feminism and ecology.[164] Ecofeminism has evoked the criticism of many liberal feminists while being applauded as a compelling theoretical premise elsewhere. Some feminists believe that associating women with nature harkens back to a time when the basis of the oppression of women was their biology and specifically their ability to reproduce. Others argue that by becoming re-associated with nature, women are celebrating their strengths and spiritualism—facets of womanhood that have been devalued by patriarchy. Judith Plant observes:

> [The] aims [of ecofeminism] are not the same as those associated with the dominant liberal feminist position. This means that ecofeminists do not seek equality with men, as such, but rather want us to recognize that women's liberation means liberation for women as *women*. They have a specific understanding of what 'being a woman' involves, and they believe that women's liberation will require a positive revaluation of those activities and sites of activity traditionally associated with women—giving birth, nurturing and the domestic arena.[165]

Feminism is currently besieged by internal disputes, largely about which social values should be given priority. To the liberal feminist, the priority is gender-free equality of opportunity; to the Marxist, the focus is on class as well as sexual oppression; to the socialist, the connections between the dominant economic systems and gender expectations are paramount; and to the radical feminist, the most important thing is the primacy of biological distinctions and reproductive roles as the vehicles of oppression.[166] For ecofeminism to emerge as a dominant stream, it will be necessary to transform all of these current differences and make the 'ecofeminist perspective central to feminist theory and practice'.[167] This will require a convergence of the various voices and perspectives within the ecofeminist movement:

> [Ecofeminism] not only recognizes the multiple voices of women, located differently by race, class, age, [and] ethnic characteristics, it centralised those voices. Ecofeminism builds on the multiple perspectives of those whose perspectives are typically omitted or undervalued in dominant discourses. . . . An ecofeminist perspective is thereby . . . structurally pluralistic, inclusivist, and contextualist, emphasizing through concrete example the crucial role context plays in understanding sexist and naturalist practice.[168]

Women have long been associated with nature, for example in metaphors such as 'Mother Earth' or 'virgin' forest. The life cycles through which women pass—menstruation, lactation, and menopause—are considered 'natural'. Women have also traditionally been responsible for child care, the nurturing of others, the care of elderly parents. Ecofeminists believe that women and men should celebrate those values associated with women and, in doing so, make people more conscious of the nature and the joy and happiness that emanate from being nurturing: 'Home is the theatre of human ecology, and it is here that we can effectively think feelingly.'[169]

Another corollary of the ecofeminist point of view is what Eckersley terms the oppression argument. By virtue of being oppressed, women are in a better position to evaluate ecological practices. Because women have been less implicated than men in activities that cause ecological destruction (the military, boardrooms, science, and bureaucracy), women are viewed as being in a better position to offer suggestions about ecological reconstruction.[170] Indeed, many women have been on the leading edge of local and grassroots movements and are seen as credible spokespeople for their communities. In the Canadian case, the role of women in leading the protest to stop the clearcutting of ancient rainforests on Clayoquot Sound has been well documented in such films as *The Sound and the Fury*. Lois Gibbs (see Box 1.3), a member of the Love Canal Homeowners Association, is often hailed as an important figure in the ecofeminist movement. In 1978, she and other residents of the Love Canal began to mobilize in order to protest about the health effects of hazardous waste disposal by Hooker Chemicals and Plastics Corporation in Niagara Falls, New York. Although men were involved in the protest, working-class women who had never before been politically active took the lead using the argument that their children and their homes were in danger. Conducting research on their community (consisting of some 1,200 households) themselves, the women discovered that only one of fifteen pregnancies resulted in a normal baby. In addition, a significant number of women in the community had developed breast and uterine cancer and one twelve-year-old girl had had a hysterectomy.[171]

Like the other currents of theoretical influences, the particular contribution of ecofeminism to a comprehensive and coherent green political theory has been contested. In certain respects, the critique by ecofeminism of development and modernization in the Third World[172] and its call for environmental activism there may have more salience than its contribution to the environmental movement in the developed world. That said, however, ecofeminism does add something important to the philosophical discussions surrounding the human domination of nature and the role of women in the environmental movement.

All God's Creatures

The first animal rights organization was the Royal Society for the Prevention of Cruelty to Animals, which was founded in England in 1824. Subsequently, similar organizations were founded in Canada and other Western countries. All advocated legislation to criminalize certain acts that were thought to violate

Box 1.3 Lois Gibbs and the Love Canal

'Love Canal actually began for me in June 1978 with Mike Brown's articles in the *Niagara Falls Gazette*. At first, I didn't realize where the canal was. Niagara Falls has two sets of streets numbered the same. Brown's articles said Love Canal was between 99th and 97th Streets but I didn't think he meant the place where my children went to school or where I took them to play on the jungle gyms and swings. Although I read the articles, I didn't pay much attention to them. One article did stand out, though. In it, Mike Brown wrote about monkeys subjected to PCBs having miscarriages and deformed offspring.

'One of the later articles pointed out that the school had been built over the canal. Still, I paid little attention: it didn't affect me, Lois Gibbs. I thought it was terrible, but I lived on the other side of Pine Avenue. Those poor people over there on the other side were the ones who had to worry. The problem didn't affect me, so I wasn't going to bother doing anything about it, and I certainly wasn't going to speak out about it. Then when I found out the 99th Street School was indeed on top of it, I was alarmed. My son attended that school. He was in kindergarten that year. I decided I needed to do some investigating.'

Source: Lois Marie Gibbs, *Love Canal: The Story Continues. . . .* (Gabriola Island, BC.: New Society, 1998), 26–7.

After being told that the local school board would not allow her to transfer her son from the elementary school built on the perimeter of the dump to another school because it would 'set a precedent', Lois Gibbs did not just get angry—she got organized. She founded the Love Canal Homeowners Association, which persuaded the government to conduct environmental tests and human health studies. After years of lobbying and rallies, President Jimmy Carter, in October 1980, finally signed the bill that advanced the funds for the residents of the Love Canal to be moved. Lois Gibbs went on to found the Citizens Clearinghouse for Hazardous Wastes, which works with over 8,000 grassroots groups in the United States faced with existing or proposed environmental threats.

the ethical rights of animals.[173] Some theorists, including Peter Singer (author of *Animal Liberation*, 1975) and Tom Regan (author of *The Case for Animal Rights*, 1983), claim that animals have certain natural rights, are moral subjects in many of the same ways that humans are, and, as such, belong to our genuine sphere of ethical concern. Each year billions of sentient animals are used as food by humans. Millions more are killed each year in biomedical research. This area is one in which the debate rages with emotions running high on both sides of the issue.

A starting point is the recognition that all living things have some form of intrinsic value—that is, their reason for being is not simply to serve the needs of humans. From this point, perspectives differ. In his important book, *Animal Liberation*, Pete Singer acknowledges that there are ethical problems in applying such concepts as equality. He states: 'The basic principle of equality does not require equal or identical *treatment*; it requires equal *consideration*. Equal consideration for different beings may lead to different treatment with different rights.'[174]

It is impossible, in any practical sense, to advance the idea of absolute equality between humans and the plant and animal worlds. In Canada, many of our citizens are employed in agriculture, fishing, and food production. Moreover, at least some form of research using animals will probably continue to be necessary. Most animal rights organizations are cognizant of these practical constraints. As it relates to the use of animals in medical research, their emphasis has been on more humane treatment of research animals and the use of other research methods that do not require animal subjects. Some advocates have called for the total elimination of any laboratory research involving primates, except under the most exceptional circumstances.[175] Even though objectionable agricultural and medical practices will probably continue, there are other issues that can be addressed within the broader area of animal liberation. First and foremost is the infliction of *unnecessary* suffering. Jeremy Bentham once wrote:

> But a full-grown horse or dog is beyond comparison a more rational, as well as a more conversable animal, than an infant of a day or a week or even a month old. But suppose they were otherwise, what would it avail? The question is not, can they *reason*? Nor can they *talk*? But, can they *suffer*?[176]

The unnecessary killing of animals and the infliction of pain is seen as an ethical issue because mankind has traditionally destroyed and killed other creatures for its own convenience. Miller notes: 'Ethically, however, convenience does not constitute necessary moral justification for practices leading to the suffering of other creatures.'[177] While there is considerable support among the public to restrict the suffering of animals that are used for research, what about the treatment of animals that ultimately end up on our dinner plates?

> Hundreds of thousands of cattle today are penned up in feed lots—standing all day confined in their own filth, and inoculated regularly with antibiotics and other drugs to prevent disease—in order to maximize both profits to the entrepreneurs and the tasty fat content of the meat. Broiler chickens are placed in windowless sheds with no possibility of movement during their entire lives. They are kept in darkness to prevent the cannibalism that would otherwise occur in such overcrowded conditions. . . . Similar techniques are used in the production of rabbits and turkeys.[178]

The major issues of concern to the animal-rights movement in Canada during the past twenty years have been the Atlantic coast seal hunt, trapping, the use of animals in research laboratories, and the well-being of livestock. Those campaigning against the Newfoundland seal hunt included both animal-rights organizations, such as the International Fund for Animal Welfare, the Animal Fund, the Animal Protection Institute; and environmental organizations, such as Greenpeace and Paul Watson's Sea Shepherd Society. The original rationale for Greenpeace's involvement was that the harp seal was an endangered species. By 1978, however, it was clear that quotas on the seal hunt imposed in 1971 had resulted in an expansion of the seal population. Greenpeace's more recent concern with the hunt has focused on the issue of animal rights, and concern for the pain and death suffered by the individual seal.

As is the case with many groups in the environmental movement, there is wide diversity within animal liberation groups in Canada. It has been estimated that over 300 animal protection groups are operating in Canada.

Conclusions

Many diverse theories have contributed to the development of green political theory. Many environmentalists remain convinced that green ideas and values can be used by governments and policy makers without a dismantling of the modern day nation-state. Moreover, the rights and freedoms enjoyed by citizens can be protected while at the same time improved and enhanced by a greener world. Many citizens continue to believe that humankind has the collective ability to solve our most serious environmental problems. Although they have been called Pollyannas by more radical greens, there is little question that many environmentalists and environmental groups believe that nation-states could implement green programs and policies within the liberal democratic tradition.

Although liberal democracy has continued to be the dominant system of governance in North America and elsewhere in the Western industrialized world, and will likely continue to be in the foreseeable future, new currents of thought developed in the 1960s and 1970s have challenged its legitimacy on both environmental and human-rights grounds. The ideology of ecologism is fundamentally different from that of environmentalism. It constitutes a significant challenge to the political, economic, and social consensus that dominated the late twentieth century and has continued into the twenty-first century. Environmentalism, on the other hand, is a managerial approach to the environment consistent with present-day political and economic practices. While environmentalism tends to be premised on an optimism that technology can solve the problems that it creates, ecologism does not. Finally, unlike environmentalism, which is premised on slow and incremental change, ecologism holds that a sustainable and fulfilling existence presupposes radical changes in our social, economic, and political structures. Distinguishing between these two very different green views has been necessary in order to explain why certain green organizations object to each other's tactics and strategies. In addition, it helps to explain why government announcements about green initiatives are often applauded by some greens but condemned by others. In Canada, as we shall see in Chapter 2, the range of green groups is as wide as the spectrum of green political thought that has been discussed in this chapter.

Suggestions for Further Reading

Elgin, Duanne, *Voluntary Simplicity* (New York: William Morrow, 1981).

Glendinning, Chellis, *My Name Is Chellis, and I'm in Recovery from Western Society* (Boston: Shambhala, 1994).

Gordon, Anita, and David Suzuki, *It's a Matter of Survival* (Toronto: Stoddart, 1990).

Naess, Arne, *Ecology, Community, and Lifestyle* (Cambridge: Cambridge University Press, 1989).

Sessions, George, 'Deep Ecology as World View', *World-View and Ecology*, M. Tucker and John Grim (eds) (Lewisburg, Pa.: Buckell University Press, 1993), 207–27.

Watson, Paul, *Nature and Madness* (San Francisco: Sierra Club Books, 1992).

Suggestions for Small-Group Discussion

1. What laws and regulations are there in Canada that govern and restrict the use of animals in medical research? What is the position of government officials? What is the position of animal rights groups? To what extent are the differences in perspectives ethical? To what extent are they political?

2. Why do liberal feminists and radical feminists feel threatened by the views of ecofeminists? To what degree is ecofeminism a strong or weak current in feminist thought?

3. Under what conditions might the principles of deep ecology transcend those of liberal democracies?

Chapter Two

Environmentalism as a Social Movement

'The Green movement aspires to be the political expression of a wider effort to reconcile the false separation between humanity and the natural world.' Brian Tokar, *The Green Alternative*, 33.

The two green world views described in Chapter One help us to understand the Canadian Green movement and the international movement in which Canadian greens and environmental organizations are but one of many participants. As would be expected, some groups choose to seek incremental change in their efforts to make liberal democracies more green. These groups try to influence government policy by penetrating political and economic structures and to present themselves as partners in decision making. They do not attempt to undermine the existing administrative and political structures, and they tend to present their points of view by peaceful means. At times they form alliances or coalitions with like-minded groups in order to attract support and favourable media coverage. Other green groups—those embracing deep-ecology views—tend to be more radical in their demands, and they may adopt more controversial tactics in order to gain publicity for their causes. In most environmental groups there are disagreements between the moderate and more radical members.

It would be inaccurate to depict the environmental movement as a cohesive group of like-minded individuals and groups joined together by shared opinions and goals. In the United States there are estimated to be a dozen or more new ecological ideologies, 'each with its cadre of articulate advocates and ardent followers'.[1] To some, this diversity is a weakness of the environmental movement. To others, a synthesis of disparate and, at times, antithetical ideas is seen as necessary if the objective is to influence decisions and the cultures of civil institutions, academic disciplines, economic philosophies, and religions.[2] Over and above this diversity, the green movement also varies from country to country.[3] This diversity has been referred to by Manuel Castells 'as a cacophony of theory and practice that characterizes environmentalism as a new form of decentralized, multiform, network-oriented, pervasive social movement.'[4] Although there have been many well-publicized disputes between the moderate and radical elements of organizations in the environmental movement, many of these have revolved around leadership, tactics, and language and not the objectives of environmentalism. When the principles and goals of these groups are examined, considerable evidence is found that there is a strong consensus 'linking up the defense of specific environments to new human values'.[5]

In order for a movement to become a social movement, however, a number of criteria must be met. This chapter, in a very brief way, discusses social movement theory in determining whether or not the green movement qualifies as a social movement. The chapter also develops a categorization system for the various types of green groups in Canada and describes examples of the different groups.

Social Movement Theories

There is a rich theoretical literature on the necessary preconditions for groups of individuals to evolve into a social movement. Interest groups within broad-based social movements are diverse and heterogeneous, ranging from being socially conservative to revolutionary. Moreover, their causes and objectives can be seen as being either good or bad.

In this important sense, they are best understood as symptoms of problems in our societies.[6] Manuel Castells views them as 'meaningful signs of new social conflicts, and embryos of social resistance'.[7] Alaine Touraine has contributed to this body of social-movement theory by establishing a typology of social movements that include a movement's identity (what it is, on behalf of whom it speaks), the self-definition of the movement, the movement's adversary, the movement's principal enemy, and lastly the movement's vision or goal (that is, what kind of social order the movement wants).

The success of a social movement is usually measured according to whether or not it has resulted in a significant transformation of both behaviour and values. In the case of the environmental movement, its success is contingent on a transformation of modes of production and consumption, as well as on social organization and personal lives.[8] Although this transformation has not yet occurred on a mass scale, there is nevertheless a growing awareness of and support for environmental goals.

Other theorists believe that a social movement is a term used to refer 'to the form in which new combinations of people inject themselves into politics and challenge dominant ideas and a given constellation of power'.[9] A nineteenth-century example was the labour movement, in which there was a mobilization of people objecting to harsh industrial working conditions. In the latter part of the twentieth century, the women's movement and the environmental movement are considered to be 'new' social movements that have challenged 'a new set of dominant ideas and another constellation of power.'[10] Like earlier social movements, both contain radical elements and espouse a new world view.

Environmental movements are seen as possessing post-materialist values that challenge the dominant materialist values of contemporary society. Strongly premised on Maslow's 'hierarchy of needs', the post-materialist argument is that 'having largely fulfilled the more basic needs of safety and security, parts of advanced industrial society are able to pursue the "higher", more luxuriant causes, such as love and a sense of belonging, beyond the old politics of material existence.'[11] A clean environment falls within the realm of post-materialism. Although a number of First World environmental movements do embody post-materialist values, this is not true for all of them. Moreover, the post-materialist thesis does little to explain the origins and character of environmental movements in the Third World, where many citizens lack the most basic material necessities.

An alternative explanation of the origin of environmental movements is the post-industrialist thesis. According to this argument, 'advanced industrialism, championed by both the market systems of latter-day capitalism and the state-centred models of Soviet-style socialism, has pushed the Earth, its habitats and its species (including humans) to the brink of extinction. The industrial/development paradigm has promoted economic growth at all costs.'[12] Contemporary environmental movements are, therefore, often explained as reactions to this industrial-development strategy.

For the most part, environmental movements have developed within the non-institutional and more informal parts of society. Dubbed 'politics-of-the-people' groups by social-movement theorists, many are dynamic, amorphous networks, associations, grassroots groups, and alliances, which in large part are not governed by formal rules of association, such as constitutions.[13] These kinds of loosely knit groups are very visible in environmental politics in Canada. Some

Table 2.1 Typology of Green Groups

Type	Identity	Adversary	Goal
Conservation of nature	Nature lovers	Uncontrolled development	Wilderness
Defence of own space	Local community	Polluters	Quality of life and health
Counter-culture, deep ecology, ecofeminism	The green self	Industrialism, technocracy, and patriarchy	Ecotopia
Save the planet	Internationalist eco-warriors	Unfettered global development	Sustainability
Green politics	Concerned citizens	Political establishment	Counter-power

Source: Based on Manuel Castells, *The Information Age: Economy, Society and Culture*, Vol. II, *The Power of Identity* (Oxford: Blackwell, 1997).

groups, however, have followed the same pattern as non-environmental groups and have become increasingly institutionalized in order to survive. Levels of organization, research capabilities, and strategies, therefore, are as varied as the green groups themselves. Thus it is difficult to classify green organizations.

Nevertheless, Castells, borrowing substantially from Touraine's classification system, has developed a useful typology of green groups that distinguishes among types of groups on the basis of type, identity, adversary, and goal.

Conservation of Nature

The first use of the term 'conservation movement' has been attributed to the natural-resource advisers to President Theodore Roosevelt in 1907.[14] Alarm at the massive shrinking of public lands from some 1.2 billion acres to just 600 million acres by 1912 led to a push to take a broader view of the public-lands question in the United States. Early efforts to come up with a holistic plan were opposed at their early stages by the American Forestry Association and other groups and by a number of state governments. It has been argued that conservation movements peak at times of economic anxiety, and there were spurts in group activities in the late 1920s and the late 1950s. The goal of conservation groups is not to slow down economic activity but to remind people 'enjoying the hedonism of affluence of the need for efficiency and frugality'.[15] By the 1980s, old and new mainstream environmental organizations in the United States came together in an alliance known as the Group of Ten.[16] Although the member groups differ in their organization and emphasis, they use the same strategy of defending conservationist causes through the institutional system.

As a mass-based movement, the Canadian conservation movement developed later than its American counterpart. For instance, the oldest national conservation organization, the Canadian Nature Federation, was not founded until the late 1930s.[17] Until the 1960s, however, most Canadians expressed 'little interest in wildlands preservation. . . . At best, only a small upper and middle income urban élite shared an appreciation of the physical, aesthetic, and spiritual values of wilderness.'[18] In the United States, the leading conservation group was the Sierra Club, which was founded in 1891 by John Muir. The adversaries for North American conservation groups are uncontrolled development and unresponsive bureaucracies, and their goal is to conserve wilderness areas.

Local Communities

Grassroots, loosely organized, and volunteer-driven groups constitute the fastest-growing type of environmental organization.[19] As far as an event that prompted this kind of action and mobilization is concerned, many activists point to the infamous Love Canal incident of 1978 which involved the dumping of industrial toxic waste in New York state. Lois Gibbs, a local resident who emerged as the leader of the Love Canal citizens' group, went on to establish the Clearinghouse for Hazardous Wastes. This group, which was not well financed or particularly sophisticated in its tactics, took on the local school board, the state of New York, and federal authorities and demanded that a hazardous waste site be cleaned up.[20] Since the Love Canal incident, communities across North America have organized against such activities as the construction of expressways, urban development, and the use of pesticides in public parks. Some current Canadian examples of grassroots movements include the Save Saltspring Campaign in British Columbia and Save the Oak Ridges Moraine, a small coalition that has taken on land-development companies north of Toronto. The tactics used by both these groups will be discussed further in our case studies of various green groups.

Counterculture

In most social movements, a counterculture emerges when some members of the movement make a deliberate attempt to live according to norms that are different from, and to some extent contradictory to, those institutionally enforced by society, and oppose traditional institutions on the basis of alternative principles and beliefs.[21] From the early days of the Industrial Revolution, utopian ideals have been embraced by certain social activists, including the Owenites and the Luddites in Great Britain. Later, the Transcendentalists, including Emerson and Thoreau, rejected progress and development and chose to live simpler lives. This ethos of counterculturalism exists within some of the more radical environmental groups, including Earth First!, the Sea Shepherds, members of the animal liberation movement, and ecofeminist groups. In certain respects, ecofeminism is clearly distant from the 'macho-tactics' of some of these movements, but 'they share the principle of absolute respect for nature as the foundation of liberation from both patriarchalism and industrialism.'[22]

In many ways, the principles of deep ecology espoused by counterculture groups can be credited with crystallizing the differences between it and light-green environmentalism. Unlike light-green environmentalism, it is critical of industrial society, technological culture, and capitalism. At the same time, this radicalism has alienated more moderate environmentalists from the movement, particularly rural, blue-collar workers:

> Not only do deep ecologists moralize about consumerism and believe in reducing human standards of living—neither of which are popular notions among people living close to the edge—but they tend to sanctify the species workers see as threatening their standard of living. The way to a logger's heart is not through the nest of a spotted owl.[23]

If the Transcendentalists were the counterculture during the Industrial Revolution, the new environmentalism espoused by the sixties generation was the counterculture of the modern industrial state. Its emergence was part of a broad, incremental process of social and political change that had its roots in the late 1950s in mass protests associated with the Suez Crisis, the Cold War, the threat of nuclear war, and the injustices of racial inequality.[24]

Save the Planet

In the last two decades, some environmental organizations have become international in scope in order to tackle global issues. Greenpeace has popularized global environmental issues by its media-oriented, non-violent, direct actions. Members of Greenpeace are motivated by a sense of urgency and a Quaker-inspired attitude of bearing witness, both as a principle for action and as a strategy of communication. Over time, this organization has evolved from a loosely knit organization to a more institutionalized group and has developed a business-like, pragmatic approach to environmental activism. For groups like Greenpeace, the adversary is development that is characterized by a lack of concern with its consequences on life on the planet. They mobilize to enforce the principle of environmental sustainability as the overarching principle to which all other policies and activities must be subordinated.[25] Above all, groups such as Greenpeace are internationalists, and they see the nation-state as the main obstacle to the control of unfettered destructive development. The evolution of this group is discussed in more detail later in this chapter.

Green Politics

In some cases, greens and other groups have created political alliances that have evolved into political parties. The most famous and successful of such coalitions was the West German Green Party (Die Grünen) in which greens, feminists, peace activists, and anti-nuclear activists joined forces in the early 1980s. The decision to move from autonomous social movements to a formal political party was a contentious one that caused a permanent fissure within the environmental movement. Not wanting to be seen as a 'typical' political party, the Green Party adopted a number of operating principles in order to present themselves as an anti-party committed not to conduct 'politics as usual'. Included among these were fixed terms and the rotation principle for their members of parliament. Part of the German Green Party's success can be explained by the political climate that existed in Germany in the early 1980s. Financial political scandals, such as the Flick affair, had rocked the political reputation of most of Germany's political parties, and widespread cynicism among the German population made the time ripe to organize social protest around a new kind of political party.

Waves of Environmentalism

First-Wave Environmentalism

In the United States, first-wave environmentalism is largely associated with the wilderness movement spearheaded by John Muir (1838–1914), whose vision led to the founding of the Sierra Club in 1892 and the creation of six national parks. Wilderness tourism flourished, and Muir's articles and books appealed to a national audience that soon embraced wilderness protection: 'Probably more than anyone else in American history, he developed the wilderness philosophy that wild nature was a healing escape from the urban industrial society which America had become.'[26] Like the Transcendentalists, Muir abhorred materialistic greed and was critical of modern science. And like Thoreau, who retreated to a small cabin in Walden, Muir left society behind to seek refuge in Yosemite Valley. His fame grew and his message spread. By 1915, '335,000 visitors enjoyed the growing national park system, compared to only 69,000 in 1908.'[27]

The founders of the American conservation movement, including John Muir, Aldo Leopold, and Robert Marshall, were all impassioned amateurs who were not motivated by a desire to become professional environmentalists. To these lay activists, environmentalism 'was a love, not a labor. They were free to demand whatever they felt was necessary for the protection of the wild, regardless of how their views sat with people of money and influence.'[28] This devotion to a cause, some argue, is much less evident in the second wave.

In Canada, first-wave environmentalism was slower to take root. In 1929, a journalist offered the following explanation to an American conservationist: 'You cannot expect from the Canadian public anything like the response . . . in the United States, because . . . you have suffered and lost much of your wilderness and we are merely in the process of losing it.'[29] Naturalist organizations, which did not become established until the early twentieth century, were inspired particularly by the nature writings of Ernest Thompson Seton, who in 1898 published *Wild Animals I Have Known*, and Charles G.D. Roberts, who published *The Kindred of the Wild* in 1902. Nature writing was given a new impetus with the writings of Grey Owl (see Box 2.4), an Englishman who successfully posed as a Canadian Indian. Also, the experiences of cottaging, canoe-tripping, and going to summer camp became an important part of the lives of many urban Canadians and strengthened their association with the land and nature. Possibly the most visible manifestations of a growing affection of Canadians with nature were the paintings of Tom Thomson and the Group of Seven. Painted after the First World War, they took their inspiration 'directly from the tangled disorder of black spruce, swamp, and wind-chopped northern lakes.'[30] The popularity of these paintings helped to foster a growing affection of city dwellers for the beauty of Canada's natural landscape.

Second-Wave Environmentalism

Second-wave environmentalism first took root in the United States, for a variety of institutional and cultural reasons. Given the strong social democratic tradition in northern Europe and the badly damaged infrastructure in much of western Europe after the Second World War, there is a certain logic in presuming that environmentalism would have begun there rather than in the United States. But, despite the growing affluence and prolonged period of prosperity after the war, Americans became concerned with the negative effects of urban and industrial forces: 'The environmental movement in the 1960s pointed to the connection between these problems [including limited and contaminated water supplies, and

Box 2.1 Grey Owl (Wa-Sha-Quon-Asin)

'First, though, you must know that all through this forest that is so dark and mysterious, with its strange animals and people, there run a great many rivers, which are used as highways not only by the Indians in their swift canoes, but by many water beasts such as the beaver, otter, mink and muskrats. And in the woods are countless trails, although perhaps you could never find them, on which the animals that live on land travel as though upon a road. For all these creatures are continually on the move. They, as well as the humans on the land, are always busy. They have their living to make, and their young ones to take care of and feed. Some live alone, with no settled home, and others keep together in large numbers, having good-sized towns tunnelled out beneath the ground, the different houses of each family joined, in groups by passages. The very wisest among them, such as beaver, build themselves warm houses, store up water in which to swim, and put up large supplies of food for the winter months, working almost like men, often talking together when resting from their labours; and they all have, each in their own way, a great deal to attend to. . . . All animals, however small or apparently useless, have their own proper place, and the Indians know this, and never bother them without good reason; and because they share with them the hardships of this forest life, they call them Little Brothers.'

Source: Grey Owl, *The Adventures of Sajo and Her Beaver People* (London: Lovat Dickson & Thompson, 1938).

inadequate collection and disposal of waste and sewage] and the way in which industrial society in general treated nature.'[31] Moreover, the United States had a rich history and tradition in conservation. Coupled with widespread scepticism about industrialization and urbanization, it provided fertile ground for the development of an environmental movement.

> Where the United States in the 1950s and early 1960s was characterized by a strong conservation movement and a relatively uncontrolled urbanization and industrialization, Europe—in particular northern Europe—had a relatively weak conservation movement and a highly regulated urban and industrial development. Thus, the environmental movement in northern Europe did not have the same favourable mobilization conditions as the movement in the United States and, as a result, it was formed a few years later.[32]

The seeds of a new culture of scepticism were sown during the 1950s, when most of North America was still basking in the prolonged affluence that marked the post-war years. On the surface, the 1950s appeared to be a time of apparent calm, and voices of dissent were subdued by the economic prosperity or intimidated by the Red scares of that decade. The fifties were a difficult time for anyone who sought to question the existing order. However, beneath this contentment and affluence, there was an embryo of protest forming:

> The contentment and conformity of the late 1950s was apparently superficial, for there was in truth a deep and latent discontent, particularly among the young. Although the United States in the 1950s appeared calm and equanimous, and the 1960s by contrast were marked by activism and change in politics and society, the struggles that brought reform in the 1960s were already emerging in the 1950s. Postwar prosperity obscured the more significant reality of economic inequality; although the share of national income received by the wealthiest 5 percent of the American population had fallen in the Depression and war years, it remained constant at about 21 percent thereafter. Similarly, the poorest 20 percent of the population received a constant 5 percent of the national income.[33]

The very affluence that was enjoyed by middle-class young Americans brought with it a marked increase in their hopes of what their environment *should* be like. Increasingly, they lost confidence in the 'system', which included the government, the military-industrial complex, and universities. In other words, for a variety of reasons the 1960s and 1970s became an era when there was a significant reconsideration of the liberal democratic tradition that had dominated Western political thought for decades. For the most part, this era of general protest, which included environmentalism, feminism, the civil rights movement, and the peace movement, tended to be identified as an adjunct of the New Left committed to revising socialist theory. However, in the case of second-wave environmentalism, because many of its issues had regressive social and economic consequences such as higher prices for commodities that would result from environmental abatement measures as well as higher unemployment, the environmental movement was often perceived as an élitist, middle-class phenomenon that threatened the standards of living of the working class.[34] (Second-wave feminism in both Canada and the United States experienced this same criticism.) 'The environmental movement as a whole was very much a Republican, white, middle-class affair, having little spiritual affinity with the growing protest movements in the country.'[35]

Despite these critical evaluations of the environmental movement, by the mid-1960s a genuine counterculture had emerged which shook the foundations of the values Americans had come to take for granted.[36] Coupled with this value change was a growing sense of urgency as air quality declined and lakes and rivers were dying after prolonged periods of uncontrolled dumping of sewage and industrial wastes. So the second wave of the environmental movement cannot be understood as a social movement with roots in democratic socialism, liberalism, or conservatism. Rather, it had its roots in a distinctive change in values combining elements of the existing ideological trilogy with specific green ideals, such as sustainable society, participatory democracy, social justice, peace, and communalism. The sense of urgency felt by more radical environmentalists also meant that moderate incrementalism associated with liberal reform movements would not be a workable strategy. As a social movement, therefore, second-wave environmentalism was driven by value change and was based on ideals and political beliefs that championed the common good rather than individual self-interest.

There were three distinct currents within the environmental movement. Reform or moderate environmentalism called for a stronger regulation by government within the liberal democratic framework. This was the current in which Rachel Carson's *Silent Spring* can best be associated. There was also a revisiting of Malthus and the Transcendentalists, referred to by Eckersley as the survivalist school and the emancipationist school respectively. These currents of environmentalism were home to a number of non-democratic ideas, such as collectivism, a centralized state, and a strongly regulated and weakened capitalist economic system. Thirdly, there was a much more radical current that called for a toppling of the liberal democratic regime and its replacement by decentralized bioregions.

In the Canadian case, however, the new environmentalism did not emerge until the 1960s, when a growing number of people realized that wilderness was becoming scarce. A new environmental consciousness was 'fueled by the environmental impulse and the outdoor recreation boom . . . [and] expanded among a generally younger, better educated, and physically more active population.'[37] In a number of provinces, the emphasis was initially on the highly mechanized and year-round timber operations. With the construction of gravel roads, many recreationists became aware that modern industry was clashing with the wilderness retreats in such natural areas as Algonquin Park and the wilderness of British Columbia. By 1965, the National and Provincial Parks Association of Canada became an effective non-governmental watchdog over all Canadian park agencies.[38]

Key Events in Second-Wave Environmentalism
Rachel Carson's Silent Spring

> It is not my contention that chemical insecticides must never be used. I do contend that we have put poisons and biologically potent chemicals indiscriminately into the hands of persons largely or wholly ignorant of their potential for harm. We have subjected enormous numbers of people to contact with these poisons, without their consent and often without their knowledge. If the Bill of Rights contains no guarantee that a citizen shall be secure against lethal poisons distributed by other private individuals or by public officials, it is surely only because our forefathers, despite their considerable wisdom and foresight, could conceive of no such problem.
>
> Rachel Carson, *Silent Spring* (1962), p. 30.

It is the view of many in the modern environmental movement that Rachel Carson's 1962 bestseller *Silent Spring* marked the intellectual starting point of the modern environmental movement. For thirty-one weeks, this book was on the

New York Times bestseller list. With a lifelong interest in nature, particularly the oceans, Carson sounded the alarm that synthetic poisons, particularly chlorinated hydrocarbons such as DDT, were poisoning the entire globe. For some twenty years, DDT had been seen as the saviour in the war against pests and had even won its Swiss inventor, Paul Müller, the 1948 Nobel Prize.

What was so amazing about Rachel Carson's work was that it challenged a powerful corporate member in the American economic system—the chemical industry. A diminutive, soft-spoken nature writer had done what many others had failed to do—her work planted seeds of doubt in the minds of Americans about the primary activity of large American industry. Despite vigorous attacks on Carson as an 'uppity' and alarmist female, as well as questions about her scientific credentials and research, she provided a credible analysis of the dangers of DDT. Most important, *Silent Spring* offered a new form of criticism that deliberately combined science and advocacy on the grounds that evidence of public danger entailed a moral duty to warn about existing and potential harm. Carson's biographer concluded: 'The debate between Carson and the scientific establishment was not fundamentally over scientific fact or institutional objectivity. It was a quarrel about values, and consequently, about power.'[39] (See Box 2.2.)

Box 2.2 Rachel Carson (1907–1964)

Rachel Carson was born in Springdale, Pennsylvania in 1907. From the time she was a little girl, her desire was to become a writer, but she also had a passion for nature and enjoyed a particular romance with oceans. By the time she was eleven, she had published her first story, 'A Battle in the Clouds', which appeared in the children's magazine, *St Nicholas*, in 1918. In 1925, Rachel entered the Pennsylvania College for Women in Pittsburgh, Pennsylvania. Although her main area of study was composition, she studied biology in her second year and a new passion was unleashed. By her third year, she had changed her major to science. Upon graduating in the spring of 1929, Rachel was offered a full-tuition scholarship to graduate school at Johns Hopkins University in Baltimore, Maryland. That summer she served as a 'beginning investigator' at the Marine Biological Laboratory at Woods Hole. At long last, she was going 'seaward' and would have the opportunity to study the oceans. In 1932, she was awarded her master's degree and had every intention of pursuing her doctorate in zoology. However, her family (which consisted of her mother, brother, sister, and two nieces) had fallen on hard times and Rachel was forced to drop out of her doctoral program in early 1934. She hoped to find work as a writer but had no success until the following year, when she was hired by a radio science show to write scripts for seven-minute programs, referred to as 'seven-minute fish tales'. She also found work with the government writing general introductions for scientific brochures. In February 1936, she sold her first article, on the decline of the shad fishery, to the *Baltimore Sun*, and her career as a nature writer had officially begun.

Over her distinguished career, she wrote numerous articles and several books, including three books about the sea, *Under the Sea-Wind* (1941), The *Sea Around Us* (1951), and *The Edge of the Sea* (1955). However, she is best known for *Silent Spring*, which was first published in 1962. Her concern about pesticides can be traced back as far as 1959, when she discovered irrefutable evidence about losses of wildlife and the effects on human health of the government's pesticide program. What is miraculous about her publication of *Silent Spring* were the many obstacles she had to surmount while writing it. For years she had been responsible for the financial support of her elderly mother, her brother, her two nieces, and a great-nephew. After the death of a niece in 1956, just before she turned fifty, she adopted her five-year-old great-nephew. In March of 1960, Rachel was diagnosed with breast cancer, from which she never recovered.

It was her literary agent who suggested she call the book *Silent Spring*, in reference to several lines from 'La Belle Dame sans Merci', a poem by the English Romantic poet John Keats. The lines were 'The sedge is wither'd from the lake,/And no birds sing.' And so *Silent Spring* was born. With its publication in 1962, controversy erupted. The pesticide industry was outraged at the so-called misrepresentations in the book, calling it a 'disappointment'. Despite its detractors, *Silent Spring* went on to become number one on the *New York Times* best-seller list. Other criticisms came from the Department of Agriculture and the United States Drug Administration. She gave several interviews, including one with Eric Severied for CBS *Reports* in November 1962, in which it was evident that Carson's health was failing.

By her own admission, Rachel Carson did invoke the rhetoric of the Cold War and the tone of moral crisis to persuade her readers of the urgency of her message. For her, the crisis over the misuse of pesticides was perfectly analogous to the threat from radioactive fallout. For these reasons, she felt justified in her criticisms of the government and the scientific establishment and in her call for citizen action.

Rachel Carson died on 14 April 1964 just before sunset. It was as she had written in the final section of *The Edge of the Sea*: 'For all at last to return to the sea—to Oceanus, the ocean river, like the ever-flowing stream of time, the beginning and the end.'

Source: Based on Linda Lear, *Rachel Carson: Witness for Nature* (New York: Henry Holt, 1997)

Earth Day, 12 April 1970
Just as the spontaneous Women's March for Peace (1961) became the defining event of the second wave of the North American Women's Movement, Earth Day in 1970 was the pivotal event in the second wave of North American environmentalism. Many view it as the advent of modern environmentalism in the United States because it was accompanied by widespread public support and the creation of a new federal bureaucracy—the Environmental Protection Agency (EPA).[40] In the United States, schools and parades gave voice to concerns about the deteriorating environment. Furthermore, both Houses of Congress recessed in order to allow elected representatives to join their constituents in observing the event.[41] Although this day generated enthusiasm and raised environmental consciousness among citizens, many environmentalists believe that interest has waned since those heady times. During the 1980s, the Reagan administration emphasized deregulation and cuts to the budget for the EPA, and public concern about the environment was soon replaced by worries about a sluggish economy, inflation, and international events, including the Iranian hostage crisis. By the end of the 1980s, environmentalism began to regain some of its lost momentum. Although Earth Day 1990 was viewed as a success—an estimated 200 million people took part in 140 countries—public attention was again waning by 1995.[42] This was particularly discouraging for supporters of the Clinton-Gore administration, for environmental protection had been presented as an important issue during the 1992 presidential campaign.

Third- and Fourth-Wave Environmentalisms
Although many environmentalists believe that the movement can best be understood as having two waves, others believe that there were two subsequent waves in the 1980s and 1990s. These newer waves, which were much smaller than the first two, each reflect a different approach to the environment. Third-wave environmentalism has been characterized by a more conciliatory attitude. Earlier environmentalists were interested in only the toughest possible regulations concerning the environment, and they used litigation as an important weapon against polluters. What characterizes the next two waves was a certain flexibility and a recognition that any solutions needed to make use of the marketplace. To this end, there has been a willingness on the part of some green groups to sit down with business and discuss compromises. 'The current buzzwords of third wave environmentalism are market-based incentive, demand side management, technological optimism, non-adversarial dialogue, and regulatory flexibility.'[43] The meanings of these words are ambiguous at best and have fuelled internal dissension within a number of groups that this strategy is nothing short of a 'sell-out' to corporate interests. In terms of tactics and strategies, the 'essence of third wave environmentalism is the shift from the courtroom to the board room.'[44] Examples of third-wave environmental measures are emission-reduction credits, which were allowed in the 1990 amendments to the *US Clean Air Act*.[45] In

Canada, two recent examples are the conflict-resolution process undertaken in the Campaign to Save BC's Ancient Rainforests and the Lands for Life initiative of the Ontario government.

Campaign to Save British Columbia's Ancient Rainforests
For many years there has been conflict between logging companies, First Nations, and environmentalists over the forestry practices used in British Columbia. Forestry companies have traditionally used the clearcutting method which, opponents argue, has seriously damaged the province's fragile ecosystems. Furthermore, the forests being clearcut are ancient temperate rainforests, which are irreplaceable. The first protests by environmentalists and First Nations involved prolonged blockades of logging roads, as in the case of the Clayoquot Sound demonstrations. More recently, however, some organizations, including Forest Ethics (formerly the Coastal Rainforest Coalition), the Rainforest Action Network, and the Sierra Club of British Columbia embarked on a very different kind of campaign in order to draw attention to the continued deforestation of Great Bear Rainforest, which has been called one of North America's biological gems. It is the home of the rare white Kermode, or 'Spirit', bear. This is an area of some 7 million hectares of temperate rainforest, fjords, inlets, islands and glacial mountains in central and coastal British Columbia that is predominately Crown land with unresolved Aboriginal claims. The essence of the campaign has been to disrupt the international market for BC forest products by persuading large purchasers to buy only certified wood products. The first forest-management certification program was Smart Wood, which was founded in 1989. It is a program of the Rainforest Alliance, an international non-profit environmental group based in New York City. Certification—its proponents argue—provides a commercial incentive for forest managers to adopt sustainable forestry practices. Not only are certified forest products labelled, but companies that process, manufacture, or sell products made from certified wood are also certified, through 'chain of custody'. (In order for a product to be certified, a chain-of-custody audit must confirm that certified wood is being used in the product line.) This certification is voluntary, and all producers of timber and companies that process or sell forest products from certified sources are eligible to apply.[46] The certification agency in Canada is the Forest Stewardship Council (FSC). Its certification process involves a ten-point program, which includes avoiding old-growth cutting and obtaining the informed consent of indigenous groups to log. Chain-of-custody rules forbid FSC wood from even being stored with other wood. Because Canadian consumers have been less insistent than Europeans on having certified wood products and because of the length of the certification process, there are only a handful of FSC-certified forests in Canada.[47]

Nevertheless, there is some evidence that the campaign may be working. In Canada, 'good wood' is a new buzz word in furniture and hardware retailing. Home decorating retailers, such as Ikea, Home Depot, and Restoration Hardware, have all jumped on the good-wood bandwagon—largely in response to the growing number of consumers who are demanding certified furniture.[48] In August 2000, Home Depot's main US competitor, Lowe's Cos., announced that it would immediately stop buying lumber from endangered forests, including the Great Bear Rainforest on the BC coast. This decision was denounced by the chief forester with Vancouver-based Western Forest Products for targeting a particular region, and a spokesperson for the industry lobby group, Forest Alliance of BC, expressed the fear that 'as an opinion leader, they will create a domino effect that could lead to real hardship.'[49] Of greater concern were fears that this ban could disrupt sensitive negotiations between the forestry industry and environmental groups that are currently underway to develop a conflict-dispute mechanism.

The negotiations, known formally as the Joint Solutions Project, were described as 'unique' by the facilitator who has been selected to broker an agreement. According to a vice-president of Weyerhaeuser, a large forestry company: 'The conflict between us had reached the point where we felt it had become institutionalized and we were both prepared to push for a breakthrough.'[50] Parties to the negotiations have agreed to a conflict-free period, and forestry companies have promised to shift workers from areas where logging is deferred so that most jobs will be saved. The purpose of the joint initiative was to develop a proposal for an ecosystem-based method of forest management and conservation on the central and north coast of British Columbia. This initiative was sponsored by four companies (of an original six that began)—Canfor, Fletcher Challenge Canada, Western Forest Products, and Weyerhaeuser—and four environmental groups—the Coastal Rainforest Coalition, Greenpeace, the Rainforest Action Network, and the Sierra Club of BC. According to the announcement, the scientific and technical work will be done in co-operation with First Nations and local stakeholders, and the framework was tabled in the fall of 2000. This will be the starting point for discussions with coastal Aboriginal leaders, the Central Coast Land and Resource Managing Planning process (LRMP), government, and other decision-making authorities.

This collaborative attempt to resolve a long-standing dispute over forestry practices represents a fundamental shift in the strategies and tactics of environmental groups associated with the forestry industry in British Columbia. There are some signs that these discussions may still be fragile, however. In July 2000, two forest companies—International Forest Products (Interfor) and West Fraser Timber—withdrew from negotiations. Furthermore, Greenpeace has embarked on a postcard campaign to encourage Japanese buyers of BC wood products to switch from Interfor and West Fraser to companies that are developing sustainable, ecosystem-based forestry practices.[51]

On 4 April 2001, the government of British Columbia and its partners in the Joint Solutions Project announced what was described as the 'largest rainforest conservation measure in North American history'.[52] Some 3.5 million acres of the Great Bear Rainforest will be immediately protected or logging will be deferred.

Forest-protection organizations, including the Rainforest Action Network, Forest-Ethics, and the Natural Resources Defense Council, have called on US and international corporations to continue their boycott of products derived from ancient rainforests to ensure that this plan is indeed put into effect over the next two years.[53] These organizations have undertaken to 'provide regular updates to the marketplace' and to continue monitoring the forestry companies to ensure that they are complying with the agreements. The plan calls for the immediate protection of twenty ecologically critical valleys in the Great Bear Rainforest and the deferral of logging for one to two years in sixty-eight other valleys while a management plan based on ecological principles is developed. Forest companies will be allowed to continue clearcutting in areas not covered by the agreement, but they acknowledge that the annual allowable cut on the coast will be substantially reduced which will 'inevitably result in changes to employment.'[54] As far as First Nations are concerned, there has been some success. A protocol has been established between many coastal First Nations and the Province of British Columbia, although two coastal First Nations that have chosen not to sign the protocol continue to participate in the government's Land and Resource Planning Process and the Turning Point process sponsored by the Suzuki Foundation. (Both processes have adopted ecosystem planning practices in their logging operations.)

ForestEthics believes that the market-based strategy was instrumental in persuading the BC logging industry and the government to adopt sustainable forest practices.[55] In particular, they credited a number of companies such as Home Depot, Ikea International, the German Pulp Producers Association, Lowes, and Centex—large lumber retailers in the US—for their support of this initiative.

Lands for Life
In the spring of 1999, the Premier of Ontario announced that the Province would add an estimated 2.4 million hectares to parks in northern Ontario. In making the announcement, Harris claimed that the government had kept its promise to complete 'the best provincial parks system in Canada'. After the announcement and a month before he called a provincial election, the World Wildlife Fund gave Harris a grade of B + for wilderness protection. This plan was the final piece of the 1999 Ontario Forest Accord, which spelled out how Crown land would be used for the next 99 years. This accord divides up 39 million hectares of northern Ontario—the Lands for Life—into parks, forestry, and other uses. The signatories to the forest accord were the lumber industry, a coalition of wilderness groups called the Partnership for Public Lands (which includes the World Wildlife Fund Canada, the Wildlands League, and the Federation of Ontario Naturalists), and the Ministry of Natural Resources. The most influential group in the deal was the World Wildlife Fund, which has been described by its critics as being 'among the best-bankrolled groups in the world and the best connected to business and conservative politicians in Canada.'[56] Moreover, it has been called a 'cloak of green' for corporations, and its board of directors include forest, energy, and mining

executives.[57] At the time, many environmental groups applauded the accord as being a step forward and defended it as the 'best deal' that could be had. According to the Partnership for Public Lands, without a deal, unfettered mining, hunting, and logging would have continued on the 2.4 million hectares.

Since the announcement, there has been a cacophony of criticism. First Nations were excluded from the talks, as were many environmental groups. However, subsequent announcements and additions to the uses allowed in these park lands have caused divisions in the environmental movement. In fact, some have labelled the deal as a crisis of conscience. This is captured in the following letter to the editor of the *Toronto Star*.

> The Lands for Life deal is an insult to every environmentalist who ever blockaded a logging road to protect an old-growth forest, to every volunteer who helped on a campaign or attended rallies, and especially to anyone who donated to groups such as the World Wildlife Fund, the Wildlands League, or Earthroots, in the mistaken belief that these organizations stood for adequate levels of protection for public land, an end to clearcut logging, no cutting of old-growth red and white pine, no hunting and mining in parks and full respect for the inherent rights of aboriginal peoples in Ontario.[58]

Critics of the accord point to two provisions. First, the deal honours existing licences for mining and lumbering and allows the companies to expand their operations, provided that additional lands are added to the protected parks. It also permits existing logging roads and new ones. Fishing and hunting are also permitted, as are trailer parks and motels. One editorial commented: 'And what remains of the protection for the "protected" areas? Really, only the trees get protection—except those to be cut down for mines and roads.'[59] Clause 24 of the accord also, its critics argue, 'supports initiatives towards the orderly development of areas north of the area of the undertaking . . . permitting commercial forest management in lands north of the area of the undertaking.'[60]

This more conciliatory wave of environmentalism is not without its critics. Indeed, some argue that it has opened the door for some of the worst environmental offenders, including Dupont, Chevron, Monsanto, and Mobil Oil, to improve their images by becoming significant environmental donors. In the United States, American groups led by third-wavers, including the National Wildlife Fund, National Audubon, and the World Wildlife Fund have been among the largest recipients of corporate support.[61] To say the least, many environmentalists do not agree with the policies of third-wave groups. While the stated intention of third-wave environmentalism is the protection of the environment, there is considerable doubt about its ability to achieve these objectives given its corporate connections.

The momentum of the third wave may have been slowed as a result of controversy in the environmental movement, but a new wave—perhaps best exemplified by the new type of protest seen in Seattle—appears to be growing:

But as the third wave washes back into history a massive swell of new environmental passion is gathering force. Democratic in origin, populist in style, untrammeled by bureaucracy, and inspired by a host of new ideologies—the fourth wave should crest sometime early in the twenty-first century. . . . At present, the fourth wave has no single defining quality beyond its enormous diversity of organizations, ideologies, and issues. It is part wilderness preservation, part toxic abatement, part ecological economics, part civil rights, part human rights, part secular, part religious, and parts of many ecologies. There are, however, some encouraging common characteristics among the parts. Anger, for example, and energy, a commitment to democratic processes, and its multivarious participants' urge to restimulate the environmental imagination and expand our concept of environment and environmentalism.[62]

It is widely expected, therefore, that this fourth wave will be inter-generational, multi-class, and multicultural. It has the potential to invigorate old second-wavers and mobilize a new generation of young people who have grown sceptical about corporate commitments to human rights and the environment. If history shows that Seattle was a watershed, the mobilization of a coalition forged from organized labour, civil rights activists, and environmentalists will likely be seen as a rebirth of political activism. Like the earlier three waves, there will, in all probability, be clashes between moderate and radical reformers. The latter is likely to be less amenable to sitting down with multinational corporations and more predisposed to protest and call for boycotts. Early indications are that it will be more militant than third-wave environmentalism and will rely more heavily on market strategies. In February 2000, the Canadian companies McCain Foods and Seagram Distillers both announced that they would soon stop using genetically modified potatoes and corn, respectively, in their products. And in February 2000, Loblaws became the first supermarket in North America to specifically stock and promote foods that are not genetically modified. These announcements were largely seen as corporate responses to many of the concerns that have been raised in Europe and more recently during the Biosafety Protocol meetings held in Montreal in January 2000. A British food-industry consultant has observed that the North American food-retailing industry is at the point that Europe was at a few years ago and that once one major chain announces that it will not sell genetically modified food, others will follow. These victories by consumers' groups have caused farmers to question their decisions to grow crops from genetically modified seeds.

Towards a Typology of Green Organizations in Canada

Although the Castells classification of British environmental groups is useful in a number of respects it does not take into account several other important characteristics, including organization, tactics and strategies, and targets. Because of Canada's federal system, the shared jurisdiction over environment, health, and natural resources, and our modified Westminster parliamentary system, environmental interest groups operate in a different way in this country.

For the purposes of this discussion, green groups and organizations in Canada will be divided into environmental non-governmental organizations (ENGOs), international green organizations, local or grassroots environmental groups, and advisory environmental groups. As in all efforts to classify groups, there are some organizations that have characteristics of more than one type.

Environmental Non-governmental Organizations (ENGOs)

Some examples of environmental NGOs are the Canadian Nature Federation, Pollution Probe, Canadian Wildlife Federation, Ducks Unlimited Canada, and the Nature Conservancy of Canada.

Some writers, including G. Bruce Doern and Thomas Conway, argue that all groups, be they Greenpeace Canada, Pollution Probe, or Ducks Unlimited Canada fall into an amorphous group called environmental non-governmental organizations (ENGO).[63] This lumping together of all environmental organizations into one group, however, is misleading because it disregards important differences among them. For instance, some of these organizations receive government grants while others do not. Some are considered charities and can issue tax-deductible receipts to donors; others are not. Some groups are important partners at meetings with government agencies and business leaders, while others shun this kind of collaboration. Occasionally, ENGOs receive some initial government funding, but most rely on membership dues and support from foundations. All attempt to influence environmental policy, although they do not all use the same strategies in doing so. Some groups (including the Sierra Defence Legal Fund and the Canadian Environmental Law Association) use litigation as their primary strategy. Others use civil disobedience to attract publicity for their cause (Earth First! and some animal rights groups are examples). Yet others embark on market campaigns—that is, they urge Canada's trading partners not to buy products that are logged, mined, or produced in ways that are harmful to the environment. As mentioned above in connection with the BC rainforest campaign, Greenpeace has used this strategy to disrupt markets for certain BC forest products that are derived from clearcut ancient rainforests. Many other groups use lobbying as their main strategy—attempting to influence politicians and policy-makers in the environmental field. The tools used in this kind of lobbying include media and education campaigns.

There is little question that environmental non-governmental organizations are the most visible players in environmental politics both in Canada and around the world. Within the policy areas associated with the natural resources and the environment, the organizations may vary. However, across the country they are present in both the predominantly non-institutional domain of social-movement politics and in the institutionalized milieu of political parties, administrative systems, governments and beyond.[64] Although business may sponsor ENGOs, the label ENGO is rarely applied to businesses. There was a huge proliferation of these organizations during the 1970s and 1980s: approximately 13,000 in developed countries alone, 30 per cent of which had been formed in the previous decade.[65]

'[The] core adherents [of ENGOs] are deeply dedicated to the long-term mission.'[66] Almost every group is unique in its philosophy and ideology. As in Robin Eckersley's various strands of environmentalism, a number of these groups are underpinned by their commitment to human-welfare ecology; others are concerned with preservation and conservation; yet others are committed to animal liberation. These contrasting philosophical currents lead to much fragmentation among groups. Moreover, many environmental groups have been plagued by internal divisions about 'vision'—liberal environmentalism as opposed to deep ecology. In the United States, high-profile groups such as the Sierra Club and Friends of the Earth have experienced ideological splits that have resulted with the ousting of radical presidents by more moderate members. On occasion, these problems have become so contentious that they have undermined the credibility of many organizations.

Another problem encountered by ENGOs is that they suffer from the '*free-rider*' problem. As Doern and Conway explain, 'This problem involves a situation in which ordinary Canadians are able to benefit from the work of ENGOs—in short, from the public goods that they produce—without ever having to join or pay fees to the group.'[67] Because of the free-rider weakness and group fragmentation, many ENGOs have been forced to rely on favourable media coverage to counter the cohesiveness and financial resources of the business lobby in Canada. At present, the data base of the Canadian Environmental Network (CEN) contains some 2,000 groups. These groups vary widely in philosophy, resources, and objectives, and from time to time they may compete with one another for scarce resources, including government grants.

Canadian ENGOs face a number of institutional barriers that their American counterparts do not, and that influences the types of strategies they employ. Because of the strict party discipline that characterizes Canada's version of the Westminster system of parliamentary government, lobbying of individual MPs has little influence. While individual members of Parliament do have the forum of their respective party caucuses in which they are free to express their points of view, it is change at the *level of government* that must be achieved. For this reason, considerable time is spent by Canadian environmental groups lobbying at the ministerial level. Complicating this lobbying process is Canada's federal system. Since jurisdiction over environmental matters may be federal or provincial, lobby groups must target their efforts to influence both the federal and provincial levels, as well as in some cases the municipal level.

Another institutional characteristic of the Westminster parliamentary system is the diffusion of power from legislative institutions to government bureaucracy. In recognition of the considerable power that rests at the bureaucratic level, lobby groups have traditionally attempted to influence officials employed at both political levels. Because the Opposition in the House of Commons—particularly in the case of majority governments—lacks any real power to alter government agendas or to advance their own, lobby groups are forced to look elsewhere to find support for their causes. This helps to explain why media coverage of protests or environmental issues is critical in raising public awareness about environment matters.

Although a limited amount of third-party advertising is now permitted during elections under the Canada Elections Act,[68] Canadian groups, unlike American ones, are disinclined to use electoral strategies such as block voting or campaign contributions. For example, in the 1992 presidential election in the United States, the Sierra Club contributed an estimated $680,000 to congressional candidates.[69] In addition to their tactics of lobbying and media campaigns, Canadian groups have also increasingly used the tool of litigation, as have many American groups. Impressed with the effectiveness of litigation as a means of environmental protection, the Sierra Club in December 1990 established the Sierra Legal Defence Fund (SLDF), which provides free legal services to Canadian conservation groups and concerned citizens. It is funded by public donations and foundation grants and has over 20,000 individual supporters across Canada.[70] SLDF is a completely separate organization from the Sierra Club, although the two groups do work together. SLDF also maintains an 'informal, collegial connection with its sister organization in the United States—Earthjustice Legal Defense Fund (formerly the Sierra Club Legal Defense Fund)'.[71] This group, which now has offices in Vancouver and Toronto, is dedicated to bringing lawsuits against corporations. Recently, as companies (particularly resource-based ones) have recognized the threat from these suits both in terms of corporate image and costly settlements, environmental law has developed to the point that it is now a legitimate legal specialty.[72] In the United States, litigation has been an important tool for environmental groups more than any other social movement largely because they have been well funded. Moreover, the American legal system allows suits to be brought against government. In Canada, this funding has not been as forthcoming. More important, our legal system does not allow for suits to be brought against governments. Although the courts have been used by environmental groups against private interests (for instance, in the case of several dam proposals in the late 1980s, when the federal government was ordered to conduct environmental assessments), success has been limited. Most litigation has been used by the Canadian Environmental Law Association and the Sierra Legal Defence Fund.

Aside from financial resources, the greatest crisis facing many Canadian ENGOs relates to faith and commitment to their directions and tactics. After more than two decades of experience, the Canadian environmental lobby has evolved into an active, technologically sophisticated, and politically knowledgeable network of organizations. They have learned to use the power of television and new information technologies including the Internet, phone banks, direct mail, and fax machines. Like most other types of lobby groups in the country, ENGOs have been forced to adapt in order to stay competitive and influential. And, as in the case of most policy communities, the major mainstream groups increasingly co-ordinate their activities to maximize resources and areas of expertise even as they compete (albeit usually quietly) with one another for members and leadership in their various policy niches.[73]

By the 1990s, it had become evident that many of these groups had shifted away from working with government to working against government. In Canada as elsewhere, the politics of neo-liberalism characterized by fiscal conservatism and pro-business proclivities have forced ENGOs to adapt with the changing times. Their tactics have changed from lobbying government regulators to influencing consumers, from bringing lawsuits to making markets work, from entreating legislators to getting voters to force government to be more responsive. In this sense 'the mainstream groups are admitting what many activists have long argued: environmentalists cannot compete in the politics of interests. Fighting the moneyed lobbyists is a futile proposition. The future involves going directly to the people and changing the way they think and act. It involves the politics of *values*.'[74]

The 'politics of values' is far more complex than playing on the feelings of the public with emotional issues such as saving whales or preserving important natural landscapes. Instead, it challenges prevailing societal norms and assumptions. In this fight, the environmentalists' most intractable opposition comes from groups loosely organized around private property rights and 'wise-use' banners. Borrowing from the conservative ideas of the Wise Use Movement in the United States (which is discussed at greater length later in this chapter), these groups oppose any action that restricts their freedom and the freedom of business. What unites these groups, particularly in western Canada and in the Rocky Mountain states, is a staunch defence of the traditional multiple uses allowed on publicly owned lands, combined with concerns about what they see as misconceived attempts by urban interests to end long-standing ways of life. Those who are part of the 'wise use' cause 'consider themselves the real conservationists, lovers of the outdoors who hunt and fish, believe in scientific management of natural resources, and chafe at charges that they are despoilers of the Earth. In many ways this battle is but the latest permutation of a century-old split between conservationists who emphasize the "managed use" of natural resources and the arguably more absolutist dictates of preservationists going back to John Muir.'[75]

Anatomy of an ENGO—MiningWatch Canada

MiningWatch Canada (MWC) is a not-for-profit organization headquartered in Ottawa, with membership from labour, Aboriginal organizations, and environmental and social justice groups. What is interesting about this group, which was founded in April 1999, is that it is governed by a thirteen-member board of directors composed of a range of experts, community leaders, and activists from across the country. The founding members, who are no strangers to the environmental movement, include the Environmental Mining Council of British Columbia, the Canadian Nature Federation, the Canadian Environmental Law Association, Northwatch, the Innu Nation, the Yukon Conservation Society, and the Canadian Arctic Resources Committee.[76] Although the founding members have long had a concern with mining operations, they decided that the time was right for an organization whose primary focus was mining. Despite the promise made by mining companies in 'multi-stakeholder' agreements such as the Whitehorse Mining Initiative (which will be discussed in Chapter 4), to become more environmentally friendly, many have fallen short of what was mutually agreed to. The mining industry and its interests have continued to dominate at the public-policy level. Too often, communities have been blackmailed into accepting the short-term benefits of jobs at a high long-term cost, such as contamination of the land and water.

MiningWatch Canada serves as an industry watchdog with a mandate to publicize the real costs of mining in Canada, including the loss of wilderness, pollution of air, water, and land, unfair tax concessions, and occupational diseases for the miners. Its watchdog role has three parts. First, it examines the records of Canadian mining operations in Canada. Second, it scrutinizes the environmental and human-rights records of Canadian mining interests abroad, particularly in the Third World. Lastly, it counteracts what it sees as propaganda spread by the mining industry lobby—the Mining Association of Canada. It sees itself as an organization that protects the interests of workers, Aboriginal peoples, communities, and taxpayers.

One of the greatest concerns for this group is the environmental havoc that mines leave behind. According to MiningWatch Canada, enough arsenic trioxide has been left at the Giant Mine in Yellowknife to poison all of Great Slave Lake.[77] It also collaborates with other groups such as the Mineral Policy Center in the United States, the Mineral Policy Institute, and MineWatch UK, and issues joint releases condemning mining operations in the developing world. In August 1999, for example, it issued a press release condemning Ok Tedi Mining Ltd, a subsidiary of Broken Hill Proprietary, for failing to meet its legal obligations to compensate landowners for the environmental damage caused by the Ok Tedi gold and copper mine in Papua, New Guinea. A Canadian company, Inmet Mining Corporation, owns 18 per cent of Ok Tedi Mining Ltd. The Ok Tedi mine dumps an estimated 80,000 tons of contaminated waste rock and tailings into two nearby rivers every day. By the company's own admission, the environmental effects on the surrounding environment '[were] far greater and more damaging than predicted'.[78] One Australian NGO noted: 'BHP would never have been allowed to dispose of toxic mine waste directly into rivers in Australia. Yet BHP does this in Papua, New Guinea, and continues to do so'.[79] More recently, in March 2000, on the heels of a major cyanide spill at a mine in Romania, a World Bank report called on BHP to close the troubled mine immediately.

Over and above its concern with the environmental implications of mining operations both at home and abroad, MiningWatch also monitors human rights and labour violations by Canadian mining operations abroad. In December of 1999, massive layoffs occurred at the Tarkwa mine of Goldfields Ghana Ltd, and a number of miners were shot by the police. Goldfields Ghana is 18.9 per cent owned by Repadre Capital Corporation of Toronto.[80] MiningWatch Canada believes that the federal government, whose policies support the activities of Canadian mining operations in the developing world, must be held accountable. Therefore, a major role played by MiningWatch is to educate an unsuspecting public by attending conferences held by other NGOs and issuing publications and news releases on their web site.

As an organization that watches the mining industry, MWC examines the claims made by the Mining Association of Canada, which speaks for the mining industry. Yet, a 1999 environmental progress report from the Mining Association of Canada contained data from only seventeen companies, and none of the data, which claimed that toxic substances from mines have declined, were independently verified. It is too early yet to know whether MiningWatch Canada will be an effective watchdog of the mining industry in Canada. However, it appears to have the backing and support of a number of powerful environmental groups and has collaborated with other international ENGOs that are concerned with the environmental implications associated with mining.

International Green Groups

Examples of international green groups are Greenpeace, Earth First!, and the Sierra Club.

International green groups often have their origins as small national groups that have sprung up in response to a single environmental issue. As a matter of group survival, they have been forced to broaden their scope in order to attract more members and media attention. Accordingly, they have become more professional and are increasingly becoming more international.

Anatomy of an International Group—Greenpeace

Perhaps the most well-known and most controversial green group in Canada and around the world is Greenpeace. Paul Wapner suggests, 'It is the target of two sets of criticisms emanating from different sides of the political spectrum.'[78] That is because of the division in the values and beliefs that characterize green political theory. This polarization was discussed at considerable length in Chapter 1. On one hand, Greenpeace has been viewed as a group of radical extremists who use outrageous tactics that threaten the livelihoods of many who are employed in the logging and mining industries in Canada. Direct-action protests such as parachuting from the tops of smokestacks are seen as confrontational and offensive, not only to corporate owners but to unions as well. There are others, however, who argue that Greenpeace is not radical enough. These critics argue that

Greenpeace is more concerned with attracting media attention to the group than to the issue itself. To its detractors, Greenpeace is viewed as nothing but 'glorified banner hangers'.[82] In many respects, its evolution from a single-issue group concerned with nuclear testing in 1971 to a highly institutionalized green interest group is the classic case of organizational change that has been theorized by A. Paul Pross, among others. As Pross observes, many single-issue groups come and go as issues are resolved or disappear from the political agenda. In order to survive, interest groups require institutionalization which, among other features, leads to an expansion of the scope of a group, a permanent headquarters, permanent staff, and links with government agencies or departments. Through adaptation and organizational sophistication, these groups become more influential and gain legitimacy as important 'voices' on political issues.

Greenpeace is one environmental group that has adapted and expanded. The issues on which Greenpeace International prepares briefs and undertakes research run the gamut from dioxins in eggs in Belgium to fisheries management to the preservation of ancient forests, among many other issues. It has been estimated that the organization has over 4,000 full-time employees. Some critics of Greenpeace believe that it has moved away from a group characterized by passion to a cause to one now defined by a corporate personality. The co-founder of Greenpeace, Robert Hunter, makes no apologies about this change: 'If we were going to hope to generate the kind of money we needed, we had no choice but to adopt a successful corporate model. If there were to be budgets, someone with a professional background was going to have to implement them and ride herd on everyone involved.'[83]

Early Beginnings of Greenpeace

Greenpeace began in 1971 as a group of disillusioned peace activists sitting in the basement of a Unitarian church in Vancouver lamenting the testing of atomic bombs on the island of Amchitka in the Aleutian Islands, off the coast of Alaska. As the story goes, one of the members, Marie Bohlen, said that the only way to stop the testing was to sail a ship into the test area. The group sprang into action, and Greenpeace was born. Over the next few months, two old ships were sent into the test site. The National Film Board documentary, *The Greenpeace Years*, shows compelling film footage of the group on one of the ships. From the start, it was a media event that struck a resonant chord among student and peace activists alike across North America. As a point of fact, the first boat was not ready to sail in time to get its story on the national news, and in order to meet the time line, it did a mock sailing out of the harbour only to return later. The departure did take place the next morning.

In part, the group's appeal can be directly related to the time at which it was founded. The United States was in the early years of the Vietnam war. Although the ships were not successful in stopping the planned detonation and two additional ones, four further tests were postponed by the American government, largely as a result of the protests of peace groups, including Greenpeace.

Internal Organization

Since the founding of Greenpeace in 1976, a series of organizational changes have been made, largely to comply with the federal Income Tax Act. There are essentially four arms of Greenpeace: The Greenpeace Canada Charitable Foundation (which existed from 1976 to 1995), Greenpeace Environmental Foundation (created in 1995), Greenpeace Canada, and Greenpeace International.

In financial terms, Greenpeace was registered as a charity in 1976, so that it could issue tax receipts to donors. This status was not challenged until its standing was first revoked in 1989 amid charges that it was not a true charity. In the opinion of Revenue Canada, a charity must provide some benefit to the public and it could not be assumed 'that remedying any and all forms of pollution always conveys a public benefit'. Citing an example that competing interests must be weighed, the decision argued that 'closing down a polluting mill may make for a cleaner town and a healthier population, but it may also propel that population into poverty.' To satisfy Revenue Canada, the Greenpeace Canada Charitable Foundation was formed—a group that was to operate separately from Greenpeace. An audit of this organization revealed a number of irregularities and a series of non-compliant activities which showed the charity had failed to devote all its resources to charitable activities. As a result, charitable status was revoked in 1995 (and an appeal dismissed in 1998). A new charity, called the Greenpeace Environmental Foundation, was then formed, but Revenue Canada called it 'a convenient way to avoid the consequences' of its past troubled charities and refused to register the group. Revenue Canada claims that the fact that Greenpeace is raising public awareness does not necessarily mean that it is preserving the environment. Furthermore, pamphlets on the destruction of forests along the Amazon or the BC coast or on pollutants emanating from smokestacks in Sudbury have little 'measurable impact on the environment'. In June 1999, the Reform Party's natural resources critic applauded the decision: 'It appears that there is resolve on the part of the Canadian government not to give back status to an organization that's obviously practising political suasion.' Greenpeace's Canadian operations are increasingly being run from Europe because the group has found it increasingly difficult to raise money in Canada.

Tactics and Strategies

It has often been charged that Greenpeace does outrageous things to capture media attention. Greenpeace activists have hung banners on bridges, placed radioactive stickers on British ships carrying nuclear weapons in Halifax Harbour, and spray-painted the fur of whitecoat seals with green paint to disrupt the seal hunt off the coast of Newfoundland. More recently, the group has resumed its anti-logging activism in British Columbia, where it erected a giant Home Depot sign in a cut block north of Vancouver and described the American hardware giant as a 'major player in the destruction of the world's remaining ancient forests'.[84] In December 1999, members of the group laid the corpses of oil-slicked birds on the steps of Petro Fina corporate offices after an oil slick from a sunken tanker washed up on the beaches of France. All of these actions can best be described as 'direct actions'. The purpose of direct action is not simply to capture media attention (although it invariably does), but to allow people to act according to their convictions. These actions are based on the notion of 'bearing witness'—a practice associated with the Quakers. If a person has observed a morally objectionable act, it is incumbent on him or her either to take action to ensure that this act does not happen again or to stand by and witness its occurrence.[85] By publicizing Greenpeace's direct actions, the media make it possible for the viewing audience actually to bear witness to the act, too. In this way, the world will know about the ecological injustices that are perpetrated. Taken to its extreme, people who participate in dangerous direct actions are prepared to risk their lives in order to show the injustice to the world. It is evident, therefore, that many of the kinds of direct actions that Greenpeace involves itself in require a passion for a cause. This may help to explain why a number of these actions tread a very thin line between the legal and illegal and why the actions of the group are so controversial.

Because Greenpeace is an international group, there have been disagreements among various branch offices. By the mid-eighties, the Vancouver office (where it had all begun) was in serious debt and had become resentful that the better-funded US group had, for all intents and purposes, appropriated the group's name and hard-earned reputation. This dispute came to a climax when the Vancouver Greenpeace office sued the office in San Francisco for violation of trademark agreements. The San Francisco office retaliated with a slander suit. Ultimately a compromise was reached through the intervention of one of the original founders of Greenpeace, David McTaggart, who now worked out of the European office but who was still influential in the Canadian operation.[86] Eventually a new funding formula was established, as well as a new co-ordinating body, Greenpeace International, under whose umbrella the debts of the various branches were cleared. Although local and national groups were free to pursue local fund raising, the confederated structure was intended to preclude future competition among national or sub-national branches.[87]

Another important adaptation made by Greenpeace has been the development of its scientific expertise. More scientific staff have been hired in efforts to heighten the credibility and legitimacy of the organization's claims. In this respect, Greenpeace also is an advisory organization, although this is not its dominant function. Scientific authority has always been important when one makes claims about social problems, and for many years the claims of environmental groups were rebutted by competing scientific claims by corporations and governments. In the past few years, local residents affected by environmental accidents (such as the Hagersville tire fire and the fire at a recycling plant in Hamilton) have solicited the scientific assistance of Greenpeace. As a result of their reports and media coverage of them, the provincial government was induced to conduct more extensive environmental investigations.

Recently the tactics used by Greenpeace have changed noticeably. In certain respects, the organization has abandoned direct action at least for the time being, and now recognizes that if forestry companies are to make significant changes in their practices, pressure must come from the market. If foreign markets can be persuaded not to buy products obtained through unsustainable practices, the profits of major corporations will be reduced. Increasingly, Greenpeace is using market campaigns to apply pressure on corporations. At present, it is engaged in a postcard campaign, in which supporters are asked to send cards to Interfor Japan and to the Canadian ambassador in Japan demanding action to preserve the biodiversity of the ancient temperate rainforests of British Columbia.

Local and Grassroots Organizations

Some examples of local and grassroots organizations are the Save Salt Spring Campaign, Friends of Clayoquot Sound, and Save the Oak Ridges Moraine.

Local and grassroots organizations are the most plentiful category of green group. They include groups that mobilize, often spontaneously, around an issue of community concern. Across the country, groups of people have joined together over such varied issues as the use of pesticide in community parks and the protection of wetlands and animal habitats. Traditionally, these groups are run by volunteers and lack any formal structure. Depending on the issue, grassroots organizations may exist for short periods of time or may have long periods when they are inactive.

Anatomy of a Local Group: The Save Saltspring Society

There has been a long history in British Columbia of campaigns led by women to protest against forestry operations that are destroying ancient rainforests and wreaking serious damage on the ecosystem. What makes the Save Saltspring campaign an interesting one to examine is that the issues are somewhat different from those of Clayoquot and the strategies used by this group are unique. The story at Saltspring began on 1 November 1999, when almost 5,000 acres—over one-tenth—of Saltspring Island were purchased by the newly formed Texada Land Corporation with the intent of building houses. These lands are not only home to ancient rainforests and fjords, but they also contain a number of rare and endangered ecosystems and species such as river otters and mink. In addition, there are a number of First Nations sacred sites on the property.

As part of the land development process, Texada is logging the land heavily and has the legal right to do so because the lands have been designated Forest Land Reserve. At current rates of logging, over 1,000 acres of forest will disappear by the end of the year 2000. Because the company has the right to log this land, the citizens' group has decided to pursue a different strategy (besides protesting) to protect this part of Saltspring Island. In conjunction with the Land Conservancy of British Columbia and its many partners (which include Capital Regional District Parks, the Salt Spring Island Conservancy, the Islands Trust Fund, and the

Nature Conservancy of Canada, among others), they have embarked on a massive fundraising effort to buy the land back from Texada Land Corporation. In conjunction with the Green Party of Canada and the BC Green Party, this organization has established the 'Green Conscience Fund of Salt Spring Island'. In order to keep costs of protecting these lands at manageable levels, the lands will be leased or sold to private buyers, and covenants and stewardship agreements will be entered into. In other words, people may purchase individual parcels of land that have conservation covenants placed on them. Some of the properties acquired may be used by the community for eco-forestry and agricultural activities in order to offset some costs, should the campaign succeed.

The campaign has raised more than $1 million, far short of the $40 million that Texada has asked for the property. The group has a web site that outlines the ecological significance of the land and shows pictures of some of the damage done by clearcutting on the Island. Over and above donations and the sale of T-shirts, the group has also embarked on a letter-writing campaign. The list of persons on the mail list include the federal and provincial ministers of the environment, the BC Premier, local MLAs and MPs, the President of Texada Corporation, and Manulife Financial. However, perhaps the most unusual part of the group's campaign is the sale of 2001 calendars illustrated by photographs in which a number of the women associated with the campaign have literally bared all. Sales of this nude calendar, which was inspired by a group of English women who did the same thing to raise money for charity, have raised $150,000.[88] At this point, it is too early to tell if the group's efforts to purchase the property will succeed, but their campaign is unique in that it is not just about blocking logging roads or chaining themselves to trees. It is also a massive fundraising campaign and includes a new strategy to preserve natural areas through the use of covenants. And, of course, in the Canadian context, the calendar idea is a new one in raising environmental awareness.

Anatomy of a Local Group: Save the Oak Ridges Moraine (STORM)

The group calling itself STORM mobilized around the issue of suburban development along the Oak Ridges Moraine, a natural area that stretches 160 kilometres from the Niagara Escarpment to the southern shore of Rice Lake in central Ontario. The moraine is a natural wildlife and wetland area and home to the headwaters of some thirty rivers and streams that provide York Region, which is one of the country's largest urban areas, with its drinking water. Over the next twenty years, the York, Durham, and Peel regions have planned for residential development on the moraine for an estimated 98,000 people.[89] Other groups that have joined forces on this issue with STORM are the Kettle Lakes Coalition, Save the Rouge Valley System, the Federation of Ontario Naturalists, and Earthroots. In early February 2000, 465 local and international scientists provided a much needed boost for STORM when they called for a temporary halt to development on the moraine until an action plan for development was undertaken.[90] Although this group of scientists is not opposed to minor expansion of existing residential areas or small infill development on the moraine, they do advocate a total ban on development in moraine forests and wetlands. The adversaries of this coalition are the municipal governments of Uxbridge, King City, and Richmond Hill. In addition, because land-use planning is under the jurisdiction of the province of Ontario, the provincial government has been heavily lobbied to freeze development on the moraine until it has a development policy. Developers argue that a freeze violates their rights to develop the land they own. The coalition's tactics and strategies have been to express its opposition at municipal council meetings and to spread the word through favourable media coverage. As well, it has objected to rezoning applications and has made presentations to the Ontario Municipal Board (OMB)—the quasi-judicial body charged with hearing objections to rezoning and other land-use applications in Ontario. In February 2000 the organization embarked on a new strategy when volunteers delivered to local residents 20,000 small plastic bags full of wood chips collected from a forest on the moraine that had been felled to make room for road expansion.[91] This dispute is typical of land-development issues across Canada where the rights of property owners are pitted against the public's demand for sound environmental decisions by politicians and bureaucrats.

Advisory Green Groups

Two examples of advisory green groups are the Canadian Environmental Law Association and the Sierra Legal Defence Fund.

Anatomy of an Advisory Green Group:
The Canadian Environmental Law Association
The Canadian Environmental Law Association (CELA) describes itself as 'a non-profit, public interest organization established in 1970 to use existing laws to protect the environment and to advocate environmental law reforms.'[92] It was formed by a group of young law students and community activists. Supported by small employment grants and the dedication of a number of volunteers, CELA survived the 1970s.[93] In 1977, CELA began to receive core funding from the Ontario Legal Aid Plan, a community-led legal clinic system. This was the first time the organization had stable funding.[94] CELA has been instrumental in inducing governments to pass legislation on such diverse topics as waste sites, urban lead pollution, and mercury pollution in the English-Wabigoon river system. It considers its most important accomplishment to be its part in persuading the Ontario government to pass a bill of rights for the environment in the early 1990s.[95] More recently, CELA was chosen by Concerned Walkerton Citizens (CWC) to represent them in the Walkerton Inquiry that began in October 2000.

    CELA plays a number of roles in the environmental policy community. From time to time, it has assisted governments in the drafting of environmental legislation. Its involvement in both domestic and international law has required it to become expert in a wide range of issues from hydrogeology to international treaties and laws.[96] CELA has prepared background reports on environmental issues and has joined forces from time to time with other environmental groups, including the Canadian Environmental Defence Fund, Forests for Tomorrow, the Canadian Environmental Network, and the It's Not Garbage Coalition.[97] It also publishes a quarterly journal named *Intervenor*.

Two other issues that CELA has worked on are pesticides and their effect on children's health, and the air transport of plutonium. In collaboration with the Ontario College of Family Physicians, CELA submitted a brief in November 1999 to the House of Commons Standing Committee on Environment and Sustainable Development about pesticide standards to protect children's health. The research was funded by the Laidlaw Foundation and its purpose was to study existing pesticide regulations and to make recommendations. As yet none of the recommendations have been implemented.

In February 2000, CELA issued a legal opinion on the legality of a plutonium airlift in January. This opinion was requested by several groups, including the Campaign for Nuclear Phaseout, the Canadian Coalition for Nuclear Responsibility, the Sierra Club of Canada, Northwatch, Greenpeace Canada, the Mohawk Council of Akwesasne, and the Concerned Citizens of Renfrew County.

Green Political Parties

In their earliest incarnation, green political parties were seen as anti-parties, different from traditional parties both in the way they functioned and in their structure. It is evident, however, that by virtue of entering the political party system, they saw a strategic value in crossing the line from their previous roles as autonomous interest groups working on the fringes of the public sphere. Of course, this decision in itself was contested as the purists—the radicals, or 'fundis', as they were called in the German Green Party—continued to believe that party politics was not a desirable forum. Although there have been green parties in municipal politics in Canada as well as in several of the New England states in the US, they have found their greatest support and influence in Western Europe, especially in Germany. In many respects, their ascendancy in Germany was not surprising. Because there was not a wild frontier there to pillage for thousands of years, there has been a tradition of stewardship with virtually no political opponents to environmentalism.[98]

In attempting to be seen as a different kind of party, however, Greens have experienced difficulty finding electoral support and have achieved varying degrees of success.

> The emphasis that the Greens place on individualism and self-realization conflicts dramatically with the bureaucratization of contemporary living. Similarly, their long-term, socially-oriented, holistic criteria as a basis of policy clashes with the traditional, short-term criteria of economic profitability which is the basis of most political decision making.[99]

In their desire to be perceived as more than one-issue parties, most have adopted broader policy stances that have included critiques of technological culture, strong anti-nuclear platforms, and opposition to the policies and institutions generated by the Cold War.[100] They have only been successful in winning national seats in those Western European countries that have proportional representation. There have been two critical electoral successes of note. In 1983, just three years after their founding conference, the Green captured 5.6 per cent of the popular national vote of the Federal Republic of Germany. This translated into twenty-seven seats in the Bundestag, and two of its founding members, Petra Kelly and Gert Bastian were elected[101] (see Box 2.3).

When the freshmen group of Green legislators first entered the Bundestag, they each placed a seedling tree on their desk to symbolize the new growth of the environment and German politics. They also presented a shrivelled pine tree distorted by acid rain to the newly sworn-in Chancellor, Helmut Kohl. These theatrics endeared the Greens to their supporters, who were convinced that this party was different from the others. While there is no question that their positions on the environment did attract a degree of measured support from the German public, the Greens owed at least part of their success to the smouldering cynicism among West Germans about the corruptness of the mainstream political parties. There had been a continuing investigation into corrupt campaign contributions by the Flick Company to members of various parties. In other words, the Greens rode the crest of its anti-party, morally superior image in the 1983 election. In the next election, in 1987, they continued to gain support, winning 8.3 per cent of the popular vote and 44 seats, although a number of fissures had started to develop within the party itself. The party had long been committed to the idea of the principle of rotating its members of parliament every two years so that they would not become corrupted by power, but Petra Kelly refused to rotate in 1985, thereby alienating herself from the other members of her party. Also, a growing tension had arisen between the moderates within the party (Realos) and the more radical wing (Fundis). This tension had resulted in the resignation of another founder of the Greens, Gert Bastien. In 1990, the party suffered from the stampede towards German reunification and failed to win any seats when it did not receive the required 5 per cent of the popular vote. The party had not been embraced by East Germans, who were more enthusiastic about industrial expansion and modernization than about the environment. Not only did the Greens suffer a loss in support after reunification, but their two charismatic leaders, Petra Kelly and Gert Bastien, were shot dead in October 1992, allegedly in a murder-suicide. Despite this tragedy, the Greens have enjoyed a renaissance in the 1994 and 1998 elections when they received 7.3 per cent and 6.7 per cent of the popular vote respectively. The party has made some major changes to its internal operations, dropping the rotation rule and replacing it with a two-term fixed limit. And, for the first time in its history, it has several positions, including that of environment minister, in the coalition cabinet. The division between the moderate and more radical wings of the party, however, is a continuing problem.

Box 2.3 Petra Kelly and the German Greens

Petra Kelly was born in 1947 in the Bavaria region of Germany to German parents and moved to the United States in 1959, after her mother re-married. After graduating from American University in 1968 with a B.A. in international relations, she attended the Europa Institute in Amsterdam to study European integration and graduated the following May with a diploma (the equivalent of an American M.A.). She commenced her doctorate at Heidelberg but never finished it.

Although Petra had left Germany as a young child, she developed an affinity for German politics as soon as she started working for the European Commission in 1970. By 1972 she had joined the German Social Democratic Party out of 'utopian hope' in the new leader, Willy Brandt. Encouraged by the ecologists in France, who had won 10 per cent of the vote in some local elections, a movement for a new national political party in West Germany began. In June 1978, a West German environment conference was convened with 100 delegates and 1,000 observers. A committee (including Petra) was established to prepare for the 1979 European elections. In order to play an active role in these elections, she took a ten-week leave of absence from her job in Brussels.

The European elections were contested by many ecology parties, including Les Verts in France, the Ecology Party in Great Britain, and Ecolo and Agalev in the French- and Flemish-speaking regions of Belgium. As well, links were made with radical parties in both the Netherlands and Italy. It was the beginning of a political force in Europe to be reckoned with. In West Germany, delegates from various regional political associations came together in March 1979 to create the Alternative Political Alliance—the Greens. The Alliance captured 3.2 per cent of the popular vote and received DM4.8 million (a 'refund' of electoral expenses calculated according to the party's share of the vote) and a nation-wide platform for its campaign for a nuclear-free Europe of the Regions. The conditions were in place for the birth of a new party.

The 'vision' for the new party was that it was to be a new kind of party beyond the politics of the left and right. This vision ultimately led to a protracted struggle between traditional conservative views and socialist opinions as to which of them would 'possess the new party's soul'. This tension haunted the party from its very beginning. Eventually an agreement was reached, and the leaders of each side signed a piece of paper on which were listed the legendary 'four pillars' of Die Grünen: (1) ecology, (2) social responsibility, (3) grassroots democracy, and (4) non-violence.

In 1983, the Greens captured 5.6 per cent of the popular vote and won twenty-seven seats in the Bundestag. Among the twenty-seven elected/

selected (from the party list) were Petra Kelly and Gert Bastian. The factionalism within the German Green Party continued between the Realos (prag-
matists who believed that the party should work with other parties) and the
Fundis (darker greens who believed that the Green's role was to oppose the
entire system). It did not take long for disillusion to set in. There was constant divisiveness within the party between the Realos and Fundis. The
Fundis were starting to get more radical and to advocate violence. They also
refused to meet with East German Greens. For the January 1987 elections,
Petra was selected for fifth place on the party list and it appeared that her
career was over. To the shock of almost everyone, the Greens won 8.3 per
cent of the popular vote and forty-four seats, twenty-five of which were won
by women. By 1989, the rotation rule had been replaced with a limit of two
terms; therefore, Petra was ineligible for a third term. In 1990, the Greens
made global warming their central issue, but the party was stung by the
stampede towards German reunification. In the election held that year, the
Greens failed to win any seats as they did not reach the necessary 5 per cent
threshold vote.

Source: Sara Parkin, *The Life and Death of Petra Kelly* (London: HarperCollins, 1994).

In Canada, the Green Party has been registered as an official party under the
Canada Elections Act in the past few federal elections. In the 1997 general elec-
tion, the Green Party ran seventy-nine candidates in the 301 federal ridings.[102]
Popular support for the party tended to be concentrated in Ontario and British
Columbia. Approximately 55 per cent of the total Green Party vote (30,442 votes)
was in British Columbia, while 32 per cent of the vote (17,928 votes) came from
Ontario residents. This trend continued in the 2000 election, although this time
Ontarians cast more votes for the party (39,763) than British Columbians did
(34,294). In 1997, twenty-seven of the party's candidates (34 per cent) were
women. In total, the Green Party of Canada captured an estimated 0.4 per cent of
the total votes cast in the federal election in 1997 and 0.8 per cent in the 2000
election. Although it received the sixth-highest popular vote nation-wide in both
elections and almost doubled its 1997 vote in 2000, it trailed behind the four
national political parties and the Bloc Québécois by a significant amount as illustrated in Table 2.2.

In Canada's political party system, it is most unlikely that the Green Party of
Canada will ever be more than one of the parties that are described as 'other' or
minor parties. In part, this is because the single-member plurality electoral system disadvantages minor parties such as the Greens. However, even if there were
a threshold of 5 per cent of the popular vote, it appears that it would take either a
sea change in voter support for the Green Party or an environmental disaster to

Table 2.2 Number of Valid Votes, by Party, 1997 and 2000 General Elections

	1997	2000
Liberal Party of Canada	4,994,277 (38.5%)	5,251,961 (40.8%)
Reform/Alliance Party of Canada	2,513,070 (19.4%)	3,277,037 (25.5%)
Progressive Conservatives	2,446,705 (18.8%)	1,566,894 (12.2%)
New Democratic Party	1,434,509 (11.0%)	1,093,748 (8.5%)
Bloc Québécois	1,385,821 (10.7%)	1,377,820 (10.7%)
Green Party of Canada	55,583 (0.4%)	104,502 (0.8%)
Natural Law Party	37,085 (0.3%)	16,573 (0.1%)
Marijuana Party	66,310 (0.5%)	

Source: Elections Canada, http://www.elections.ca.

mobilize enough support for the party to win any seats. Moreover, its ability to raise money is hampered by its anti-business platform. From 1994 to 1997, the Green Party of Canada raised only $227,058, which amounted to a per capita contribution of $180. Per capita contributions for other parties are listed in Table 2.3.

There are also provincial Green Parties, which are strongest in British Columbia and Ontario. Neither has won seats in their respective legislatures, and the BC Green Party has been plagued with internal dissension at a time that many of its supporters thought was opportune for a breakthrough.

Under the new leadership of Adriane Carr, the BC Greens began to build momentum in anticipation of an election. By the time the legislature was dissolved and the election was called for 16 May 2001, speculation mounted that the Greens were about to make an electoral breakthrough in Canadian politics. This opportunity for a breakthrough was buttressed by Adriane Carr's strong performance in the televised leaders' debate. By 9 May 2001, a public opinion poll reported that the Liberals had 65 per cent of the popular vote, and that the Greens had overtaken the NDP with 15 and 14 per cent of voter support, respectively. (It should be noted that this poll, conducted by MarkTrend, had a relatively small sample of 500 and margin of error of 4.4 per cent.)[104] This same poll and others were all predicting a clean sweep by the provincial Liberal Party. Neither the Greens nor the NDP were expected to win any seats.

As a last-ditch strategy, Premier Ujjal Dosanjh was warning BC voters that a vote for the Greens was like a vote for Ralph Nader in Florida. He also attempted to capitalize on the NDP's wealth of legislative experience as opposed to the inexperience of the Greens. Another logistical problem faced by the Greens in this election was the wide polarization among voters. There were thirty-six parties running candidates. On the eve of the election, a Compas poll indicated that the

Table 2.3 Party Finances, Canada, 1997

Party	No. of contributions	Value of Contributions	Per Capita Contribution
Liberal Party	42,043	$17,480,718	$ 415.78
New Democratic Party	51,965	14,011,983	269.64
Bloc Québécois	18,886	2,140,103	113.31
Progressive Conservatives	26,590	10,982,253	413.02
Reform	77,014	8,799,544	114.25
Canada Party	61	3,551	58.21
Canada Action Party	26	1,349,282	51,895
Christian Heritage Party	26	166,004	6,384.76
Green Party	**349**	**62,824**	**180.01**
Libertarian Party	31	1,741	56.16
Marxist-Leninist	7	22,165	3,166.42
Natural Law Party	365	248,261	680.16
Party for the Commonwealth of Canada	429	21,481	50.07

Source: Elections Canada, Table 8, http://www.elections.ca.

Liberals had dropped slightly to 61 per cent of the popular support, while the NDP had overtaken the Greens with 16 per cent as compared to 12 per cent support for the Greens.[105] On election night, the hopes of electing a Green Party member to the BC Legislative Assembly came crashing down. As pundits had been predicting for several weeks, when voters actually got to the ballot box, they would ultimately vote for an opposition party that was experienced. Ultimately, this lack of parliamentary experience and the tendency of the single-member-plurality electoral system to over-reward the party capturing the largest number of votes works against a third party such as the BC Greens.[106] In the election, seventy-seven of the 79 seats in the legislature went to the Liberals, two to the NDP, and none to the Green Party. But the popular vote tells a different story: 57 per cent for the Liberals, 21.5 per cent for the NDP, and 12.4 per cent for the Greens.

Green parties have had good success in parts of Western Europe, but have been only minor parties in Canada's political system. Electoral support for the Greens at the national level has been sparse for a variety of institutional and non-institutional reasons. Furthermore, their modest financial resources do not allow them to publicize their platforms in any mass way. Hence, it is unlikely that these parties are destined for federal or provincial electoral success in Canada under current circumstances. What is more likely is that the larger parties may become greener as a result of environmental activism.

Environmental Values and Beliefs

In North America and elsewhere, there have been two distinct periods of environmental activism (described earlier in this chapter as first- and second-wave environmentalism). By the mid-1990s, it was estimated that 80 per cent of Americans and over two-thirds of Europeans considered themselves environmentalists.[107] Although evidence abounds that things are slowly changing—public relations campaigns by corporations expounding on their environmental practices, for example, and political candidates who talk about the environment on the campaign trail—it is evident that there is a significant gap between environmental attitudes and environmental action.

Between 1965 and 1970, environmental groups proliferated, as did other groups propounding post-materialist values. As argued by Ronald Inglehart, post-materialism, which emerged during the prosperous and relatively secure years following the Second World War, included such ideals as peace, human rights, and a clean environment.[108] These new kinds of values and beliefs, which supplanted many of the older, materialist values such as income, job security, and the need for food and water, became the principle issues around which social, economic, and political discourse revolved. Underpinning these new values was an ethos that questioned the legitimacy of many of our economic, political, and social institutions. It was the time of Watergate, Woodstock, the assassination of President Kennedy, and Trudeaumania. Characteristic of these new times was the sense of urgency—indeed, crisis—that suddenly pervaded public discussions of environmental issues. Business was cast as an enemy of the environment, and all sorts of new comprehensive environmental legislation was adopted. As Sharon Beder notes, 'business found its political influence seriously eroded by a new set of interest groups.'[109]

Attitudes and Beliefs of Canadians toward the Environment

As was explained in Chapter One, there is a variety of opinions within the environmental movement that are largely explained by where an individual or group sits on the anthropocentric-ecocentric environmental spectrum. Cross-national value changes have been tracked for decades, and since 1970 the World Values Survey (WVS) with its twelve-choice measure of materialism and post-materialism has been conducted regularly. The 1990–1 World Values Survey covered a wide range of domains from politics to sexual and family norms, religious values, attitudes toward war, state-market relations, and the environment.[110] In total, forty countries participated in the Survey. In their analysis of the data from the 1990–1 WVS, Abramson and Inglehart attempted to determine if there was a correlation between mean per capita income and post-materialism. The mean score on the values index of the seven wealthiest countries was 35.5. (The higher the score, the more post-materialist the societies.) Some anomalies, or 'underachievers', a term used by Abramson and Inglehart, were observed. Norway, for example, had a values index score of 15.3, and the United States had a values index score of 20.4. The importance of being able to measure post-materialism is that it is a strong predictor of other value orientations. On the basis of multivariate analysis undertaken by Inglehart in a subsequent study in which the effects of education, age, occupation, and sex were controlled, the link between post-materialism and pro-environment attitudes was clearly evident.[111]

What can the World Values Survey tell us about value change in Canada? On the basis of the 1981–3 survey and the one conducted ten years later, it has been possible to measure value change in Canada. In the 1981–3 survey, the percentage difference index (PDI)[112] for the four-value item index was –6. In other words, there were more materialists than post-materialists. By 1990–1, this score had changed to 14, which represents a shift of +20.[113] The evidence appears conclusive that over this period, an increasing number of Canadians had value orientations that were more post-materialist than ten years earlier. This change is important because post-materialist values are seen as fostering pro-environmental orientations.[114] Abramson and Inglehart acknowledge that post-materialism will not rise indefinitely since it is unlikely that incoming cohorts will always be more post-materialist than the preceding generations: 'Unless the values of newly entering cohorts are more post-materialist than those of the second youngest cohort, the trend toward post-materialism will slow down and eventually end.'[115]

In Europe, they suggest, the biggest factor reversing the trend toward post-materialism will be the economy: 'Young Europeans will face problems . . . adjusting to the complex demands of a changing economy.'[116] As Inglehart himself acknowledges, the thesis of a materialist-post-materialist shift has been controversial, particularly in light of the growing realization that Western youth is highly materialistic and concerned primarily with meeting survival needs.[117] However, he and others believe that the evidence is convincing that important value changes have occurred and are continuing at a global level. The use and interpretation of data from the WVS has not been without its critics. As the survey has expanded to include more countries, questions of interpretation and cultural differences serve to challenge the validity of its findings.

Social scientists have traditionally assumed that values relating to policy matters can best be represented in terms of a left-right political orientation; advocates of the New Politics, however, are able to make a convincing case that these attitudes and beliefs are best represented on the materialist-post-materialist dimension. Deep ecologists would claim that the dimension having the most relevance for organizing environmental attitudes would be the ecocentrist-anthropocentrist continuum. Yet others would suggest that attitudes and beliefs towards the environment and environmental problems depend on whether one is motivated more by individual or community interests.[118] What is evident is that there are a variety of factors underpinning the values and ideals associated with environmental issues. The difficulty is that, since these factors may differ among people and societies, macroanalysis is difficult and problematic.

In 1993, the International Social Survey Programme (ISSP) conducted an environment survey in twenty countries. These environmental surveys and their interpretation by Jon H. Pammett and Alan Frizzell were published in 1997 by Carleton University Press under the title *Shades of Green—Environmental Attitudes in Canada and around the World*. Unless otherwise stated, results of these surveys will highlight attitudes towards the environment found in Canada, the United States, Great Britain, the 'greenest' country, and the 'greyist' country.

This survey consisted both of questions and of statements to the respondents, and asked them for their opinion using a six-point 'feeling thermometer' (strongly agree, agree, neither agree nor disagree, strongly disagree, and can't choose). For the purposes of this discussion, 'strongly agree' and 'agree' have been consolidated into 'agree', and 'disagree' and 'strongly disagree' have been consolidated into 'disagree'. One of the first questions asked about the relative importance of the environment and the economy, specifically jobs and prices. On this question Canada tied for the top ranking on the greeness scale. Respondents said that the environment was an important issue that warranted our attention. The countries that were more concerned with economic factors such as prices and jobs (and no doubt taxes and incomes) included Ireland and the United States.

More than anything else, the question highlighted in Table 2.5 attempts to determine the level of citizen efficacy as it relates to environmental issues. Not only did Canadians believe that they had the power to make a difference, but they surpassed the second-most efficacious country in the survey (Italy) by 8 per cent. The lowest score, registered by Bulgarians, was typical of former Soviet Bloc countries.

Another question (see Table 2.6) measures the extent to which Canadians would be prepared to pay higher taxes in order to protect the environment. At a time of high taxes and a period when governments are struggling with how best

---

Table 2.4 Prices and Jobs

'We worry too much about the future of the environment and not enough about prices and jobs today.'

Country	Agree	Neither agree nor disagree	Disagree	Can't choose
Canada	25%	14%	58%	3%
United States	40	14	41	5
Great Britain	36	13	47	3
(greenest) Australia	26	16	58	1
(greyest) Ireland	55	7	38	1

Source: Based on Table 1 in Jon Pammett and Alan Frizzell, eds, *Shades of Green* (Ottawa: Carleton University Press, 1997), 3.

Table 2.5 Progress and Environment

'It is just too difficult for someone like me to do much about the environment.'

Country	Agree	Neither agree nor disagree	Disagree	Can't choose
Canada	12%	12%	74%	3%
United States	24	13	56	7
Great Britain	33	16	46	5
Italy (greenest)	22	12	66	1
Bulgaria (greyest)	70	7	15	9

Source: Based on Table 3 in Jon Pammett and Alan Frizzell, eds, *Shades of Green* (Ottawa: Carleton University Press, 1998). 5.

Table 2.6 Environmental Taxes

'And how willing would you be to pay much higher taxes in order to protect the environment?'

Country	Willing	Neither willing nor unwilling	Unwilling	Can't choose
Canada	37%	21%	38%	4%
United States	38	19	37	6
Great Britain	38	26	33	4
Spain and Japan (most willing)	43	18/26	37/29	3
Ireland (most unwilling)	23	8	67	1

Source: Jon Pammett and Alan Frizzell, *Shades of Green* (Ottawa: Carleton University Press, 1998).

to spend (or save) excess revenues, this question on taxes is important. Some governments (such as those of Ontario and Alberta) believe that taxpayers should receive the lion's share of benefits that have accrued with balanced budgets. Other governments and social groups believe that the savings should be used to restore funding levels in such areas as health care, post-secondary education, and social programs. Environmental groups have made the case that environmental ministries should be re-staffed so that environmental laws can be better enforced. One of the problems with the wording of the question is that 'much higher' taxes is not quantified. What the figures in Table 2.6 do tell us, though, is that 37 per cent of Canadians surveyed were either very willing or fairly willing to pay much higher taxes in order to protect the environment. This figure ranked below the Netherlands (48 per cent), Israel, Japan, and Spain (43 per cent), Russia (41 per cent), and Great Britain and the United States (38 per cent). This tells us that support among Canadians is not overwhelming for either a green tax or increased taxation that is specifically targeted for environmental purposes. Thirty-eight per cent of Canadians surveyed were fairly unwilling or very unwilling to pay much higher taxes in order to protect the environment.

Table 2.7 shows the views of citizens about the effects on air quality of the gas emissions from cars. Sixty per cent of Canadian respondents believed that car emissions were either extremely dangerous or very dangerous to air quality and were willing to see emission standards raised.

Table 2.7 Cars and Air Pollution

'In general, do you think that air pollution caused by cars is . . . ?'

Country	Extremely dangerous for the environment	Very dangerous	Somewhat dangerous	Not very dangerous/not dangerous at all	Can't choose
Canada	24%	36%	35%	3%	2%
United States	17	30	38	8	8
Great Britain	21	27	43	7	2
Japan (most willing)	22	42	30	4	3

Source: Jon Pammett and Alan Frizzell, *Shades of Green* (Ottawa: Carleton University Press, 1998).

Canadian Survey Research

As well as international survey data, a considerable amount of survey data have been collected by Canadian researchers. This discussion will focus on research conducted in British Columbia, which arguably has been the hotbed of environmental activism in Canada. Several surveys were conducted by researchers at the University of British Columbia in the 1990s. Rather than testing opinions on various environmental questions, this research has attempted to find the relationship between attitudes and behaviours. This research also attempts to determine the nature of environmental concern, be it local or global. It has been observed that 'It is easier to mobilize people in response to environmental problems that have immediate impact, where the targets and remedies are easily identified, than . . . in response to problems that have more distant or diffuse effects or that appear more intractable.'[119]

In a 1995 survey, British Columbians ranked the environment second (18.1 per cent) behind unemployment (26.6 per cent) as the most important problem facing British Columbians. When the respondents were asked to rank environmental issues by importance, the top four issues were motor-vehicle exhaust (20.2 per cent), logging practices (13.4 per cent), ground-water contamination (11.8 per cent), and air pollution (11.3 per cent). (It is interesting to note that environmentalists themselves were chosen by 1.1 per cent of the respondents.)[120] This study also distinguished between two different kinds of behaviour—green consumerism and green activism. The top three 'consumerism' activities (all having over 80 per cent response rates) were turning off lights when leaving the room, turning down thermostats at night, and recycling newspapers. In terms of activism, the study found that activities which take less time and are more individualistic—donating money to environmental causes, signing petitions, and boycotting particular products—received the highest response rates. British Columbians were less inclined to engage in collective and time-consuming actions such as protests, working in election campaigns, and joining environmental groups.[121]

The researchers also tested certain hypotheses about environmental attitudes—that differences may be attributable to such characteristics as income, age, and sex. They did find that education did make some difference in intensity of concern, although the differences were small and 'ambiguous'. However, sex was an important factor, for the study found women to be 'substantially greener than men'. Age, too was significant: surprisingly, perhaps, the study concluded that the greenest age group was the middle-aged. This group scored particularly high when it came to local issues. Region proved to be statistically insignificant.[122]

Another variable that did have an influence on environmental concerns was political values. The researchers constructed post-materialism, neo-conservatism, and populism scales, on which respondents were ranked according to their responses (see Box 2.4) and tested to determine if the attitudes measured by them were predictors of environmental concern. This research confirmed the widely held view that there was a strong correlation between post-materialist values and environmental concerns. It was also concluded that neo-conservatism was an important determinant of anti-environmental attitudes. Even though the researchers concluded that 'there is a greater potential for environmental issues to be caught up in the struggle between left and right in British Columbia than in other jurisdictions,' they nevertheless concluded that the potential exists to mobilize across ideological boundaries.[123] This finding is significant in the Canadian case because provincial and federal politics in Canada are increasingly ideological. With the recent creation of the Canadian Alliance Party at the federal level and the continued success of provincial conservative parties, ideology has emerged as an important variable in attitudes and beliefs on social, economic, and environmental issues.

Box 2.4 Political Value Measures

Populism

Respondents were asked to indicate the extent to which they agreed or disagreed with the following statements, using a scale from 1 to 7:

- We could probably solve most of the big political problems if government could actually be brought back to people at the grassroots.
- Communities grow best through private decisions by individuals who know their own needs.
- A high priority should be placed on giving people more say in important governmental decisions.
- What we need is a government that protects the environment without all this red tape.

Populism scores are an average of the responses, yielding a scale that runs from 1 (low populism) to 7 (high populism). The sample mean is 5.4.

Neo-conservatism

Respondents were asked to indicate the extent to which they agreed or disagreed with the following statements, using a scale from 1 to 7:

- The government should do more to protect the environment, even if it leads to higher taxes.
- To prevent the destruction of natural resources, the government must have the right to control private land use.
- Protection of the environment requires more extensive regulation of business by government.

Neo-conservatism scores are an average of the responses adjusted so that higher scores are associated with opposition to government action in each case. The sample mean is 3.4.

Post-materialism

This scale is based on the work of Ronald Inglehart. Respondents were asked to indicate whether they give high priority, medium priority, low priority, or no priority to each of the following twelve goals:

Materialist

- maintain a high rate of economic growth
- make sure Canada has strong defence forces
- maintain a strong economy
- fight rising prices
- maintain order in the nation
- fight against crime

Post-Materialist
- give people more say in important government decisions
- progress toward a less impersonal, more humane society
- see that people have more say in how things get decided at work and in their community
- protect freedom of speech
- protect nature from being spoiled and polluted
- progress toward a society where ideas are more important than money

Each respondent was given a score of +1 for each post-materialist value assigned high priority. An additional point was added for each materialist value considered to have low priority or no priority at all. Finally, a point was subtracted for each materialist value viewed as high priority. The scale has a theoretical range from −6 to +12. In fact, however, the highest point obtained in the sample was +8. The sample mean is 1.2.

Source: Donald E. Blake, Neil Guppy, and Peter Urmetzer, 'Being Green in BC: Public Attitudes towards Environmental Issues', Appendix, *British Columbia Quarterly*, no. 112 (Winter 1996–7).

The Environment as a Political Issue

The 1997 general election campaign was the seventh national election during which samples of voters were asked essentially the same series of questions. The respondents were asked the relative importance of a variety of factors in making their voting decision. As well as being asked the usual questions about leaders and local candidates, voters were asked to select the issues that influenced voting decisions. Although the 1988 election was dominated by the Free Trade Agreement, issues have not usually been decisive in contemporary national elections. As Table 2.8 illustrates, 'resources, environment' as an issue cluster was not chosen by voters as the most important election issue in the elections of 1988, 1993 and 1997. In fact, it is more accurate to describe this issue as a non-issue in the three most recent federal elections, when only 2 per cent, 0 per cent, and 1 per cent, respectively, of voters ranked it as the most important issue.

According to Harold D. Clarke et al., in order for an issue to have a bearing in an election, it must meet three conditions. First, the issue must be salient to the voters—that is to say, they must have an opinion on it and they must consider the issue to be somewhat important.[124] Second, different positions on the issue must be associated with different political parties. And, third, opinion on the issue must be strongly skewed in a single direction. 'At the extreme, such an issue becomes a *valence* issue, one for which there is a high level of agreement of opinion on its resolution.'[125] In the case of the environment, all parties at one time or another tend to make passing reference to the environment and its

Table 2.8 Most Important Election Issues, Canada, 1988–1997

Issue	1988	1993	1997
Unemployment, jobs	1%	44%	24%
Economy	1	8	4
Deficit, debt	2	18	10
Taxes	1	—	3
Free trade	82	1	—
National unity, Quebec, separation	1	4	13
Resources, environment	2	—	1
Social issues	2	4	10
Government, trust, accountability, etc.	2	7	3
Other	3	4	3
None, don't know	5	10	29

Source: Alan Frizzell and Jon H. Pammett, *The General Election of 1997* (Ottawa: Carleton University Press, 1997), 235.

importance. Its failure to emerge as a valence issue helps to explain why it has never emerged as a decisive issue in federal general elections.

The most recent provincial election campaign in Ontario (in June 1999) was described as one of the nastiest in the country's history. All three of the mainstream provincial parties (the Progressive Conservatives, the Liberals, and the New Democrats) adopted US-style attack or negative advertisements designed to discredit other party leaders and their policies. From 4 January 1999 to 1 June 1999, public opinion was tracked by fifteen polls conducted by four different companies—Ekos Research, Angus Reid, Environics, and Compas. One open-ended question asked, 'For you, personally, what is the SINGLE MOST IMPORTANT issue in the current provincial campaign?' Table 2.9 shows the responses to this question for an Environics poll commissioned by the Canadian Broadcasting Corporation and published on 28 May 1999.

The results of this poll reveals much about the importance that Ontario voters placed on environmental issues. The two main issues identified by voters—education and health care—became important issues in the platforms of all three provincial mainstream parties, while the environment received scant attention.

Neo-conservativism and the Environment

Since the mid-1970s, a major restructuring project—known as a neo-conservative agenda by its critics and fiscal prudence by its advocates—has been undertaken in Canada and elsewhere. As part of this new project, 'politicians have begun to give priority to deficit reduction over job creation, to free trade over state-promoted

Table 2.9 Single Most Important Issue in 1999 Ontario Election Campaign

Issue	%
Amalgamation/reorganizing local government	1
Conservative/Harris government	3
Crime	*
Deficit, public debt	3
Economy, devaluation of the dollar, interest rates	3
Education	21
Gambling/casinos/VLTs	—
Goods and Services Tax (GST)	*
Government scandals, dishonesty, patronage	1
Government spending, waste	1
Health/OHIP/cost of health care/doctors extra	33
Hospitals-services, closing	1
Moral/social problems/quality of life/drugs/alcohol	1
National unity, Quebec	—
Pollution, environment, acid rain	**1**
Social services—cuts too severe	1
Social services—government spending too much	*
Strikes, labour unrest	*
Taxes—income taxes	7
Taxes—property taxes	2
Unemployment	4
Welfare—cuts too severe	*
Welfare—government spending too much	*

Source: 'Ontario 1999: Polls', *CBC News Online*, 4 June 1999, http://www.ontario99.cbc.ca.
Note: The asterisk (*) means a response of less than 1%. This survey was conducted by telephone between May 25–27, 1999 among a probability sample of 1,010 adult residents of Ontario (age 18 or older) who were eligible voters. The sample, which was stratified by region and by community size, was estimated to be accurate within approximately three percentage points, 19 times out of 20.

development strategies, and to spending restraints over social programs.'[126] Although some analysts argue that conservative governments lack an electoral mandate for these policies, the political and economic restructuring continues. In the most recent Ontario election, in June 1999, 56 per cent of the voters did not support the Harris Conservatives, who, nevertheless, won a second majority government. Robert Paehlke, among others, claims that neo-conservative reforms have been implemented and pursued largely because they have not been successfully challenged by alternative visions that appeal to mass publics:

Moderate progressives have had little new to say. Many articulate young people believe that the excesses of liberal progressivism are at the root of our contemporary economic dilemmas—and few seem able to articulate a response to such a perspective. Neoconservatism is thus the intellectually dominant ideology of the 1980s largely by default.[127]

The influence of neo-conservative ideologies on public policy is explored in greater detail in Chapter 3.

The Suppression of Environmentalism: Conspiracy Theory?

In North America and elsewhere, the response by business to environmental activism was twofold. First, businesses increased the number of lobbyists and trade organizations that were charged with advocating their interests at the national and sub-national levels. Second, corporations in the United States, Britain, and Australia supported and funded scholars whose views were compatible with the corporate view in non-university research institutes, sometimes known as think tanks.[128] These groups and institutions were effective in countering the influence of environmental interest groups in the late 1970s and throughout the 1980s.

By the end of the 1980s, public anxiety was once again sparked by a series of environmental accidents and scientific confirmation that the environment was deteriorating. Once again, business responded with a new wave of corporate activism: 'Environmentalism was labeled the life and death PR battle of the 1990s.'[129] In part, this was because lobbying and public relations had become an industry in themselves both in government and outside it. Politicians and political parties began to be marketed in many of the same ways as commodities were. Voters were treated as consumers and were bombarded with political advertising both during election campaigns and between. Corporations took steps to give the impression that they were becoming greener and claimed to be good environmental citizens. Their public affairs departments and consultants ensured that these messages reached the public. With the collapse of communism, the rhetoric and discourse that had guided politics for half a century, pitting east against west, good against evil, and capitalism against communism, left a vacuum. According to Brian Tokar, the last obstacle to the complete hegemony of multinational corporate capitalism was the growth of ecological awareness in the industrialized countries.[130] In many respects, environmental groups have been cast in the role of David, greatly out-resourced by the corporate Goliaths.

Besides using public relations to promote the corporate agenda and counter environmentalism, corporations have been highly successful in convincing politicians that they enjoy the support of grassroot groups and individuals. 'Using specially tailored mailing lists, field officers, telephone banks and the latest in information technology, these firms are able to generate hundreds of telephone calls and/or thousands of pieces of mail to key politicians, creating the impression of wide public support for their client's position'.[131]

This broad-ranging loose-knit coalition of hundreds of corporations in the United States has been called the Wise Use Movement (WUM), and it promotes a conservative agenda. According to Beder, the WUM is 'stage-managed by Ron Arnold and Alan Gottlieb from their base at the Center for the Defense of Free Enterprise, a non-profit "educational" foundation devoted to protecting the freedom of Americans to enter the marketplace of commerce and the marketplace of ideas without undue government restriction.'[132]

It has been claimed that a similar loose coalition, called the Share movement, operates in Canada. Its member groups have attempted to mobilize workers in the primary industries such as forestry and fishing by arguing that environmental protection costs jobs and threatens their livelihoods. They also attempt to discredit environmentalists by claiming that they care more about animals and plants than people.[133] It is evident from the titles of some recent books, such as *Greenwash: The Reality behind Corporate Environmentalism* and *Hijacking Environmentalism*, that many environmentalists believe that corporations are undermining the green movement. Eloy Casagrande Junior and Richard Welford claim that international trade increases cross-border pollution and therefore has a negative impact on the environment. For example, goods that are exported create waste in the exporting country, and the long-distance transportation of goods also has repercussions for the environment given that the means of transportation are largely derived from fossil fuels.[134] In their view, the existence of large, transnational corporations creates unequal access to technology and often causes different countries to compete to attract investment. As they note, these factors contradict the basic assumptions of free trade.[135] The influence and power of these corporations are pervasive. According to Casagrande Junior and Welford, 'They are in control of more than 70 per cent of total international trade, helped by the European Union (EU), the Organisation for Economic Co-operation and Development (OECD), the Group of Seven industrialized nations (G7) and trade organizations such as the World Trade Organization (WTO), the North American Free Trade Agreement (NAFTA) and similar agreements in Asia and South America.'[136] According to *Business Week*, the profits of the top twenty-five transnational corporations amounted to about US$83 billion in 1996.[137]

Environmentalism and the Old and New Media in Canada

Since many environmental groups are not well funded, few have had been able to conduct sophisticated public relations campaigns. As competition among newspapers was eroded as a result of continuing mergers and sales, and news wire services became shared resources, fewer journalists were assigned to sectoral areas such as the environment. Although the large national newspapers continue to have one or two reporters engaged in this kind of investigative reporting, other questions have been raised about why the old media of newspapers have failed to report on environmental stories. NewsWatch Canada has recently published a study entitled *The Missing News*, which examines whether there are systematic and pervasive patterns of omissions in the Canadian news media. They discovered a number of filters that had the effect of screening out various important social, environmental, and cultural issues. The authors have termed these omissions 'blind spots'. For the purposes of our discussion here, only the filters affecting environmental stories will be discussed.

The report concludes: 'Given both the global and national stakes of systemic environmental decline, it is a disappointing surprise that so many stories concerning environmental degradation appeared on our "Most Under-Reported" lists during the 1990s.'[138] The examples cited included the mismanagement of the cod fisheries, military pollution, the dark side of fish farming, and cleaning up after AECL, to name just a few. In part, the news media were more interested in covering environmental crises such as the Exxon Valdez oil spill than the 'systematic and ongoing connections between global environmental degradation and the ordinary every-day workings of the economy, including the pursuit of corporate profit and the promotion of consumerism and materialism as the path to personal fulfilment.'[139] The authors speculate that there are two filters that have resulted in the sensational, spotty attention given to environmental issues. First, in the 1990s reader polls consistently ranked the environment lower on a list of news priorities than had been the case in the late 1980s. So reporters have been reassigned to other, higher-interest areas. And second, the media has difficulty covering 'the byzantine world of research and science'.[140] As a result of these two filters, the news media have tended to focus on the obvious environmental threats at the expense of 'open-ended issues which are continental and extend over long periods of time.'[141]

Because of their frustration with traditional news reporting, green groups have become expert at using visual images suitable for television to publicize their causes. The visual images of a number of Greenpeace actions from spray painting the furs of whitecoat seal pups to scaling bridges have brought considerable publicity to their campaigns. The visual images of oil-slicked birds and sea life washing ashore after oil spills and of animals caught in leg-hold traps are etched on the minds of the viewers. However, though pictures are important and powerful, they often do not tell the whole stories and backgrounds of environmental issues and perpetuate the sensationalist journalistic tradition. Most of these issues are so complex that they cannot possibly be explained in the ten-second sound bites on which television news is based.

Environmental groups have increasingly turned to the new media in attempting to raise awareness about issues and have been very effective. New media—computer-based information technologies that include the Internet—are very influential in Canada. According to an Angus Reid survey, 56 per cent of Canadians used the Internet between November 1999 and January 2000.[142] Although earlier studies concluded that the World Wide Web was dominated by a small, technologically sophisticated conservative minority,[143] much has changed since then. While it is true that many old media with conservative biases have web sites and provide links that may also be conservative, there are also a number of more progressive sites. Admittedly, these may be more difficult to find; however, their very existence on the Internet does allow those organizations a visibility that the older media do not. Increasingly, information on the web is used by students and people doing research for work. The power of the new media has not been lost on environmental groups, many of which have web sites that explain the history of the group as well as its mandate, allow new members to sign on, and provide copies of their reports, often free of charge. The research for this book relied heavily on the new media for copies of newspaper stories as well as more formal publications. As Canadians continue to embrace these new media as important sources for their news and political information, it is expected that environmental groups will continue to make these sites more educational and informative. Of course, many of these sites will be countered by sites operated by the corporate and organizational adversaries of the environmentalists. However, the opportunity to post their unfiltered and unmediated messages on the Web is a strategic advantage that rarely existed in the old media.

thegreenpages.ca

'thegreenpages.ca' is a web site that is owned and operated by university students; it was developed initially in 2000 by Rex Turgano in order to help students obtain environmental information. As a fourth-year Environment and Resource Studies co-op student at the University of Waterloo, Turgano's goal was to provide a searchable database of environmental links for student research. One of Canada's first web sites dedicated to environmental students and ecologically minded people, the site currently lists over 900 Canadian links categorized into more than fifty themes. The web site has received several honours. In the summer of 2000, Turgano received an Environmental Citizenship Award from Environment Canada and in May 2001, he was named one of the five finalists in the 'Volunteer of the Year' category of the 2001 Canadian New Media Awards. The site, which has received no grants, is self-financed. The many organizations and institutions that have already linked to thegreenpages include Environment Canada, the *Globe and Mail*, the World Wildlife Fund, Nature Conservancy of Canada, Canadian Parks and Wilderness Society, Yahoo Canada (as well as Yahoo.com, Yahoo India, and Yahoo UK), and the University of Guelph. David Suzuki will also be posting a regular column on the site. As of May 2001, the site has had more than 20,000 visitors. What is unusual about thegreenpages is that it was founded and is run by volunteers.[144]

The success of this web site shows the growing influence of new media as a source of information about the environment for the public, researchers, and students alike.

The Legacy of the Battle of Seattle

Some members of the environmental movement are confident that the protests in Seattle which disrupted the trade talks of the World Trade Organization may have marked a turning point in public opinion and attitudes towards the environment. In Seattle, environmentalists joined forces with trade unions and civil liberty groups to protest against the continued and unquestioned globalization of the economy. This kind of coalition has not been seen since the 1960s, when students, peace activists, civil rights activists, and feminists mobilized in efforts to challenge existing centres of power. Although environmentalists may have different objectives than their allies, all of these groups share the same misgivings about globalization and its attendant humanitarian, labour, and environmental abuses. Institutions were the Goliath of the 1960s. At the start of the twenty-first century, transnational corporations are seen as the new threat. Despite the optimism among environmental groups and others that these protests are influencing public opinion, Matthew Mendelsohn and Robert Wolfe have argued that they have little influence on political discourse in this country:

> Over the past three years, protestors disrupted one international meeting after another. Dozens of Canadian NGOs were formally accredited to the WTO meeting in Seattle, and busloads of Canadians participated in the street demonstrations. Yet even the NDP, which expressed serious reservations about NAFTA and the WTO, centred its 2000 campaign on health care, not trade.[145]

Only time will tell if the Battle of Seattle will be seen as a flashpoint calling into question the role of corporations and trade in the world.

Conclusions

Unlike other movements, such as the civil rights movement, where there was a solidarity of purpose and goal, the environmental movement in Canada is diverse and heterogeneous. Since the early decades of the twentieth century, there have been several waves of environmentalism, which were generated by a series of different social, economic, and political forces. Each wave was then followed by long periods of non-activism. These peaks or waves, as they have been described here, are important because they have demanded a government response. Between these periods of intensity, however, there have been periods in which environmental ideals and beliefs have been counteracted by corporate commitments to become more green. Also, there have been prolonged periods where other issues have been considered more important.

Green groups and their members vary in ideology, organizational structure, and strategies used in attempting to influence policy makers. In order to survive, they have had to adapt to the changing political climate. Most moderate ENGOs are guided by a light-green ideology and use conventional lobbying methods. That means that in Canada's Westminster-style cabinet parliamentary system, they have concentrated their efforts at the ministerial and bureaucratic levels and have implored business to become better environmental citizens. Darker-green groups have resorted to a number of other tools such as media campaigns, protests, and boycotts. When necessary, a number of these groups have joined together in a united front. At the same time, there have been occasions when groups have been pitted against each other. Given that the Green Party of Canada will not likely ever be an important party in our single-member-plurality electoral system, green groups will remain the most important representatives of environmental views in this country. The 2000 election campaign, which took place against the backdrop of Walkerton and Seattle, was devoid of environmental discourse. The pro-business agendas of Canada's dominant political parties, scant media attention, and a retreat from a regulatory state have all had a role in weakening environmentalism over the past six years. Rather than having a crucial influence on public policy, environmental groups have been relegated to the back seat by governments and business. However, as noted at the beginning of this chapter, there is a historic pattern in which the growth of environmental groups and activism mirrors the ends of periods of sustained economic expansion. We may well be witnessing such a period at the beginning of 2001 amid growing speculation that North America may be entering a recession. Only time will tell if this pattern holds true.

Suggestions for Further Reading

Biographical Profiles of Leading Environmentalists
Parkin, Sara, *The Life and Death of Petra Kelly* (London: HarperCollins, 1994).

Lear, Linda, *Rachel Carson: Witness for Nature* (New York: Henry Holt, 1997).

Green NGOs
Hunter, Robert, *Warriors of the Rainbow: A Chronicle of the Greenpeace Movement* (New York: Holt, Rinehart, and Winston, 1979).

Lee, Martha, *Earth First! Environmental Apocalyse* (Syracuse, NY: Syracuse University Press, 1995).

McTaggart, David, *Greenpeace III: Journey into the Bomb* (London: Collins, 1978).

Taylor, Bron Raymond, ed., *Ecological Resistance Movements* (Albany, NY: State University of New York, 1995).

Documentaries
The Greenpeace Years, The National Film Board of Canada, 1992.

Web sites
Greenpeace International—http://www.greenpeace.org

see http://www.thegreenpages.org/rresource_centre for a comprehensive list of Canadian environment-related organizations, institutions, and individuals

Suggestions for Small-Group Discussion

1. What are the advantages and disadvantages of direct action?
2. Has Greenpeace forgotten its ideals of peace and ecological justice?
3. Should Greenpeace be considered a charity under the provision of the Canadian Income Tax Act?
4. How effective are market campaigns? Under what circumstances would you use your buying power to protest the environmental records of corporations?
5. *Thegreenpages.com* says that its web site will 'empower' students and users. In what ways do you think the new media will influence public opinion?

Chapter Three

The Governmental Role in Environmental Policy

As noted in the previous chapter, environmental interest groups began to spring up in the 1960s, largely in response to increasing alarm about pesticides, scarcity of resources, and the loss of wilderness areas. For the most part, these organizations advocated more management and regulation by governments. Most of them did not support intrusions onto private property or limits on individual rights and freedoms. In many ways, these groups were proponents of a moderate (light-green) environmentalism that was compatible with the ideals of liberal democracy. At the same time, some groups did propose more rigid regulations and stiffer penalties. Rights and freedoms of individuals, they argued, had to be secondary to the preservation and protection of collective resources. In this sense, these groups embraced a view that was darker green and arguably less supportive of democratic principles as they pertained to individual and property rights. These differences in values illustrate just how complicated environmental policy making by governments is. In addition, the diversity of interests in the environmental-policy area creates 'organizational problems for groups attempting to represent environmental interests in the political process.'[1]

In Canada, governments at all three levels have been involved in resource and environmental issues. The fact that 90.3 per cent of Canada's surface area is Crown land illustrates just how important government policy is.[2] There have also been numerous occasions when the federal government has delegated certain environmental responsibilities to the provinces, which have further delegated certain responsibilities to the local level. Although this informal and decentralized approach to environmental policy making has sometimes involved co-operation among governments, on occasion one level of government has challenged another, either through the courts or by embarking on its own action. The result of decentralization and delegation of authority in the environmental field has been a patchwork quilt of programs and regulations across the country rather than a comprehensive approach to environmental policy making. Some have argued this haphazard approach is the direct by-product of ambiguities in Canada's constitution. Not only is the constitution silent about the right to a healthy environment, but it does not offer a clear guide to environmental protection or sustained management of resources.[3] 'Different levels of government, and a range of ministries, administrative arrangements, and statutes, comprise a significant barrier to a comprehensive policy analysis. Changes in government and constellations of participatory politics also make it difficult to understand general trends in the actors and interests represented in the policy-making process.'[4]

This chapter begins with a brief overview of the constitutional ambiguities and jurisdictional problems related to environmental protection and management. Then it examines various instruments of public policy (institutional design and redesign, legislation, regulatory regimes, advisory boards, consultative agencies, voluntary compliance regimes, certification, among others) that have been used over three eras since 1968 to explain environmental policy making. This discussion will be followed by an examination of the federal role in the environment through its lead agency, Environment Canada. Similarly, the provincial role in environmental policy making will be discussed with a particular examination of Ontario's Ministry of the Environment. Both discussions will highlight recent trends in environmental policy making, including defunding and decentralization of environmental programs and personnel. The chapter then examines the domestic and 'external' factors that have influenced environmental policy. The final section presents, as an illustrative example of these jurisdictional and administrative entanglements, the long and arduous process of passing endangered species legislation in Canada.

Constitutional Ambiguity and Political Jurisdiction

One of the critical points of tension in environmental politics in Canada is that constitutional authority over environmental protection is shared by the federal and provincial governments. At the same time, municipal governments, which have no constitutional jurisdiction except in those areas where they have been delegated authority by the provinces, play as significant a role in pollution prevention as their federal and provincial counterparts do.[5] As resource issues become more complex, there has been an increase in the numbers and types of resource users or stakeholders that have interests in resource and environmental policy.[6]

In addition to the increasing numbers of stakeholders, another barrier to effective policy making and policy analysis has been the fragmentation of policy issues and jurisdictions.[7] Furthermore, the courts have played a prominent role in strengthening the hand of one level of government over the other. Because of the jurisdictional ambiguity and overlapping, 'double unilateralism' has been a continuing problem, particularly in some policy areas. This term refers to different and, at times, contradictory actions taken by the two levels of government in the same general policy area. In the past, this has happened in the areas of water-pollution regulations and air-quality regulations.

Although the environmental policy arena has tended to be characterized by tension and jurisdictional disputes, 'double unilateralism' has not been as serious a problem here as some suggest. In fact, in many cases the federal and provincial governments have co-operated and forged successful agreements and compromises, as they did in offshore jurisdictional disputes in Nova Scotia and Newfoundland. In these cases, co-operative resource management and revenue sharing was agreed to.[8] These two successful agreements show that co-operation is possible.

The Federal Role in Environmental Policy Making

The federal government receives authority over the environment from three separate sources: section 91 of the Constitution, international obligations, and federal treaty powers.

The Constitution

As is the case with many present-day policy fields (telecommunications and aeronautics to name two others), there was no explicit reference to environmental protection in the BNA Act nor is there in the *Constitution Act, 1982*. Indeed, there is considerable latitude and *potential* for federal environmental action through the 'peace, order, and good government' clause, interprovincial and international trade, navigation and shipping, fisheries, jurisdiction over Native peoples, criminal law, and ownership of federal land.[9] The Government of Canada has a *direct* responsibility for fisheries species and their habitats under the Fisheries Act, migratory birds covered by the Migratory Birds Convention Act, and all species on federal lands (such as national parks) and in federal waters. At times, federal authority over seacoast and inland fisheries and navigation and fishing have come into conflict with provincial powers over the exploration and development of natural resources. However, since before the Second World War, many environmental functions, including resource management, pollution regulation, wilderness and species regulation, and parks services, have been legislated and administered largely at the provincial level, where they have been delegated to different ministries.[10] Thus, provinces and municipalities have critical roles to play in environmental management and regulation. This constitutional ambiguity over authority in the environmental area has led to inter-jurisdictional wrangling and political compromises. In the event that concurrent federal and provincial laws are in direct conflict, the doctrine of 'paramountcy' would give federal law precedence and provincial law would be inoperative.

At the federal level, two important developments in the environmental field have been the creation of Environment Canada which was established in 1971, and the enactment of The Canadian Environmental Protection Act (CEPA). This Act, which was the only federal environmental statute enacted in the 1980s, was justified under the 'peace, order, and good government' clause, and referred in the preamble to national concern over toxic substances in the environment.'[11]

The same clause was used to justify the constitutionality of the Ocean Dumping Control Act. The federal government has also used the Criminal Code as another means to regulate pollution, although this power has not been used often.[12] On 14 September 1999, an amended Environmental Protection Act received Royal assent. This renewed Act was the culmination of a five-year review. Its cornerstone is pollution prevention, and it gives the government several new tools for protecting the environment and human health.

International Obligations

The federal government also derives power from its international obligations. Examples of enactments under this power include the Migratory Birds Convention Act and the International Rivers Improvement Act.

Federal Treaty Powers

A third source of federal authority over the environment comes from federal treaty powers, although this authority has been contested. Section 132 of the British North America Act assigned both treaty-making and treaty-implementing powers to the government of Canada, but the section only 'expressly considered Canada's powers in relation to Empire Treaties, that is, treaties entered into by Great Britain on behalf of Canada.'[13] Although the case law of the federal treaty power has been mixed, a general conclusion has been that the federal government must be able to pursue a coherent and consistent foreign policy. Furthermore, the Vienna Convention on the Law of Treaties 'does not allow states to be excused from international obligations because of internal conflicts.'[14]

The Three Eras of Federal and Provincial Environmental Policy Making

Bipartite Bargaining (1968-72)

Although Pierre Trudeau did not campaign on a platform of improving environmental regulation, during his first administration no fewer than nine environmental statutes were enacted, including the Clean Air Act, the Ocean Dumping Control Act, amendments to the Fisheries Act, and the Canada Water Act. In large part, this activity was due to the heightened environmental awareness of the early 1970s. In this sense, this era can best be understood within the framework of the issue attention cycle (see Box 3.1). In addition, the federal Department of the Environment was created in 1971. At the time, the new department was much heralded; it not only brought together a variety of existing agencies under one roof, but it gave a heightened visibility to environmental issues and to its new Environmental Protection Service, which was charged with combatting pollution.[15] Provincial governments during this time also passed a number of new statutes and regulations, including Quebec's Environmental Quality Act (1972) and Ontario's Environmental Protection Act (1971). This era, therefore, was characterized by the traditional regulatory approach, commonly referred to as 'command

Box 3.1 Issue Attention Cycle Model

This model is an adjunct of the public-choice model that was originally advanced by Anthony Downs. In simple terms, it posits that public policy priorities change as the public's attention shifts from one issue to another. This model has been adapted within the context of environmental policy making in Canada by Kathryn Harrison of the University of British Columbia. Harrison argues that governments will respond if public opinion considers the environment to be important. When the environment is seen as the most, or one of the most, important issues (that is, a salient issue) by the public, Environment Canada and their provincial counterparts will likely see their fortunes rise. This will be manifested in increased funding and legislative activity. By the same token, when the public shifts its concerns to another issue or two, we can expect to see funding and program priorities shift accordingly. Not only does this model posit that a ministry's administrative capacity is strongly correlated to the public's attention cycle, but it also has important implications for functional capabilities. That is to say, regulators with insufficient resources to develop and implement regulations are in a weak position to coerce anyone. Thus the department or ministry is not only left in a funding shortfall, but is seriously disempowered as well.[1] Harrison's work is important because she goes beyond theorizing about this correlation and finds the evidence to be irrefutable. It has been documented by Harrison and others that federal government spending in the area of the environment (Environment Canada) corresponds with the peaks and valleys of public interest in the environment as determined by public opinion polling. During periods of low salience or when there is only latent public concern for the environment, governments rarely act since 'environmental protection offers politicians more blame [from industries] than credit [from the public]'.[2]

Notes

1. Harrison, Kathryn, 'Retreat from Regulation: The Evolution of the Canadian Regulatory Regime', in Bruce Doern et al., eds, *Changing the Rules: Canadian Regulatory Regimes and Institutions* (Toronto: University of Toronto Press, 1999), 124.
2. Harrison, Kathryn, *Passing the Buck: Federalism and Canadian Environmental Policy* (Vancouver, University of British Columbia Press, 1996), 25.

and control'. Failure to comply with these regulations resulted in either penalties or sanctions. At the administrative level, the Canadian Council of Resource Ministers was renamed the Canadian Council of Resource Ministers and Environment Ministers in 1971 and now included both resource ministers and environment ministers.[16] This organization was further refined in 1988 with the creation of the

Canadian Council of Ministers of the Environment. In some of the new bureau-cracies and laws, there was no discernible change in the way that environmental policy was made. It continued to be decentralized, and the provinces carried the lion's share of responsibility over air and water pollution. Moreover, policy mak-ing 'continued to be dominated by bipartite bargaining conducted through closed, cooperative negotiations between government and industry.'[17] Environmental groups were not well organized and were not considered important parties in this bargaining process. On the other hand, resource businesses had formidable power at their disposal, including large financial resources and control over vital information. In addition, there were some well-organized and influential sectoral organizations such as the Canadian Pulp and Paper Association.[18]

Multipartite Bargaining (mid-1980s to mid-1990s)

By the mid-1980s there was a renewed interest in the environment, and it became apparent that the state itself could no longer legitimately claim to represent envi-ronmental interests. Increasingly, suspicions were expressed about a closed sys-tem that was dominated by business interests. There were two crucial changes. First, the federal government expanded the bargaining process by including rep-resentatives of environmental interests and other groups, including consumers and labour.[19] Although this new multipartite system was more open, it did retain informal and co-operative elements of the bipartite style. Proposals for legislation or regulations were developed in face-to-face meetings under the guidance of pro-fessional negotiators who helped in the effort to reach a consensus.[20]

The second change, according to George Hoberg, was the decision by environ-mental groups to adopt legalism rather than co-operation as a new strategy and to rely on the courts to force governments to change policies. In 1989, the courts ruled on several cases brought by environmental groups involving the construc-tion of dams. The courts' decisions forced the federal government to perform environmental impact assessments.[21] To end the uncertainty about whether the guidelines of the Environmental Assessment Review Process were binding or not, the federal government tabled new legislation in June 1990—the Environmental Assessment Act. Although this bill passed the House of Commons in March 1992, it was not proclaimed until October 1994.[22] Even after the Canadian Environ-mental Assessment Act came into force, several organizations continued to use litigation in the environmental field. The Sierra Defence Fund, for example, attempted to use the courts to reform British Columbia's forest practices, but they have not had much success. As Hoberg points out, the fusion of the executive and legislature in the Westminster system of parliamentary government and strict party discipline will likely ensure that the courts will not play as significant a role in environmental policy here as they do in the United States.[23]

The rigorous environmental assessment requirements were put into place largely as a result of a number of environmental accidents by Canadian mining operations that damaged ecosystems and caused health problems such as mercury poisoning among particular Native populations. The Environmental Protection Act empowered the federal government to determine whether substances used in commerce and industry were toxic. Schedule 1 of the Act lists those toxic substances deemed to pose a risk to the environment or to human life and health. Two such substances are lead and asbestos. Critics of the legislation say this list is far from comprehensive, since some substances used in mining, including nickel, arsenic, and cadmium, have been found to be toxic but have not been included.[24] The Act also contains a number of regulations governing the import, export, and transport through Canada of hazardous wastes.

As public interest in the environment became more apparent in the early 1990s, governments realized that the public would no longer accept policy making behind closed doors. Accordingly, they began to hold more public hearings and consultations. This openness was encouraged by several judicial decisions that created new opportunities for 'increasingly sophisticated environmental groups to use the court system to lobby governments on environmentally related economic developments'.[25] This expanded role for green groups in decision making was largely brought about by a heightened public interest in environmental issues. Without widespread, intense public support, business would not have recognized the importance of appearing to be willing participants in the process. As the issue attention cycle model posits, as public interest wanes, 'the incentives of politicians to claim credit for protecting the environment will decline, and business may be less willing to co-operate in increasing its costs of production.'[26] By the early mid-1990s, this decline in public interest was palpable and a new era in policy making was ushered in.

Deregulation, Destaffing, Defunding, and Voluntary Compliance (mid 1990s–)

As public interest in the environment faded and deficit reduction moved to the top of both the federal and provincial governments' agendas, a new era in environmental decision making began. At both the federal and most provincial levels, a number of environmental regulations have been weakened in order to make investment more attractive to business. This free-market approach to public policy views all goods as private goods. It views government regulation as a barrier to economic growth and an enemy to the taxpayers. It is predicated on the fundamental postulate of neoclassical economics—that the unit of analysis on which all else is built is individual choice. According to proponents of this model, individuals make welfare-maximizing choices. In other words, there are no *externalities*, no economies of scale, no decision costs (that is, there is full information and costless information and exchange), and preferences are fixed and not interdependent among individuals.[27] Government bureaucracy is viewed as wasteful, inefficient, and less competent and disciplined than the private sector. Simply stated, government is considered an impediment to business development and growth. In many respects, the current era has witnessed a fundamental shift in ideology from government as protector and service provider in the environmental arena to government as facilitator for investment. Accordingly, the government's bureaucracy in the environmental area has been substantially reduced. At the federal level, Environment Canada's budget and staff are now smaller than those of the early 1980s.[28]

Since the early 1990s, there have been efforts by government to reform the regulatory approach to one that is seen as less coercive. However, policy makers have continued to reject more market-oriented incentives such as marketable permits and pollution taxes.[29] A second approach—called the 'right-to-know approach'—requires firms to disclose information about the pollutants they emit. Although Canada has lagged behind the United States on these types of initiative, there have been several successful initiatives based on this approach. Products are now eligible to be certified as environmentally friendly and are labelled as such as a result of a federal program. In addition, the daily readings of ultraviolet radiation (known as an ozone watch) now forms part of the weather forecast. Canada was the first nation in the world to report these daily readings.

The third policy instrument that has emerged relies on voluntary compliance by individuals and industry groups. In large part, this has come about because of growing dissatisfaction with so-called 'command and control' environmental regulation, 'which is widely criticized as economically inefficient, adversarial, and administratively cumbersome.'[30] Moreover, governments have withdrawn from regulatory regimes because they have been seen as barriers to economic development and growth. In both Canada and the United States, a number of measures rely on voluntary compliance by provinces and industry groups: 'The growing reliance on less coercive regulatory and voluntary programs reflects a trend toward greater reliance on civil society to achieve collective goals.'[31] Among these initiatives are voluntary reductions by various industrial sectors of greenhouse gases and programs that have been introduced to both promote energy efficiency and reduce emissions. These programs 'typically involve less arm-twisting in the form of explicit threats of regulation or other punitive measures.'[32] (In the United States, over 1,300 companies participated in the EPA's 33/50 program [reducing toxic emissions by 33 per cent by 1992 and 50 per cent by 1995].) In Canada, several of these voluntary initiatives have been launched by industry sectors. The most far-reaching and ambitious has been the Responsible Care program of the Canadian Chemical Producers' Association (CCPA), which began in 1977. This program was introduced for two reasons. First, the reputation of the chemical industry had been rocked by several highly publicized chemical accidents in Europe, Asia, and North America. Second, in the aftermath of these accidents, the chemical industry was afraid the government might introduce more costly and intrusive regulations.[33] In many respects, therefore, Responsible Care was a preemptive strike by the CCPA. The program includes 'a statement of policy, guiding principles, a national advisory panel, a chemical referral centre, a verification process, and six codes of practice with 152 individual elements covering community awareness and emergency response, research and development, manufacturing, transportation, distribution, and hazardous waste management.'[34] CCPA represents seventy chemical manufacturers, most of which are medium-sized firms with 150 to 500 employees. Smaller companies, for the most part, are not inclined to participate in the program because the short-term savings are less than the costs.[35] Although Responsible Care has improved the chemical industry's public image, its critics argue that one of the most dangerous features of government involvement with voluntary initiatives is that the process is liable to be dominated by the industry sector. It is also feared that international trade serves to lower the standards of Responsible Care and that the pressure for increased competitiveness will lead to restructuring, downsizing, and less interest in environmental issues.[36] Despite these criticisms, there is no question that Responsible Care has had considerable success in improving both the chemical industry's environmental performance and its relationship with the government.[37]

A broader voluntary program for preventing pollution is the Accelerated Reductions/Elimination of Toxics (ARET) Challenge, which began in 1994. This program challenged industry participants to achieve certain goals by the year 2000.[38] The program began when representatives of industry, government, environmentalists, and labour came together and drew up a list of toxic substances and ranked them for action. However, implementation became a sticking point and subsequently the environmentalists and labour representatives withdrew from the program.[39] Critics have charged that questionable methods of data collection and a lack of verification have weakened the credibility of the program. Moreover, most industry sectors do not have full participation. Some critics also believe that new regulations might have achieved more than a voluntary initiative. Supporters of ARET counter that the reductions achieved under ARET are significantly higher than what could have been required by the federal government under the Canadian Environmental Protection Act, which lists only 10 per cent of ARET's 117 substances.[40] In addition, the program has been cost-effective, requiring only a modest investment of $1 million by Environment Canada.[41] Two other programs of this nature are the Canadian National Packaging Protocol (discussed briefly in the section on municipal solid waste in Chapter Five) and the Voluntary Challenge and Registry pertaining to greenhouse gases (also discussed in Chapter Five).

The success of these kinds of voluntary programs has been mixed. On one hand, even though they are voluntary the participants may still be subject to certain rules and compliance audits. In the case of Responsible Care, all members of the Canadian Chemical Producers are required to participate. One member has been expelled from the association for persistent non-compliance.[42] At the other end of the spectrum are environmentalists such as Elizabeth May, who has described the forest certification initiative as a 'scam'.[43] There is no question that these programs offer industry participants the opportunity to improve their public images by appearing to be environmentally responsible citizens. At the same time, governments are less inclined to regulate, which is both cost-effective and business-friendly. In the final analysis, however, a heavy reliance on these kinds of programs may not result in industry compliance and may not achieve the desired results. Environmental groups have not been persuaded that these programs are an effective alternative to regulation.

Environmental Policy Making

Environment Canada

The Early Years (1971–1985)

The fortunes of Environment Canada have waxed and waned according to fluctuating public attitudes and opinions toward the environment; this relationship illustrates the strength of the issue-attention-cycle model at the federal level. Between 1970 when 69 per cent of Canadians polled said that pollution was a very serious problem, and 1985, when the percentage fell to an all-time low of 46 per cent, Environment Canada was on a roller coaster ride. Because the environment was no longer considered important by the public, it did not receive much attention from the government: 'the department was subjected to the organizational shuffles and ministerial rotations usually reserved for the more inconsequential . . . agencies.'[44] In its first fifteen years of existence, Environment Canada had no fewer than ten different ministers. Condemned to the political back-burner, environment ministers were offered little opportunity to shine in the political arena.

Although Environment Canada was introduced as a department that would be given considerable operational latitude, it evolved into a horizontal portfolio with co-ordinating responsibilities across many ministerial portfolios. Compounding this operational constraint was a resistance in a number of other departments, including Fisheries and Oceans and Energy, Mines and Resources to handing over their authority. With the introduction of the Policy and Expenditure Management System, one of the nine spending envelopes was social development, which contained the 'quality of life' programs. Environment Canada was assigned to this envelope and was dwarfed by higher-profile departments. Moreover, because it was categorized as a 'social-program' Environment Canada had little opportunity to wade in on program matters related to the economy-environment interface.[45]

The Second Fifteen Years (1986–2001)

Many of the factors that had served to undermine Environment Canada in its first fifteen years—public indifference, bureaucratic resistance, lack of political visibility—changed by the beginning of 1986. Public opinion surveys indicated that the public's beliefs and values were undergoing a significant change. In response to an open-ended query as to the most important problems facing Canada, the 'environment' became significant for the first time in 1987, when 3 per cent deemed it the most important problem, a figure which increased to 17 per cent in 1989.[46] The reasons for this significant change in public opinion have been contested. Some point to the post-materialist thesis of Ronald Inglehart and others, which was discussed in Chapter 2. Yet others contend that a series of accidents, including the explosion in 1986 at the Chernobyl nuclear power plant in the former Soviet Union, was a major contributory factor. Whatever the causes, the evidence appears to be convincing that values and attitudes did change in the mid-1980s. In addition, after being excluded from economic talks, the National Task Force on Environment and Economy—which was created in 1986 in response to the call by the Brundtland World Commission on Environment and Development for Canada to examine the relationship between resource exploitation, investment, and technological development—concluded that 'environmental and economic concerns must go hand in hand.'[47]

After the federal election in 1988, Prime Minister Brian Mulroney demonstrated that his government was intent on making the environment a priority. He appointed Lucien Bouchard, a long-time friend whom he had personally recruited into federal politics, as Minister of the Environment. He also shifted a highly regarded bureaucrat, Len Good, to Environment Canada as Deputy Minister. Both of these appointments were seen as lifting Environment Canada 'from the junior to the heavyweight ranks in Cabinet and the federal bureaucracy.'[48]

In December 1990, Mulroney announced the release of Canada's Green Plan, which called for a $3 billion investment on a number of environmental measures over five years. With little fanfare or public outrage, the Green Plan was terminated in 1995 with only 28 per cent of its original commitment spent ($847 million).[49] Since 1994, there have been continued reductions in spending and cutbacks in federal environmental programs, including a 45 per cent cut to the budget of the Council of Ministers of the Environment, the intergovernmental bureaucracy.[50] It can be argued that since 1995, the Liberal government's preoccupation with fiscal matters, increased productivity, and encouraging investment has supplanted its concern about the environment. Public opinion has tended to support this agenda and as long as it does, it is likely that a pro-business ideology will continue to guide environmental activities by the federal government.

Provincial Role in Environmental Policy Making

There is general agreement that the provinces are the lead environmental policy makers in the Canadian federal state. In part, this is because they have exclusive authority in certain areas. In addition to their jurisdiction over provincially owned lands and resources, much legislation related to the environment has been enacted under the provinces' authority over local works and undertakings (s.92 [10]), property and civil rights within the provinces (s. 92 [13]), and matters of a local or private nature (s. 92 [16]).[51] After the passage of the Constitution Act in 1982, section 92A assigned provinces exclusive jurisdiction over the development, conservation, and management of non-renewable resources in the provinces, including forestry and hydroelectric facilities. Because environmental pollution offences, for the most part, have been considered civil (not criminal) offences, provinces have also been given the authority to control water, land, and stationary (not ambient) air pollution.[52] Their authority in environmental matters has also been strengthened as a result of 'federal abdication of regulatory power and delegation of administrative or enforcement authority to the provinces.'[53]

This overlapping of political jurisdictions can be seen in many environmental policy areas, including air quality. While the provinces have the primary responsibility for the protection and the enhancement of air quality, the federal government has the authority, under the Clean Air Act, to regulate air emissions. Municipalities are primarily responsible for preventing pollution in the areas of drinking water, sewage treatment, hazardous waste discharged to sewers, and solid waste disposal.

Ontario Ministry of the Environment

The Ontario Ministry of the Environment was created in 1971 shortly after the federal environment department was formed. As was the case with the federal department's bipartite approach to environmental policy making, the Ontario ministry soon developed a close relationship with waste-generating industries.[54] Moreover, as in the federal case, the policy process was essentially a closed one with little involvement by the public or environmental groups. It has been documented by the Canadian Institute for Environmental Law and Policy that the budget of the Ontario Ministry of the Environment was smaller in 2000 than it had been in the mid-1970s. Moreover, the ministry has even more responsibilities than when it was created in 1971: 'Between 1991–92 and 1997–98, the ministry's operating budget was sharply reduced by 68 percent in real 1998 dollars and its staffing by 40 percent, forcing a metamophosis in the ministry's mandate in the areas of scientific research and monitoring, implementation, and enforcement.'[55]

Although the cuts have been more pronounced since the Harris Conservatives came to office in 1995, the first large cuts were made by the NDP government led by Bob Rae when he reduced the ministry's overall budget by $200 million in an effort to control the mounting government deficit.[56] For the most part, these cuts were made to the capital budget and there were few changes to personnel or operating budgets. By comparison, in the first two years of the Harris administration (1995–97), the cuts to ministry staffing were deep. In total, some 750 positions were eliminated and a further 350 staff were laid off. Unlike in the cutbacks of the Rae government, however, the operating budget—not the capital budget—was significantly reduced. These cuts limited the ability of the ministry staff to conduct environmental assessments and enforce regulations, among other things.[57]

In addition, there were comparable cutbacks to the other major environment portfolio—the Ministry of Natural Resources. In the past, Crown lands in Ontario have been held in a public trust for future generations of Ontario. However, this future legacy has been seriously threatened by several actions. First, provincial operating grants to Ontario's Conservation Authorities were reduced by 42 per cent in 1997–8 against the 1994–5 base year[58] (see Figures 3.1 and 3.2). Table 3.1 shows that the budgets of the environment and natural resources ministries have shrunk by 39 and 21 per cent respectively.

Table 3.1 Operating Expenditures, Selected Ontario Ministries, 1994/5 to 2000/1 (in millions $) during Harris's Conservative Government

Ministry	1994/95	1995/96	1996/97	1997/98	1998/99	Interim 1999/00	Plan 2000/01	Changes from 1994/95 to 00/01
Agriculture, Food and Rural Affairs	409	263	324	306	309	328	446	9%
Citizenship, Culture and Recreation	363	302	316	300	365	455	398	10%
Community and Social Services	9,364	8,816	7,965	8,047	7,648	7,604	7,504	-20%
Consumer and Commercial Relations	150	140	123	92	136	135	146	-3%
Economic Development, Trade and Tourism	463	385	192	140	89	94	99	-79%
Energy, Science and Technology	14	13	11	69	83	128	241	1621%
Environment	258	226	146	142	162	174	158	-39%
Health	17,599	17,607	17,760	18,284	18,868	20,600	21,988	25%
Natural Resources	478	519	417	405	542	458	376	-21%
Northern Development and Mines	54	66	52	62	82	114	274	407%
Transportation	598	1,054	879	709	607	618	537	-10%

Source: Ontario's Fiscal Plan, Budget 2000, App. B

Figure 3.1. Ontario Ministry of the Environment, Operating Budget, 1993/4–2000/1

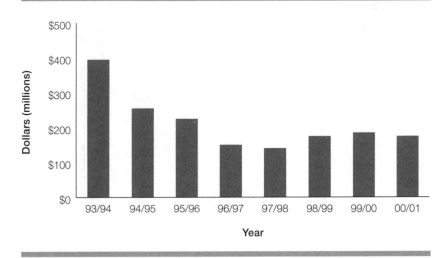

Source: Canadian Institute for Environmental Law and Policy, "Ontario's Environment and the Common Sense Revolution—A Fifth Year Report" (Toronto: The Institute, 2000).

Second, the 'Lands for Life' process—which was hailed by the government as a much improved plan for ensuring the preservation of Ontario's wilderness areas and which was discussed in the previous chapter as an example of third-wave environmentalism—has been heavily criticized by a number of environmental groups. Although additional lands were set aside as 'protected areas' and parks in March 1999 as part of the Lands for Life/Living Legacy settlement, there is some question as to whether these satisfy the international definition of protected areas. Among the activities permitted are mining, sports hunting, commercial trapping, and the use of logging roads by the public. Several environmental groups did initially support the province's plan, but there has been considerable debate within the environmental community as to whether this support was premature and ill-founded. Moreover, this Lands for Life/Living Legacy settlement has opened the door for the province to negotiate long-term (100-year) leases of forest Crown land, amounting to almost one-half of Ontario's land, with private forest companies.[59]

There appears to be little question that Ontario's environmental policies have been strongly influenced by an ideology that is pro-business, anti-regulation, and grey. Environmentalists have been cast as enemies of economic growth and regulation as barriers to investment. The opportunities for public participation and outside expert input in environmental decision making have been reduced as a result of the closing of a number of public advisory boards. This signals a return to a closed, bipartite relationship between the ministry and affected industries.[60]

Figure 3.2. Ontario Ministry of the Environment, Capital Budget, 1993/4–2000/1

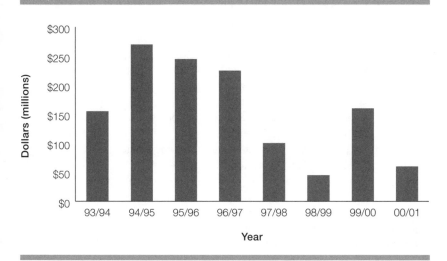

Source: Canadian Institute for Environmental Law and Policy, "Ontario's Environment and the Common Sense Revolution—A Fifth Year Report" (Toronto: The Institute, 2000).

Although there is some optimism among environmental groups in the province that the tragedy at Walkerton may lead to public pressure to restore funding and personnel back to the ministry, it appears (at the time of writing) that the province continues to be committed to pro-business environmental policies.

Intergovernmental Dimension of Environmental Policy Making

The Canada-wide Accord on Environmental Harmonization (1998)

An example of a joint federal-provincial effort to harmonize regulatory processes is the Canada-wide Accord on Environmental Harmonization and the Sub-Agreement on Environmental Assessment. This Accord was signed in 1998 by all the members of the Canadian Council of Ministers of the Environment except the Quebec minister. The overlapping of federal and provincial environmental assessment processes had been a source of tension between the federal and provincial governments since the Canadian Environmental Assessment Act was passed in 1995: not only was there a potential for overlap when one application was subject to two or more environmental assessments, but the 'federal principle of self-assessment meant that proponents were required to deal with several federal departments on a single proposal.'[61] This was frustrating and often time-consuming and costly for an applicant, and the potential for conflicting decisions was high. The Canadian Environmental Assessment Agency estimates that between 80 and 100 projects a year are subject to both federal and provincial environmental assessments.[62] In order to simplify the rules of environmental assessment by applying uniform standards, federal and provincial governments adopted the Canada-wide Accord on Environmental Harmonization in January 1998. This accord, which included a 'Sub-Agreement on Environmental Assessment', was to be implemented through a series of bilateral agreements between the federal government and each of the provinces. By the end of 1999, agreements were in effect between the federal government and Saskatchewan, British Columbia, and Alberta. The sub-agreement includes provisions for shared principles, a sharing of information, a defined series of assessment stages, and a provision for a single assessment and public-hearing process.[63] Although the accord was welcomed by most provinces, there are still a number of outstanding issues related to harmonization, including timing considerations, co-ordination, accountability, and public participation.

There has been criticism of this accord. Some environmental groups believe that the Canadian Environmental Assessment Act is more rigorous than some provincial statutes and are afraid that it may become weaker as a result of the accord. Under the new rules, provinces will become the 'lead party' responsible for the assessment process. The Canadian Institute for Environmental Law and Policy argues that some joint environmental assessments, including the Cheviot mine project in Alberta and the Comprehensive Study of the Voisey's Bay nickel mine in Labrador might not have been so successful without the strength of the federal Act: 'It becomes difficult to conceive how environmental assessment will not get weaker in some Canadian provinces.'[64] Both the accord and the sub-agreements were reviewed in 2000 by the Canadian Council of Ministers of the Environment; a more comprehensive review is scheduled for 2003. Efforts are under way to formalize the relationship between the Council of Ministers and Aboriginal groups.

Outside Influences on Environmental Policy

George Hoberg believes that the United States influences Canadian domestic public policy in two ways: by exporting costs and by exporting knowledge. As examples of the export of costs, he cites acid rain and Great Lakes water quality, where the United States literally exports its pollution to Canada.[65]

The other channel of US influence is through the exporting of knowledge. Often, Canada uses US policies as an example to emulate. Frequently, Canadian policy makers adopt American programs which they adapt to the Canadian situation. On the one hand environmental officials or policy specialists are attracted to the American example. On the other hand Canadian activists sometimes point to American standards in efforts to shame the government into acting.[66] Over and above emulation, there is also American domination in the area of science. For example, the United States is the world leader in toxicology research, and Canadian policy makers may be forced to act when American research shows a particular chemical to be dangerous. At the same time, Canada does benefit from the free-rider factor related to scientific and technical discoveries in the United States. It is also possible that Canada may choose to emulate policies from other

nations, although this is unlikely if they are not compatible with American policies. As Hoberg observes: 'Trade with other nations, multilateral trade arrangements, other international agreements, and broader international policy
communities can all affect Canadian domestic regulation.'[67]

Anatomy of a Policy—Protecting Species at Risk

Although the British North America Act of 1867 and the Constitution Act of 1982
granted various policy areas to the provinces and to the federal government, neither one assigned authority over animals and wildlife and their natural habitats
to either level of government. By virtue of this silence, it has largely been interpreted that the principle of residual power would assign jurisdiction over this
area to the federal government by default. At first blush, it appeared that the federal government would take the lead in protecting various animal species, particularly those at risk. For the most part, however, there has been a decentralized
approach to protecting wildlife in Canada, for several reasons. First, many threatened species are found on privately owned property, and property and its regulation are clearly within the purview of provinces. It has been estimated by
Environment Canada that the degradation and disappearance of habitat is to
blame in the case of about 75 per cent of the threatened or endangered species in
Canada.[68] Second, there is widespread sentiment among federal officials that
local decentralized agencies, both public and private, would be in a better position to assess the state of wildlife and take any necessary action. Third, a number
of failures of the American federal endangered species legislation have convinced
some that a decentralized system would be more effective.

In response to a large and vocal lobby demanding wildlife protection and biological diversity, Environment Canada in 1978 established the Committee on the
Status of Endangered Wildlife in Canada (COSEWIC) consisting of wildlife experts
from several universities and museums, several provinces and territories, three
national conservation organizations (the Canadian Nature Federation, the Canadian Wildlife Federation, and the World Wildlife Fund), and four federal agencies
(the Canadian Wildlife Service, Parks Canada, the Department of Fisheries and
Oceans, and the Canadian Museum of Nature). Recently, a wildlife expert was
appointed from Nunavut. Each year since its creation, the Committee has published a report which assigns species to one of the following categories:

extinct: A species that no longer exists.
extirpated: A species no longer existing in the wild in Canada, but occurring
                  elsewhere.
endangered: A species facing imminent extirpation or extinction.
threatened: A species likely to become endangered if limiting factors are
                  not reversed.
vulnerable: A species of special concern because of characteristics that make
                  it particularly sensitive to human activities or natural events.

not at risk: A species that has been evaluated and found to be not at risk.

indeterminate: A species for which there is insufficient scientific information to support status designation.

Since its creation in 1978, COSEWIC has considered more than 500 species.[69] At its annual meeting in May 2000, it added thirty-three Canadian wildlife species to the national list of species at risk. Table 3.2 illustrates the 2001 figures according to the seven categories listed above.

Critics have argued for many years that this federal-provincial-municipal patchwork system of animal protection was inadequate, and they have called for a federal regime. Recognizing that co-operation among the provinces was necessary, the Wildlife Ministers' Council of Canada established a committee on the Recovery of Nationally Endangered Wildlife (RENEW) in 1988. Part of RENEW's mandate was to ensure that no endangered species became extirpated or extinct and that no new species would become threatened. To this end, recovery plans were to be prepared for all threatened and endangered species.[70] By May 2000, recovery plans had been approved and implemented for only seventeen species.

The Evolution of Endangered-Species Legislation

This discussion will highlight the roles of various stakeholders in arriving at a new legislative initiative protecting endangered species including those groups, such as the Fraser Institute, that have been particularly critical of this proposed legislation.

Lobbying for Wildlife Protection

The organizations concerned with wildlife protection and management in Canada range from well-known national organizations such as the Canadian Wildlife Federation to smaller, less well-known groups such as Baillie Birdathon and the Oceans Blue Foundation. The main co-ordinating group is the Committee on the Status of Wildlife in Canada (COSWIC), an umbrella group responsible for designating the conservation status of indigenous species. There are eight subcommittees (or species specialist groups) and twenty-eight voting members.[71]

Industries

The Fraser Institute contends that industry has done a great deal to protect species and their habitat in Canada:

> In some cases, resource companies have voluntarily relinquished oil, gas, mineral, or logging rights and donated land to protect habitat. For example, in 1992 Shell Oil donated a large holding in British Columbia to the Nature Conservancy of Canada. Forest companies have a long history of donating land. Cathedral Grove, one of the best-known old-growth forests in the country, was donated by MacMillan Bloedel in the 1940s, and wetlands have been periodically donated by Bowater-Mersey Forest Products Ltd. in New Brunswick.[72]

Table 3.2: Numbers of Species at Risk in Canada, by Major Category and Taxonomic Group, 2001

Taxonomic Group	Extinct	Extirpated	Endangered	Threatened	Special Concern	Total Listed	Recovery Plans
Mammals	2	4	15	14	24	59	4
Birds	3	2	21	6	24	56	11
Reptiles	0	2	5	6	8	21	1
Amphibians	0	0	4	3	9	16	1
Fish	6	2	10	18	42	78	0
Invertebrates	1	4	10	1	3	19	0
Plants	0	2	49	33	43	127	0
Lichens	0	0	1	0	3	4	0
	12	16	115	81	156	380	17

Source: Committee on the Status of Endangered Wildlife in Canada, Species at Risk, 2000 (Ottawa: The Committee [News Release], 3 May 2001).

After the death of Bill C-65, it was believed that more co-operation was necessary in developing species-at-risk legislation. In 1998 a group was formed that included representatives of the Sierra Club, the Canadian Nature Federation, the Canadian Wildlife Association, the Canadian Pulp and Paper Association, and the Mining Association of Canada. It was known as the Species at Risk Working Group. In October 2000, this working group presented its proposed amendments to the Species at Risk Act (SARA) to the Standing Committee on Environment and Sustainable Development.

For industry groups, a major problem appears to be the lack of compensation and the protection of species as a shared good. These concerns are highlighted in the statement made by the Mining Association of Canada:

> The idea behind this principle [that the protection of species is a shared good] is simple. Citizens who live and work in downtown Toronto cannot escape responsibility for Canada's species at risk simply because decades of urban growth long ago destroyed the habitat of the Massasauga rattlesnake or king rail, thus making direct action by Torontonians impossible. Similarly, ranchers living in southern Alberta, woodlot owners or mineral explorationists, should not have to bear the entire burden of protecting species at risk that happen often by chance to dwell on their property or on lands on which they work.'[73]

Legislative Initiatives

The federal government has always recognized that any successful measures to protect endangered species and their habitats would require the co-operation of the provinces and territories. In 1996, Bill C-65, the Canada Endangered Species Protection Act, was introduced in the House of Commons, but it died when the 1997 election was called. The death of Bill C-65 was not mourned by everyone with an interest in endangered-species legislation. In particular, there were concerns that the legislation did not recognize the need for partnerships among the various stakeholders, including provinces, territories, municipalities, private landowners, and farmers, among others.[74] One of the bill's biggest critics was the Canadian Wildlife Federation, which was critical of the legislation's 'intensive care ward' style of protection and advocated a broader approach that would take into account the importance of biodiversity and ecosystem protection and long-term planning on wildlife conservation.[75] The federation also concluded that the Act failed to answer the concerns of private landowners and to outline mechanisms for mitigating the effects of land uses on species at risk. Most important, the group argued, 'implementation and enforcement can not be achieved through the existing resources of Environment Canada.'[76]

With the appointment of a new minister (David Anderson), who had long been a supporter of environmental causes, enthusiasm began to grow about the prospect of new and improved legislation. Judging by the failures of the Canada Endangered Species Protection Act, it was clear that the federal government needed a fall-back position in the event that provinces and territories were not willing to co-operate. To this end, it was imperative that any new legislation prohibit the continued destruction of natural habitats. As stated in the federal press release, 'The proposed federal approach would balance the rights of individual landowners and the roles of other jurisdictions with the need to ensure that a critical habitat safety net is available as a backstop when other measures fail.'[77] It is the form of this habitat safety net that has provoked outrage and criticism. The authority to deploy the critical-habitat safety net on provincial or private lands is

> rooted in a part of the Government of Canada's Constitutional authority called the criminal law power. The use of the criminal law power does not mean that an infraction of proposed SARA habitat regulations would be a Criminal Code offence, or that violators would have a criminal record. The criminal law power is the basis for prohibitions in many federal statutes, such as certain sections of the *Canadian Environmental Protection Act*, the *Competition Act*, and the *Food and Drugs Act*.[78]

Environmental groups and think tanks representing private landowners and corporations have been quick to criticize the new federal legislation protecting endangered species—the Species at Risk Act (SARA). The Sierra Legal Defence Fund and the Canadian Nature Federation, which have been particularly outspoken, objected to the composition of the Committee on the Status of Endangered Wildlife in Canada (COSEWIC). The committee was originally intended to be an independent body with responsibility for identifying species at risk, but critics charge that more and more its membership consists of government officials rather than independent scientists.

In 1999, the Fraser Institute published a report, entitled *Cry Wolf* which charged that a number of environmental groups had let 'emotion overcome reality' as it related to animal protection legislation. This report states further:

> They are so convinced that this heavy-handed approach to conservation is necessary that they are unwilling to consider the possibility that this may not be the best way to protect wildlife although, as the evidence in the United States suggests, it may actually further threaten them. Besides these extreme environmental groups' 'crying wolf', the media that get more attention when they report a crisis, politicians and corporations anxious to appear 'green', and bureaucrats with incentives to expand their empires increase the support for more command-and-control regulation.[79]

In responding to criticisms of the lack of compensation provided for in the ill-fated Canada Endangered Species Protection Act, and in recognition that the economic burden of protecting threatened or endangered species should not be borne by individual landowners, land users, or Aboriginal peoples, the proposed SARA does contain provisions for compensating private landowners: 'Compensation should ensure fairness so that particular individuals do not have to bear the costs associated with a public good.'[80] Compensation could come in the form of land swaps and financial assistance in changing to alternative land uses or land-management practices. And in order to encourage private ecological gifts, the Income Tax Act has been amended to allow gifts of wetlands and habitat for endangered species to be allowable deductions. For Aboriginal peoples, compensation would be based on the value of their normal use of reserve lands.

Although the provisions for civil suits are no longer being considered for the new Act, violations of SARA would constitute statutory offences that could be prosecuted in the courts.[81]

Conclusions

Despite several periods of public attention to environmental issues over the last thirty years, comprehensive government action on long-term environmental protection and resource management and stable funding have not been forthcoming. Although the federal Green Plan was viewed as innovative and promising at the time, the policies derived from it have been limited and disappointing. Similarly, innovative institutions, such as the Council of Ministers of the Environment, have not been given the power or funding to function in the ways that were envisaged when they were created. Under the current conditions—that is, the government's preoccupation with increasing productivity and wealth coupled with low public interest in the environment—it appears unlikely that there will be any dramatic new environmental policies. However, as environmental regulations are relaxed and as the capability to enforce them by environmental ministries declines, the federal and provincial governments will be more and more vulnerable to environmental disasters, such as the one in Walkerton, Ontario. Such incidents may lead governments to question the ideology on which their policies are based and may also rouse public opinion from its current latent interest in the environment to a stronger concern. However, in the 2000 election, there was no mention of the environment. This raises the question whether the issue-attention cycle has been obliterated by the market-driven model and voluntary compliance. Under these circumstances, it is difficult to predict when, and if, the environment will emerge once again as a government priority. In the meantime, the environmental agencies have lost much of their capacity to develop policies and enforce regulations. In the event that the environment once again becomes an important issue for the public, environment-department staffs will have to be enlarged significantly, and poorly maintained water and sewer infrastructure will have to be upgraded. The short-sightedness of the federal and provincial governments over the past decade will probably cost millions and potentially billions of dollars more than if there had been steady and incremental funding and regulations. The Ontario government's compensation package to the citizens of Walkerton, announced in February 2001, is a reminder of what the costs can be.[82]

Suggestions for Further Reading

Boardman, Robert, and Karen Beazley, eds, *The Politics of the Wild* (Toronto: Oxford University Press, 2001).

Gibson, Robert B., ed., *Voluntary Initiatives and the New Politics of Corporate Greening* (Peterborough: Broadview Press, 1999).

Harrison, Kathryn, *Passing the Buck: Federalism and Canadian Environmental Policy* (Vancouver: UBC Press, 1996).

Hessing, Melody, and Michael Howlett, *Canadian Natural Resource and Environmental Policy* (Vancouver: UBC Press, 1997).

VanNijnatten, Debora L., and Robert Boardman, eds, *Canadian Environmental Policy: Context and Cases* (Toronto: Oxford University Press, 2001).

Related Web sites

< www.policy.ca > Launched in November 2000 in collaboration with the University of British Columbia's Public Knowledge Project, this Web site describes itself as a non-partisan resource for the public analysis of Canadian policy issues in 16 general areas (e.g., education, fiscal and monetary policy, environment), each of which is monitored by an academic volunteer affiliated with a university. Each general area is divided into subcategories (e.g., under environment, air, toxic substances, and climate change). Under each of these headings can be found various documents including government legislation, conference papers, and position papers by interest groups. The current director of policy.ca is Professor George Hoberg of the School of Forest Resource Management at UBC. Policy.ca also includes teaching tips about how to use the site as a teaching and learning tool.

Suggestions for Small-Group Discussion

1. How has federalism complicated environmental policy-making in Canada?

2. Are you optimistic or pessimistic about the success of voluntary initiatives? What else might governments do (besides regulation) to persuade companies to meet environmental targets?

3. One difficult issue in endangered-species legislation relates to species-at-risk located on privately owned lands. How do other countries with endangered-species legislation address this problem? What ideas might Canada borrow?

4. Assess the success (or lack thereof) of the Canada-wide Accord on Environmental Harmonization.

Chapter Four

Natural Resources in the Canadian Commons

Until recently, natural resources were defined either as renewable—that is, capable of regeneration and existing in infinite supplies—or as non-renewable—that is, not capable of natural regeneration and existing in finite supplies; that is, once gone, they were gone forever. Soil (and by implication the production of food) and forests were considered renewable resources, and all other resources were considered finite in supply and non-renewable. By the mid-1980s, however, this distinction had become less clear. Environmentalists who have been adamant in their position to the clearcutting of ancient forests in, for example, British Columbia, Alberta, and the Temagami region of Ontario, claim that these forests are irreplaceable and that they constitute important elements of larger ecosystems and of the biodiversity of their respective regions. The planting of millions of young saplings will not restore and repair these damaged systems once the ancient forests are clearcut and harvested. Therefore, the renewability of forests has been contested by a number of green groups and scientists. In terms of soil and its agricultural capability, recent droughts in the summers of 1998 and 1999 in the western provinces have raised concerns about permanent and irreparable damage. Quantifying the influences that shifts in climate patterns may have for agricultural production also raises concerns about future soil capabilities. Once again, on several fronts, the renewability of soil and the unlimited production of food have been challenged. For these reasons, it is considered more fruitful to abandon the traditional distinctions of renewability and non-renewability and treat all our natural resources as having limits, while recognizing that certain of these—namely fisheries, mineral resources, and energy resources—are more limited than forests and soil (and therefore agriculture). For that reason, the discussion in this chapter does not distinguish between renewable or non-renewable.

This analysis of Canada's natural resources begins with a theoretical discussion of the various perspectives from which Canada's natural resources have traditionally been viewed, followed by an examination of five natural resources: fisheries (Atlantic and Pacific), minerals, agriculture, forests, and water.

The Three Perspectives on Natural Resources

The Innisian Perspective: Resources as Staples

Canada has always been known as a country with rich and abundant natural resources. These resources have formed an important part of our national identity and are a source of pride to Canadians. These same natural resources have also served as the backbone of our domestic economy, and their use, exploitation, and sale have been critical to the development of the nation's wealth and in the creation of jobs. Unlike many countries of the developed world, Canada is not yet facing a resource crisis where limits of land, water, and food have been reached. So, Canada's resources and their 'value' in Canadian society continue to be viewed primarily from a political-economy perspective. In other words, many producers, resource owners, and workers perceive their value strictly in economic terms and believe that governments should not interfere in the market.

Harold A. Innis, Canada's most famous economic historian, was the first scholar to reflect on the importance of these natural resources, or *staples* as he called them, to Canada's historical economic development. Before Innis's theory of political economy, history had traditionally been studied mainly through the examination of a series of formative events—wars, revolutions, droughts, and plagues to name but a few. Innis, however, argued that Canadian history could best be understood through the study and analysis of dominant staples. The *staples theory*, which he developed in conjunction with his study of the fur trade in Canada, posited that each stage of Canadian history was defined by a dominant staple and the technologies that were developed in order to exploit and transport it. For instance, wheat was the dominant product in the Canadian west at the turn of the century, and the transcontinental railway was the necessary technology developed in order to transport this product to the east and other markets. Similarly, after the discovery of oil in Leduc, Alberta, that became the region's dominant staple and spawned the technologies of pipelines, processing plants, and refineries. A third example relates to the increased mechanization related to the development of the fresh and frozen fish industries. For example, salt as a preservative yielded to ice, and the schooner to the steamship, the railway, and the trawler.[1]

These staples also shaped the society and political beliefs of the inhabitants of the regions where the resources were being exploited. Using the wheat staple again to illustrate, the nature of farm life and the size of farms in the western provinces led to the development and emergence of co-operatives, which allowed for the sharing of expensive farm equipment and grain elevators. In turn, this led to group cohesiveness and a sense of joint purpose that made political mobilization more easy. This helps to explain, Innisians would argue, why the west has traditionally been the birthplace of protest and populist movements, as well as third parties. As further evidence, Innis pointed out that the cod fishery had a profound influence on the political traditions of Newfoundland.

> The balancing of interests through divergent interests which provided a setting for the growth of responsible government was absent in Newfoundland. In Nova Scotia commercialism lent its support to it. In Newfoundland the same commercialism made it extremely difficult. In Newfoundland, sectarian and racial divisions were intensified, whereas in Nova Scotia they provided the basis for tolerant compromise.[2]

The staples theory also posited that the end of a staple, or its exhaustion, left social and political upheaval in its wake, including the loss of élite status by certain social groups. If Innis were alive today, he could argue that the collapse of the east coast fishery and consequent massive unemployment means that fishers and fish-plant workers and owners, who were formerly an élite group, may need to leave the province in search of work. Others would argue that many of Newfoundland's fishers have little education and skills and that their experience in the fishery is, for the most part, not transferable to other kinds of work. The development of the Hibernia oil reserve off the coast of Newfoundland will not create a land of new opportunities for unemployed fishers and will likely foster the emergence of new élite groups and a new technical class. Similarly, Patricia Marchak argues that when recession hits the forest sector, employment alternatives for laid-off forestry workers are minimal.[3]

In his staples theory, Innis warned that a staples-based economy was inherently unstable. An economy dependent on the export of raw resources for processing elsewhere left itself extremely vulnerable to fluctuations in commodity prices on international markets and ran the risk of remaining limited to the role of a resource hinterland and not a mature industrial economy. Without a secondary manufacturing sector or a vibrant research and development sector in a domestic economy, an economy based on staples was doomed to lead a country down the path to economic peripheralization.

Harold Innis's objective was to develop an approach to the discipline of political economy relevant to Canada's economic and political realities. To Innis, fish, furs, timber, wheat, and oil were commodities to be traded on the international market just as cars and ships were. Innis was therefore not concerned with environmental management or the preservation and conservation of Canada's natural resources. Although in his musings about the social and political upheavals that followed a shift in staples, he indirectly recognized that there were physical limits, he did not address the issues of 'scarcity' or 'sustainability' in his theory. Moreover, Innis wrote and thought in a time when sovereign nation-states were economic and political entities in and of themselves. Globalization was a term that had not yet been coined. Although Innis's later work in communications theory did see the continental integration of information and media as both inevitable and threatening to civilizations,[4] he did not apply that theory to economies or the environment. While some might view it as a stretch of Innisian analysis, his work does hold some relevance to the politics of the environment. One of the greatest legacies of his work may be the stern warning to policy makers in Canada: encourage economic diversification or run the risk of remaining a resource colony of the United States. Developed further, with a slightly greenish cast, this warning implied that Canada's resources would be defenceless against exploitation by foreign economic interests and that governments would not be able to do much to prevent it.

Over much of the twentieth century, Canada's natural resources were considered as resource staples to be exploited and used in the creation of wealth. The thought that these resources—particularly so-called renewable ones—had limits has been a relatively recent phenomenon largely associated with the works of deep ecologists.

The Economic Theory of Common Property

David Ralph Matthews has argued that there was a fundamental shift in natural-resources policy—and specifically in fisheries management—during the 1950s and 1960s. He describes this theoretical change as the *economic theory of common property*: he states: 'Before the common property perspective gained acceptance, regulation of the fishery was concerned primarily with biological conservation. By contrast, the common property perspective treated the fishery as an economic and social system that had to be regulated on the basis of considerations other than biological.'[5] Matthews believed that the term 'common property' was fraught with misunderstanding and conceptual problems largely because of disagreement as to whether property was a *thing* or a *right*. In his view, 'common property' was an ideal type of property ownership that rarely (if ever) existed in reality. What was usually referred to as common property, he argued, was 'actually some form of usufruct property, wherein access to and the use of the property was determined by one's membership in a "community" of users. . . . Such communities typically assumed that they had the right to deny access to certain members of the community as well as to outsiders.'[6] Accordingly, there are usufruct property rights[7] that stem from community membership (such as those found in the regulation of the fisheries), as well as usufruct property rights associated with private ownership or state ownership, including those granted to corporations engaged in such activities as oil exploration or forest harvesting.[8] In his analysis of the Canadian fishery in 1954, Scott Gordon argued that the fishery was a common-property resource, to which everyone had rights of access.[9] 'The rational action for each individual in a common-property, open-access fishery would seem to be to take as much catch as possible before it is appropriated by others. The only alternative Matthews could envisage involved some sort of regulation: the commons must in some way be "fenced in" in order to turn it into private property.'[10] Garrett Hardin made a further contribution to this theory when he argued that this theory could be applied to any resource characterized by this system of owner-ship. In his view, the result of this system of ownership was invariably the deple-tion of the common resource: 'Freedom in the commons brings ruin to all.'[11] This perspective embodies the view that common property is essentially state prop-erty. In the case of private property, 'individuals or groups can claim the right both to use the property in question and to exclude others from its use. In addi-tion, they have the right to sell the property. It is this right to dispose of ownership that appears to be the distinguishing characteristic of private property.'[12]

Common-Pool Resources—Managing the Commons

In various parts of the world, common-pool resources (CPRs) have been regulated by traditional rules, which in many respects have been successful in sustaining resources. In state regimes, against the backdrop of the conservation, wilderness, and environmental movements, a new way of examining natural resources has emerged. From this perspective resources are entities having both implicit and explicit value that should be conserved, preserved, and sustained through responsible management. Rather than short-term profit taking, adherents of this point of view take a long-term view and assume that natural limits exist. Rather than being viewed from an economic perspective, CPRs are viewed from an insti-tutional perspective where ownership and management will vary depending on the nature of the resource and the issues that surround it. Advanced by political theorists, including Elinor Ostrom, the 'new institutionalism' is premised on the idea that institutions can make an important difference. According to Elinor Ostrom, they have the ability to address issues that individuals cannot.

> Institutions help individuals with fundamental problems of exchange, collective choice, and collective action . . . in the real world there are social dilemmas, agency costs, nonsimultaneous exchange. . . . However, all these problems exist, and insti-tutions ubiquitously deal with the trade-offs they create, providing opportunities for beneficial transactions that would not take place in the absence of institutions.[13]

The new-institutionalism approach to policy making is premised on the assump-tion that there is no one 'institutional' solution for all policy problems. Indeed, many institutional options and arrangements are possible. In other words, the focus is not on determining the best resource policy but on finding the best insti-tutional design that will optimize resource policy.[14]

The significant differences among these three theories of how resources or staples should be viewed helps to explain why conflict has characterized the development of Canada's natural resources. Producers and resource owners have historically embraced the staples-as-product approach in their management policies, while environmentalists have subscribed to the CPR or managing-the-commons perspective. In other words, the differing views of various stake-holder groups have led to occasional conflict among them. These conflicts have generally pitted corporations against governments, environmentalists, and Native groups. In some instances, environmental organizations have been pitted against alliances of corporations and governments. With increased globalization linking international economies and the proliferation of new information technologies, the use of the term 'commons' now must also embrace the notion that resources are transnational. This does not mean that the Innisian theory has become irrelevant. However, for the most part, 'managing the commons' as embodied in the CPR perspective has increasingly been given voice by the knowledge and science sectors, environmental groups, Native groups, and (occasionally) the media.

Each of the resources that are discussed in this chapter has been the subject of extensive studies, which have examined the exploitation, management, technology, and labour-related issues associated with each resource. Some are highly specific in examining one or two particular issues associated with the resource. For example, in Patricia Marchak's 1983 analysis of the BC forest industry entitled *Green Gold*, her primary concern was the lack of diversification in the industry itself and the class implications. In particular, she was interested in what this lack of diversification meant for employment opportunities in the BC forest industry.[15] Secondarily, she was concerned about the isolation and other social ills of single-industry towns. Larry Pratt and Ian Urquhart's study, *The Last Great Forest*, provides a chronological account of how the government of Alberta, in seeking to diversify its economy, allowed sizable parts of its boreal forest to be pillaged by Japanese multinational corporations. For them, the question was: who should control the resource—governments or multinational corporations? In their view, this was a critical issue as the control of the resource ultimately determined the nature of the industry.

Not all our resources have had the same problems. Therefore, the discussion of them will not necessarily be symmetrical or balanced. For the most part, for each resource the following themes will briefly be examined: a brief history from the political economy perspective; an identification of the stakeholder groups associated with the resource and how these have changed over time; an overview of the critical environmental issues (current and past) associated with each; new trends associated with the 'managing-the-commons' perspective; and the role of government in managing and regulating the resource.

Canada's Natural Resources

The Fish Resource

When John Cabot returned to England after his first voyage of discovery to Newfoundland in 1497, he described 'a sea so teeming with cod that they could be dipped out with baskets.' Similarly, years later Sir Francis Bacon declared the fisheries resources of Newfoundland to be of greater value 'than the tin mines of Peru'.[16] Indeed, the cod of the Grand Banks were the impetus for the founding of English settlements in America, and one of the first parts of the American continent to become known to the Mayflower settlers was named Cape Cod.[17]

However, at the beginning of a new century, the continued viability of the celebrated Atlantic cod and the Pacific salmon is threatened. Some believe that these species are likely 'to follow in the path of the haddock, the passenger pigeon, and the buffalo herds as another melancholy sacrifice to man's short-sighted greed and stupidity.'[18] Table 4.1, which shows statistics for commercial landings on both the Atlantic and Pacific coasts from 1972 to 1999 for four categories of fish, clearly illustrates the first collapse that occurred in 1974–1976 and the more recent collapse of groundfish and pelagic and other finfish, which continues to the present.

This overview of Canada's fish resources in both Atlantic Canada and in the Pacific Northwest will focus on four key areas:

- the evolution of public policy in the areas of the *industrialization* of the fisheries and in the *management* of the fisheries
- the decline and collapse of the fisheries
- current issues facing the Canadian fish resources
- the future of the Canadian fish resource

The Fisheries and Public Policy—The Atlantic Fishery

Stage One: Modernization, Subsidies, and the 200-Mile Limit, 1942–1974
It was not until the end of the Second World War that the need for public policy for the fishery in Atlantic Canada became evident, although scientists had observed a noticeable decline in stocks since the 1800s. With the post-war push to increase food production and the development of new technologies, the exploitation of ocean fish stocks greatly increased. The robust economy following the war also stimulated the demand for fish products. Catches grew very rapidly in the 1950s and 1960s, the increase averaging over 6 per cent a year. New technological developments, including plastic nets, mechanical net hauling, and electronic aids to locate fish, all stacked the odds against the fish. In addition, freezing facilities on trawlers and bigger boats enabled the fishermen to fish farther from shore.[19] From 1949 to 1966, the catch of cod increased by 66 per cent, and in Canada alone it frequently topped 600 million pounds a year. By 1969, however, the figure had dropped to slightly more than 539 million pounds.[20]

Technological advances in the design and construction of fishing vessels and fishing gear contributed to a decline in the cost of catching fish as well as increased efficiency. Most noteworthy of these newly efficient technologies were the large and powerful factory trawlers and similarly large and well-equipped purse-seiners.[21] The unmistakable success of these new technologies heavily influenced the federal government's first foray into fisheries policy. The larger catches, lower costs, and greater efficiency that would result from a modernization of the antiquated east coast fleet led the federal government to jump on the bandwagon. It was evident to all involved—the government, the province, fishers, and related industries—that the economic future of Atlantic Canada was largely dependent on the success of the fishery. The Department of Fisheries

Table 4.1 Atlantic and Pacific Coast Commercial Landings, 1972–1999

Year	Groundfish[a]	Pelagic and Finfish[b]	(metric tonnes, live weight) Shellfish[c]	Other[d]	Total
1972	553,970	460,578	79,003	33,440	1,126,991
1975	448,667	379,697	109,967	36,397	974,728
1980	774,807	327,966	183,241	28,802	1,314,816
1985	829,139	408,666	164,868	27,420	1,430,093
1990	785,543	565,474	251,498	43,394	1,645,909
1995	230,122	312,093	308,510	29,566	880,290
1996	257,124	318,471	311,571	30,699	917,865
1997	260,716	315,071 (est.)	338,322	33,319	947,428
1999 (est.)	298,708	296,563	396,276	18,646	1,010,192

[a]Includes cod, haddock, redfish, halibut, flatfishes, Greenland turbot, pollock, hake, cusk, and catfish.
[b]Includes herring, sardines, mackerel, tuna, alewife, eel, salmon, skate, smelt, and capelin.
[c]Includes clams/quahaug, mussel, oyster, scallop, squid, shrimp, and crab.
[d]Includes marine plants and lumpfish roe.

Source: Department of Fisheries and Oceans, Statistics Office. http://www.ncr.dfo.ca

embarked on a radical modernization policy under the stewardship of Ernest Bertrand as Minister. This policy led to government subsidies for construction of draggers and modification of schooners for trawling gear as well as funding for research into the development of new equipment. Among these was government sponsorship of an experimental inshore boat design—the longliner. The government's intent was to upgrade the efficiency of both the independent producer and the corporate fishery.[22]

This two-pronged policy of modernization and subsidization continued to guide the federal government's policy in the Atlantic fishery for the next thirty years, with mixed results. There was no question that the factory trawlers were instrumental in increasing the size of the catch:

> Factory trawlers were capable of fishing at great ocean depths (1,000 metres or more) in almost all weather conditions and, since they could stay out for months at a time, could pursue trawl fisheries practically all over the world. The purse-seiners with their high-tech electronic equipment could pinpoint schools of pelagic species with a high degree of accuracy and scoop them up in gulps of hundreds of metric tonnes at a time with their huge and powerful purse seines.[23]

Between 1956 and 1964, 'federal and provincial governments provided an average of 84 per cent of the financing (17 per cent through federal boat construction assistance and 67 per cent through provincial loan boards) for Atlantic Canadians purchasing 50 to 60 foot fish draggers, which at the time cost around $50,000.'[24] The grand vision for a modernized and industrialized Atlantic fishery was cut short by a collapse of North Atlantic groundfish stocks in the late sixties and early seventies. Although this collapse was partly attributable to the over-exploitation of stocks by foreign fleets, it was also an unintended consequence of the federal government's modernization policy.

An additional consequence of the subsidy program was that it fostered a culture of dependence among fishers, who were enabled to modernize their operations without investing from their own money. For example, as a cash down-payment, fishers paid only about 16 per cent of the purchase price of new boats and equipment.[25] On the other hand, fishers have argued that they were left with little choice: modernize and upgrade their equipment or get out of the business. Without assigning blame, it can be said that this federal policy changed the face of fishing on the Atlantic coast forever and left fishers dependent on the government for subsidies to modernize their operations and for financial support during the off season.

Canada was not alone in this modernization effort. Indeed, sixteen countries were exploiting the resources of the northwest Atlantic, and scientists were warning this intensive fishing would reduce the abundance of fish. In response to this growing international problem, some eighty-six states came together in Geneva and, by a two-thirds majority, agreed to adopt a Convention of High Seas Fishing, which for the first time set limits to the traditional freedom of fishing on the high seas.[26] This convention directed fishers to respect any conservation measures adopted by any signatory states.[27] However, mechanisms to enforce these measures were non-existent. Although Canada was a signatory on this convention, it failed to achieve its goal of establishing its own exclusive fishing zone off its shores. In both 1958 and at a subsequent Law of the Sea Conference in 1960, Canada failed to extend the exclusive fishing zone from its traditional three-mile limit to twelve miles. This issue was unresolved until 1970, when the Canadian government established twelve-mile fishing zones off both east and west coasts that would be exclusive to Canada.

Despite these successes in the international arena, many believed that the die had been cast for the east coast fishery with the federal government's post-war emphasis on modernization, an increased world demand for fish, and anarchy on the high seas. As a harbinger of things to come, in August 1963, W.R. Martin of the Canadian Research Fisheries Board presented a report entitled *Trends in Canadian Mainland Fisheries, Past, Present and Future*, which concluded: 'Increased human population will lead to increased demands for fish, and to meet these requirements increased landings . . . are expected. Wise use of the resources will require development programs and international management to avoid waste.'[28]

Stage Two: Regulation, Restrictions, Licences, and Unemployment Insurance, 1974–1992

> There are few success stories in the Canadian fishery to match the recovery of the northern cod stock off Newfoundland and Canada since Canada imposed its 200-mile economic management zone on January 1, 1977.[29]

The collapse of the groundfish fishery in the early 1970s (see 1975 landings in Table 4.1) necessitated a major rethinking of federal fisheries policies. The government had little choice but to change its emphasis from industrial development and modernization to the creation of stock and control of access to marine resources. In short, the fundamental problem facing the industry was no longer inefficiency but survival. The concern about technologies was

> replaced by a biologically-grounded perspective that insisted the industry had too many fishers pursuing too few fish. The proposed solution was the development of a more refined, sophisticated, and comprehensive management and regulation regime to limit and control access to marine resources through mechanisms such as licences and quotas.[30]

This necessitated a new regulatory task for federal officials—the policing of both fish catching and processing.

In response to the crisis in 1973 at the Law of the Sea Conference, Canada attempted to gain international consent to extend its jurisdiction over fisheries to 200 nautical miles from its coastline. When this was slow in coming, Canada threatened to declare a 200-mile fishing limit unilaterally. Ultimately, the multinational conference granted Canada the right to extend its jurisdiction over fisheries to 200 miles effective 1 January 1977.[31] Also in 1973, Canada announced that it would introduce licensing for east coast fishers. The licensing system, which operated essentially as a registry, made no distinction between full- and part-time fishers. In addition to fishers' licences, the system would now require licences for boats (of all sizes) as well: 'The impetus for licensing was the federal government's expectation that its 200-mile fishery jurisdiction would allow it to set quotas and regulate catches throughout the whole East Coast fishery.'[32] There is little question that the rationale for this regulatory policy was that access to the fishery needed to be limited and the number of people working in the fishery needed to be reduced.

This new regime required a rethinking of just who owned and controlled the marine resource. For years, small-boat fishers had had a sense of ownership of the resource—each took what he or she needed and could catch. It was a resource that was shared by the fishing community. The new federal policy, however, marked a shift from an individual or community-based ownership of the resource to control by the federal government. The government argued that it had a constitutionally legitimated proprietorship of ocean territory and had the authority 'to grant *individuals* the *privilege* of access to ocean resources through licencing, as long as licence holders adhered to the specifications of their licences, for example, species fished and quantity and type of gear used.'[33]

This shift in understanding of *who* owned the marine resource was critical to policy making. In many respects, this change implied that the fishers themselves were responsible for the collapse of the ground fishery. The 'competitive anarchy' that prevailed on the high seas among self-seeking fishers who were intent on maximizing their profits had necessitated government intervention. Critics have argued that this 'big-stick' approach by federal officials showed little knowledge of local-level notions of proprietorship, common stake, and access management. Anthony Davis argues that this policy was not only heavy-handed but ultimately led to a long period of conflict between governments and fishers:

> The government's limited entry licensing policy, said to be necessary for the good of the industry as well as the economic conditions of fishers, collided with and contradicted local-level, consensual and co-operative modes of behaviour and organization. With the power of sanctions at hand, the government compelled compliance and, in so doing, engaged in a form of intervention that fueled conflict between itself and fishers.[34]

In effect, by blaming the fishers and instituting a regulatory regime that depended on policing and compliance, the federal government continued to ignore the biological and ecological considerations for ensuring a future for the industry. It also failed to draw correlations between high capitalization and overexploitation of the fish resource. This second stage of federal fishery policy was a disaster on many fronts. The very industries that the government had nurtured in the post-war period—independent catching and processing enterprises—had been retooled and made dependent upon a regular access to fish. For this group, the federal policy was nothing short of a betrayal. Moreover, as Davis has observed, the regulations and policing created an industry-wide atmosphere of distrust and conflict.[35]

Although the federal government did shift its emphasis to regulation, its policy was still driven by a desire to modernize and expand. Within a few years, it was apparent that there were a number of problems with the regulatory and enterprise-allocation program. Furthermore, the objectives of limiting access and working towards a sustainable fishery were being compromised in several ways. First, small fishers complained that government policy continued to disproportionately reward the bigger operators and was 'pro-dragger'. Furthermore, a direct consequence of this program was significant under-reporting of landings by commercial fishers. Because there were quotas for boats, and their seasons would end once the official allowance for the boat had been recorded, fishers had an incentive to under-report sales. Indeed, it has been reported that a few of the larger boats may have *doubled* their legal annual catches. Estimates by fishery officers of unreported catches during the mid-1980s usually ranged between 20 per cent and 40 per cent of the total legal quotas for the entire fleet.[36] Although enterprise allocations were not made officially transferable until 1990, it was well known that many fishers found ways to transfer fish to someone else. There were also widespread under-the-table sales which 'became common after the implementation of the enterprise-allocation program.'[37] The program also encouraged wasteful practices. It has been alleged that high-grade fish were targeted by fishers and smaller, less valuable fish, were discarded. Because a boat was limited to a certain weight of fish, it was crucial to maximize the value of the fish sold. It is difficult to know the extent of such discarding, but it reportedly occurred both at sea and at the wharves of the fish plants.[38] Although it was recognized that the enterprise allocation system had inadvertently led to illegal and destructive fishing practices, the program, with modifications to allow a slight increase in the temporary leasing of licences, was extended another three years (1987–9).[39]

Several other problems that began in the mid-1980s would come to dominate the future of the fishery. Foremost among these was the discovery that cod were becoming smaller and slightly more difficult to find.[40] From a 1985 high of 480,471 metric tonnes, only 12,438 metric tonnes were caught in 1995 (see Table 4.2). Haddock, flatfish, and redfish also had precipitate declines. Fishers adapted to the smaller size by placing liners in their nets.

During the first seven or eight years of the federal government's regulatory and management regime, there was a widespread belief that Canadian stocks, particularly cod, were recovering. Many fisheries observers pointed out that the Total Allowable Catches (TACs), or quotas, introduced as a management technique with the extension of jurisdiction, increased progressively for most species and stocks. In the important northern cod industry, for example, the TAC increased from 135,000 tonnes in 1978 to 260,000 in the 1984–1988 period. In addition,

Table 4.2 Atlantic Coast Commercial Landings, Various Years

Species	1972	1975	1980	1985	1990	1995	1997	1999
					(metric tonnes, live weight)			
cod	219,146	145,917	422,092	480,471	395,266	12,438	29,605	55,047
haddock	17,206	19,447	54,262	37,095	22,148	7,933	9,670	10,555
flatfish	116,980	91,952	104,887	89,113	63,665	10,686	10,792	17,115
redfish	109,917	102,916	48,982	71,388	81,451	17,953	18,200	19,679
hake	15,522	12,498	18,269	15,147	15,185	21,444	8,486	16,987
Total Groundfish	**521,459**	**420,892**	**739,784**	**768,083**	**646,231**	**95,866**	**117,123**	**151,041**
herring	304,045	241,914	176,915	193,400	260,272	193,260	184,433	201,908
mackerel	16,143	13,552	22,136	29,862	21,790	17,769	19,752	16,353
salmon	1,525	2,218	2,391	957	688	103	77	1
capelin	4,367	4,789	22,219	36,080	126,917	293	21,800	23,536
Total Pelagic	**337,420**	**280,703**	**241,941**	**271,370**	**423,210**	**232,173**	**234,696**	**249,842**
scallop	43,723	66,651	70,472	47,208	83,278	68,467	65,745	57,896
shrimp	1,384	4,712	13,317	12,955	37,279	54,582	72,917	115,903
lobster	15,054	17,489	20,088	32,638	47,857	40,465	38,941	43,721
crab (Queen)	7,020	7,040	28,725	43,247	26,177	65,372	71,369	95,115
Total Shellfish	**72,355**	**103,750**	**174,363**	**148,484**	**230,047**	**279,150**	**315,614**	**373,215**

Table 4.2 *(continued)*

Species	1972	1975	1980	1985	1990	1995	1997	1999
					(metric tonnes, live weight)			
marine plants	33,172	36,082	27,919	27,412	41,517	26,671	28,541	13,305
Total Other	**33,440**	**36,397**	**27,919**	**27,420**	**42,940**	**29,277**	**32,939**	**18,263**
Total Landings	**964,674**	**841,742**	**1,184,007**	**1,215,357**	**1,342,428**	**636,465**	**700,372**	**792,360**

groundfish classification includes: cod, haddock, redfish, halibut, flatfishes, Greenland turbot, pollock, hake, cusk, catfish
pelagic and other finfish classification includes: herring/sardines, mackerel, tuna, alewife, eel, salmon, skate, smelt and capelin
shellfish classification includes: clams/quahaug, mussel, oyster, scallop, squid, lobster, shrimp, crab–Queen, crab–other
other classification includes: marine plants and lumpfish roe

Source: Department of Fisheries and Oceans, Statistics Office. http://www.ncr.dfo.ca

encouraged by government policies, considerable consolidation and reorganization occurred among the largest fish processors. Emerging from this process were two vertically integrated companies, Fishery Products International and National Sea Products, which dominated the processing of groundfish, shrimp, and crab as well as offshore harvesting.[41]

After Canada threatened in 1973 to declare a 200-mile fishing limit unilaterally, the multi-national Law of the Sea conference eventually granted Canada the right to extend its jurisdiction over fisheries to 200 miles effective 1 January 1977,[42] although the UN Convention on the Law of the Sea, which gave exclusive sovereign rights to coastal states to 'explore, exploit, conserve, and manage their fisheries within 200 nautical miles (370.4 kilometres) of their shores',[43] did not come into force until November 1994. In the months ahead, Newfoundland substantially expanded its offshore trawler fishery for groundfish. At the same time, a new near-shore sector was created and fish species previously ignored, such as crab, capelin, and shrimp, became targets for commercial harvest.[44]

Stage Three: Moratoriums and Collapse, 1992–
It is widely agreed that irreparable damage was done to the cod industry between 1982 and 1987 as a result of overfishing by both domestic and foreign fishers. Although there were periods of good fishing and high prices during this time, gill-net fishers, who had been steadily reducing the size of their mesh since the 1970s, were clearly encountering more difficulty in finding fish, and the fixed-gear fishers of the southwest coast were suffering great reductions in catches.[45] By 1984, cod-trap fishing along the northwest coast, which had been the backbone of the fixed-gear fishery for decades, ceased to be a reliable source of income.[46] In response to this crisis in the fishery, the federal government appointed an independent panel in 1989 to review the northern cod stock. The panel's report, issued in February 1990, confirmed the suspicions that fish populations were not growing, and it called for dramatically reduced harvests. The panel also acknowledged that the difficulty in scientifically quantifying the problem was a serious weakness of this study.

> In attempting to assess the capacity of any such system to sustain a relatively stable yield of a particular species such as northern cod, we must clearly contemplate not only the variability of naturally incurring phenomena on yield but, as well, the effect of human intrusions through, for example, the exploitation of other species. At present our knowledge is deficient in both respects. We neither comprehend fully the complexities of the natural world that northern cod inhabit nor realize the full impact of natural adjustments to human activities.[47]

The Canadian government responded by reducing total allowable catches (TACs) for Northern cod and adopting many of the panel's other recommendations, including the establishment of a special scientific task force on Northern cod.[48]

When stocks continued to decline, the government closed the fisheries ahead of schedule in 1992, and in July of the following year declared a moratorium, closing the entire Northern cod fishery. The estimated 30,000 fishers and plant workers affected were offered compensation as well as vocational training, at a cost of approximately $1.9 billion over five years.[49] The purpose of the moratorium was to allow the northern cod population to increase without interference. Fisheries officials believed that this moratorium would allow the remaining stock to grow into spawners and since their offspring would also be protected, the population would be able to grow again to an exploitable level.[50]

On 1 January 1994, a second moratorium—this time for the Gulf cod—went into effect. Despite the moratorium on both the Northern and Gulf cod, it must be understood that draggers were not tied up to wharves with their crews drawing compensation. Many draggers continued to fish for other species. In fact, they were forced to continue fishing in order to earn enough insurable weeks to qualify for unemployment insurance. (The required number of weeks worked was raised from ten to twelve in 1994.)[51] The main species for draggers were shrimp and scallops, although a new limit on each vessel's yearly catch of shrimp was imposed.

The Current State of the Atlantic Fishery, 1994–

Although the closing of the Northern cod fishery has been the most publicized of the fishing moratorium, virtually all groundfish fisheries as well as commercial Atlantic salmon fishing have also been closed owing to declining stocks. In the case of Atlantic salmon, a five-year moratorium was declared in 1992, along with a volunteer buy-out. Over 90 per cent of licensed Atlantic salmon fishers sold their licences back to the Canadian government at a total cost of $20 million. As of 1999, shrimp, crab, lobster, and lumpfish fisheries continue, but at best, they provide five to six thousand seasonal jobs of a few weeks' duration.

There is no question that significant human suffering resulted from the fishing moratoriums, particularly for families and local communities in Newfoundland. This social upheaval harkens back to Innis, who warned that social and political upheaval would follow in the wake of a disappearing staple. While the social costs of this collapse are clearly apparent, much of the debate following the closing of the groundfish fishery has revolved around the issue of who or what is to blame for the collapse. There is no single reason for the collapse, nor is there agreement about the reasons. Cold water temperatures, more seals, and other ecological factors may all have contributed to the collapse of the Northern and Gulf cod stock. However, there appears to be little question that the primary reason was overfishing. Because of the size and complexity of the fishery ecosystem, scientific knowledge about the cod and other species is imperfect. In fact, it has been difficult for scientists to confirm with complete assurance that the stock is even declining. This is particularly true with the Gulf cod.

Except when they are young (up to 50 centimetres in length), cod are bottom feeders capable of consuming a wide variety of prey including capelin, herring, redfish, other cod, hake, sand dollars, marine worms, mussels and combjellies, to name only some. Cod prefer cool temperatures within a fairly wide range from −0.5°C to 10°C and are capable of adjusting quickly to transitions from warmer to colder water by generating internal 'antifreeze' within several days. Although government scientists remain convinced that environmental change has been significant in bringing about the recent collapse, evidence from the Atlantic area, at least, suggests that changes in water temperature and other environmental factors have not been sufficiently radical to produce such a consequence. . . . Nevertheless, state managers and fishers remain unconvinced, and both have had to plan their strategies for dealing with the declining catches in the context of uncertain knowledge.[52]

This uncertainty among scientists has made them an easy target for blame. It is now evident that the earlier estimates of population growth were often based on unrealistic assumptions. From 1978 to 1986, the abundance of Northern cod was arbitrarily estimated as the midpoint of the estimates derived from commercial catch (by the Canadian otter trawler fleet) and data from surveys by Canadian research vessels. Both these estimates, which were based upon the non-randomly collected commercial catch rate data, suggested that Northern cod had increased threefold between 1978 and 1985.[53] Compounding this problem of unreliable measurement techniques was the frequent use by managers and their political masters of the most optimistic of alternative estimates. It has also been alleged that the bureaucracy in the fisheries department was highly politicized and that the staff was pressured to tell the politicians what they wanted to hear.[54] In fairness to the fisheries bureaucrats, it must be recognized that population dynamics in the fishery are complex and highly variable. Although rumours of overfishing and discarding practices among fishers served to undermine their own credibility, some critics of the federal regime claim that the views and opinions of fishers were often overlooked: 'The opinions of fishermen or others with first-hand experience in the marine environment were courteously dismissed as anecdotal since such information could not be readily quantified.'[55]

Other 'culprits' in the collapse of the fishery were high-efficiency technologies. Their widespread adoption and the expansion of the fisheries fleet resulted in significant increases in the size of catches. For instance, in 1969, the total number of Newfoundland offshore trawlers (usually greater than 100 feet in length) was 43. By 1981, no fewer than 124 trawlers were operating in the waters off Newfoundland. New technologies, including better navigational equipment, now allowed the largest ships to fish virtually all year round. In the short term, these technologies had the effect of increasing the size of the catch and expanding employment by nearly 2,000 jobs, including many in support and maintenance occupations.[56] The fishery also diversified into shellfish and lobster, which became a partial saviour for fixed-gear fishers with lobster licences. However, the limits on new licences made the lobster fishery unable to take in significant numbers of new participants.[57]

A consequence of the industrialization of the fishery was that it led to a stratification among fishers themselves. Smaller, fixed-gear fishers were being outfished and outearned by trawler fishers. These difficulties in the fixed-gear fishery finally led to the formation of the Newfoundland and Labrador Fixed Gear Association in 1987. This group did not call for the abolition of the dragger fleet, but it did seek protection for the fixed-gear fleet. Not to be outdone, the draggers responded by forming the Otter Trawler's Association to offset what they felt was unjustified negative publicity. The conflict between fixed-gear and mobile-gear (dragger) fishers had now become institutionalized in separate industry organizations.[58]

Other important stakeholders in the fishery policy community were those employed in the fish-processing industry. With the increasing industrialization of the fishery, fish processors had became more and more dependent on the fish caught by the dragger fleet. This represented one more group that was pressing the government officials for a response. Clearly, federal bureaucrats with Fisheries and Oceans were in a conundrum, as was shown by a certain ambiguity in federal policy.

> On the one hand, the fixed-gear fishers were right in assuming that there was still a general commitment to dragger technology as the fishery of the future. On the other hand, however, state officials were reluctant to discuss what was meant for the fixed-gear fishery and much of the population of the region. Many dragger fishers were also correct in their view that the future dragger fishery envisioned did not necessarily include their particular enterprise.[59]

The end result was that both dragger and fixed-gear fishers felt abandoned and betrayed by the state during this period. Dragger fishers pointed to the new buffer zones (where fishing is not allowed) as evidence that they were being restricted in order to ensure the future of the fixed-gear fishery. Although they had always blamed lax enforcement as the root cause of illegal fishing practices, the imposition of user fees for increased enforcement was perceived as unfair because it placed an unfair share of the blame on the dragger fleet.[60] By 1995, the Newfoundland fisheries employed only 10 per cent as many people as it had during the late 1980s. However, this significantly smaller work force generated approximately 20 per cent of previous export earnings.[61]

After the collapse, a number of mechanisms have been put into place to address some of the underlying problems with communications and reporting. An independent advisory committee, the Fisheries Resource Conservation Council (FRCC) was created in 1993, with appointees from the private and public sectors. The mandate of this organization is to examine scientific assessments and advise the government on management.[62] There have also been a series of efforts to develop closer links, both formal and informal, between various fisher organizations and government.

Foreign Fishing Fleets

The extension of national fishing zones has not resolved the problem of over-exploitation. Often, in fact, foreign fishing is replaced with an expansion of domestic fishing. Displaced foreign fleets have been obliged to move outside the 200-mile zone where they can continue to harvest the same stocks as before. A critical challenge, therefore, is the management of transboundary fish stocks. The difficulty in addressing this challenge was made abundantly clear in March 1995, when Canadian fisheries patrol boats attempted to board a Spanish trawler, the *Stai*, suspected of fishing Greenland turbot illegally just outside Canada's 200-mile limit. Refusing to be boarded, the boat cut her trawl nets adrift and attempted to flee. In the ensuing chase, warning shots were fired by the Canadian vessel and the *Stai* was boarded. The trawler's skipper was placed under arrest and the trawler towed to St John's. Not long after, the ship's nets were retrieved from the ocean bottom and displayed for the media. The nets contained illegal liners of smaller mesh specifically designed to trap undersized turbot. The government also claimed they were in possession of several thousand pounds of what the Northwest Atlantic Fisheries Organization (NAFO) agreements have termed to be banned species.[63]

Canadian officials never claimed that the *Stai* was fishing within its 200-mile limit. Rather the issue was that the ship was using undersized mesh for the express purpose of catching undersized turbot stock (known locally as Greenland halibut). Though an interim agreement signed on 16 April 1995 did give Spain a larger allocation of turbot than was originally provided by NAFO, Canada also won some concessions. The agreement stipulated that impartial, third-party observers would be posted on all foreign fishing vessels operating off Canada's coast. The agreement also expanded the use of satellite tracking and called for the immediate introduction of new, larger mesh to minimize damage to juvenile fish. Canada also won some concessions relating to monitoring and was granted the authority to carry out offshore inspections where there were reasonable grounds to suspect violations were occurring.[64] A permanent solution to the transboundary stocks problem has still not been worked out. One hurdle concerns the issue of implementation. At the present time, NAFO has no regulatory authority and is strictly an advisory body.

Aboriginal Fishing Rights

The issue of Aboriginal and treaty fishing rights has become an explosive one in Atlantic Canada, culminating in violence between Aboriginal lobster fishers and officials from the Department of Fisheries and Oceans in the summer of 2000 at Burnt Church, New Brunswick. This was the most recent confrontation that began with a Supreme Court decision and subsequent 'qualification' to the decision, commonly referred to as the Marshall case. Although the Maritime lobster industry is not as strong as it used to be, it generates $60–70 million in revenue and employs some 2,000 workers.[65] Combined with related work in the processing of lobster, the industry has sustained many communities. The tension between Native and non-Native lobster fishermen began in the early 1990s, when eight natives from Burnt Church were charged under the Fisheries Act with selling lobster without a valid licence.[66] A decision in this case was delayed pending a decision in the Marshall case.

The case concerned Donald Marshall, a Micmac Indian, who was charged in 1998 with three offences set out in federal fisheries regulations. He was charged with selling eels without a licence, fishing without a licence, and fishing during the closed season with illegal nets. In two lower-court hearings, he admitted that he was guilty of all three offences but argued that he possessed a treaty right both to catch and to sell fish under treaties of 1760–1 that exempted him from the federal regulations. The prosecutors in the case argued that the Micmac trading entitlement set forth in the treaty entitled them only to trade with the British and was terminated in the 1780s when the system of licenced traders died out. The Supreme Court of Canada, in a majority decision issued on 17 September 1999, held that Marshall had established that a local Micmac treaty right to carry on a small-scale commercial eel fishery had been infringed upon.[67] However, the court's decision also left open the possibility for federal intervention in the fishery should it be justified:

> Aboriginal people are entitled to be consulted about limitations on the exercise of treaty and aboriginal rights. The Minister has available for regulatory purposes a full range of resource management tools and techniques, provided their use to limit the exercise of treaty right can be justified on conservation and other grounds.[68]

Moreover, the court ruled that Donald Marshall, along with other east coast Aboriginals, had the right to fish for food, for ceremonial purposes, and to make a *moderate* income. DFO officials and non-Native groups argued that the wording of the Supreme Court's decision should be read for what it says about the *justification* of fishing regulations. In the view of these groups, this wording clearly left the door open for the limitation of this right under certain circumstances. However, the effect of this decision—which was interpreted by Aboriginal fishers in Nova Scotia and New Brunswick as exempting them from federal regulations governing the lobster industry—was the immediate placement of some 4,000 lobster traps in the water in open defiance of a federal fisheries directive to cease and desist from lobster fishing. The initial decision by the Supreme Court, which was thought to award Aboriginal peoples special concessions as it related to fishing rights, enraged non-Native fishers and handicapped DFO officials in regulating the fishery. What ensued in October 1999 was an altercation in which Native lobster traps were damaged, threats exchanged, and trucks set on fire on the Burnt Church wharf in northeastern New Brunswick. Non-Native fishers warned that the fishery could be damaged, even wiped out, unless Native fishers were forced to comply with the federal regulations. They demanded that the federal fisheries minister, Herb Dhaliwal, order a temporary halt to the disputed fishing.[69]

The West Nova Fishermen's Coalition applied (in November 1999) for a rehearing of the appeal of the Marshall case and also sought a further trial limited to the issue of whether the application of the fisheries regulations to the exercise of a Micmac treaty right could be justified on conservation or other grounds. The other parties involved (Marshall, the federal government, and several Native organizations) all opposed the rehearing. A motion to rehear the case was rejected on 17 November 1999; however, in its ruling the Supreme Court used language that has been referred to as a 'qualification' to the existing decision handed down in the Marshall case: 'The paramount regulatory objective is the conservation of the resource. This responsibility is placed squarely on the Minister and not on the aboriginal or non-aboriginal users of the resource.'

Many Native groups were outraged by the qualification to the Marshall decision. Matthew Coon Come has said that First Nations people should be allowed the right to fish in their own waters and to use their own instruments of self-patrol, such as constables and peacekeepers.[70] Twenty-nine other reserves have made agreements with the DFO; however, the Burnt Church First Nations have refused to do so. Whereas the deal accepted by the other reserves calls for a forty-trap limit, band leaders at Burnt Church argue they have the right to drop as many as 5,000 traps in the Atlantic.[71] This dispute clearly reflects three visions. Native fishers see the lobster fishery as a common-property resource for Aboriginal fishers, in which they will regulate themselves in order to sustain it now and in the future. Non-Native fishers view this as a collective resource to which they have had their access limited by DFO regulations, which do not, however, bind other groups (Natives) in the same way. DFO believes that the conservation of the fishery is *the* most important issue and that limiting fishing is justified.

Some groups have argued that these judicial decisions have opened the door to reckless and greedy fishing practices by Native peoples at the expense of the sustainability of coastal and freshwater fisheries. These kinds of fears need to be tempered by the fact that Native fishers stand to lose their livelihoods if the fisheries are not harvested at sustainable levels.

Before the Supreme Court's qualification in the Marshall case, it was reported that the Fisheries Minister Herb Dhaliwal was prepared to spend as much as $500 million over five years to buy out non-Native fishermen in the Atlantic provinces and transfer their licences to Aboriginal fishers. Should this plan be approved, it would give Aboriginal groups a major role in managing the fish resource.[72] It would also take away the livelihoods of non-Native fishers, many of whom are second- and third-generation fishers, and lead to the decline of a number of communities for whom fishing has traditionally been their economic mainstay. Since the qualification, however, it appears that Ottawa is determined to flex its muscle as the lead regulator of Canadian fisheries. Until this conflict over fishing rights is resolved, it appears likely that there will be more violence.

The Future of the East Coast Fishery Resource

The future of the east coast fishery is uncertain, at best. As a resource, its regeneration is questionable. As a livelihood, fishing will never be the mainstay of the Atlantic region that it once was. Indeed, on the east coast, there may be long periods of unemployment in the harvesting sector and related industries. It also appears that Canadian taxpayers will no longer be sympathetic to heavy state subsidy of the fishery and fishers themselves. Moreover, it is unlikely that international trade organizations such as the WTO will look favourably upon subsidies:

> The rise of large regional trading blocs, founded at least in part on the principle of relatively unimpeded trade, poses new challenges for these island societies. With the removal of most, if not all, trading barriers within supranational associations such as the European Union or the North American Free Trade Agreement, issues of productivity and cost effectiveness will become highly important in maintaining or expanding market share. They will certainly be key to any effort by any island society to increase the amount of additional, value-added processing done within its territory and the employment associated with it.[73]

All of these factors combine to form a formidable challenge to policy making in the fishery. In order for the fishery and related processing activities to become efficient and sustainable, a dramatically different management system will be necessary. This will be difficult: 'Throughout much of the island's European settlement, the inshore fishery has been considered the employer of last resort: when no other work could be found, one could always fish. Unemployment insurance for fishermen, introduced in 1957, has further entrenched this tendency.'[74]

There has been widespread agreement that a major overhaul of the management of the Atlantic fishery is long overdue, and in May 1999, the Minister of Fisheries and Oceans directed his department to launch a comprehensive public review of fisheries management policies for the Atlantic fisheries—named the Atlantic Fisheries Policy Review (AFPR). The review will be conducted in two phases. In the first phase, the Department of Fisheries and Oceans released a discussion paper called *The Management of Fisheries on Canada's Atlantic Coast.* On the basis of this report, the government held a series of meetings in the Atlantic provinces, Quebec, and Nunavut during 2000 and 2001. By May 2001, these discussions had been completed, and it is anticipated that sometime in the fall of 2001, the Department will issue a new policy framework that will 'define a set of objectives and principles to guide the long-term management of the Atlantic fisheries.' The second stage will draw up an implementation plan that will outline the responsibilities of the various stakeholders and identify the mechanisms needed to put the new framework into effect.[75]

Of course, Canada is not the only country that has suffered a serious blow to its fishery. Accordingly, it may be useful to examine policies that have been adopted by other countries to solve the problems of fishery management. One of the most promising management regimes of the past ten years is based on property rights. This approach 'attempts to remedy the common property problem through bestowing property rights in the fisheries. The most prominent of the rights-based fisheries management systems is the Individual Transferable Quota (ITQ) system that has been introduced in various important fisheries around the world, most notably in New Zealand, Iceland, and Australia.'[76]

In the minds of greens, the collapse of the east coast fishery is primarily an environmental problem. For those who have relied on fishing, both directly and indirectly, it is an economic or employment problem, as is borne out by unemployment statistics and low incomes. However, the collapse also has an important social dimension. A range of social relations and customs have evolved in connection with the traditional organization of the fish resource. During a period of adjustment—as the moratoriums and collapse certainly are—there may be a great deal of social friction and many civil disturbances. This is evident in the Burnt Church dispute. Also, with the passage of time and the out-migration of fishery workers, certain social structures and values are likely to be irretrievably lost.[77]

As far as the Canadian fishery is concerned, regeneration of the traditional resource is not the only objective that has been pursued. Like other countries, Canada has tried to develop new forms of fisheries, such as aquaculture. This relatively new economic endeavour is growing so quickly all around the world that the United Nations Fisheries and Agriculture Organization has estimated that aquaculture could supply up to 39 million tons of fish by 2010—70 per cent more than today.[78] Not everyone, however, believes that aquaculture is environmentally friendly or healthful. Fish farms have had negative repercussions for wetlands, and the escape of farmed species has been devastating to wild fish. Moreover, it has been estimated that for every kilogram of farmed salmon produced, five kilograms of wild fish are needed for fish meal.[79] Farmed salmon, it has been discovered, are particularly susceptible to certain diseases, including infectious salmon anemia and bacterial kidney disease. Outbreaks of the former in Norway in the late 1980s and early 1990s cost the country an estimated $100 million in economic losses.[80] In April 2001, a federal study commissioned by the Department of Fisheries and Oceans was obtained through an access-to-information request by the David Suzuki Foundation. The report, entitled *Impacts of Freshwater and Marine Aquaculture on the Environment: Knowledge and Gaps*, revealed several disturbing facts about this new industry. Most disconcerting was the discovery of drug residues in wild fish and shellfish collected near fish farms. These drug levels exceeded accepted levels for human consumption and constitute a threat to human health if eaten.[81] Nevertheless, the Department continues to support programs and incentives to increase the competitiveness of Canada's aquaculture industry.

The Pacific Northwest Fishery

> From his work [that of the biologist William Ricker from the 1940s to 1980s] we can begin to imagine what a spectacle it must have been during the 'big year' sockeye runs to the Fraser River, when perhaps as many as 160 million sockeye salmon moved through the Strait of Georgia, across the shallow sandheads of the estuary and into the mainstream, and then on through the mountains to their natal creek-fed lakes. The movement of an organic mass of that size across the face of the globe must have represented a colossal ecological event on the continent's landscape, on a scale equal to the migratory convergences of great buffalo herds on North American plains. Nothing of this kind has been seen on the Fraser in living memory: the average annual return of Fraser River sockeye during the late twentieth century has been about 7 million fish.[82]

Although some of the problems of the Pacific Northwest fishery are similar to those on the east coast, there are a number of important differences. First and foremost, the diversity of species in the Pacific fishery makes it far less dependent on one species than the Atlantic fishery was. For example, while there is only one variety of Atlantic salmon, there are five distinct varieties of salmon spawning in Canadian and American waters of the Pacific Northwest fishery: sockeye, pink, chum or keta, chinook or spring, and coho salmon.[83] This diversity in the Pacific fishery has made the west coast fishery less vulnerable to a shutdown in the event that one species became threatened. Nevertheless, even though the outright collapse might take longer, Terry Glavin claims that warning signs of a troubled resource already exist:

> So while it is true to say that what happened in Newfoundland could not happen here (because there is no single biomass that accounts for the vast majority of BC's fisheries jobs), it is also true to say that it has already happened here, and it is happening here. And if the prevailing fisheries policies on this coast are not soon abandoned, it will likely continue to happen here until it is all gone. . . . Instead, our fisheries are more likely to die a long and painful death, fishery by fishery, stock by stock, species by species, creek by creek.[84]

Another difference between the two fish resources is in the range of the habitats of the Pacific fishery: 'Unlike the Grand Banks and Georges Bank of the Canadian and US East Coast, the primary resources of the West Coast's fisheries are not confined to a single, common range. So our fisheries are less likely to be wiped out by one horrific, deathdealing blast.'[85] There are also other important differences. American fishers are an important factor in the west coast fishery, as are natural factors such as El Niño and the influence of other wildlife species, including seals and sea lions. Whereas the north Atlantic is getting colder, the north Pacific is getting warmer, and fish are changing their ranges, spawning habits, and travel patterns.

For much of its history, nature kept a balance in the salmon runs through periodic disasters such as floods, droughts, and landslides. In more recent times, human activities have contributed to the growing problems faced by the Pacific fishery. Organic and inorganic pollutants generated by mining pose one threat. Logging exacts a heavy price on the fishery by destroying the spawning beds, by eroding streams and creating heavy silting that smothers the eggs in the gravel, and by denuding the forest so that there are fluctuations in stream levels, ranging from heavy floods to virtually dry stream beds. Dams are also considered major man-made fish killers.[86]

The Pacific fishery has had several near collapses before. In particular, halibut and herring have been threatened at one time or another. On both occasions, there was a partial recovery, which may serve to explain why fishers have not taken recent predictions as seriously as they might have. Pacific herring, which ranks second only to salmon in value to the commercial fisheries of the coast, was almost fished into extinction in the late 1960s. Fortunately, populations rebounded in the early 1970s. The herring is not simply important as a commercial product, but is invaluable as a food for various fish (including the chinook salmon), mammals, and birds. In other words, the disappearance of a species like herring has profound implications for the marine ecosystem at large. More recently, a new herring roe fishery was begun, 'to meet the demand for a delicacy produced almost exclusively for the Japanese market. By 1995, the roe herring fishery was supporting 150 seine boats and more than 1,000 gillnet boats that land between 30,000 and 45,000 tons, worth up to $80 million annually.'[87]

Perhaps one of the more contentious issues in the west coast fishery is the fishing practices of American fishers in Alaska, Washington, and Oregon. As early as 1995, the seeds were sown for a lengthy dispute between American and Canadian fishers. In the summer of 1995, Fisheries Minister Brian Tobin blamed Alaskan overfishing for endangering BC's chinook salmon stocks. The dispute centred on Alaska's insistence on a chinook allocation of 230,000 to its troll fleet, most of which spawned in rivers in BC, Washington, and Oregon. In the absence of an agreement under the Pacific Salmon Treaty, Canadian scientists—with the support of BC's commercial, recreational, and Aboriginal fishing communities—called for the Alaskan fishery to keep its chinook catch below 138,000 fish.[88] The agreement that was reached later resulted in increased opportunities for British Columbia's northern commercial trollers, but what was unforeseen was the impact of the province's sports fleet on the stocks.

There has been much finger pointing as to who and what are to blame for the crisis confronting the Pacific Northwest fishery. According to some fisheries experts, many distinct fish populations are already as 'commercially extinct' as the cod and many fish populations have been extirpated from much of their former range.[89] Unlike the situation on the east coast, the declines have not been as noticeable because of the diversity of the fishery. Like the collapse of the surf smelt fishery in the waters around the mouth of the Fraser River in the early

1970s, declines tend to be comparatively piecemeal and inch by inch so that hardly anyone notices.⁹⁰ As was the case with the east coast fisheries, one of the villains in the plight of the Pacific fishery has been increased mechanization:

> The worldwide trend towards the rapid emergence of highly mobile big-boat fleets and the increased concentration of catching power and wealth among fewer and fewer companies and fewer and fewer boats has played out on Canada's West Coast, at the expense of abundance, sustainability, small-scale fisheries and community stability.⁹¹

Another issue in the Pacific fishery relates to the different fishing practices and traditions. Small-scale fisheries tend to be inshore operations that require a wide variety of special skills and cultural knowledge. They usually depend on specific, localized fish populations and an intimate familiarity with specific fishing grounds. Large-scale fisheries, on the other hand, are almost exclusively offshore fisheries that rely heavily 'on massive capital investment, large-scale industrial technologies rather than cultural knowledge, and generalist, semiskilled wage labour in place of localized and inherited knowledge and custom.'⁹² Observers of these two different types of fisheries claim that small-scale fisheries are far more likely to be sustainable because they tend to be rooted in long-standing, sometimes ancient traditions. Large-scale fisheries simply do not have the same stake in sustaining fish populations.

Current Issues in the Pacific Northwest Fishery

In June 1999, Canada and the United States signed a new salmon treaty, which has been described as a conservation-based agreement. Canada came to the negotiating table with two main objectives—to increase Canada's take of Fraser River sockeye and to reduce Alaskan interceptions of endangered Canadian coho.⁹³ This treaty was the culmination of a long dispute with American fishers and a series of bans and regulations imposed by the federal government. Earlier in the summer of 1999, the federal government banned the fishing of coho salmon in northern British Columbia because it needed time to intermingle with healthier stocks. What enraged Canadian fishers, however, was that US fishers were under no restrictions. By June 1999, the Alaska Department of Fish and Game estimated that 800,000 coho salmon had been caught. This catch was considered an extraordinary fishing season.⁹⁴ Of this total, according to DFO estimates, 200,000 were Canadian coho and 6,000 of these were of the weakened coho stock.

The new ten-year salmon agreement signed on 3 June 1999 ended a six-year dispute and many failed efforts to reach an accord. The agreement was endorsed by the Fisheries Minister, David Anderson, the governors of Alaska, Washington, and Oregon and representatives of twenty-four US Indian tribes. The agreement calls for the Americans to contribute US $140 million to a fund that will be jointly managed by Canada and the United States for the purposes of rebuilding salmon spawning grounds. The agreement also establishes mechanisms for co-operative scientific research.[95] But it has not been without its detractors. The Government of British Columbia, which was excluded from the 1999 negotiations, criticized the accord for failing to protect endangered BC coho and 'for giving the Alaskans more than their fair share.'[96] Former provincial Premier Glen Clark claimed the 'Anderson Deal' would 'eventually turn British Columbia into a hatchery for American fishermen.'[97] According to Bud Graham (a former federal director of fisheries management in DFO and BC's assistant deputy minister), Canada obtained only insignificant concessions from Alaska to reduce coho interceptions, while the Fraser River treaty slightly increased America's share.[98] There have also been difficulties in regulating salmon fishing, particularly by Native peoples. In July of 1999, thirty people—mostly members of the Cheam band—were charged with defying a ban on sockeye fishing on the Fraser River.[99]

The Fisheries Resource: Summary

It is evident that both of Canada's coastal fisheries face serious problems that have been complicated by uncertain scientific information and transboundary problems. In these two specific areas, Canadian action alone cannot lead to a regeneration of threatened species. However, when one examines the ways in which Canadian fisheries resources have been viewed by various observers and participants, it is evident that each perspective described at the beginning of this chapter has not only provided a way of understanding the problems but also has helped in the search for solutions. Since the partial collapse of both the east-coast and west-coast fisheries, the perspective that is usually invoked is the effective management of the commons because scarcity is seen as the dominant issue. As Canada's fish resources face limits, fishers have been thrown into socially detrimental competition with each other for shares in the available catch. This has been particularly evident in the sometimes violent confrontations between Native and non-Native fishers and between Canadian and foreign fishers. All too often, the results of these conflicts have been excessive fishing effort, and loss of income.

A second uncertainty lies in the market returns for fish catches which render those who work in the fishery highly vulnerable. Fishers and fish processors who specialize in only one or two species of fish severely limit their options when those species become scarce. Over the years, specialization has been both encouraged and heavily subsidized by a plethora of federal and provincial measures. Increasingly, this has led to significant debt both for fishers and the government. Often, specialization involves new technologies which require more investment by the fishers. This situation 'amplifies the operational vulnerability of fish catching and fish processing enterprises to reduced resource supply and depressed market conditions.'[100]

Turning to the common-property perspective, the overcapitalization and eventual overexploitation that results when individuals compete to harvest as much of a common-property resource as quickly as possible in order to avoid losing the resource to competitors only compound the fisheries' problems. In this sense 'the common use or ownership' of the resource is problematic. Through set allocations to individual enterprises, a degree of private property ownership is introduced. The benefits of this strategy, it is argued, are to reduce the need to maximize short-term harvests and to overcapitalize, both of which result when each producer strives to increase his or her share of the total. Ideally, this limitation on investment reduces the tendency to overexploit the resource and may even produce greater interest in its long-term conservation.[101] In theoretical terms, enterprise allocations are seen by advocates as a means of avoiding the 'tragedy of the commons' often thought to be inherent in common-property resources.[102]

Mineral Resources

> Government and mining industry assertions aside, Canada's system of environmental laws affecting mining have failed to strike a fair balance between the interests of the mining industry and the interests of the public. Significant reforms to strengthen the existing regime at the federal and provincial levels are required to protect the environmental and economic interests of Canadians. Governments must move Canada toward a sustainable approach in the extraction and use of metals and other materials.[103]

On 30 January 2000, a cyanide spill from a containment dam at a gold mine in Romania contaminated several rivers in nearby Hungary and Yugoslavia and killed tons of fish and other life forms in these ecosystems. This incident served as a stark reminder of some of the environmental hazards of mining operations. Closer to home, an impasse between Inco and the Government of Newfoundland has developed over the province's demands that an environmental assessment under Canada's Environmental Assessment Act be conducted in Newfoundland and not Ottawa. At issue are the lands in the vicinity of the Voisey's Bay mining site. Inco has argued that the requirements are too onerous and has threatened to abandon this mining project altogether. Large mining companies such as Inco also have extensive mining rights outside of Canada in countries where regulations are not as stringent. When they threaten to suspend their Canadian operations and go elsewhere, there is always a risk that Canadian towns, communities, and miners will be the victims of this power play between mining companies and government.

The mineral industry has always been an important sector in the Canadian economy. Not only does it represent about 4.4 per cent of Canada's GDP, but it also employs an estimated 300,000 persons in jobs ranging from mining to metal fabrication.[104] Historically, it is a resource sector marked by highs and lows, and in 1994, for the first time since 1989, more mines opened (twelve) than closed (nine).[105] Part of the problem facing Canada's mineral sector, mining experts claim, is that the regulatory regime is unattractive for investors. Since the Supreme Court of Canada ruled against Alberta's case that federal intrusion into provincial jurisdiction over resource management was unconstitutional, most large projects must now undergo environmental assessments at both levels of government. This has served to increase the time reached for project approvals.[106]

For many years, staples such as minerals have been viewed as non-renewable because they are finite and, once exhausted, will be gone. However, Paul Harrison tells us that mineral reserves defy all the laws of arithmetic. 'Take the curious case of copper. In 1950 copper reserves amounted to 100 million tonnes. Over the following thirty years, 156 million tonnes were consumed. And at the end of that period reserves stood at 494 million tonnes—five times the 1950 level.'[107] Because exploration has the effect of expanding reserves, it is difficult to estimate the extent of reserves and to predict accurately when they will be exhausted. For example, in 1950, the experts said that oil reserves would be exhausted in eighteen years.[108] Another indication that minerals are not in scarce supply is the decline in commodity prices between 1948 and 1989. It has been estimated that in that period commodity prices fell by almost 45 per cent in relation to manufactured goods.[109] Other materials 'that had been the mainstay of economic growth earlier this century were also used more efficiently or sparingly. In 1988, for example, developed countries were using 39 per cent less steel per dollar of GDP than in 1961. In the USA the amount of steel and cement used per person began to fall from about 1970 onwards.'[110]

But mineral exploration and the discovery of new mineral reserves should not lead to complacency:

> At some point, probably towards the end of the next century, scarcity of minerals could limit either our population, or our economic growth, or both. We could face a conventional resource crisis. If past history is any guide, the crisis need not be followed by collapse, as the Limits-to-Growth scenarios suggest. More likely it would lead—like the agricultural and industrial revolutions—to adaptations, substitutions, in some cases reductions in consumption.[111]

Although the economic importance of the mining industry to Canada's economy is undeniable, the environmental issues associated with the domestic mining industry are considerable. In particular, the process of environmental assessment, the issuance of permits, the environmental regulatory process, land access, land claims, and Aboriginal self-government are all difficult problems.[112] For the most part, mining operations fall into one of four categories—exploration; mining and milling; smelting and refining; and mine closings. Each phase of mining carries with it the potential for environmental impact.

As with other resources in Canada, jurisdiction over mining is shared between the federal government and the ten provinces and three territories, although the provinces have primary jurisdiction. Federal involvement in mining within provincial boundaries most commonly occurs where approvals under federal legislation related to the protection of fish habitat or navigable waterways are required for a proposed project.[113] The federal government also has responsibility for resources on federal lands within provinces and in the Yukon and Northwest

Territories. Resources in Nunavut are controlled with resource-management agreements under the Nunavut Agreement.[114] Provinces have full jurisdiction over mineral exploration, development, conservation, and management, which means that they have legal power to control most aspects of mining: environmental monitoring, remediation, and monitoring of closed mines.[115] Although the Constitution is quite clear about these responsibilities, there have been claims, from time to time, about federal interference over some aspects of mining exploration and operations. As was discussed in the previous chapter, the provinces and the federal government did work together on a harmonization framework which was ratified in January 1998. Critics of this framework, as it pertains to mining regulation, have argued that its greatest impact will be on environmental assessment.[116]

The enforcement of regulations related to mining practices in Canada is under a great deal of pressure to change owing to a complex set of factors, including globalization of the economy, deregulation, federal-provincial relations, and the influence of the mining industry on regulators.[117] As far as globalization is concerned, the mining industry has been described as 'aggressive in its threats to move investments away from jurisdictions imposing stringent regulatory standards.'[118] In the early 1990s, the mining industry launched a public relations campaign called 'Keep Mining in Canada'. As part of this campaign, it lobbied for increased subsidies and tax write-offs, among other concessions. In response, the federal Department of Natural Resources and House of Commons Standing Committee on Natural Resources issued a report in 1994 that recommended changes to the tax system to encourage mineral exploration and development.[119] Despite a number of environmental disasters caused by mines both here and elsewhere, Canadian governments have been persuaded that the industry needs regulatory relief and federal subsidies. As was discussed in the previous chapter, the pro-business ideology that has been embraced in Canada appears to have won out over the voices of Aboriginal peoples, ENGOs, and many Canadian citizens.

Aboriginal peoples have been particularly affected by mineral operations, because many of their communities are located in remote, mineral-rich areas. Although there have been improvements in their right to participate in mining decisions and their ownership rights to minerals in some parts of Canada, they continue to be victims of disrupted ecosystems from mining operations. They continue to be pitted against a formidable and strong interest—the mining industry—and have had mixed results even though their own bargaining power has improved in recent years. Another adversary of the Canadian mining industry are ENGOs, which have long had an interest in mining issues.

Because of the power of the mining industry, combined with its importance to the Canadian economy, both the federal government and the provinces have embarked on a number of measures that have weakened environmental protection. Instead of imposing more stringent regulations, governments at both levels and industry associations have relied on voluntary measures. Though a number of these measures have had some success, they are no replacement for regulation because they cannot be enforced.

The Whitehorse Mining Initiative

In 1993, in response to concern expressed by many stakeholder groups, industry and labour leaders, deputy ministers of mines, members of Aboriginal communities, and environmentalists met in Toronto to discuss the ways in which the mining industry could be both competitive and sustainable. This collaboration was given the name 'Whitehorse Mining Initiative' because it was first suggested at a conference of Canadian mines ministers held in Whitehorse in 1992.[120] This kind of collaboration recognized that there were many stakeholders in the mining policy community, and it offered the prospect that the environmental problems of mining could be solved. In the ensuing years, however, the optimism surrounding the so-called Whitehorse Initiative began to fade. In order to counteract the strength of the mining lobby, a new organization named MiningWatch Canada (MWC) was formed in April 1999 (see Chapter Two). Although a number of established green groups had long had an interest in the poor environmental records of Canadian mining companies, both here and abroad, it was believed necessary to establish one organization that would oversee this industry and collaborate with similar mining watchdog groups in the United States and Latin America. One of the most important goals of this new organization was to develop a strong working relationship with Aboriginal organizations and First Nations.[121] In June 1999, the Innu Nation and MWC co-hosted a workshop on the impact of mining on First Nations; over seventy-five Aboriginal leaders as well as technical workers from over thirty communities were in attendance. Four provinces and the three territories also sent representatives.[122] Abandoned mines were a major issue, given that there are as many as fifteen abandoned mines on traditional Aboriginal lands.[123]

Current Issues in Mining

Generally speaking, mining in Canada may be subject to two types of approvals —a general assessment approval, and license or permit requirements under mining and environmental protection legislation. In addition, environmental assessments and specific permits may be required by both the federal and provincial governments, depending on the circumstances and nature of the proposed mining operation.[124] This does not necessarily mean, however, that a new mining operation undergoes an environmental assessment before it begins operations. In fact, the timing of the environmental assessment is controversial.

Another contested issue in the mining industry relates to overlap between the Canadian Environmental Assessment Act (CEAA) and provincial environmental assessment processes. The CEAA applies to projects for which the federal government has decision-making authority, whether as a proponent, land manager, source of funding, or regulator. An environmental assessment is required when a mine's operation will alter fish habitat or deposit deleterious substances into waters or if a bridge needs to be built over a navigable waterway to provide access to a mine site. Permits under these two relevant federal statutes (Fisheries Act and Navigable Waters Protection Act) cannot be issued until an environmental assessment under the CEAA has been completed.

At the provincial level, all provinces have either an environmental assessment act or another form of regulation requiring environmental assessments for certain projects, although assessments vary greatly.[125] This overlap was one of the reasons for the Canada-Wide Accord on Environmental Harmonization adopted in January 1998. Sub-agreements on environmental assessment were to be implemented through a series of bilateral agreements between the federal government and each province. By the end of 1999, these agreements were in force between the federal government and all of the western provinces.

Mining-industry analysts point to a strong worldwide downturn in mining exploration and have argued that rigid land-use policies and the antipathy of provincial governments toward mining have only aggravated the problems of the industry here in Canada. The difficulty for policy makers is that mining interests are often located in areas where there are a host of other users, including First Nations, recreationalists, environmental interests, and other industries.[126] For that reason, mining is subject to a variety of statutes and regulations. In British Columbia, for example, mines are required to post reclamation bonds under the Mines Act. They are also subject to other statutes, including the Contaminated Sites Regimes of the Waste Management Act. At the end of 1999, however, the Ministry of Energy and Mines, backed by the mining industry and the British Columbia Business Council, presented a proposal to exempt mines from these provisions and from retroactive liability under the pollution-abatement and pollution-prevention-order provisions of the Waste Management Act. The current measures, they argue, are unfair to industry and investors.[127] Critics of this proposal argue that if mines are excused from retroactive liability, other resource industries may ask for the same treatment. Ultimately, the taxpayers would be left holding the responsibility for any damages that might be caused by a mine.

Mine abandonment is a major environmental problem. Despite the fact that most provinces and territories require closure plans and financial assurances from mining operations as conditions for the issuance of a permit, it has been estimated that there are more than 10,000 abandoned mines in Canada, and at least 6,000 abandoned tailings sites. In Ontario alone, there are thought to be approximately 6,000 abandoned mines, for which the clean-up costs are estimated at between $300 million and $3 billion.[128] It has estimated that less than 20 per cent of the lands disturbed by abandoned metal mines have ever been reclaimed. Mining companies claim that reclamation and rehabilitation rates have been low because the costs of doing so are excessive. The Mining Association of Canada has placed the cost of remediating abandoned mine sites in all of Canada at $6 billion, a cost which is likely to have to be paid by Canadian taxpayers.[129] The seriousness of this problem is illustrated by the collapse of a tailings dam at the Matachewan Mine in Northern Ontario in 1990, which contaminated the water supply of three communities with lead and other toxic substances. The provincial government spent about $2 million on clean-up. The mine had ceased operations in the 1950s.[130] Therefore, the problem is not simply the abandonment of mines; rather many of these 'orphan mines' that have reverted to Crown ownership are hazardous. The legal ramifications of this situation are immense. In Ontario, companies that voluntarily surrender their mines to the Crown after reclamation activities are 'complete' are exempt from any future liabilities, even if the company is at fault.[131]

A second critical issue—often related to the issue of abandonment—is water pollution. Water used in mining operations may be extremely acidic or alkaline and 'may contain suspended solids, residual mine-mill chemicals, heavy metals, ammonia, and in the case of uranium mines, radioactive substances. . . . Cyanide collection reservoirs and contaminated tailings left behind by heap-leaching, a new technology for extracting gold from very low-grade ores using cyanide solutions, pose major threats to wildlife and groundwater.'[132] Moreover, tailings dam failures can result in the contamination of water supplies with heavy metals and other toxic substances, destroy fish and wildlife populations and their habitat, and threaten downstream communities with flooding.[133]

There has been a long history linking mining with air pollution. In his historical analysis of transboundary smelter smoke in North America, John Wirth chronicles the case of Cominco's smelter in Trail, BC. Beginning in 1925, the Consolidated Mining and Smelter Company accepted responsibility for environmental damage to the properties of landowners and farmers in Stevens County, Washington. Eventually, this dispute reached the highest levels of the Canadian and US governments. The case was not resolved until 1941, but the Trail settlement has been 'celebrated as the first international ruling on transboundary pollution and for its affirmation of the "polluter pays" principle in international law.'[134] Wirth concludes that, despite this early success, bi-national co-operation and action on air pollution caused by mining has been slow. Indeed, he concludes: 'It is high time to recognize a shared responsibility for airborne pollution in the region as a whole, because acting alone, no one nation of North America will be able to protect adequately its domestic environment or its citizens from pollutants transported along continental pathways.'[135]

Another critical problem related to mining concerns the environmental records of Canadian mining companies working in other countries. By late 1996, over forty Canadian companies had interests in sixty-five mineral properties in seven countries of the former Soviet Union. Canadian mineral investment in Central Asia has escalated as state-owned mining properties are offered for sale under pressure from the International Monetary Fund. Canadian companies involved in the region include World Wide Minerals, Placer Dome, and Tech. As was noted in the earlier discussion of MiningWatch, a number of Canadian companies have been less than exemplary environmental citizens.

Conclusions

As demonstrated in the previous discussion, the mining policy community in Canada has been characterized by a powerful industrial lobby, (until recently) a fragmented environmental lobby with particular interests, and a relatively powerless Aboriginal community. As a resource Canadian mining reserves appear to be relatively stable. However, the issues facing the various stakeholders in the mining policy community are complex and have many implications for the environment, both here and abroad. Government involvement in enforcing domestic environmental regulations has been largely counteracted by industrial 'blackmail' (that is, the threat to move elsewhere) and the industry's poor environmental record of remediation. Moreover, poor environmental records further afield by Canadian companies have not been as carefully scrutinized by Canadian officials as they should have been. Although the Whitehorse Mining Initiative and its multipartite approach to environmental planning appeared hopeful at the time, this early promise has largely been lost as we enter the twenty-first century.

The Agricultural Resource

Although only about 7 per cent of our land is capable of significant food production, most Canadians take our reasonably inexpensive and safe food for granted and give little thought to the environmental implications of the production system. Farming, however, has become far more complex than the simple production of food. Today, it is a most important landscape designer and determiner of environmental quality, facts that are important to all Canadians.[136] Given that the supply of food has rarely been an issue, Canada's policy makers have concentrated on other aspects of the country's agriculture. For example, a good deal of Canada's agricultural policy has been aimed at saving the family farm. Governments have created a maze of programs and subsidies designed to preserve this system—with mixed results. Although ownership and the continued viability of the family farm continue to be important social and economic issues within the agricultural sector, others have emerged that have important ethical, health, and environmental implications. Although there are many issues that could be discussed here, including Canada's efforts to alleviate malnutrition in the Third World and nutrition here in Canada and elsewhere,[137] I will concentrate on five 'domestic' topics that have particular relevance for the philosophical and agricultural objectives of sustainability and sound management. First, fertilizers, insecticides, and herbicides remain vital tools used extensively by farmers and agri-businesses to ensure an adequate supply of crops for both humans and animals. Governments continue to support research and development into new products that offer promise in sustaining or increasing crop yields. Second, as an alternative to crop protection, biological controls have been tried, albeit with only limited success. Third, many farmers and agricultural businesses have embraced biotechnology, such as genetically modified organisms. As it relates to research and development in the chemical and fertilizer industry, governments have provided seed money and committed research funds to exploring new technologies that offer the promise of increased resistance and improved hardiness of crops. Fourth, and less well known, has been the rise in organic farming. Because this kind of farming produces smaller crop yields and less aesthetically pleasing crops, agri-business and governments have been disinclined to embrace its virtues. It has generally been consumers themselves and some farmers who have been responsible for the emergence of organic farming. And lastly, the environmental implications of large-scale industrial farms will be examined.

Insecticides and the Environment

The real revolution in agriculture began in the 1940s with the widespread adoption of DDT (dichlorodiphenyltrichloroethane), the first important synthetic insecticide. As chronicled by Rachel Carson in her insightful book *Silent Spring*, the use of DDT eradicated many beneficial insects along with destructive pests. Over time, the wholesale application of this chemical led to resistance which ultimately contributed to the now well-known phenomenon of food-chain magnification.[138] This occurred when DDT accumulated in scavengers and predators at the top of the food chain to the point where their reproduction, and thus their survival, was threatened. Ospreys, eagles, and falcons were among the many wildlife species that suffered. Since the 1970s DDT and related compounds have been banned or severely restricted in North America, but they are still used in other countries from which Canada imports produce.

Over and above the DDT issue, other environmental consequences of chemical use have emerged. Because arable land is often cultivated close to the edge of streams and rivers, fertilizer runoff from fields and wastes from feedlots may escape to cause damage downstream. Pesticide use and misuse and accidents all combine to affect lands and waters, to the detriment of organisms living on and in them. Usually the alarm about pesticides comes only after obvious disasters such as fish kills. However, it is the water in rock and soil beneath our feet that is of particular interest; this groundwater moves slowly, and contamination may not be suspected because the effects are not readily seen.[139] It has been documented that waters may become over-enriched and eutrophic. The eventual buildup of nitrogen (particularly in the form of nitrates) in groundwater, and the relationship of such increases to agriculture, is also a contentious issue, since high levels of nitrates have been shown to be harmful to human health. Recent surveys of farm wells in Ontario found that 13 per cent had nitrate levels exceeding Canadian guidelines for maximum acceptable levels.[140]

Although most environmentalists would advocate a moratorium on the use of chemicals and fertilizers and the adoption of alternative treatments, these chemicals will continue to be used for the foreseeable future. Their continued use dictates caution—using the minimum amounts, taking great care to avoid spills and accidents, and targeting pests much more accurately in terms of their life cycles.[141]

Many provinces have embarked on programs to reduce the use of pesticides. Ontario's Food Systems 2002 program, for example, has as its objective a 50 per cent reduction in pesticide use by 2002. According to agricultural scientists, from 1983 to 1993 pesticide use in Ontario declined 28.5 per cent, as measured by weight of active ingredient. Over the same period, there was a 10 per cent reduction in total area of land farmed and a 16 per cent increase in tonnes produced per hectare.[142] In other words, the reduction in pesticide use did not adversely affect productivity.

Crop scientists point to a number of reasons why pesticide use has lessened. In part, new kinds of pesticide sprayers and improved sprayer calibration have enabled farmers to use much lower doses.[143] Other changes in farming practices—such as crop rotation—have reduced the need for pesticides. However, perhaps the most significant reason is the adoption of innovative biological controls, including integrated pest management (IPM).

Biological Controls

Although chemicals continue to be the crop protection of choice for many farmers, other less invasive methods are available. Great advances have been made in integrated pest management (IPM), which combines biological and cultivation techniques with a minimum of chemical treatment to control a problem. IPM has been quite successful with crops as diverse as cotton and apples.[144]

> These technologies have been also referred to as biological controls and have contributed to the attack of pests by predators, parasites, or disease vectors. Although spectacular gains have been observed in some cases, this is true only in a fraction of cases. Sometimes, it may be impossible to find the appropriate agent. On other occasions, the process is so labour-intensive that the control may be so slow in developing that a crop may be lost. Still, research into biological methods is a very active field, and every success story represents a lessening of chemical dependency.[145]

A successful biological control program requires considerable expertise and involves time-consuming and expensive research. The behaviour of a 'control' species as well as the species to be controlled must be understood. How does one species interact with another and with the dynamics of the ecosystem? And how will control methods affect the target species and the entire ecosystem? An example of biological control concerns the problem of flies in large swine operations, where they are a nuisance both to workers and to animals. Depending on the species of fly, they may also spread disease and cause the animals to lose weight.[146]

To address this fly problem, a tiny (pteromalid) wasp was recommended as a biological control. Pteromalid wasps that are reared for the express purpose of controlling flies attack the pupal stage (an inactive immature stage) of the fly but do not sting animals or humans. A female wasp lays an egg in a fly pupa, the egg hatches, and the wasp larva feeds on the developing fly, thereby killing it. One female wasp, which lives for about a week, is capable of laying eggs in fourteen pupae a day. Because the development of a wasp from egg to adult takes about three weeks, whereas a fly can develop in about two weeks, wasps would have to be released at least once every two weeks to keep pace with the flies.[147] Although this experiment was not successful (it proved to be too expensive and the wasp population could not perpetuate itself), it does illustrate an example of a biological control.

Biotechnology, Genetic Engineering, and Genetic Modification
There are thousands upon thousands of acres of genetically modified crops growing in Canada. It has been estimated that more than half the canola, about a quarter of the corn, and some 20 per cent of the potatoes grown each year are now grown from genetically modified seeds. Other crops, including squash, tomatoes, and soybeans—to name just a few—have also been extensively modified. Many farmers and their associations sing the praises of genetically modified organisms (GMOs). Not only are they economical for farmers to use, the claim is made that less chemical is needed in farming them. To their supporters, GMOs are a winner both for farmers and the environment. On a broader scale, some scientists are convinced that GM food will be the key to survival in the twenty-first century as land becomes scarce and the population increases. Since 1994, these crops and packaged foods made from them have been finding their way on to the shelves of Canadian grocery stores. Ottawa has approved some forty-two different genetically modified foods as safe.[148]

Before such a food can be approved for general release, the Canadian Food Inspection Agency (CFIA) assesses it for its environmental effects, and Health Canada's Health Protection Branch evaluates it for its effects on human health. Critics of GMOs argue that these government agencies rely on studies produced by biotechnology companies. Spokepeople at the CFIA dispute this claim: 'There's a lot more that goes into a decision than just a company's information.'[149] The use of these foods is so widespread that many Canadians do not realize the extent to which they have become parts of their diets: 'Whether you like it or not, GMOs were probably in your breakfast cereal, in the cookies you ate with your lunch, in the dressing you poured on your salad for dinner and in the potato chips you munched on last night while watching TV.'[150]

Genetic modification or engineering has been a highly controversial technology because of ethical as well as health and environmental considerations. In the genetic engineering of food, genes from one organism or species are added to the blueprint of another. It has been discovered, for example, that a fish gene added to a strawberry plant makes it more resistant to the cold.[151] Genetic modification has also been used to eradicate certain pests and weeds and is making contributions to pest resistance in plants. These transgenic plants literally have a built-in advantage when attacked by pests. Biotechnology is also heralded as a new way in which to produce greater short-term yields of domestic plant strains.

Innovations in biotechnology are supported by some scientists, governments, farmers, consumers, and gigantic life sciences companies with money to invest in research.[152] Although many scientists and government officials alike espouse the benefits of biotechnology, others have issued warnings. One crop scientist observed, 'We're moving genes around that we don't have any idea what they are going to do.'[153] Others have warned that the insertion of antibiotic-resistant bacteria into genetically modified seeds may have adverse effects on the use of antibiotics in humans:

> You have an infection, your doctor prescribes an antibiotic for you and the food that you are eating. Because it has an antibiotic resistant bacteria in it as a marker, it would neutralize the antibiotic, so the bacteria would just run through your system and the antibiotic would be completely ineffective. That is a theoretical possibility.[154]

Other critics claim that pesticide-resistant vegetables inadvertently kill some insects such as Monarch butterflies.[155] Another unintended consequence of genetic modification, opponents argue, is that pollen from fields of GMOs altered to resist herbicides could blow onto a field of weeds. That could make the weeds resistant to herbicides. The same thing could happen to insects that feed on certain crops.[156] In a twist of irony, a consequence of new biotechnologies, detractors allege, is that our food plants are becoming dramatically *more* susceptible to insects and diseases.[157]

Although many people enjoy fat yellow corn and round red tomatoes, not all consumers are enthusiastic about GMOs. In fact, a number of Canadian groups have lobbied (unsuccessfully so far) for the labelling of genetically modified foods. Despite mandatory labelling in Europe and parts of Asia, Health Canada demands labelling only when the nutritional quality of a food is changed or an allergen is introduced.[158] Pressure from European consumers has led some Canadian and US food industries to begin working on a labelling program; however, in the absence of long-term studies or reported health problems caused by genetically altered food, Health Canada does not appear likely to change its policy. In both Canada and the United States, governments have embraced biotechnology as an important new tool in the hands of their agricultural industries.

There is mounting evidence, however, that the North American love affair with biotechnology may be over. A number of groups have mobilized, including the Campaign for Food Safety (formerly the Pure Food Campaign) which is affiliated with the Organic Consumers Association, Greenpeace, the Council of Canadians, and the Canadian Health Coalition, urging governments to require the labelling of genetically modified food. An organization 'dedicated to building a healthy, safe, and sustainable system of food production and consumption', the Campaign for Food Safety describes itself as a 'global clearinghouse for information and grassroots technical assistance'.[159] Its campaign strategy consists of a variety of tactics including 'public education, targeted boycotts, grassroots lobbying, . . . and public relations, activist networking, and direct action protests and media events.'[160]

Although a growing number of groups are questioning the merits of biotechnology, for the most part North American governments appear to have climbed on the biotechnology bandwagon with little or no debate. Elsewhere, however, many governments are refusing to approve the sale of genetically modified foods while others have approved them only if they have been labelled as such.[161] In Great Britain, the campaign was led by the late Linda McCartney and since her death has been championed by others, including Prince Charles. A number of analysts have concluded that the debate about GM foods in Britain has been heavily influenced by BSE (mad cow disease—see Box 4.1), dioxin scandals in Belgium, and recent reports that sewage had been used in animal feed in France.[162] In order to reassure a nervous citizenry, the British government enacted a European Union law requiring the labelling of all GM foods. By 1999, the government went even further and required that all pubs, cafés, and restaurants list GM ingredients on their menus.[163]

Box 4.1 Bovine Spongiform Encephalopathy (BSE) (commonly known as Mad Cow Disease)

Mad cow disease is formally known as 'bovine spongiform encephalopathy', or BSE. BSE is the cow version of a larger class of diseases called 'transmissable spongiform encephalopathies', or TSEs, which can afflict sheep, deer, elk, cows, mink, cats, squirrels, monkeys, humans, and other species. In all species the symptoms of TSEs are the same—progressive destruction of brain cells leading to dementia and death. Mad cow disease appeared in British dairy cattle for the first time in 1985, and the British authorities spent the next ten years assuring the public that there was no danger from eating the meat of infected cows. They said a 'species barrier' prevented mad cows from infecting humans. A 'species barrier' does prevent many diseases from crossing from one species to another—for example, measles and canine distemper are closely related diseases, but dogs do not get measles and people do not get distemper.

In cows, the latency (or incubation) period for mad cow disease is thought to be about five years, meaning that cows have the disease for five years before the symptoms begin to appear. The epidemic of mad cow disease was caused by an agricultural innovation—feeding dead cows to live cows. Cows are, by nature, vegetarians, but modern agricultural techniques changed that. Cows that died mysteriously were sent to rendering plants, where they were boiled down and ground up into the consistency of brown sugar, and eventually added to cattle feed. It was later determined that mad cow disease was being transmitted through such feed, and especially through specific tissues—brain, spinal chord, eyes, spleen (known collectively as offal), and perhaps other nerve tissues.

After the mad cow scandal erupted, the British government attempted to eradicate the disease by requiring that all cows older than thirty months be slaughtered. By 1990, twenty-three non-European Union countries, including Canada, had banned imports of British beef. By September 1999, more than 2.5 million British cows had been destroyed. Despite these radical measures, an estimated 1,600 new cases of mad cow disease are still being reported each year in England.

While the British government was assuring people about the species barrier, British citizens began to die of a new disease, called 'new variant Creutzfeld-Jakob disease' or nvCJD. A similar disease, CJD (Creutzfeld-Jakob disease) has been recognized for a long time but it almost never occurs in people younger than thirty; nvCJD, on the other hand, strikes people as young as thirteen. There are several other important differences between CJD and nvCJD, so nvCJD is indeed something new. As of January 2000, nvCJD has killed forty-eight people in England and one or two others elsewhere in Europe. The main feature of both mad cow disease and nvCJD is the progressive destruction of brain cells, inevitably leading to total disability and death.

After a link was found between mad cow and human CJD, the banning of British beef was accelerated. France and Belgium both banned the importing of beef, and McDonald's stopped serving British beef in its 660 restaurants in the UK. All of the EU banned British beef. By late 1998, the EU decided Britain had taken adequate measures to halt the spread of mad cow disease and the ban was lifted. But more recent developments indicate that mad cow disease has not been halted in its tracks. In November 2000, France discovered its first homegrown case of BSE, and Germany acknowledged that two cows born and raised on German soil were infected. Spain and Portugal have also discovered the disease in their food chains. In all four countries, the beef industry has been devastated as the demand for beef products from countries in the EU has declined dramatically. The European Union has introduced measures to keep mad cow disease from spreading further. In France, for example, every animal older than thirty months that is slaughtered must now have its brain tissue tested.

Should Canada worry about BSE? As of January 2001, there has only been one reported case of a cow infected with BSE in Canada. In that case, the animal was found on a farm near Red Deer, Alberta, in December of 1993 and had been imported from Britain. Immediately, Mexico temporarily banned imports of Canadian beef, and the United States sent observers to see how Canada was dealing with the problem. The Alberta Ministry of Agriculture called for the slaughter of all animals imported from Britain between 1982 and 1990, as well as their offspring. In total, 363 animals were destroyed. During the summer of 1995, the human variant of BSE was discovered after two people (who, incidentally, had donated blood to the Canadian Red Cross) died of Creutzfeldt-Jakob disease. Initially, it was feared that CJD might be spread through the blood supply; however, this has never been proved.

Currently, Canada does not import meat or bone meal from nations where cows have been found to have BSE. Nevertheless, a European Commission report published in 2000 placed Canada in the second rank of risk for mad cow disease (a top rank designates almost no risk). In part, this is because before 1992, meat and bone meal were routinely fed to Canadian cattle. Given the incubation period of BSE, it was concluded that Canadian beef is at some risk. The Canadian Food Inspection Agency has announced that it will appeal this ranking to the European Commission's scientific steering committee.

Sources: Rachel's Environment and Health Weekly, #683—'Mad Cow Disease and Humans', 20 Jan. 2000. CBC News Online, Indepth: 'Mad Cow: The Science and the Story' (accessed 12 Jan. 2001). CBC News Online, 'France Struggles with Mad Cow Crisis', 12 Jan. 2001. CBC News Online, 'Should Canada worry?' 12 Jan. 2001. *Related web site:* www.mad-cow.org

The question in the minds of many, though, is: are GM foods dangerous to human and animal health? The frustrating answer is that no one seems to know. The *New Scientist* reports, 'Standard toxicology tests don't work for food. It is often difficult to feed lab animals enough GM fodder, whether or not they find it palatable, to see if it has undesirable effects compared with unmodified foods.'[164] Because conventional food has not been tested for toxicity, scientists are unsure where to start. Moreover, because genetic engineering can alter a plant's DNA, it is difficult to know when a change is a problem. Debora MacKenzie explains:

> The production of a novel protein is only one of the potentially harmful changes that occur when a foreign gene is inserted into a plant. Because the positioning of the novel gene within the plant's DNA is essentially random, it may alter the plant's expression of its own genes—with unpredictable effects. It is this kind of change

that stymies conventional toxicology. Food is a complex mixture of substances that occur in different quantities in different varieties of crops and in the same variety grown under even slightly different conditions. When is a change in one or several of those substances a problem?[165]

In Canada genetically engineered food (also called novel food) is regulated in the same manner as foods produced by conventional methods. Once it has been evaluated by Health Canada under the Novel Food Guidelines of the Food and Drugs Act, it may or may not be approved for safety before reaching the food production system. Although the issue of labelling continues to be debated, there have been efforts to consolidate the control of food inspection and quarantine services under one agency. In April 1997, the Canadian Food Inspection Agency (CFIA) began operations; it was to provide services formerly provided by Agriculture and Agri-Food Canada, Health Canada, and Fisheries and Oceans Canada.[166] This agency, which reports to the Department of Agriculture and Agri-Food is responsible for 'all inspection services related to food safety, economic fraud, trade-related requirements, and animal and plant health programs.'[167] Biofertilizers, regulations and guidelines for animals derived from biotechnology, livestock feeds, and plants with novel traits all require approval by the CFIA. Some critics of the regulatory regime, including the Canadian Environmental Law Association, argue that the Minister of the Environment might be more objective in this process given that the agriculture department promotes the biotech industry.[168] Others, including some scientists in the Food Directorate of the Health Protection Branch, are opposed to the transfer of authority for inspections. On 30 September 1999, a letter signed by a number of these scientists was sent to the Minister of Health, Allan Rock. Part of this letter reads as follows:

> The CFIA is currently in an unacceptable conflict of interest position. It reports to the Minister of Agriculture and promotes production and trade while concurrently enforcing the food safety legislation in the Food and Drugs Act. This type of conflict of interest has been recognized internationally by consumers, producers and food manufacturers as being a major threat to both food safety and to the economy (e.g. mad-cow disease in Britain). . . . We strongly recommend that Bill C-80 be withdrawn and replaced with legislation returning investigation of food poisoning incidents and enforcement of the Food and Drugs Act from the CFIA to Health Canada. Failure to do so will be disastrous to the health of infants, children and adults, as well as to Canadian food producers and manufacturers.[169]

The Case against GMOs in Canada

In Canada, the Sierra Club, Greenpeace, and the Council of Canadians have taken the lead in publicizing the environmental and medical risks of GMOs. Citing studies by groups such as the British Medical Association suggesting that GM foods *could* have dire consequences for human health, advocacy groups are demanding that more research be conducted.[170] To this end, a group of scientists and academics have joined together to form an organization named GE Alert. Using the web site of the Council of Canadians, this group, in January 2000, released a paper entitled 'Food Safety of GM Crops in Canada' written by Dr E. Ann Clark, a professor at the University of Guelph. Among other findings, this study revealed that the testing of toxicity and allergenicity of genetically engineered crops by Health Canada had not been conducted on 70 per cent of the forty-two GM crops.[171] The explanation by federal officials for the lack of testing is the assumption that humans will be exposed to GM plant toxins only by eating oil. Because toxins are removed in the refining of oil, they claim there is no risk.[172] Clark's study claims that the oil processing leaves a protein-rich byproduct that is commonly fed to livestock and then enters the human food chain. Moreover, GM crops used in animal feed are not subjected to rigorous testing.[173]

GE Alert, the Council of Canadians, and the Council of Concerned Scientists are calling on the federal government to introduce mandatory labelling of GM foods as well as lobbying for those foods to be removed from grocery stores until they are proved safe. This campaign has drawn on the efforts of British grassroots groups, which persuaded major grocery chains such as Sainsbury's and Marks & Spencer to stop carrying GM foods. Other large food companies, including Cadbury, Nestle, and Unilever have reduced their stock of GM products in Europe. In Canada, though, it has mainly been scientists themselves who have given voice to concerns about the safety of GMOs. They claim that governments have taken their 'hands-off' approach largely as a result of an over-reliance on studies provided by multinational companies and the biotechnology industry.[174] They point to recent American studies about the health implications of the cauliflower mosaic virus, a gene used in the genetic modification of corn, potatoes, and soybeans. According to the Sierra Club, this gene is toxic.[175] The anti-GM food campaign has had some success. Heinz Canada has begun removing all genetically modified additives, including corn starch, soy lecithin, and vegetable oil, from its baby food.[176]

Biosafety Protocol

In January 2000, environment ministers from 138 countries spent a week in Montreal trying to agree on trade rules for genetically modified organisms used in crops, research, and pharmaceutical products. This protocol comes under the umbrella of the UN Convention for Biodiversity. The talks revealed the deep division between the world's exporters of genetically modified crops, led by the United States, Canada, and Argentina, and the importers, composed mainly of European countries and developing countries.[177] A deal was finally reached, although several provisions of the draft agreement were not supported by exporting countries. Most contentious was the provision that a country does not need scientific proof that a GMO is dangerous in order to block its import. Based on the 'precautionary principle', its inclusion in the draft accord was not supported by exporting countries such as Canada and the United States, both of which continued to object to labelling on the grounds that it is both cumbersome and costly.[178] Those countries not supporting the PP—dubbed the Miami Group and including Canada, the United States, Argentina, Chile, Uruguay, and Australia—argue that this principle stakes out such a high moral ground that countries not supporting it are seen as irresponsible for adopting the 'better sorry than safe' viewpoint.[179] The European Union and the Like-Minded Group, which represents more than 80 developing countries in Asia, Africa, and South America, continue to support the freedom of nations to bar genetically modified foods. The European Union has refused to import genetically modified crops such as canola because of concerns there may be risks to human health.[180]

Despite the fact that the Montreal meetings were useful in finding points of agreement, there continues to be some question about the relationship of the Biosafety Protocol to other international agreements and organizations, in particular the World Trade Organization. A molecular scientist in Canada believes that the public debate on GM foods has not been a rational one because of the scientific nature of genetics. He states:

> The public debate on GM technology . . . suffers from an apparently deliberate campaign of emotional pleadings based on scientific misinformation, misinterpretation, and simply misunderstanding, peppered with occasional invective and sometimes personal attacks by both proponents and opponents. This may make exciting tabloid copy but does nothing to advance the cause of informed public deliberation. The underlying foundation of this debate, GM technology, is scientific. We must, unfortunately, rely on scientists to provide the fundamentals. I say unfortunately because, in general, the public doesn't like to rely on scientists.[181]

Only time will tell how the debate over genetically modified foods will be resolved. As long as Canada is dependent on the United States as a trading partner and remains a signatory to NAFTA, no major regulations are likely to be made in the areas of genetic engineering unless compelling scientific research about health hazards materializes. The agreement reached at the Biosafety Protocol meetings in Montreal illustrates the dilemma for exporting and importing nation-states: err on the side of caution or trust multinational corporations and the bureaucrats charged with protecting the public interest.

Organic Farming

At the opposite end of the spectrum from biotechnology and GMOs is a return to natural, chemical-free farming. Primarily conducted on a small scale, organic farming has had wavering support from government. However, according to the Canadian Organic Growers (COG), there was a 20 per cent increase in the number of certified organic producers between 1998 and 1999, with Saskatchewan reporting a dramatic increase of 48 per cent.[182] A number of organic farmers across the country have joined forces to share information; they include the Canadian Organic Growers and the Canadian Organic Livestock Association. There are also a number of provincial organizations that have formed alliances promoting the benefits of organic farming. For example, the Ontario Farm Environmental Coalition consists of thirty farm organizations committed to improving nutrient management in Ontario agriculture.[183] These organizations hold conferences across the country and publish newsletters for their members. Some have also created web sites on which they post news releases and other information to members.

Organic farmers avoid mono-cropping and intensive livestock production because these attract pests and diseases.

> Multiple livestock and crop species with sufficient space and good conditions will spread out the workload, reduce pest populations and promote good health. This will reduce the impact in the unlikely event of a problem, realizing that the farmer cannot fall back on pesticides and antibiotics, and thus spread out the risk and the cost of a crop failure or the market failure of any one product.[184]

For those consumers who wish to avoid genetically engineered foods, organic farming and its products offer a different approach to farming. This 'holistic approach' which emphasizes the functional relationship between all aspects of food production, acquisition, and use offers consumers an alternative as well as the potential for sustainable food production. Organic farms are by nature long-term—requiring long-term commitment by government and institutions to succeed. Any future that they have in the agricultural food resource in Canada will require a change in how we think about agriculture.[185]

Industrial Farms

Industrial farming has become much more prevalent in the past ten years as a result of economies of scale that lower production costs and the prices of commodities in the marketplace. One of the central features of industrial agriculture is the cultivation of one crop, a practice called monoculture. The planting of the same crop, year after year, may result in soil depletion, which increases the need for fertilizers. Concentrated livestock operations put large numbers of animals in close proximity to each other, often under unnatural conditions. As a result, animals may become more susceptible to disease, creating a large market for antibiotics, medications, and vaccines. It becomes a vicious and self-perpetuating cycle—huge scale becomes necessary to afford the great expense of developing medicines and pesticides.[186] One of the difficulties with industrial farms is that there appears to be some dispute over which level of government should regulate them. In some provinces, municipalities have adopted guidelines as part of a regulatory framework. Only three provinces—New Brunswick, Quebec, and Saskatchewan—have adopted specific legislation in response to the intensification of the livestock industry and the growing concern that they may cause significant environmental damage. In some cases (Quebec, Manitoba, British Columbia), the lead role has been played by provincial environment ministries. In the remaining provinces, departments or ministries of agriculture have been the main government actor. In part, this rather weak and disjointed response can be explained by the importance of agriculture in the Canadian economy. In Ontario alone, agriculture (the province's second-largest industry) contributes $25 billion to the provincial economy and employs some 640,000 people.[187]

Criticism of waste management on large industrial farms had been made across the country months before the Walkerton contamination problem, but there is little question that the events at Walkerton and the possibility that livestock run-off may have caused the contamination have fuelled the debate. For the purposes of clarity, the terms 'intensive' and 'industrial' have been used by governments and groups across the country to distinguish between large-scale operations and smaller family farms. It has been argued that these intensive livestock facilities are not farms in the traditional sense, but factories, which are often owned by corporations or absentee owners.[188] Recently, a town in southern Alberta rejected the plans of a Taiwanese company to build a $41 million hog factory in the middle of the Palliser Triangle, citing civic and environmental reasons.[189] Had it been approved, fourteen barns housing some 150,000 hogs would have been constructed. Although it is not known whether the decision will be appealed, the company is actively pursuing a development permit for the same project in central Alberta.[190] Controversy also broke out in Brandon, Manitoba, after the Government of Manitoba granted a licence to Maple Leaf Meats for a large hog-processing plant without holding Clean Environment Commission hearings.[191] Several citizens' groups organized a 'citizens' hearing' in an attempt to compensate for the lack of such a process before the licences were granted. Twenty-nine presentations were made at the hearing. Although this meeting had no legal status, a number of important issues were raised regarding the effects of such industrial farms in the United States, where they have existed for some twenty years. Hog-processing plants have been described as 'water-greedy', because they use from 700 to 1025 litres per hog for processing. The Maple Leaf plant in Brandon, which draws water from the Assiniboine River, will require about 4.5 million litres per day per shift.[192] Beyond the water-use issue lies the potential for increased pollution of the Assiniboine River. Several municipalities and First Nations obtain their water for domestic use and crops from this river.

In February 2000 the Canadian Environmental Law Association (CELA) presented a brief on intensive agricultural operations in Ontario to the Ministry of Agriculture, Food, and Rural Affairs and the Ministry of the Environment in response to a Ministry of Agriculture discussion paper. As noted in CELA's report, there has been a growing concern among rural residents that large industrial farming operations were not only causing a decline in property values and marginalizing small-scale farmers, but were also posing major environmental threats. Primarily, they were worried about the leaching of nutrients into water sources. The task force heard from more than 700 people and listened to 140 delegations. It also received 200 written submissions and 420 completed questionnaires.[193]

Statistics cited in the CELA brief indicate that one hog produces two tons of manure a year. In fact Ontario's 4 million hogs produce as much raw sewage as the entire population of the province.[194] The problems caused by this quantity of animal manure range from odour, health implications associated with the odour, and water contamination, to manure spills. Since 1988, operators of intensive farm operations have been shielded from common-law suits for nuisance from noise, odour, and dust if these are caused by 'normal farm practices' as defined in The Protection of Farm Practices Act.[195]

Despite a strong farm lobby and the continued importance of agriculture to the Canadian economy, it appears that resistance is growing among rural dwellers across the country to large-scale industrial farms. Although many of the proprietors of these facilities are not careless in their management of animal wastes, some are. As one scientist put it, 'most outbreaks of food-or-water-borne disease are not acts of God. They follow a series of events and management.'[196]

Conclusions

It was estimated that by 2000, even using low inputs of fertilizers and pesticides, developed countries would be able to feed 60 per cent more than their expected populations from their own lands.[197] At the other end of the scale, there are sixty-four countries with over one billion inhabitants, which will be unable to feed their projected 2000 populations from their own lands if they were using low inputs. Twenty-nine of these are in Africa, and they are home to 60 per cent of the continent's population.[198] Maintaining sustainable agriculture, therefore, is important not only for Canadians but for many others in the developing world. In its final report before being dissolved by the federal government, the Science Council of Canada identified the principles of sustainable agriculture as follows:

- thorough integration of the farming system with natural processes
- reduction of inputs most likely to harm the environment
- greater use of the biological and genetic potential of plant and animal species
- improvement in the match between cropping patterns and land resources to ensure the sustainability of present production levels
- efficient production, with emphasis on improved farm management and conservation of soil, water, energy, and biological resources
- development of food processing, packaging, distribution, and consumption practices consistent with sound environmental management.[199]

Although Canada's agricultural sector will likely continue to encounter challenges in the years ahead that may harm agricultural production, its continued strength as a resource staple in many parts of Canada appears to be secure at the present time. The perspective that appears to be most applicable to our farming resource is its effective and sustainable management. Red flags have been raised about the desirability of industrial farms, and it appears that governments, largely in response to growing complaints from rural residents and family farmers, are seriously reviewing the current standards and regulations. Similarly, government responses to the GM food debate will be more likely as consumers and scientists continue to express their concerns. Although Canada appears to have its hands tied by the American position on GMOs and a strong agricultural lobby, if exports are harmed by market restrictions elsewhere, mandatory labelling may be forthcoming.

The Forestry Resource

More than any other resource—cod included—the great appeal of Canada for British colonists was its forests. In the 1830s, in particular, the Saint John and Miramichi valleys were 'treated like quarries, their rich veins of pine timber floated to tidewater and exported to Britain'.[200] The bulk of this rich pine forest had largely disappeared from New Brunswick by 1870, and the British then moved on the forests of the Ottawa Valley. Here fast-flowing rivers drained 80,000 square miles of virgin timberland, and every spring, the logs were rafted to Quebec as soon as the ice broke up.[201] With the reduction of the Imperial Preferences in the 1840s, the United States slowly began to surpass Britain as the most important market for Canadian wood.[202] Although markets have changed in the ensuing years, many of Canada's other valuable forest reserves have been seriously depleted. Despite a number of attempts to adopt the ideas of conservation and sustainability, the regulation and management of the forestry industry has been beset, from the very beginning, with uncertainty and a certain irrationality:

> It often unfolded in unpredictable ways, as political actors inside and outside of government maneuvered through the mists of uncertainty and the swirling political currents, searching for the most advantageous course. At the centre we find cabinet ministers and their advisors gathering advice about the technical and political merits of different policy options and trying to process this advice into judgements about risks, opportunities, priorities, and imperatives.[203]

Much of the literature on Canada's forest industry has focused on the disputes that have occurred in British Columbia[204] expressly because the policy paths chosen by alternating Social Credit and New Democratic governments have been so different. Nevertheless, other studies have been more national in scope. Larry Pratt and Ian Urquhart, although principally concerned with Alberta's northern forests, talk about the extent of Canada's boreal forest in their compelling book, *The Last Great Forest*.

> In Canada, this forest covers 3.24 million square kilometres—nearly one-third of the nation—and accounts for approximately 80 per cent of the country's forests as it stretches from the Yukon territory in the west to Newfoundland in the east. Despite its vastness, scientists know remarkably little about this ecosystem. The boreal forest remains a great unknown, a wilderness shrouded in mystery and ruled by the ghosts of Native hunters, fur traders, and bush pilots.[205]

The forest resource has been a major focus of governments because much of it is located on Crown lands. In both British Columbia and Alberta, for example, some 95 per cent of the provincial lands are publicly owned. This compares with only 9 per cent in the southern United States, a region that is the source of more than 60 per cent of American pulp production and softwood lumber.[206]

This question of public ownership is at the heart of the current softwood lumber dispute between Canada and the United States. (The Canada-U.S. Softwood Lumber Agreement expired at the end of March 2001.) This dispute has been going on for some twenty years. American forest companies have long alleged that the Canadian softwood lumber industry is subsidized by government. They argue that the price of Canadian softwood is significantly lower than that of American lumber because the government sets the prices. Unlike most US states, Canadian provinces do not use competitive bidding to arrive at a price that forest companies must pay for the wood they cut. Rather, the government (not the market) sets the price through a system called administered pricing, also known as stumpage rates. American forest interests argue that by keeping stumpage rates low, governments in Canada are effectively subsidizing forestry operations. Canadian forestry companies counter this allegation by saying that stumpage rates are higher than they would be under a competitive pricing system.[207] In April 2001, the US Coalition for Fair Lumber Imports, an organization of US lumber companies, began legal proceedings under US trade law. The legal action calls for the imposition of a 39.9 per cent countervailing duty on Canadian softwood and an additional anti-dumping penalty of between 28 and 38 per cent to compensate American lumber mills for Canadian wood exported south below cost. If successful, this case could mean a maximum penalty of 77.9 per cent. Former Ontario Premier, Bob Rae, was retained by the Canadian Free Trade Lumber Council as legal counsel. Many observers on both sides of the border viewed this legal challenge as one of the first tests of Canada's relationship with the United States under President George W. Bush. On 10 August 2001, the US Department of Commerce determined that Canadian softwood lumber exports to the United States were subsidized by 19.31 per cent. As a result, retroactive countervailing measures, in the form of cash deposits or bonds, were applied to shipments made on or after 20 May 2001. Some ten days later, the Canadian government announced that it would challenge these measures at the World Trade Organization and under NAFTA.

The importance of the forest industry to Canada's economy cannot be understated. It 'contributes more to Canada's foreign exchange earnings than agriculture, mining, fishing, oil and gas combined. One dollar in seven, or 15 per cent of all value added in manufacturing, is derived from the forest sector.'[208] It is also important to employment:

> Estimates are that some 300,000 Canadians are employed directly in the forest products industry and, because this industry has relatively strong backward and forward linkages with the rest of the economy, it has been estimated that the sector as a

whole accounts for a million jobs in Canada. In other words, one Canadian in ten depends on the forest.[209]

Whereas forests were once thought of as a resource that would be able to supply our needs in perpetuity, it now appears that one of the most heavily forested countries in the world now faces a wood supply crisis.[210] In part, there is no question that governments saw lumber and wood products as commodities and staples like any others, to be traded on international markets. This policy, which was evident as recently as the late 1970s, saw both the provincial and federal governments putting back into the forest only five cents for every dollar extracted in revenue.[211] 'As forest landlords, governments in Canada have behaved like many other landlords, treating their property as a resource of current revenue. It has always been easy to ignore the future of the forest resource, especially when a bright future necessarily depends on expensive programs of continuous and attentive management.'[212]

Three Eras of Forestry Policy in British Columbia
Pre-Second World War—Clearcutting and Slash Burning
Although there was some early government involvement in the management of the forest industry, after 1912 governments had little, if any, role or control over the actual conduct of logging operations. Companies rarely employed foresters, and logging operations were conducted according to the principles of engineering efficiency. In terms of techniques, research by E.T. Allen on the ecological characteristics of the Douglas fir in 1901 established clearcutting as the proper silviculture (the cultivation of forests for the production of wood) technique to use. Allen's report concluded: 'To secure regeneration of the species on the public lands, foresters should cut everything which can be utilized and clear the ground for a healthy seedling growth.'[213]

Slash burning was also viewed as a technique that was useful in reducing the fire hazard and effective in clearing away the layer of 'duff', exposing the mineral soil that provided fir with its best opportunity for establishment.[214] In their submissions to a 1909 royal commission, it was generally agreed by forestry 'experts' that the greatest threat to the perpetuation of the forests was fire, not logging methods.[215] Although the Forest Act was adopted in British Columbia in 1912 and a professional bureaucracy to oversee cutting in the Crown forests was established, little attention was given to reviewing forestry practices or introducing conservation methods. As had been the case with similar legislation passed in Ontario, New Brunswick, and Nova Scotia, the public ownership of most of British Columbia's resource base did not necessarily imply a more systematic pursuit of conservation.[216]

In concert with the Forest Act, timber sale licences were introduced in 1912 in order to create a competitive market for the harvesting of timber on Crown land. However, by 1940, while nearly 3,000 companies held forestry licences, 58 of them controlled 52 per cent of timber land.[217] Although British Columbia adopted the sustained-yield model of forest management during the 1940s, it was unwilling to control the way logging was done.[218] In 1943, the government of John Hart announced its intention of establishing a royal commission to inquire into the state of the forest industry in British Columbia, for the purposes of 'protecting the lumber industry'. In part, the impetus for the commission, it has been claimed, came from the larger firms, 'which were faced with both competition from Scandinavian and Baltic nations and a diminishing resource base at the coast'.[219]

Post-Second World War—The Sustained-Resource Model
According to Wilson, in the post-war period the exploitation of natural resources was only minimally regulated. Forests were viewed primarily as stockpiles of timber, and policy debates centred on the frontier challenges of how to get at this wealth and translate it into benefits for society.[220] In 1945 British Columbia established its first forest service at the urging of a relatively weak group of scientific managers led initially by H.R. MacMillan. But they were confronted by a determined forest industry committed to limiting the scope of government efforts to conserve the resource, extract rent, and control speculative activity, and fared rather poorly.[221] In the late 1930s, however, and with the help of the Sloan Royal Commission of 1945, discourse began to be changed by the use of measures such as sustained yield, or liquidation conversion. Soon after, it became accepted practice that harvesting practices should be tempered by measures designed to promote conversion to a new, second-growth forest.[222] This era was important because, for the first time, the forest resource was perceived as one that if properly managed, could supply long-term economic benefits.

By the mid-1950s, British Columbia and the dominant forestry companies had settled into a comfortable relationship based upon a monopolistic tenure system that imposed few meaningful restrictions on the method and rate of cutting.[223] Ten years later, 'the forest industry was in the midst of an expansion that saw annual timber production increase from 22 million cubic metres in 1950 to 54.7 million cubic metres by 1970.'[224] In the same period, pulp production increased more than eightfold, and the number of pulp and paper mills in the province grew from seven in 1945 to twenty in 1970.[225]

During this era, conservation issues had little influence on the debate surrounding forestry practices, although the effects of logging on fish, wildlife, and recreation were frequently discussed at sessions of the British Columbia Natural Resources Conferences, which met annually or biennially from 1948 to 1970.[226]

1960s–1980s—The Integrated-Resource Model
The trend towards domination of forestry by a handful of large companies continued. By the time of the Pearse Commission, established in 1974, eight companies controlled 82 per cent of the provincial harvest. However, by the middle 1960s, the sustained-resource model was being challenged by those who believed

that a more expansive and integrated view of the forest resource was necessary.

Increasingly stakeholders in the forestry sector realized that the resource had more than simply economic value but had recreational and environmental value as well. It gradually became accepted that 'the liquidation project had to be tempered not only by measures designed to ensure conversion but also by constraints aimed at protecting and enhancing these other values.'[227] This challenge was not without its struggles:

> From the time of the Barrett NDP government onwards, two opposing conceptions of integrated resource management battled for supremacy within the policy-making system. Environmentalists and their allies within parts of the bureaucracy promoted a broad, interagency notion, while the industry and its bureaucratic and political allies tried to maintain a narrower concept centred on control by the Ministry of Forests (MOF).[228]

The extent of this integration of industrial, recreation, and tourism uses is evident from user rates of wilderness areas in British Columbia. It has been estimated that 400,000 people (about 80 per cent of whom are British Columbians) buy sport fishing licences yearly, 125,000 buy hunting licences, and three to four thousand people work at trapping or guiding. In total, more than 60 per cent of British Columbians use a provincial park each year. According to a brief prepared by the Ministry of the Environment in 1990, 'Wilderness-oriented adventure tourism is a $135 million industry in BC and is expected to grow at a rate of 15 to 21 per cent per year.'[229]

1980s—the Conservation Model

By the 1980s, debates about forest land use were strongly influenced by the rapid ascendance of environmental groups, which espoused conservation biology, a 'mission-oriented' branch of biology determined to develop and promote the tools that would reverse the deterioration of Earth's diversity. Employing the concept of biodiversity and related ideas, the proponents of these views emphasized the terms 'rainforest' and 'ancient forests' to build support for the notion that old-growth forests were complex ecosystems containing a great wealth of ecological diversity.[230] While this vision was certainly embraced by a large number of environmental groups, the industry itself and its importance to the economy posed a dilemma for British Columbians. Environmentalists argued that the long-standing notion of sustained yield was in need of significant revision to capture the idea that sustainability needed to be applied to the whole forest ecosystems and not just to the trees themselves.[231]

The Current State of the Forestry Resource—Problems and Stakeholders

The contrasting visions and types of forestry management described previously continue to this day; they characterize the current debates about the forestry resource across the country. One of the elements in the debate is the issue of tenure. The stakeholders in the BC forestry policy community have been the forest industry (and its workers), environmental groups, and government institutions. More recently, Aboriginal groups have claimed a place within this community. An analysis of the evolution of these stakeholder groups helps to explain the shifts in policy outcomes that have occurred.

The Question of Tenure

The system of tenure that specifies the rights and responsibilities of the grantee as well as the rights and obligations of the Crown has been controversial. The one irrefutable fact about this system is that 'neither governments nor private companies have provided the ecological stewardship required to sustain coniferous forests over very long periods of time.'[232] The greatest flaw, therefore, with the tenure system is that immediate revenues or profits have always won out over the long-term health of the forests. First established in the mid-1940s to provide employment and stability in rural regions of the province, the tenure system had the secondary objective of encouraging reforestation in logged-out areas. Although this system was quite successful in meeting the employment objectives, the reforestation part of the program had much less success.[233] Private companies argued that there was no incentive to reforest unless they had long-term security of tenure. Although there are a number of different forms of tenure, Forest Licences and Tree Farm Licences cover the most acreage and allow for the greatest volume of timber cutting. Generally speaking, the licences are granted for twenty and twenty-five years and are renewable every five years.[234] These are considered to be 'volume-based' licences and are granted to companies that maintain, establish, or expand processing facilities such as sawmills and pulpmills.[235] Although the forest companies are required to provide management plans every five years, the government has been guided more by economic and political requirements than by environmental considerations.[236]

By the 1990s, new licence forms were introduced amid the growing rhetoric of 'sustained yield'. Despite this talk of sustainability and conservation, with each new era of licencing, the volume of wood cut has grown.[237]

The Forest Industry and Forestry Workers

One of the difficulties in understanding the British Columbia forest industry itself is its heterogeneity. Not only is it divided sectorally into wood products and pulp-paper sectors, but it is also divided regionally into Interior and Coast sectors.[238] To this day, it remains an 'export-oriented and cyclical industry whose profitability depends on the health of markets and its ability to maintain access to Crown timber at reasonable rates.'[239] The markets for wood products are diverse as well:

In 1993, about 24 per cent of wood products went to Canadian markets, with 47 per cent of production shipped to the USA and 21 per cent to Japan. . . . Pulp and paper markets are more diversified—10 per cent of production went to Canadian markets, 28 per cent to USA, 23 per cent to EU nations, 32 per cent to Japan and other Pacific Rim countries.[240]

As was seen in the case of the fishing industry, new technological advances both in logging and in the processing of forest products have exacted a toll on those employed in the industry. By 1994, approximately 10 per cent fewer jobs were available in this sector than was the case in 1970.[241] Those employed in forestry are estimated to earn two-thirds of the income generated by BC's forestry industry, while about 27 per cent of the wealth goes to the industry and 6 per cent to the Crown.[242]

Although the forest industry complained that it was being unnecessarily burdened with changes in policy by the alternation of NDP and Social Credit governments, by the late 1980s their complaints were falling on increasingly unsympathetic ears. Determined to fight back, 'both COFI (Council of Forest Industries) and MacMillan Bloedel initiated advertising campaigns with estimated yearly price tags of more than $1 million, using the electronic and print media to plug their message that the industry could be counted on to ensure "forests forever".'[243] By the 1990s, it appeared that public opinion about the industry was becoming more favourable. To ensure that the momentum would continue in their favour, several of the major companies hired Burson-Masteller, 'a New York firm known for, among other things, its handling of high-profile corporate public relations disasters such as that visited on Union Carbide by the Bhopal gas leak.'[244] This firm quickly mounted an effective campaign to neutralize the influence of environmental groups in the province. Funded by more than $1 million supplied by thirteen forest companies, the BC Forest Alliance was founded in April 1991. It ran a series of television infomercials in which it attacked industry critics. Within a year of its founding, the Alliance counted some 4,000 members and named the long-time president of the International Woodworkers of America-Canada (IWA), Jack Munro, as its first chairman.[245] Workers in the forest industry also began to organize against the increasingly vocal and influential wilderness movement. By 1990, 'a loose network of groups such as Share the Stein, Share our Resources, Share our Forests, North Island Citizens for Shared Resources, among others, were pushing the argument that multiple use would allow for the preservation of industry jobs as well as recreational opportunities.'[246] Environmentalists cried foul, claiming that these 'share' groups were instigated and bankrolled by the forest companies, and they linked the share movement to the American 'wise use' forces (discussed in Chapter Two).

By the mid-1990s, forest workers and spokespersons for forest-dependent communities had become powerful and aggressive advocates of industry positions on a range of issues.[247]

Another feature of the forestry industry has been the extent of concentrated ownership and increasing levels of foreign ownership:

> At the time of the Pearse Report (1976), between 70 and 90 per cent of all timber licences in the six forestry districts were held by the ten largest companies; the same companies also owned about 35 per cent of the lumber facilities, 74 per cent of the plywood and veneer companies, 90 per cent of the pulp facilities, and all the paper facilities. Seven of these companies were owned outside BC, five of them outside Canada. Thirteen of the top twenty were foreign-owned, although five of the largest were owned in Canada. . . . The degree of concentration changed little over the next two decades, although by 1990, nearly 25 per cent of timber rights were controlled by two large entities, Noranda Forest and Fletcher Challenge Canada.[248]

Foreign ownership of the forestry industry has been extensively documented by Pratt and Urquhart in their analysis of Japanese ownership of sizable tracts of Alberta's boreal forest. The overseas expansion of Japanese pulp and paper companies, which began in the 1980s, was largely attributed to strict Japanese regulations that prevented the company from adding pulp and paper capacity in Japan. In other words, it is evident that it was a corporate strategy to transfer pollution-generating operations to other countries.[249]

The rationale for concentrated ownership in the forestry industry is similar to arguments advanced in other corporate sectors. In industries that are subject to the volatility of international markets, large companies are more stable and less likely to close down during recessions. And, as in other industries with concentrated ownership, representatives from these companies occupy prominent spots at the top of provincial corporate hierarchies. Wilson cites, as an example, the case of Adam Zimmerman, who in the 1980s and early 1990s, was chairman and CEO of Noranda. In addition, he was a member of the board of MacMillan Bloedel and Northwood Pulp and Paper and also 'sat on the Board of Southam, Inc., one of the country's two large media conglomerates and the owner (through Pacific Press) of Vancouver's two daily newspapers, the *Vancouver Sun* and the *Vancouver Province*.'[250]

British Columbia Wilderness Movement

The British Columbia wilderness movement comprises dozens of organizations with thousands of members. The movement can be divided into four distinct components: fish and wildlife clubs and their umbrella organization, the BC Wildlife Federation; naturalist groups and their provincial organization, the Federation of BC Naturalists; clubs for hikers, climbers, and other 'non-consumptive' outdoor recreationists; and groups concerned mainly with environmental advocacy, including the Sierra Club. These groups have goals that range from local and regional to province-wide and multi-issue.[251] Because this movement is diverse and draws members and supporters from a variety of different interest groups, its greatest sources of strength are 'its broad public support, its large and intensely committed pool of activists, its diversity, and its access to important allies both inside and outside the province.'[252]

Other Interest Groups
Outside of the wilderness movement, other environmental groups have been influential in the area of forestry policy. Greenpeace has had a growing interest in rainforest preservation, and other organizations, such as the Forest Action Network and the Friends of Clayoquot Sound, have bolstered the radical end of the spectrum, while the emergence of BC Wild and the Sierra Legal Defence Fund, and the ascendancy of groups like the Canadian Parks and Wilderness Society have strengthened the more moderate end.[253] Despite criticisms of these groups by forest companies and forestry workers, these groups are not dominated by middle- and upper-income city dwellers. Evidence exists that these groups receive support from all economic and social classes. Nor have these groups confined themselves to criticizing the forest industry or government policy. The Sierra Legal Defence Fund, the Suzuki Foundation, and Ecotrust have undertaken sophisticated analyses of the forest economy and have published reports based on detailed monitoring of industry and Ministry of Forestry performance.[254] While most of their efforts are designed to educate the Canadian public about the crisis in the country's forest industry, these groups have also sought to influence international public opinion: 'Since 1990, BC groups and a growing network of international allies have encouraged consumers of BC forest products to voice their dissatisfaction with provincial forest practices and to back those protests with talk of boycotts.'[255]

Interest groups associated with the forestry resource continue to face three particular difficulties—access to forestry officials, weak financial support, and internal dissension. Access to government forestry officials has been inhibited by a series of reorganizations. At one time, forest-land-use policy in British Columbia was controlled by the Ministry of Forests. Since 1991, the lead agency has been the Ministry of Environment, Lands and Parks. As for funding, most groups continue to be plagued by inadequate financial support. When rainforest preservation became a popular issue in the early 1990s, however, several American foundations, including the Pew Charitable Trusts and the Bullitt Foundation, made large donations to groups such as BC Wild and the Western Canada Wilderness Committee.[256]

However, most environmental organizations have been forced to rely on fundraising drives and the recruitment of new members. They have also faced internal discord, in part because of the competing groups that have traditionally found their political home with the province's New Democratic Party. On one hand, party stalwarts believed that many of the leading activists were middle and upper-middle income people who were unsympathetic to the plight of workers in the forestry industry. At the same time, some of the activists believed that they were being made the scapegoat for the layoffs in the industry.[257]

Governments

In theoretical terms, there are advantages and disadvantages to public ownership of resources, and provincial governments in Canada have had to weigh these carefully. There are many prototypes for public ownership in Canada—PetroCan, the Saskatchewan government's takeover of the potash industry, the Province of Quebec and asbestos, and the Alberta government's Alberta Energy Corporation.[258] Wilson maintains that if British Columbia had taken over the forest industry in the 1940s, 1950s, or the 1960s, it might have been able 'to establish resource policies to favour companies that re-invested in more diversified industries throughout the province. Possibly it could have sought diverse markets and reduced the economy's dependence on the United States.'[259] Another problem for the British Columbia government is the question of tenure. As discussed previously, the tenure system allows for the logging of timber or other uses of public lands.[260] The dilemma faced by governments is this:

> Governments are supposed to assume responsibility for the stewardship of natural resources in the public interest. At the same time, however, they are rewarded for investments in social infrastructure, not for long-term supports for nature. Indeed, the way the tenure system has been structured, governments obtain stumpage fees (resource rents) when the forests are cut, not when they are conserved. Furthermore, resource rents have underwritten many social and other services that the British Columbia population has enjoyed.[261]

Aboriginal Communities

Increasingly, Aboriginal communities are becoming involved in a number of resource sectors as a result of resource development and native land claims. As their involvement has grown, disputes have become more common. One of the most publicized disputes occurred in Alberta between the Daishowa company and the Lubicon Lake Cree. At the centre of the controversy was the territory around Buffalo Lake, some 105 kilometres east of the town of Peace River. This was the first time that this area had been disturbed by resource exploration. Between 1979 and 1984, over 400 oil wells were drilled within fifteen miles of Little Buffalo and destroyed what had been a viable traditional hunting and trapping economy.[262] The objections of Aboriginal communities at this time were largely ignored by the provincial government. Several years later, a gigantic pulp mill was proposed. This time the Lubicon gained the support of organizations such as the Canadian Council of Churches, and the government became obliged to work towards resolving an outstanding land claim. When negotiations with the government broke down the Lubicon took matters into their own hands and erected checkpoints and barriers on all the main roads into their territory. Eventually the RCMP stepped in and twenty-seven people were detained.[263] The dispute intensified in the months ahead, and in November 1990, arsonists torched a logging camp run by a Daishowa sub-contractor, some fifty kilometres northeast of Little Buffalo. Thirteen people—dubbed the Lubicon 13—were charged in connection with the arson.[264]

With the support of a large number of organizations and companies, including Knechtel's, the YMCA, Cultures Fresh Food Restaurants, and the Body Shop, a boycott of Daishowa paper products and cancellation of contracts ensued. By July 1993, the Friends of the Lubicon claimed that at least twenty-six companies, representing over 2,700 retail outlets, had joined the boycott. Daishowa retaliated with a Strategic Lawsuit against Public Participation (SLAPP) in an attempt to prevent the Friends of the Lubicon from continuing the boycott. The courts, however, ruled in favour of the Friends of the Lubicon, who were represented by the Sierra Legal Defence Fund. A SLAPP is a lawsuit brought by a plaintiff to intimidate his or her opponents and discourage them from speaking publicly about controversial issues. Examples of alleged SLAPPs include MacMillan Bloedel's suit against the Galiano Conservancy Association for lobbying local governments to take actions that would potentially affect MacMillan Bloedel's corporate interests. British Columbia introduced a new law in March 2001 called *The Protection of Public Participation Act* (Bill 10) to prevent these types of legal actions.

Conclusions

The forest resource remains a vital part of Canada's economy. For the most part, wood and wood products have been viewed as staples to be sold in the marketplace, and this attitude has guided federal and provincial forestry policy. Because it was believed that reforestation would replace the forests that were felled, there was little worry about clearcutting logging practices. By the mid-1980s, however, this attitude changed as attention began to be focused on the loss of Canada's ancient forests. Environmentalists argued that these forests and the fragile ecosystems of which they were a part were irreplaceable. Much of the environmental activism that was unleashed in the mid-1980s took place in British Columbia, where forestry practices were hotly debated. Many coastal rainforests are on lands that are home to many First Nations peoples. As noted earlier in this book, many of these groups have formed alliances with forest-conservation organizations in other countries and have engaged primarily in market strategies, such as calling on large businesses to boycott British Columbia forest products, particularly those that are not certified. In May 2000, Bell Canada, Kinko's Canada, Roots, and the Citizens Bank of Canada received awards from the Market Initiatives coalition for their commitment to the world's ancient rainforests. Bell Canada's letter to the coalition said: 'It is our intention to favour those wood-based product suppliers who will have adopted sustainable practices which do not contribute to the destruction of irreplaceable natural treasures such as ancient forests.'[265] In a few cases forest companies have agreed to alter their logging practices, as was discussed in Chapter Three, with the signing of the Great

Bear Rainforest Agreement in April 2001. However, there are still companies that do not practice sustainable forestry. As long as there are such companies, it is likely that environmental groups will continue their protests.

The Forest Action Network (FAN), a network of over 500 forest activists and twenty-two organizations throughout British Columbia, North America, and Europe, has as its objective the end of industrial forestry and its replacement with 'ecologically-sound, First Nations and community-controlled ecoforestry.'[266] To groups such as FAN and to the First Nations, the system that has governed the forest resource in Canada has been ecologically unsound. And, while there are some indications that some industrial groups may be prepared to make some concessions along these lines, the common-pool-resource model appears unlikely to be adopted at the present time.

Water—Resource or Commodity?

> Humans consume water, discard it, poison it, waste it, and restlessly change the hydrological cycles, indifferent to the consequences: too many people, too little water, water in the wrong places and in the wrong amounts. The human population is burgeoning, but water demand is increasing twice as fast.
>
> Marq de Villiers, *Water*, 15.

As Canadians, we have water thundering over Niagara Falls; countless fresh-water lakes, rivers, and streams; frozen water in the snow, ice, and icebergs of the Arctic; oceans of water coursing underground; and one of the largest land masses in the world on which to catch rain and snow from the sky. In fact, we worry more about flood than famine.[267] In Canada, which has 9 per cent of the world's renewable water supply, but less than 1 per cent of the world's population, water-management traditions have grown out of the mistaken impression that Canadian water resources are infinite.[268] Now, however, many experts have recognized that supply is becoming increasingly eroded by demand. A University of Alberta water ecologist, David Schindler, has warned that 'without increased funding for freshwater research and a national water strategy, fresh water will become Canada's foremost ecological crisis early in the twenty-first century.'[269] He attributes this impending scarcity to a combination of climate change, acid rain, human and livestock wastes, increased ultraviolet radiation, airborne toxins, and biological invaders.[270] Climate change has caused the glaciers to thin and has increased rates of evaporation. Wetlands are particularly vulnerable to rising evaporation rates, and it has been predicted that many lakes on the Prairies will disappear, as they did during a warm period 4,000 to 6,000 years ago.[271] Climate warming also helps to spread non-native biological invaders such as zebra mussels.

It was estimated that, in 1997, some 436 million people around the world did not have enough water. It has been projected that the percentage of the world's population without enough water will increase fivefold by 2050.[272] In some regions, this scarcity is particularly pronounced. In Africa, the Middle East, India, and China, the scarcity of water is already critical. There is also evidence that this problem is also slowly developing in the developed world. There are signs that water in the United States may be becoming scarce in certain regions, for the underground aquifer that supplies one-third of the water for the continental United States is being depleted eight times faster than it is being replenished.[273] Compounding the water scarcity is the problem that more than 300 river systems cross national boundaries.[274] This characteristic of rivers and watersheds sets the stage for future conflicts and even wars over water.

This section will explore three themes related to water issues in Canada: (1) the use, management, and regulation of water; (2) the trade of bulk water on the international market; and (3) the circumstances under which Canada should be obliged to share its water with the rest of the world.

Use, Management, and Regulation of Water in Canada
The right to use water in North America has traditionally not cost anything. At present, no Canadian federal or provincial statute binds consumers to include water conservation as part of any industrial or municipal program. Instead, water use is governed by a variety of non-legal guidelines and policies. In fact, a good many of these policies encourage wastefulness by failing to charge realistic prices and by not relating costs to the volume used.[275] The result of this laissez-faire approach to water management and conservation has been that Canadians now are among the world's most wasteful water users, consuming more per capita than any other country except the United States. Moreover, the prices charged for water are among the lowest in the world. Water costs in Canada are

> 33 to 50 per cent of those in France and Germany, for example, while the per capita consumption on a residential basis is more than double that of those countries. Water rates in most municipalities are in fact set at 65 to 75 per cent of the real cost of delivering water and sewage services, so there is little incentive to conserve.[276]

The largest Canadian water user is the electric-power generating sector, which uses more than 26 billion cubic metres a year (1986 figures). Second is manufacturing, at about 8 billion cubic metres a year, followed by municipalities (water for drinking, washing, lawn-watering, and firefighting) at about 5 billion, agriculture at about 4 billion, and mining at less than 1 billion.[277] Even the manufacture of computer wafers used in the production of computer chips requires water—up to 18 million litres a day worldwide. Around the world, the computer industry uses 1.5 trillion litres of water a year and produces 300 billion litres of waste water.

The ownership of water raises a series of other questions. In Canada, most municipalities run their own water systems, whereas inspection and infrastructure are the responsibility of the Province. In Ontario, municipalities are responsible for reporting the results of water tests to the Province, which is no longer responsible for monitoring the quality of drinking water. For the most part, though (Ontario notwithstanding), water inspections and quality controls are administered by public agencies.

It is a difficult enterprise to quantify Canada's fresh-water supply, particularly the groundwater. For example, like surface water (lakes and rivers), groundwater is constantly on the move. Over the years or decades or centuries it eventually finds its way into 'the channels of rivers and streams and then back to the sea. . . . Somewhere around 10 to 20 per cent of rain finds its way into underground water systems.'[278] Despite advances in computer technologies and tools of measurement, the quantifying of underground water supplies is haphazard. Also, although remote sensing and tracer techniques can help track groundwater, its movement is extremely difficult to follow.[279] Aquifers present another series of problems. Water can be stored not only in the pores of rock but also in cracks and fractures, which can become subterranean streams or even rivers having the capability of swelling surface rivers dramatically during heavy rains: This is 'why aquifers are almost impossible to clean up once they have become polluted, and why pollutants, leaching through the soils from waste dumps, landfills, and agriculture, can occasionally be found alarmingly long distances from the polluting source.'[280] It is also difficult to determine the bottom depth of aquifers. For years, the city of Tucson, Arizona, relied entirely on groundwater wells. Over time, the depth of the wells had to be increased from 150 metres to 450 metres. Beginning in 1980, Arizona began to regulate groundwater overdrafts and required low-flow appliances like water-saving toilets. Although these measures have reduced water use to about 375 litres per person per day—one of the lowest rates in the United States—the depletion of the aquifer is irreversible.[281]

Water for Sale and Water Mining

The sale of fresh water in Canada may take two forms—bottled spring water and bulk water exports. In the past several years, the bottled-water industry in Canada has mushroomed. For the most part, this industry has been unregulated by government, although permits are required for large extractions. These extractions have become increasingly controversial, however, particularly in communities that have suffered through long periods of drought. Local residents in Artimesia Township in Grey County, Ontario, appealed the Ministry of Environment's decision to grant Echo Springs Water of Mississauga (Ontario's third-largest water bottler) a water-taking permit allowing it to extract 176 million litres of water annually for two years. Their objections were based on the fear that this additional extraction would worsen the water shortages that have existed in the area over the past few years. The decision of the ministry was upheld by Ontario's Environmental Appeal Board in December 1999.[282] Canadian bottled water is included in NAFTA, whereas bulk water is not.

In response to alarm bells being sounded by environmental groups and others, including the Council of Canadians, about the sale of bulk water on international markets, the Ministry of Foreign Affairs announced in March 1999 the imposition of an export moratorium that will remain in place until all the provinces can agree on a method to ban water exports permanently. This inter-governmental co-operation is necessary because of the shared jurisdiction over lakes and rivers in Canada. Although this decision was applauded by some provinces and environmental groups, it was criticized by some who see Canada as a 'future OPEC of water' that stands to make huge profits from exporting water.

The moratorium has given governments and environmental groups time to examine the scope of the domestic water industry. And the scope is massive. In Newfoundland, McCurdy Enterprises announced plans to 'harvest' 13 *billion* gallons of water a year from Gisborne Lake, an eleven-square-mile lake in Newfoundland. McCurdy planned to withdraw water from the lake and transport it, by pipeline, five miles to the coastal town of Grand LaPierre. From there, it would be loaded into scrubbed, former oil tankers. McCurdy Enterprises also plans to open a water-bottling plant in Grand LaPierre that would employ 150 people. The local municipality approved the plan, as did the province, but a final decision on the permit was put on hold because of the moratorium announced by the federal government. For a region hit hard by the collapse of the fisheries, these jobs were much needed, and the government's moratorium was heavily criticized. In a startling announcement made on 20 October 1999, Newfoundland's Premier, Brian Tobin, reversed his position, stating, 'Newfoundland's water is not for sale.'[283] Another Canadian company, Global Water Corporation, has a bulk-water purchase agreement with the Alaskan community of Sitka, which would allow the company to take 5 billion gallons of water a year from the glacier-fed Blue Lake for export to China in five-gallon jugs.[284]

The sale of water and the private management of water systems became more commonplace in the 1980s and 1990s. In Britain and France in particular, private companies manage not only their own systems, but systems in other countries as well. Lyonnaise des Eaux became the largest water company in the world after merging with another French company, and it now distributes water to some 68 million people in thirty countries. It also has contracts with several Canadian municipalities including Montreal.[285]

Is Canada Obliged to Share Its Water?

The search for international law on the sale, use, and misuse of water has been elusive. The only agreement, the UN convention on the Law of the Non-Navigational Uses of International Watercourses, was adopted in 1997 but, as of 1999, had still not been implemented.[286] Despite continued efforts to codify international water law, few tools are available to policy makers. There are some 2,000 treaties and instruments related to international watercourses and aquifers, and yet the hands of policy makers continue to be tied.

It is expected that the coming water bankruptcy will be felt first in China. It is expected that annual industrial water use will rise from 52 billion tons to 269 billion tons in the next thirty years, owing to a huge increase in the population and rising incomes that allow more people to have indoor plumbing. In fact, it has been predicted that China 'will be the first country in the world that will literally have to restructure its economy to respond to water scarcity.'[287] All of this raises questions about ownership. Does Canada or any other country 'own' its water? De Villiers argues: 'Water is not "ours" or "theirs" but the planet's. We use water, and it passes on, and then it comes back to us. But it is not, surely, something we should either hoard or prevent others from using.'[288]

Water and NAFTA

Canada has water to spare, and Mexico virtually none. It makes for an interesting ménage.[289]

Opponents have represented the Lake Superior proposal as the first tiny breach in the watertight dike, a breach that, once made, will become a rushing torrent, as thirsty Americans use trade instruments like NAFTA to plunder our hydrological resources, while water worshipping Canadians stand by, impotent.[290]

Under the terms of NAFTA, Canadian bottled water is a tradable commodity. Where the agreement is less clear is whether Canadian bulk water is subject to continental exploitation. Moreover, there is a concern that the difference between a litre of bottled water and a supertanker of bulk water may turn out to be merely a matter of size and semantics.[291]

Proponents of free trade in water want it to be regarded as a commodity, something to be bought and sold, perhaps included as an integral part of NAFTA. This makes environmentalists shudder because even a modest export of water would set a precedent that could open the floodgates. One of the first proposals for the bulk sale of water, which was made by the Nova Group of Sault Ste Marie in 1997, involved the export of 600 million litres of Great Lakes water by cargo ship to Asia. The ship would travel down the St Lawrence River, down the east coast of North America, and through the Panama Canal. Nova never revealed what the freight charges would be or who its customers were.[292] After a public outcry on both sides of the border, the permit was withdrawn; however, the issue of bulk water sales has not yet been resolved.[293]

The free-trade argument that was invoked by the Nova Group was essentially that Canada sells all its other natural resources, so why not water? Moreover, what would stop Americans from pumping water from the Great Lakes on their side? Canadian companies might as well profit from this operation if their American competitors are going to do the same. On the other side of the argument were water sovereigntists—anti-freetraders. Their argument was that 'under Chapter 11, the non-discriminatory clause of NAFTA, once a permit has been issued—thus recognizing that water is a tradable commodity—it becomes impossible to deny equivalent permits to anyone else who wants them, and for whatever quantity.'[294]

Another legal opinion that was prepared for the Council of Canadians argues that the federal government's focus on water as a tradeable commodity has ignored the fact that under NAFTA, water is both an investment and service. Therefore, even if there is support for the notion that water is not a good, Canada stands to lose. Steven Shryman further states: 'NAFTA leaves Canadian water resources, and measures established to protect them, entirely vulnerable to foreign investor claims.'[295] Like others, he has warned that once one deal is made to sell bulk water, the national treatment and proportional sharing rules of NAFTA would render Canada helpless to restrict water exports later.[296] On the basis of this opinion, the Council of Canadians has embarked on a campaign to raise public awareness regarding the commercialization of water and the emergence of transnational corporations and concentrated ownership in the water business. Several studies indicate that these companies are competing for contracts in all parts of the world, but particularly in the developing world. Between 1990 and 1997, ninety-seven private water and sewerage projects were completed in developing countries.[297]

The private corporation is incapable of adequately managing the myriad interests involved in the management of an important public resource, not the least of which involves serving the needs of citizens. Indeed, studies indicate that 'water sector experts' promote the belief that the notion of water provision as a public good and welfare activity is being replaced by the concept of water as an economic good and as an input in economic activity.[298]

Simply stated, there are three issues—the making of a scarce resource a tradable one on international markets, the environmental issue of the depletion of Canada's surface and groundwater supplies, and the issue of sovereignty. Although the environmental implications of the trade of bulk water were important, there is no question that the critical issue was Canada's sovereignty over its water. If this battle were lost, critics argued, what would prevent foreign ships from sailing into the Canadian Arctic and taking on fresh water without detection (if global warming results in an open Northwest Passage in ten to fifteen years)?

As is the case when goods become scarce, entrepreneurs look for ways to export and sell large amounts of the scarce product. They also survey the market, looking for customers. Countries that use less than 10 per cent of their annual renewable water do not usually have supply problems. For those that use between 10 and 20 per cent there may be regional difficulties. By the late 1980s, data revealed that many countries were headed for trouble. Out of 113 developing countries, fourteen were using 10 to 20 per cent of their water. China and most of South Asia fell into this group. Another twenty-five countries were using more than 20 per cent.[299] The regions with the greatest problems are the Middle East and North Africa, where eleven of twenty countries are already using more than half their water resources. International experts have predicted that a shortage of water could result in regional conflicts. There is already evidence of local disputes over wells, canal routes, and irrigation schedules among farmers in South Asia and the Near East. But water scarcity is not just happening in the arid and semi-arid countries of the developing world. In the United States, thirsty cities in the dry states are buying water rights from farmers, whose ability to produce food is thereby reduced.[300] The Canadian Environmental Law Association reports that thirty-one countries have severe water shortages that threaten their food security.

In Ontario, there is a growing concern that the Great Lakes and the water that flows into them are for sale and that the public ownership of them may be challenged. For example, the Ontario Clean Water Agency, which manages more than one-third of Ontario's municipal water works and sewage treatment plants, has been handed over to Ontario's Privatization Secretariat. If the water agency is sold to private interests, it will constitute the biggest foothold in North America for multi-national water companies.[301] Furthermore, a number of companies are intensifying their extraction of groundwater for sale and export as bottled water. According to CELA, 'preliminary research shows that in the last two years alone, Ontario has granted water bottling companies permits for almost 3 billion litres of groundwater.'[302]

Recently, it has been reported that commercial bottlers have been given the right to drain, free of charge, more than 18 billion litres a year from Ontario's water supply.[303] 'That's 30 times the amount allocated to a company [the Nova group] planning to export Lake Superior water to Asia before a public outcry prompted the province to rescind its permission in July 1998.'[304] Although Ontario's Ministry of the Environment argues that the groundwater resource is well managed, others familiar with the issue are concerned that this drain off from Ontario's aquifers may not be sustainable. Although 'some mapping' has been done of groundwater, its extent is unknown. This uncertainty has environmental groups warning that the potential ecological effects of these water operations have not been adequately studied.

Water Pollution

Pollution leads to disease, a straight-line computation that is self-evident. Best guesses are that some 250 million new cases of water-borne diseases occur every year, killing somewhere around 10 million people—a Canada every three years.'[305]

Experts have claimed that 80 per cent of China's major rivers are so degraded they no longer can support any fish. A World Bank study in 1997 'put the cost of air and water pollution in China at $54 billion a year, equivalent to an astonishing 8 per cent of the country's gross domestic product.'[306] Canada's record on water pollution is far from impressive. Halifax and Victoria dump all their sewage, untreated, into their harbours, and it is estimated that a third of Canadians are not served by waste-treatment plants.[307]

Water-borne disease infects more than 200 million people in some seventy countries and is spreading and intensifying daily in large parts of the developing world. Closer to home, Legionnaires' disease is also caused through contaminated water. Although outbreaks are relatively rare, it is nevertheless worrying to public health officials because it is resistant to chlorine and so can infect even water that is treated to US and European health standards.[308]

Most recently, in April 2001, several hundred people in North Battleford, Saskatchewan, became ill because of the contamination of their municipal water supply with cryptosporidium, a microscopic, single-cell parasite. It is believed that contamination occurs when water is exposed to cattle feces that contain the parasite. One can also be infected by eating unwashed fruits and vegetables that were sprayed with contaminated manure. There were two major outbreaks of the parasitic illness in British Columbia in 1996, when some 2,000 residents of Cranbrook and another 10,000 people in Kelowna became ill.[309]

Beyond Water Scarcity—The Lessons of Walkerton

What angers him most, however, is not ruined health but ruined trust. Like many people here, the damage-control blitzkrieg of the past year seems to have alienated Mr Bagnato as much as the years of gross negligence that triggered the crisis. 'The huge aggravation Walkerton people have is that we have been personally assaulted,' he said. 'We got contaminated water, we got sick and we feel like all forms of government from the top right down turned their backs on us.'

Nearly a year after the public-health crisis that brought death and debilitating disease to Walkerton, a (local mother) still pays for much of the water her household consumes and her four-year old son, Joseph, still breaks out with a rash after bathing; the result, according to his doctors, of sensitivity to the high amounts of chlorine still being used to quell the dangerous micro-organisms that coursed freely through the town's water supply.[310]

A year after Walkerton, there remain many unanswered questions. What caused the breakdown in reporting? Was it simply a matter of incompetence by a local water manager? Was it an event that can best be explained by a series of events including a bad storm and deficient farming practices? The judge hearing the inquiry will not be releasing his report for months. In reflecting on Walkerton a year later, it is useful to examine some of the early coverage of the event when the residents of the town were looking for answers. Below is one story that appeared in various news media at the time the tragedy was unfolding and that was particularly critical of unsafe agricultural practices.

If a farmer wants to spread manure before a heavy rain, one that might wash it into the water system, there is no one to stop him. And yet, as the people of Walkerton discovered, cow manure may contain a new and deadly strain of bacteria, E. coli 0517:H7. Industry knew this. So did governments. The Cattlemen's Association Web site is filled with references to E. coli 0157. It has been an identified threat in Ontario since 1994. A recent study by the US National Academy of Sciences found that one-third of US cattle contained the killer strain. So why are we surprised by Walkerton? In a province literally awash with untreated animal manure, a province in which the toxic waste from large-scale farming is assumed to be somehow more virtuous than that of, say, large-scale chemical firms, this tragedy—or something very much like it—was bound to occur.[311]

Box 4.2 *Escherichia coli, E. coli* 0157:H7

Escherichia coli (*E. coli*) 0157:H7 is one of hundreds of strains of the bacterium *E. coli* that produces a powerful toxin and can cause severe illness. The disease it causes is better known as hamburger disease, although it is now known that the bacterium can also be waterborne. Most strains of *E. coli* are harmless and live in the intestines of healthy humans and animals. However, *E. coli* 0157:H7 can be lethal, as evidenced in the outbreak in Walkerton in May 2000, where seven people died and hundreds of others became seriously ill. There have also been several serious outbreaks in the United States. The long-term health implications of these outbreaks will not be known for several years. This particular strain was first identified in 1982 after an outbreak of bloody diarrhea caused by contaminated hamburgers. Although undercooked hamburgers continue to be a primary source of this strain, *E. coli* 0157:H7 has also been found in such foods as leaf lettuce, alfalfa sprouts, and goat's milk. Generally speaking, symptoms usually appear about three days after exposure but can incubate for up to nine days. One of the difficulties with identifying this deadly strain is that not all laboratories are equipped to perform the test.

Although the immediate symptoms are severe diarrhea and abdominal cramps, the infection can also cause longer-lasting disorders. In children under the age of five, a complication called hemolytic uremic syndrome can occur. This syndrome destroys red blood cells, ultimately leading to kidney failure and death in 3 to 5 per cent of cases. An additional 8 per cent of victims have lifelong complications, including high blood pressure, seizures, and blindness. Elderly victims may develop thrombotic thrombocytopenic purura (TTP) which can lead to strokes. One of the difficulties in treating the symptoms of the infection is that some antibiotics may actually cause kidney complications. Because of potential long-term health conditions associated with the deadly outbreak at Walkerton, the Government of Ontario has negotiated a tentative open-ended compensation package for those whose health and long-term well-being have been affected by the contamination.

The source of *E. coli* is generally attributed to sewage or animal waste that may be washed into creeks, rivers, streams, lakes, or groundwater by rain or melting snow. In the case of Walkerton, it is thought that at least one well was contaminated as a result of a torrential rain on 12 May 2000.

Sources: cbc.ca/news/indepth/walkerton/science.html, Health Canada, US Environmental Protection Agency, and Medline.

What *is* known for certain about the Walkerton situation is that seven people died and hundreds of others became seriously ill as a result of the outbreak of *Escherichia coli* 0157:H7 (see Box 4.2), a deadly strain of the most common bug in the human intestines, *E. coli*: 'Most E.coli is harmless, but 0157:H7 is a cause of what is popularly called hamburger disease, a sometimes lethal food contamination, as well as severe illnesses associated with bad water. It often originates in cattle intestines.'[312]

In 1991, Professor Michael Goss of the Land Resource Science department at the University of Western Ontario concluded that 30 per cent of Ontario's wells were contaminated. At the time of the Walkerton crisis, he said that half the wells used for drinking water contained some bacterial contamination and that one-third of them were contaminated with *E. coli*.[313]

There is evidence that Walkerton had problems with its water quality dating back to 1994. Three tests of the town's water system conducted by Ministry officials early in 1998 discovered *E. coli* bacteria. After these tests, the Town of Walkerton wrote to Premier Mike Harris requesting that the government take control of drinking-water testing. The request was made two years after the province had closed its labs and privatized water-testing services in 1996.[314] Walkerton's request was never answered.

Some view the tragedy at Walkerton as a stark reminder that the quality of Ontario's drinking water must be protected at all costs. These critics claim that the province's drinking water has been allowed to deteriorate because it has historically been 'safe enough' and the public has not demanded new government investment to ensure its continued quality. Others view the Walkerton story as an inevitable result of four years of government cuts to the Ministry of the Environment bureaucracy, particularly its inspection staff. Yet others see Walkerton as a major failure of the Ontario government's privatization strategy—a central objective of the Commonsense Revolution with which the Ontario Progressive Conservative Party came to power in 1995. Although well water has been contaminated elsewhere in Canada, the loss of life and widespread illness from this environmental accident are unprecedented in our nation's history. The indisputable legacy of Walkerton is that the public's confidence in both the quality of its water supply and the regulations to ensure its protection has been seriously eroded. What is less certain about Walkerton is the effect it will have on Ontario's environmental policies and on the management of the province's water supply.

In the weeks following the Walkerton tragedy, environmental organizations were optimistic that the events that occurred there would be linked to the cutbacks in both the operating and capital budgets of the Ministry of the Environment. Moreover, they were confident that further talk about privatization of public utilities would be stopped dead in its tracks. In fact, just the reverse happened. The Conservatives announced that privatization of public utilities would continue to be explored. Ironically, Walkerton became, in many respects, fuel for the new public management. This is captured in the following story that appeared in the *National Post*:

Privatization, rather than the cause of environmental risk, is the route to greater safety. Private water firms are ready to invest billions in water systems around the world. Moncton is a good example. The city got a new drinking water system this year for $23 million, about $8 million less than it would have paid for one built by the city. Water rates are lower. And the water standards are reportedly 10 times greater than national regulatory standards.[315]

Over and above the loss of human life, Walkerton *should* be remembered for a number of important reasons related directly to environmental protection and management. First and foremost, a safe drinking-water supply has historically been regarded as a 'public' good. That is, water has been such an important commodity that only governments were considered to have legitimate authority over its management. Simply stated, water was too important to become a 'private' good with profit the primary consideration. Nevertheless, the evidence—at least in Ontario—has revealed that water was partly privatized by 1996 as part of the massive cuts to government bureaucracy made by the Progressive Conservative government after it came to power in 1995. This conversion of drinking water from a public good to a partially private one was made with little fanfare, although several environmental organizations criticized these changes at the time. Indeed, most members of the public were not aware that the rules of water testing had been changed. Even if they had been made aware by media and other gatekeepers—such as Opposition parties in the Ontario legislature—it is not likely that the public would have been enraged by this significant change in environmental policy. In many respects, this conversion was ideological: that is, the government of the day believed that the private sector would do a more effective and efficient job than a bloated and ineffective bureaucracy. At the time of writing, no definitive cause has been determined; however, early indicators pointed to the run-off of livestock sewage into the town's water supply during a heavy rainstorm in May 2000. At the same time, farmers' associations and some academics in agricultural science argue that the causes are inconclusive. Meanwhile, farm organizations and agricultural scientists quickly went on the defensive.

> Farmers in Ontario are recognized as global leaders in land stewardship for their adoption of environmental farm plans and nutrient management plans. But not all participate. With 5,000 animals or 50, there are good and bad producers. Further, most studies show the prevalence of *E. coli* 0157:H7 in feedlot cattle is similar to that in range cattle. Whether it's factory farms or small organic operations, the lesson is vigilance, because bacteria will evolve and adapt to whatever food production and distribution systems humans develop. Simplistic finger pointing can in fact be dangerous as individuals may assume that such problems only happen to other people in other places.[316]
>
> Douglas Powell
> Assistant Professor, Department of Plant Agriculture
> University of Guelph

In terms of two themes of this book—managing our collective commons and the regulation of private-sector operations—the tragedy at Walkerton can be best understood in relation to both of these factors. Of course, inquiries and other investigations that will be undertaken on the tragedy at Walkerton may point to other causes—human error, bureaucratic bungling, and ineffective regulatory legislation being chief among them. However, this discussion will concentrate on the two elements of environmental politics that have been central to this book—management of the commons and the government's role in it.

Rules Governing Municipal Water Systems

Environment Canada reports that approximately 57 per cent of Canadians are served by waste-water treatment plants. This compares with 74 per cent, 86.5 per cent, and 99 per cent of Americans, Germans, and Swedes respectively.[317] An estimated 26 per cent of Canadians rely on groundwater for domestic use. This is the group that the residents of Walkerton fall into. In Ontario, 429 water and sewage-treatment plants are operated by the Ontario Clean Water Agency (OCWA), a provincial Crown corporation, whose business is 'to provide environmentally responsible and cost-effective water and wastewater services to Ontario's municipalities.'[318] Although each of Ontario's 650 municipal water systems carries a certificate of approval (COA) which is supposed to outline a municipality's legal requirements for operating the system—many of these appear to be outdated. For example, the *National Post* reported that in a small sample, some COAs dated back forty years and have not been updated to include the province's recent drinking-water objectives. Unless these objectives form part of the COAs, they are not legally binding. In other words, while some municipalities have legal obligations for both the testing of water and reporting the presence of contaminants, others do not.[319] Walkerton fell into this category. Its COA was issued in 1979 and was amended on several occasions. These amendments required the Public Utilities Commission to monitor some local wells but not its main waterworks. In the final analysis, it has been concluded that the Ontario government's guidelines for monitoring water quality and reporting any contamination were not incorporated into the COA.[320] In other words, although the town had an implicit 'obligation' to report contamination, it was not legally required to do so.

Since 1996, testing labs and water-testing services in Ontario have been privatized. In the event that private labs found contamination in water samples, their only obligation was to report these findings to the local municipal officials. Neither the Ministry of the Environment nor the Medical Officer of Health automatically received these testing results, even if they showed the presence of contaminants. Ontario's Drinking Water Objectives, last revised in 1994 (but not added to Walkerton's COA or those in several other municipalities surveyed by the *National Post*) require 'private operators of water supply systems . . . [to be] responsible for the quality of water at the consumer's tap.'[321]

To summarize, in the realm of water-supply management and testing, Ontario has a patchwork of bylaws, guidelines, and objectives but inconsistent or non-existent legally binding rules to protect its drinking water from contamination. Like a number of other municipalities in Ontario, Walkerton was not compelled to report findings of contamination to provincial officials or the local Medical Officer of Health. In other words, the town followed the reporting rules established by the Ministry of the Environment. (The equally important issues of accountability and the protection of the public interest are beyond the scope of this discussion. They are the subject of the second stage of the Walkerton inquiry.)

On the environment side, however, there is certainly some persuasive evidence that allows us to make educated guesses about what happened at Walkerton. These concern the management and inspection of drinking water. In addition, the failure of governments to require the containment of livestock sewage on privately owned property offers further insights into the Walkerton situation. In September 1999, Dr Murray McQuigge, medical officer of health with the Bruce-Grey–Owen Sound Health Unit and the man credited with alerting the public to the Walkerton situation, sent a memo to Bruce County Council warning about factory hog farms. Part of the memo read as follows:

> There have been studies that show downstream pollution by antibiotic-resistant bacteria. . . . Although this cannot be directly linked to hog farms, there is a high index of suspicion that this is the case. What is known is that in large farm productions that require large use of antibiotics, there are increasing concerns about the production of antibiotic-resistant bacteria. . . . There is increasing concern in Huron County that poor nutrient management on farms is leading to the degradation of the quality of ground water, streams and lakes.[322]

It is also evident that reductions in the operating budget of the Ministry of the Environment weakened its ability to monitor municipal water plants.

Between 1996 and 1998, the Ministry of the Environment saw its budget cut by 44 per cent and more than 800 jobs eliminated, including 220 in the field of environmental inspections.[323] Of this total, 37 district environmental officers who conducted plant inspections lost their positions. When the Progressive Conservative government privatized water testing in 1996, it laid off 42 per cent of the ministry staff dedicated to monitoring drinking water.[324] Table 4.3 shows the decline in the number of inspections of water plants since 1993/4.

Officials in the ministry were alarmed by the staffing cuts and warned in January of 1997 that severe reductions 'will have an obvious impact on the amount of work we can accomplish.'[325] The correlation between staff reductions and poor management practices will take more time to establish. However, the government did take the important step of calling for a public inquiry into what happened at Walkerton. In addition, on 12 June 2000, the government also passed legislation designed to protect government employees who testify at the inquiry. This law (referred to in some circles as whistle blower legislation) would

Table 4.3 Number of Water Plant Inspections in Ontario, by Fiscal Year

Fiscal Year	No. of Water-Plant Inspections
1993/4	470
1994/5	378
1995/6	188
1996/7	224
1997/8	186
1998/9	152
1999/00	184

'prohibit employment-based reprisals against anyone who discloses information to a commission established under the Public Inquiries Act.'[326]

Conclusions

When any commodity becomes scarce in supply, solutions are advanced that address either the 'supply' side or the 'demand' side of the problems. In the case of water, the technical solution advanced on the supply side by many international water experts is increased desalination in areas where water is scarce. An estimated 97 per cent of the water on earth is sea water.[327] Unlike the bulk trade of fresh water which is highly expensive, desalination is a technology that is being continually improved: 'The Middle East Desalination Research Centre, created in 1996 in Muscat in the gulf state of Oman, is where much of the more interesting work is being done.'[328] Another proposed solution, and one that is inherently troubling, is the redistribution of water from those countries that have water to those countries where water is scarce. Frederick Frey makes a compelling case that water is different from other renewable resources such as fish or wood:

> Water has four primary characteristics of political importance: extreme importance, scarcity, maldistribution, and being shared. These make internecine conflict over water more likely than similar conflicts over other resources. Moreover, tendencies towards water conflicts are exacerbated by rampant population growth and water-wasteful economic development. A national and international 'power shortage,' in the sense of an inability to control these two trends, makes the problem even more alarming.[329]

Although de Villiers concedes that water shortages may not necessarily lead to war, they most certainly lead to food shortages, increased poverty, and the spread of disease. Because they make people poorer, they increase the migrations of people, placing further strains on refugee camps in the developing world. As standards of living deteriorate, the potential for social unrest and violence increases.[330]

More solutions to the water problem have been advanced on the demand side. The first and most obvious is conservation of the world's water supply through reduced consumption. Economists argue that if water were priced as other commodities are, to take into account its real cost, including the cost of remedying pollution, consumption and waste would immediately be reduced.[331] Other fiscal measures designed to reduce wastefulness and promote conservation have also been suggested. One such measure is a water-depletion tax. De Villiers asks, 'Why should taxpayers subsidize the unsustainable withdrawal of groundwater?'[332] Yet another strategy, and one espoused by Cassandras from Malthus onwards, is a reduction in population growth rates, which would include improved programs in birth control.

Whatever measures are adopted by nation-states, no one country alone can solve the problems associated with water. Long-lasting and sustainable solutions to this critical problem must be solved internationally through world-wide co-operation. Although climate change will have a profound influence on freshwater supplies, climate change can be reversed only if there is an international 'will' to do so. On the management side, Walkerton has focused attention on the deterioration of water infrastructures and inspection practices. In the wake of Walkerton, the Ontario government has announced that it will be spending billions of dollars on infrastructure renewal. More important, however, it will be necessary to determine if water should be restored to its previous status of a 'public good'. If so, more money will be needed to restore the monitoring and inspection abilities of the Ministry of the Environment.

Suggestions for Further Reading

Fisheries

Davis, Anthony, *Dire Straits: The Dilemmas of a Fishery* (St John's: Institute of Social and Economic Research, 1991).

Glavin, Terry, *Dead Reckoning* (Vancouver: Douglas & McIntyre, 1996).

Palmer, Craig, and Peter Sinclair, *When the Fish are Gone* (Halifax: Fernwood Publishing, 1997).

Mining

McAllister, Mary Louise, and Cynthia Jacqueline Alexander, *A Stake in the Future: Redefining the Canadian Mineral Industry* (Vancouver: UBC Press, 1997).

Wirth, John D., *Smelter Smoke in North America* (Kansas City: University of Kansas Press, 2000).

Agriculture and Biotechnology

McHughen, Alan, *Pandora's Picnic Basket* (Oxford: Oxford University Press, 2000).

Forests

Marchak, M. Patricia, Scott L. Aycock, and Deborah M. Herbert, *Falldown: Forest Policy in British Columbia* (Vancouver: David Suzuki Foundation and Ecotrust Canada, 1999).

Pratt, Larry and Ian Urquhart, *The Last Great Forest* (Edmonton: NuWest Press, 1994).

Rajala, Richard Allan, *Clearcutting the Pacific Rain Forest* (Vancouver: UBC Press, 1998).

Wilson, Jeremy, *Talk and Log* (Vancouver: UBC Press, 1998).

Related Web sites

< www.walkertoninquiry.ca > This web site contains all transcripts of testimony given at the Walkerton Inquiry. At the time of writing the Commission has not completed its hearings.

Suggestions for Small-Group Discussion

1. Debate the issue of genetically modified foods. To what extent can Canada set its own policy when the United States continues to support the production of GM foods and oppose labelling?

2. Should the Canadian government be doing more to encourage organic farming practices? What measures have been instituted in other countries that might be useful in the Canadian context?

3. What is the current state of the fisheries on Canada's east coast and west coast? Do you believe that Canada's current practices and management can lead to sustainable fisheries?

4. Discuss the controversy surrounding fish farming.

5. Should Canadian mining companies with operations in other jurisdictions be subject to Canadian environmental regulations? To what degree should they be held accountable in the event of pollution or contamination accidents? Should there be an international tribunal to deal with cases of poor corporate citizenship?

6. In many respects, forestry policy in British Columbia appears to have been driven primarily by political considerations. Discuss.

7. To what extent do you believe that the tragedy at Walkerton will force governments to re-invest in infrastructure and their environmental ministries?

Chapter Five

The Health and Security Imperatives

The cancer epidemic is a reflection of uncontrolled, runaway industrial technologies.[1]

A team of American and Canadian scientists has for the first time found pesticides and industrial chemicals contaminating the amniotic fluid of unborn babies which could lead to the feminization of male foetuses.[2]

As we have seen earlier in this book, the public's interest in the environment has tended to wax and wane over the last three decades under the influence of various streams of green political thought. The environment, as a public-policy issue, has usually been thought of as a stand-alone issue. In certain respects, this helps to explain why it has so easily been dismissed by politicians as an election issue and why the public's interest and support has not been consistent. Indeed, in the 2000 general election, little attention was paid to the environment with the lion's share of campaign rhetoric being devoted to health care and tax cuts. There is a certain irony to the tenor of the most recent federal election campaign given the mounting evidence of a strong causal relationship between the environment and health. There is growing medical and scientific evidence of a direct effect between environmental contaminants and health disorders among adults, children, and wildlife. Linking environmentalism with health issues, in my view, would be of enormous strategic importance for the Canadian environmental movement and would mark a decisive shift in green political thought to the human-welfare ecology stream that was summarized in Chapter One. There is already evidence that this link is being taken seriously at the federal level. In May 2000 the House of Commons Standing Committee on the Environment issued an extensive report entitled *Pesticides: Making the Right Choice for Protection of the Environment*. In the same month the Canadian Environmental Law Association and the Environmental Health Committee of the Ontario College of Family Physicians published a major joint study called *Environmental Standard Setting and Children's Health*. Although the tone of these two reports and a number of their recommendations differ, both acknowledge that the correlation between environmental contaminants and health is irrefutable. Yet another study, *Human Health and Global Climate Change: A Review of Potential Impacts in the United States*, commissioned by the PEW Center on Global Climate Change, was released in December 2000. Moreover, in the aftermath of the violence related to the Burnt Church fishing dispute in the summer of 2000 and conflicts elsewhere over scarce resources, it is also apparent that there is a correlation between the environment and security.

This chapter argues that environmental degradation is increasingly being viewed through the lenses of health and security. Traditionally, health-care analysts and advocates have generally concentrated on tangible factors such as beds, equipment, and health care personnel rather than preventive measures related to the environment. If environmental groups can successfully link the policy areas of health care and the environment in presenting their views, we will witness a 'greening' of health care policy and advocacy. Similarly, assuming that peace and stability are desirable social objectives both at home and abroad, the environment will likely be viewed as an increasingly important factor. This chapter will highlight a series of issues that all have a bearing on human health and welfare, including acid rain, toxic substances, ozone depletion, pesticides, climate change, and municipal waste management. The second section of the chapter discusses the ways in which environmental issues pose a threat to security—both domestically and in the international arena.

The Health Imperative

In 1880 an American neurologist, George M. Beard, observed symptoms of 'neurasthenia' or 'American nervousness' in his patients. The symptoms included fatigue, short-term memory loss, and sore joints and muscles. The cause for this condition, Beard argued, was technological progress itself, namely steam power, the printing press, and factories.[3] This early identification of environmental factors as causal agents of health problems was all but forgotten when miasmic theory[4] was abandoned in favour of germ theory. By the 1970s, scientists turned their attention to the gene theory of disease, which has emerged as the dominant theory in all fields of medicine, including environmental medicine.

The subfield of environmental health is a growing area of public health. Environmental-health problems include not only the direct effects of pollutants that are inhaled, swallowed, or absorbed through the skin but also the indirect effects of toxic agents that damage stable ecosystems and pose further risks to the health of humans and wildlife.[5]

The Politics of Cancer: The Lifestyle Approach versus Exposure to Carcinogens

Sandra Steingraber, a survivor of cancer and an ecologist, spells out the situation regarding scientific proof of the environment-cancer link as follows:

There is no one study that constitutes what we in the scientific community would call absolute proof of a connection between cancer and the environment. Instead, what exists are many well designed, carefully constructed studies that all together tell a consistent story. So I begin to see that each of these studies is like a little piece of a jigsaw puzzle. By themselves they are provocative, but they really only make sense if you bring all the pieces together and look at how they form a kind of startling picture. And I think it's a picture that we ignore at our peril.[6]

One of the methodological difficulties in drawing linkages between environmental contaminants and illness is that there are many gaps in knowledge. For example, of all chemicals that are produced, relatively few have been tested to determine their influence on health. Moreover, except in the case of lead, mercury, and PCBs, little is known about how chemicals affect the health of children.[7] Furthermore, the findings of animal studies may not be directly applicable to humans.[8] In other words, there are gaps in our knowledge about the effects of contaminants on health. Nevertheless, there are considerable data that do point to serious health implications of environmental contaminants.

Although many other diseases are declining, cancer rates rose steadily throughout the century. The American Cancer Society has predicted that this disease will become the world's leading cause of death sometime in the twenty-first century.[9] A study, *Everyday Carcinogens: Stopping Cancer before It Starts* (1999), which was released as part of a workshop on cancer prevention at McMaster University in March 1999, concluded that cancer rates in Ontario among women rose dramatically between 1966 and 1996. These increases are particularly apparent in breast cancer (29 per cent increase), non-Hodgkin's lymphoma (106 per cent increase), lung cancer (349 per cent increase), and melanoma (116 per cent increase). For men, increases have been observed in rates of prostate cancer (102 per cent), melanoma (273 per cent), non-Hodgkin's lymphoma (115 per cent), and testicular cancer (115 per cent). For both men and women, rates of thyroid cancer have also increased by 133 per cent and 146 per cent, respectively.[10]

The general strategy adopted by western industrialized countries in waging the war against cancer has been to put increasingly large research and financial resources into gene research and the development of new drugs. As Robert Proctor says, the causes of cancer have been known for years and they include 'bad habits, bad working conditions, bad governments, and bad luck, the latter including such things as the luck of the genetic draw and the culture into which one is born.'[11] The Canadian Cancer Society continues to attribute 60 to 70 per cent of cancers to 'lifestyle choices'. This 'lifestyle' factor for increased rates in cancer has recently come under fire by a number of researchers and ecologists who argue that it is not the only explanation. As evidence, they point to some increased rates for cancer among children and wildlife. The Canadian Institute of Child Health has reported that there has been a 25 per cent increase in the last twenty-five years in cancer incidence among children fifteen years of age and younger.[12] In particular, this increase in prevalence has been observed in certain childhood cancers, including brain cancers, acute lymphoblastic leukemia, Wilm's tumor, and testicular cancer.[13] There is a parallel epidemic of cancer in wild animals. Steingraber observes: 'Animals are in some ways better to study when raising questions about cancer in the environment than humans because wild animals don't drink, smoke or hold stressful jobs. They don't have bad diets. So you can't blame lifestyle factors on the ascendant rise of cancer among fish.'[14] While ecologists are in no way suggesting that 'lifestyle' factors are not important—particularly in light of the irrefutable evidence that smoking and certain kinds of diet do pose significant risks—they do believe that the link between the environment and cancer warrants further study. In quantifying the connection between cancer and exposure to contaminants, Dr Samuel Epstein concludes that 'three-quarters of the rise in US cancer rates can be attributed to exposure to carcinogens in the environment, workplaces, food, cosmetics, and consumer products.'[15]

In her acclaimed study of the cancer-environmental connection entitled *Living Downstream*, Steingraber agrees that this current 'lifestyle' approach to cancer research and emphasis on genetic research should not be the only avenues pursued: 'collectively, fewer than 10 per cent of all malignancies are thought to involve inherited mutations.'[16] Moreover, inheritance is 'the one piece of the puzzle we can do absolutely nothing about.'[17]

The redirection of some of the limited funds for cancer research from strategies that consider cancer a problem of *behaviour* to one that also sees it as a problem of *exposure* would be a positive first step in identifying disease-causing agents.[18] Steingraber claims that the orthodoxy of lifestyle defines the public-education literature on breast cancer. Warnings about exercise, low-fat diets, breast self-examinations, family history, timing of childbirth, and mammograms are common themes in this literature. Both mammography and breast self-examination, for example, are tools that have been developed to detect cancer in its early stages. However, as Steingraber notes, 'Detecting cancer, no matter how early, negates the possibility of preventing cancer. At best, early detection may make cancer less fatal, allowing us, as the epidemiologist Robert Millikan puts it, "to live in a toxic soup without breasts or prostates, et cetera".'[19]

Contamination and Human Rights:
Towards a Human-Rights Approach to Cancer

In 1962, the biologist Rachel Carson was one of the first scientists to sound the alarm about the health risks of massive spraying regimens of pesticides. In her book *Silent Spring*, she called on the public to demand from their legislators an explanation about the frightening menace they were being asked, without their consent, to endure. She argued that humankind has an *obligation to endure*, and that part of our job is to ensure that we pass on a safe and healthy environment to succeeding generations. This obligation required humankind to investigate other forms of environmental management, including biological ones. She asserted that it was our right not only to know about the poisons that were being released into the environment, but to be protected from this contamination. One of life's ironies is that Rachel Carson, who had no family history of breast cancer, was never a smoker or drinker, and exercised and walked regularly, died of breast cancer in 1965 at the age of fifty-six.

Steingraber states that it is necessary to discover our ecological roots and ask questions about the physical environment in which we have grown up—the sources of our drinking water (past and present), wind patterns, and the agriculture system that provides our food (present and past). Rather than supporting after-the-fact regimens, this approach argues that the release and disposal of known and suspected carcinogens must be stopped.

Therefore, the debate about the environmental-cancer-health nexus is dominated by two very different approaches—the lifestyles strategy and the human-rights strategy. There is no question that anti-smoking campaigns and publicity about healthy diets have tremendous value in educating the public about the known causes for cancer. However, there is a growing scientific literature that points to considerable value in a two-pronged strategy in the war against cancer.

Other Health Effects

As well as cancer, a host of other ailments have been attributed to environmental agents; they include spontaneous abortion, asthma and other respiratory diseases, environmental chemical sensitivity, and reproductive and endocrine abnormalities. As it pertains to reproduction, much of the knowledge stems from studies of acute toxic exposure, such as the accidental exposures to PCB-contaminated oil in Taiwan and Japan, after which the rates of spontaneous abortion were unusually high.[20] Higher rates of spontaneous abortion than normal have also been found in certain occupations where solvents or pesticides are used. As for asthma, its increase—particularly in children—has been alarming. In Canada, there has been a fourfold increase in asthma in children under the age of fifteen over the last fifteen years.[21] Statistics Canada research for 1994/95 indicate that asthma prevalence among children under fifteen was 11.2 per cent (compared to 2.5 per cent in 1978/79). Furthermore, it was concluded that an estimated 672,000 Canadian children have some form of asthma.[22] Asthma is now the leading cause of hospital admission in Canada, and the most frequent trigger for an attack is air pollution.[23] Although there is no definitive study that points to environmental factors as being the primary *cause* of new asthma cases, it has been posited that the likely factors have been increased exposure to indoor allergens, including house dust mites, cats, cockroaches, and moulds whose influences have been exacerbated by more-airtight houses.[24] Similar increases in other respiratory ailments, such as bronchitis, have also been linked to long-term exposure to acid aerosols and other airborne pollutants. In addition to asthma, there has been a steady increase in new kinds of illnesses that scientists believe are related to the environment. Environmental or multiple-chemical sensitivity is a condition characterized by 'a cluster of symptoms, such as headache, breathing difficulties, fatigue, muscle aches and inability to think and function.'[25] Although there are no conclusive causes of this condition, anecdotal evidence points to low levels of chemicals.

In addition to having direct effects on human health, some pesticides and other chemicals can have indirect effects by altering the normal functioning of glands that secrete hormones. Endocrine disrupters are chemicals that have some structural similarities to normal hormones and that bind to the same receptor of the naturally produced hormone. However, unlike the normal hormone, which when bound to its specific receptor produces biochemical responses that characterize normal endocrine functioning, disrupters may either enhance normal endocrine functioning or block it.[26] Most of the research in this area has been on animals living in heavily polluted environments. Among the other effects are ambiguous or congenitally malformed genitalia in birds, reptiles, and fish; impaired fertility; and abnormal reproductive development and behaviour. Abnormalities in the thyroid and immune systems have also been observed.[27] Although the evidence is not conclusive, some studies have reported that sperm counts may also be declining. According to the World Wildlife Fund (Canada), about fifty chemicals are considered to have hormone-disrupting effects and thirty-nine of these are pesticides registered for use in Canada.[28] Another study, released in August 2000 by the Canadian Institute of Child Health, entitled *The Health of Canada's Children* concluded: 'chronic, low-level exposure to pesticides, smog, food additives, and other chemicals could also create a host of public-health problems for coming generations, including limiting the ability of prospective parents to conceive.'[29] Although the scientific evidence to confirm this finding is not conclusive, it has been speculated that there may also be a link between attention-deficit hyperactivity disorder, among other learning disabilities, and exposure to environmental contaminants. In particular, it is thought that lead, PCBs, and methylmercury may prevent proper brain development if a fetus or young child is exposed to them.[30] Other causes of concern for children are contaminants in indoor environments, where it has been estimated that young Canadians spend 90 per cent of their time. All of these studies suggest that it is imperative to assess the effect of environmental contamination on children more carefully: 'Today's children are born with a body burden of synthetic, persistent organic pollutants—the consequences of which will not be known for another 50 years or so.'[31]

Others have attempted to draw attention to the health issue by framing the problem in economic terms. For example, the Ontario Medical Association[32] estimated that health care costs caused by poor air quality would amount to nearly $630 million in 2000 and that the costs from worker sick days would amount to $566 million. Put another way, they are 'direct, out-of-pocket expenses for taxpayers, employers, and employees in this province.'[33]

The environmental lobby, broadly construed, has launched a two-pronged attack in presenting the argument that health and the environmental are related. On one hand, it has played a lead role in collaborating with medical practitioners in studies pointing to persuasive scientific data in supporting their position that environmental contaminants are having a significant influence on the health of Canadians and wildlife. Within the general framework of light green environmentalism and the human welfare ecology stream, in particular, environmentalists are calling on governments and health researchers to re-think the ways in which they spend health care dollars. They are also calling on governments and businesses to reduce the number of contaminants released into our environment. More market-oriented arguments linking environment and health have calculated the actual dollar costs of health-care spending and labour hours lost in attempting to influence public opinion, industry, and governments.

Transboundary and International Environmental Issues with Implications for Health

The discussion that follows examines a series of environmental issues that emerged in the 1970s, 1980s, and 1990s and that have implications for human and animal health. Many of these issues have evolved into critical challenges to Canada and the world because unless efforts are made to address the environmental degradation associated with each of them, there will be enormous health costs. A number of these issues, such as the thinning of the ozone layer and climate change, are linked. Several of them have resulted in international agreements, called protocols or framework conventions. This discussion will highlight the objectives of these protocols and the progress that has been made toward the stated objectives. It will also identify the political factors that are delaying the implementation of these measures. The following issues will be discussed: acid rain, toxic substances (persistent organic pollutants, pesticides, and other pollutants), the thinning of the ozone layer and the Montreal Protocol, climate change and the Kyoto Protocol, and solid-waste management.

Acid Rain

Not all acid rain is a by-product of industrialization; natural sources such as volcanoes also contribute to the problem. However, even the huge eruption of Mount St Helen's emitted the equivalent of only 1 per cent of annual US emissions from human sources. The principal culprit has been the increase in emissions caused by human activities. In 1960, global emissions of sulphur dioxide from human activities were less than 10 million tonnes; by 1980 they rose to an estimated 160 million tonnes.[34]

Acidity is measured on the pH scale, 7 constituting a neutral value. All values above that are described as alkaline, while those below are acidic. Most scientists agree that acid rain has a pH of 1.5 to 5.5. By way of comparison, vinegar has a pH of about 3 and lemon juice about 2.1. In addition to the devastating effects of acid rain on vegetation, many forms of wildlife have also been adversely affected. Some fish species, in particular, do not respond well to changes in water chemistry. For example, salmon cannot tolerate pH levels much below 6, and perch die below 5. Sweden, which has been particularly hard hit, has seen its fish stock decline in 9,000 lakes.[35] Populations of birds that depend on coniferous forest for habitats have also declined precipitately. It has also been demonstrated that acid rain can be harmful to human health, in part because people can no longer enjoy the fish and plant life in lakes, rivers, and streams. However, it has also been observed that toxic metals mobilized by acidic water 'enter human water supplies and produce chronic toxicity.'[36] These toxic metals may also leach out of plumbing pipes, solder joints, and aluminum water containers. Although definitive evidence is still not available, several studies have found an excess of aluminum in the damaged brain tissue of people with Alzheimer's disease and amyotrophic lateral sclerosis (Lou Gehrig's disease).[37]

Acid rain was first analysed and observed in 1872 by a British pollution inspector, Robert Angus, but it is not considered to have been recognized as a serious problem until the 1960s, when trees in Germany's Black Forest began to appear ill. The symptoms were discoloration, shedding of needles and leaves, thinning of crowns and canopies, and a decreased resistance to frost, drought, and disease.[38] Subsequently, it was determined that the major causes of acid rain were gases emitted by the burning of fossil fuels—sulphur dioxide and oxides of nitrogen, which in combination with moisture from rain, snow, fog, or dew on the ground, formed sulphuric and nitric acids.

Research by a number of Scandinavian scientists served as the basis for a report on acid rain presented by Sweden to the 1972 UN Environment Conference. This was the first conclusive evidence that acid rain was transported long distances in the atmosphere and that the acidity of rain had been rising steadily since the 1950s.[39] By 1989, more than half the trees surveyed in Czechoslovakia, the United Kingdom, Germany, Estonia, and Tuscany had lost over 10 per cent of their leaves. In the United States, three out of five trees had lost more than 10 per cent of their leaves. One in five had lost more than a quarter.[40]

Acid rain was described in June 1977 by then federal Environment Minister Romeo LeBlanc as 'an environmental time bomb', indeed, 'the worst environmental problem ever faced by Canada.'[41] Moreover, it was recognized that the problem was transboundary in nature and that both Canada and the United States were responsible. By 1978, both countries had monitoring networks in operation and had agreed to establish a joint scientific committee, known as the Bilateral Research Consultation Group (BRCG) to study the problem.[42] The report of the BRCG, issued a year later in 1979, estimated that American emissions of sulphur dioxide were five times greater than those of Canada and that American emissions of nitrous oxides were ten times greater.[43] Despite this sense of urgency, the Canadian negotiations encountered several formidable political obstacles in the United States. First, in response to the oil crisis of the 1970s,

President Jimmy Carter announced that $10 billion would be committed to converting oil-fired power plants to coal-fired plants. This would only worsen the acid rain problem. Second, as noted by Munton and Castle,

> the United States lacked the necessary legislative basis to deal with their acid rain problem. While the 1972 and 1977 Clean Air Acts led to significant improvements in urban air quality and a reduction in smog, there were no provisions specifically designed to combat the problem of long-range transport of air pollutants.[44]

The necessary amendments to the Clean Air Act were sure to rouse the ire of a number of powerful interests in the United States, including the coal mining lobby and a number of large coal-producing states. Although a memorandum of intent committing the two countries to negotiate an acid rain agreement was signed in 1980 by Jimmy Carter and Pierre Trudeau, the issue fell off the political agenda when Ronald Reagan won the presidential election that November. So began a war on US environmental policy, a chilling of relations between Canada and the United States, and a stalemate in the bilateral negotiations on acid rain. More evidence about the transboundary nature of acid rain was revealed in 1983 by a report of the National Academy of Sciences, which directly linked acid precipitation in the northeastern United States and Canada with industrial emissions. The report concluded that the incidence of acid rain could be reduced by placing stringent controls on industrial emissions.[45] This report was significant because it served as a reminder that acid rain was a persistent problem requiring political commitment from both the Canadian and American governments. Even with this new evidence, Washington was not persuaded to put the issue on its political agenda.

Delegations of NGOs and politicians from both Canada and the United States began to take their case directly to the Congress and to the American public in efforts to draw attention to the acid-rain problem. However, it was also apparent that Canada had to put its own house in order before it could expect the United States do the same. On the international front, Ottawa convened a meeting of western developed states—named the '30 per cent club'—in 1984 when they agreed to reduce their sulphur dioxide emissions by at least 30 per cent.[46] By all accounts, the United States was not invited to attend the meeting. With the victory of Brian Mulroney and his Conservatives in 1984 came a decided change in approach to bilateral negotiations with the Americans. Unlike the acrimonious relationship that had characterized the Trudeau government's relationship with its southern neighbour on the acid rain issue, Mulroney had gone on the record as seeking a more co-operative and conciliatory approach in US-Canadian relations. Although his campaign had identified acid rain as a critical issue, it became evident that the Reagan administration was not interested in a bilateral agreement. Beginning in 1985, Environment Canada managed to persuade the seven eastern provinces to agree to a 50 per cent reduction in their sulphur dioxide emissions;

the last province, coal-producing and coal-burning Nova Scotia, signed in 1987.[47] This federal-provincial environmental agreement has been hailed by some as one of the true success stories in Canadian environmental policy making.

In order to give the appearance that there was going to be more co-operation between Canada and the United States, Reagan and Mulroney appointed two special envoys—a former Ontario premier, Bill Davis, and a former US transportation secretary in Ronald Reagan's cabinet—to study the problem for a year. Their report confirmed what scientists had known for over thirty years: acid rain was a serious problem. Recognizing that new regulations to reduce emissions would not be well received by coal-producing states and by the coal and utility lobby, the report took a different tack, proposing a large investment by industry and government in so-called 'clean-coal' technologies. However, movement by the American government was slow, and once again an agreement on acid rain proved to be elusive, for the rest of the Reagan era.

A turning point in reaching an agreement with the Americans was the election of George Bush as the President in 1988. An important plank in his election campaign had been the environment, and after his victory, it became clear that he was serious about putting the environment back onto the US political agenda. He appointed an environmentalist to be the Administrator of the Environmental Protection Act (EPA) and he committed his administration to passing a new Clean Air Act that would contain provisions to reduce emissions of sulphur and nitrogen oxides. By 1990, the Act was passed, and a year later the Canada-US Air Quality Agreement was ratified, some thirteen years after acid rain had been first described as an 'environmental time bomb'. The US Clean Air Act mandated that by 2006 sulphur dioxide would be reduced by 10 million tons from 1980 emission levels and nitrogen oxide would be reduced by 2 to 4 million tons.[48]

The time that it took to ratify a bilateral agreement on acid rain speaks to the difficulties inherent in dealing with transboundary environmental problems. It also reflects how politics can both undermine negotiations, as was evident with the anti-environmental tenor of the Reagan administration, and facilitate decisive action, as was seen in the relatively quick action taken by President George Bush after his election in 1988.

In 1997, Canada undertook its second major review of acid rain and its effects. The 1997 *Canadian Acid Rain Assessment* revealed that both Canada and the United States had made considerable progress in reducing their emissions of sulphur dioxide.[49] By 1995, Canadian and American emissions were down from their 1980 levels by 43 per cent and 28 per cent respectively.[50] However, other findings were less encouraging. Of 202 lakes that have been monitored in southeastern Canada since the early 1980s, 33 per cent had become less acidic, 56 per cent showed no change, and 11 per cent had become more acidic.[51] In addition, new research revealed that nutrients such as calcium that are essential for healthy trees are being lost from soils exposed to acid deposition:

Our current control programs for reducing Canadian and American sulphur dioxide emissions do not go far enough to protect many of our forests and lakes. When the Canadian and US acid rain programs were established, they were expected to reduce the maximum deposition of sulphates in precipitation from levels as high as 40 kg per hectare to a target load of no more than 20 kg per hectare by 2010. Current data reveals that this means that US and Canadian emissions will have to be reduced by another 75 per cent, far higher than was anticipated.[52]

While the acid rain problem has not been eradicated in the developed world, it has, to a large degree, been controlled by a series of measures, including shifts to fuels with a lower sulphur content and stricter requirements for flue extraction. These measures have led to a reduction in sulphur dioxide emissions from OECD countries by an estimated 38 per cent between 1970 and 1988. However, acid rain is now a new threat to the vegetation and waterways of developing countries in the South as they become industrialized.

Toxic Substances

Environment Canada operates a national system of air pollution monitoring stations known as the National Air Pollution Surveillance (NAP) network. As an additional safeguard, many provinces also have their own monitoring networks. For the most part, the pollutants measured are carbon monoxide, sulphur dioxide, and airborne lead. Between 1977 and 1989, emissions of these substances from the industrial sector declined. According to Monica Campbell, big cities like Montreal, Toronto, and Vancouver have experienced a decline in industry and an increase in less polluting commercial activity over the past 100 years.[53] However, these same positive results have been absent in the transportation sector.[54] Transportation, and particularly car emissions, are a main source of air pollutants in most cities. Industry continues to be a major contributor of volatile organic compounds (VOCs), and electrical utilities are the main source of sulphur oxides. Vehicles are the primary sources of higher levels of nitrogen oxides, carbon monoxide, particulates, and benzene. It has been estimated that motor vehicles contribute up to 83 per cent of all emissions of benzene (a human carcinogen) in Canada and that petroleum refining and chemical processing contribute less than 10 per cent.[55] In Canada, it is not unusual to hear of air quality warnings that warn young children, the elderly, and those with respiratory problems not to go outside unless necessary. And, though there are more calls to emergency services during those air-quality advisories, we have yet to experience air-related illness on a large scale. The most famous historical episode of fatal air pollution occurred in London during a cold spell in 1952, when an estimated 4,000 people died within five days of exposure to a 'black fog'. This was caused by a stagnant air mass and increased burning of coal in power plants and fireplaces in which the 'resultant elevated levels of sulphur dioxide and particulates greatly increased the incidence of bronchitis, influenza, respiratory disease, pneumonia, heart disease, and lung cancer.'[56] Although smoke had been a problem for over three centuries in London, the smog of 1952 was what drew widespread attention to the seriousness of air pollution.

On 7 December 2000, Canada and the United States signed an agreement to reduce the pollution that causes smog, most of it from power plants on both sides of the border. According to this agreement, the long-term goal is to 'substantially reduce pollutants such as nitrogen oxide and VOCs, mainly from power plants, by 2010. The first step is to cut nitrogen oxide emissions by 2004.'[57] More recently, the Environment Minister, David Anderson, announced on 19 February 2001 that the federal government will spend $120 million over several years to fight smog, the largest part of the money being earmarked for motor-vehicle emissions. Beginning with the 2004 model year, there will be stricter emission standards for cars and trucks. An estimated $30 million of the total will be spent updating the air-quality monitoring stations across Canada with some $23 million targeted towards expanding a database of polluters and pollutants available to the public online.[58]

Persistent Organic Pollutants (POPs)

Described by many as the 'worst of the worst' of toxic substances, persistent organic pollutants (POPs) are a group of contaminants consisting of many industrial chemicals and some pesticides that are highly toxic to wildlife and humans. They remain in the environment for a long time because they are not easily degraded. They are soluble in fat (but not in water) and therefore become stored in fatty tissues of organisms that ingest them.[59] Examples of POPs include PCBs, dioxins, and furans, which are a trace contaminant of PCBs. At one time PCBs were widely used in a number of industrial applications, including electrical transformers, hydraulic fluids, flame retardants, adhesives, and plasticizers.[60] Despite being banned in 1970, they continue to be present in the environment because of their persistence and their continued use elsewhere. Most human and animal exposure to PCBs comes from food, particularly breast milk, fish, fatty meats, and dairy products.[61] The World Wildlife Federation states that POP levels tend to be highest in species at the top of the food chain, such as eagles, polar bears, and killer whales.[62] Some dioxins are produced naturally (by forest fires and volcanoes); however, most are a by-product of the petrochemical industry, waste incineration, and the pulp and paper industry, among others.[63] Health Canada estimates for the average total daily intake of POPs are shown in Table 5.1. Exposure is greatest among breast-fed infants and children eleven years of age and older, among people living in the Great Lakes basin, and among the Innu in northern Quebec, whose exposure is highest of all Canadians and among the highest in the world.[64] This is largely because much of their diet consists of fish and other marine life that have been heavily exposed to POPs.

Table 5.1 Estimated Exposures to POPs for Great Lakes General Population

Age Group	PCBs[a]	Dioxins and Furans[b]	DDT and related compounds[a]
0–6 months (breastfed)	808.18	57.05	701.27
0–6 months (formula)	47.96	12.56	222.85
7 months–4 years	65.60	9.54	226.35
5–11 years	45.93	4.69	121.21
12–19 years	24.73	2.25	58.68
20+ years	21.83	1.20	43.57
Average daily lifetime intake	33.00	2.60	69.51
Intake guidelines	PTDI[c]=1,000	TDI[d]=10	TDI[d]=20,000

[a] In ng/kg bw/day
[b] In pg TEQ/kg bw/day
[c] PTDI = Health Canada's Provisional Tolerable Daily Intake
[d] TDI = Tolerable Daily Intake

Source: M. Haines et al., *Persistent Environmental Contaminants and the Great Lakes Basin Population* (Ottawa: Health Canada, 1998).

Global Treaty on POPs

On 9 May 2001, the Environment Minister, David Anderson, announced that Canada will sign and ratify the United Nations Convention on POPs. This global agreement, known as the Stockholm Convention, will help to reduce emissions of twelve toxic substances known as the 'dirty dozen'.[65] Canada is the first country to announce that it will ratify this agreement. An International Negotiating Meeting for the proposed legally binding treaty on POPs had met on five occasions—the fifth and last session was held in Johannesburg, South Africa, in December 2000. Canada's policy has been to lobby for the complete elimination of PCBs, DDT, and unintentional by-products such as dioxins and furans as the long-term goal. It has also committed to provide a financial contribution to assist developing countries in meeting this goal. However, there are still a number of disputed provisions in the draft treaty. Some critics argue that it does not go far enough in promoting the use of clean safe technology to prevent the use, production, release, and disposal of POPs.[66] Others object to the supremacy clause, which would give precedence to obligations of other international trade agreements such as those under the WTO.[67]

Pesticides

Since the publication of Rachel Carson's *Silent Spring*, what have we learned about the use of pesticides in the air we breathe, the water we drink, the places we work, and the food we eat? According to a report prepared by the Canadian Food Inspection Agency in November 1998, the amount of pesticide left on fresh fruit and vegetables grown in Canada had more than *doubled* since 1994.[68] Residues long considered to be more common on imported produce are now found at more or less the same rate on our home-grown produce. The report revealed that nearly 25 per cent of all produce that was tested randomly showed signs of residues, even after their inedible skins were peeled off (see Table 5.2). Defenders of the quality of our produce and the regulations that govern it argue that one explanation for the higher levels is improved testing methods that were not used ten years previously. However, this does not explain why some produce is more susceptible to pesticide residues than others. For example, residues were found on 49.1 per cent of apple shipments but on only 8.4 per cent of blueberries.[69]

Although the lifestyles approach continues to have considerable merit in the setting of public-health objectives, it does little to ensure that unborn fetuses,

Table 5.2 What's in That Apple?

Pesticide	Shipments	Some Uses and Effects
Azinphos-methyl	59	Insecticide; suspected carcinogen; toxic to birds, fish
Captan	3	Fungicide; carcinogen; toxic to fish
Carbaryl	6	Insecticide; suspected carcinogen; decreases fertility
Chlorpyrifos	2	Insecticide; sterility in bulls; toxic to birds and fish
Diazinon	3	Insecticide; toxic to birds, fish, and amphibians
Dicofol	16	Insecticide; carcinogen; toxic to fish and aquatic insects
Dimethoate	16	Insecticide; suspected carcinogen; kidney damage
Diphenylamine	122	Fungicide; effects unknown
Endosulfan	20	Insecticide; suspected carcinogen; eye and kidney damage
Phosalone	80	Insecticide; toxic to birds, fish, bees, and crustaceans
Phosmet	12	Insecticide; suspected carcinogen; toxic to birds and fish
Propargite	20	Acaricide; fetotoxin; eye damage

Source: J.M. Samet, 'Learning About Air Pollution and Asthma', *American Journal of Respiratory and Critical Care Medicine* 149, no. 6 (1994): 1398.

children, and adults of all ages have a safe environment in which to live. The data are still not conclusive, but concern is being expressed about how pesticides affect children's health. An American study found that 'pesticide levels set for adults could damage brain functions of fetuses and children.'[70] Other studies have concluded that there is a link between pesticides and lower intelligence and less developed motor skills in children.[71]

More recently, studies have revealed disturbing amounts of pesticide in amniotic fluid. Although DDT is no longer manufactured or used in North America, a by-product of it—DDE—was found in 30 per cent of the amniotic fluid tested in a joint American-Canadian study. It is not certain what all the effects of this contamination are, but one possible effect is the feminization of male fetuses. In previous studies, DDE has been implicated as an agent that blocks the testosterone receptors in the fetuses, which are a key to sexual development.[72] Coupled with certain chemicals that occur naturally in food, such as phytoestrogens in soybeans, pesticides may damage the development of the male reproductive tract.[73]

For all intents and purposes, Canadian governments have followed the lead of the United States in setting standards for pesticide use. Not only has the American research capacity in risk management and risk assessment been superior to ours, but the need to harmonize standards as a result of NAFTA suggests that this is a logical approach. However, Canada does have its own agency—the Canadian Pest Management Regulatory Agency (PMRA)—that is responsible for evaluating pesticides. Created in 1985, it is an agency of Health Canada but it has been given a certain amount of autonomy. Critics of the PMRA continue to insist that this agency should be an independent body.

As was indicated at the beginning of this chapter, the difficulty of proving definitive links between contaminants and health has resulted in the onus being placed on scientists, environmentalists, and researchers to prove that there is risk. While banning PCBs and DDT outright in 1970, government agencies have been more inclined to develop an 'acceptable' level of risk since that time. In the absence of definitive scientific proof, a new approach that has recently emerged uses the precautionary principle as the basis for policies to protect human health and the environment.[74] In a way, this allows a government to express concern about an issue without compelling evidence. The precautionary principle has been used in numerous international treaties, conventions, and protocols (as in the Biosafety Protocol concerning GM foods discussed in Chapter 4) and has become a customary rule or norm of international law. However, its use in a *domestic* application is relatively new. Although there is no unanimity as to the explicit meaning of this term, several conventions that have developed help to clarify its meaning and purpose. Where there *appears* to be a threat of harm, the onus should be on those threatening such harm to prove that the activity in question will not cause harm to the environment or human health.[75]

The US Food Quality Protection Act, passed in 1996, was hailed as an important statutory tool to be used in the reduction of pesticide use. However, the standard of proof demanded in risk assessment in the United States has resulted in only a few reductions in pesticide use and exposure.[76]

Other Pollutants

In 1997 the North American Commission for Environmental Co-operation (CEC) —the environmental watchdog agency set up under the North American Free Trade Agreement—identified Ontario as the second-worst polluter in North America (Texas was the worst). The third annual *Taking Stock* report showed that Ontario industries released almost 68.8 million kilograms of pollutants into the environment in 1996. Although that was almost 6 million kilograms less than in 1995, Ontario still overtook Louisiana, which had been second in 1995.[77] By comparison, Quebec ranked twentieth and Alberta twenty-seventh. The rankings are based 'both on direct emissions into air, land or water and on transfers made to other sites for disposal.'[78] Approximately 170 different pollutants are measured in the report. This same report listed two Ontario companies as among the twenty-five worst polluters in Canada and the United States—Co-Steel Lasco Ltd in Whitby, Ontario, for zinc transfers, and Inco Ltd in Sudbury, Ontario, for release of airborne sulphuric acid.[79] The Ontario government has been critical of these findings on the basis of the measurement system that was used. They argue that by combining direct emissions and transfers, the report gives an unfair picture of polluters and environmental conditions. Interestingly enough, little opposition to the report's findings has been voiced by American officials or politicians.

Water pollution

Water pollution does not come just from untreated sewage that is dumped into waterways in large cities or from fertilizers and pesticides in run-off from farms and golf course. It can also be an unintended consequence of large-scale water diversions. Perhaps the most damaging case of this nature occurred in the James Bay area in the mid-1970s.

In 1975 the Nishnawbe-Aski (better known as the Cree and Ojibway) and the Inuit of northeastern Canada entered into an agreement with the Province of Quebec in 1975 when they signed the James Bay and Northern Quebec Agreement. In return for ceding much of their traditional homeland to the Province for the purpose of constructing an enormous hydroelectric project, the Native people received $350 million. The project which was undertaken in three phases, ultimately involved the construction of three dozen dams and hundreds of dikes that were to have a major impact on a land mass roughly the size of France.[80]

The project never underwent an environmental assessment, and by the time phase one was underway, the ecological devastation had begun. The waterways in the area became seriously contaminated with highly toxic methyl mercury, which poisoned the fish—an important staple of the Cree and Inuit diet. It worked its way into the blood streams of the local population, causing widespread neurological disorders and learning disabilities in children.

Health Implications of the Thinning of the Ozone Layer

In the region called the stratosphere, some twenty-four kilometres up in the atmosphere, ozone is created and destroyed, primarily by ultraviolet radiation. Ironically, the ability of ozone to absorb a range of ultraviolet rays also leads to its destruction.[81] These processes of ozone production and destruction initiated by ultraviolet radiation have sometimes been called the 'Chapman Reactions' by scientists.[82] Although it represents a very small fraction of the atmosphere, ozone is critical for life on Earth. Since the beginning of time, natural processes have regulated the balance of ozone in the stratosphere:

> A simple way to understand the balance of ozone is to think of a leaky bucket. As long as water is poured into the bucket at the same rate that water is leaking out, the amount of water in the bucket will remain the same. Likewise, as long as ozone is being created at the same rate that it is being destroyed, the total amount of ozone will remain the same.[83]

Owing to the fact that ozone molecules move about the stratosphere in changing concentrations, scientists who observed ozone at ground level were never sure whether changes in local ozone levels were due to global alterations.[84] With new satellite technology, this uncertainty has been eliminated. So too, has the uncertainty surrounding the depletion of ozone. Scientists are now confident that the ozone layer is being depleted worldwide, partly owing to human activities. This phenomenon represents a serious health hazard for both the human and non-human world.

In 1974 two scientists from the University of California, Mario J. Molina and F.S. Rowland, were the first to sound the alarm about increasing amount of chlorofluorocarbons (CFCs) being discharged into the environment and the catastrophic effects that this could have on the ozone layer:

> It seems quite clear that the atmosphere has only a finite capacity for absorbing Cl atoms produced in the stratosphere, and that important consequences may result. This capacity is probably not sufficient in steady state even for the present rate of introduction of chlorofluoromethanes. More accurate estimates of this absorptive capacity need to be made in the immediate future in order to ascertain the levels of possible onset of environmental problems.[85]

In 1982 a British scientist, Joe Farman, first discovered the ozone hole in the Antarctic. By 1984, it was estimated that the hole covered some 14 million square kilometres. Since that time, global surveys have confirmed that ozone is being lost in all regions. For example, ozone levels over Europe were 8 per cent lower in 1991 than in the previous decade.[86]

Scientists initially thought that the layer might have been damaged by supersonic flights, space shuttles, or nitrous oxide emitted by fertilizers.[87] Since those earlier studies, it has now been discovered that the main culprits are chlorofluorocarbons (CFCs), which were invented in 1928 and first used in refrigerators and air conditioners. Later they became important ingredients in cleaning solvents and aerosols. The widespread use of CFCs, on a global scale, has only accelerated this thinning:

> Global production of the two main CFCs—CFC-11 and CFC-12—soared from a mere 2200 tonnes in 1940 to 126,700 tonnes a decade later and 491,700 tonnes in 1970. . . . Most of this was in the North. Developing countries produced only 14 per cent of the 1986 emissions. . . . They are inert, stable, non-flammable and longlived and can persist up to 130 years.[88]

The thinning of the ozone layer poses a significant health risk because ozone acts as a barrier to the most damaging forms of ultraviolet radiation. It has been estimated that if CFC use continues to grow at the same rate, by 2075, there could be an additional 43 million cases of cataracts and 98 million new cases of skin cancer, including 2 million additional cancer deaths. There are also profound implications for plant life. Enhanced ultraviolet radiation reduces the yields of many plants—from 5 per cent for wheat up to 90 per cent for squash. The height and leaf area of plants are adversely affected, as are flowering and germination. Ultraviolet radiation damages the cyanobacteria that fix nitrogen in paddy fields, and could reduce rice yields. And finally, it could speed global warming by damaging trees and phytoplankton, which absorb large amounts of carbon dioxide.[89] By the mid-1980s, scientists all over the world had become convinced that ozone depletion was a serious problem and that an international effort was needed to curb the use of the substances that contributed to this problem.

The Montreal Protocol on Substances that Deplete the Ozone Layer, 1987

In 1985, under the guidance of the United Nations Environment Programme (UNEP), governments of the world arrived at the Vienna Convention for the Protection of the Ozone Layer. Governments, for the first time, made the commitment to protect the ozone layer and to share scientific information of atmospheric processes.[90] Two years later, in 1987, policy makers from around the world meeting in Montreal signed the Montreal Protocol on Substances That Deplete the Ozone Layer, an agreement that has been hailed as 'one of the most successful cases of international co-operation on environmental issues.'[91] The success of the Montreal Protocol was particularly important as it was generally seen as a model for establishing the framework for the Kyoto Protocol on Climate Change.

Since the Montreal Protocol was first signed, there have been five subsequent amendments, all of which introduced more stringent reductions in CFC use in order to eliminate the use of CFCs and other ozone-thinning substances more quickly. As amended, the Montreal Protocol contains the following provisions:

- It phases in an outright ban on both the consumption and production in industrialized countries of a variety of substances including CFCs, halons, carbon tetrachloride, and methyl chloroform. It allows some reduced

production of between 10–15 per cent of 1986 levels for developing countries to satisfy 'basic domestic needs'.[92] Developing countries must fully
phase out their CFC and halon emissions by 2010.

- It phases in an outright ban on the consumption and production of
  hydrochlorofluorcarbons in developed countries by 1 January 2020 and in
  developing countries by 2040; of hydrobromofluorocarbons by 1 January
  1996; and of methyl bromide by 1 January 2005.

The Montreal Protocol also contained an agreement to co-operate in promoting
research, development, and the exchange of information on technologies dealing
with the containment, recovery, recycling, and destruction of these substances.
By way of a financial mechanism, the Protocol called for the creation of a multilateral fund to help developing countries meet the objectives of zero production
and consumption. According to the United Nations Environment Programme,
this fund has provided nearly a billion dollars to developing countries since 1991.
Developed countries have, for the most part, met the moratorium objectives of
the Protocol, although the Russian Federation and countries of central and eastern Europe have not met their deadlines and are receiving additional help from
the Global Environment Facility.[93] Funding for those countries was agreed to in
December 2000.

China and India continue to produce and consume CFCs and halons in large
amounts. In March 2000, the Multilateral Fund's executive committee agreed to
some $150 million to fund the complete closing of China's CFC production facili-
ties by 2010 and have made a similar arrangement worth $82 million with India.[94]

The Montreal Protocol was an innovative agreement, particularly in the development of a financial mechanism, the linking of policy making with specific and
technical advice, and its non-compliance procedure. Specifically, the parties to
the Protocol are allowed to impose trade sanctions on non-participating countries
that produce the banned substances. Some scientists believe that if the Protocol
is enforced, the ozone layer could fully recover some time in the twenty-first century.[95] However, there is a need to be vigilant in the assessment of new chemical
products that come onto the market. To this end, it was agreed at the most recent
meeting, in December 2000, that the Scientific Assessment Panel and the Economic Assessment Panel should collaborate in assessing the ozone-depleting
potential of all new chemicals and should work towards a co-operative relationship with the private sector for that purpose.[96]

The Ozone-Depleting Substances (ODS) Regulations, 1998 and 2000

Canada was one of twenty-three nations that signed the Montreal Protocol and
has been a signatory on subsequent revisions to it. In 1998 Canada passed its first
regulation which committed it to the emission reductions of the Montreal Protocol and to the subsequent four amendments. In December 1999, parties to the
Montreal Protocol—including Canada—met in Beijing to discuss further moratoriums on substances, including HCFCs and bromochloromethane. In addition, an

international phasing-out of methyl bromide was added, to be complete by 2005. Amendments to Canada's regulations reflecting the agreement reached at Beijing came into force on 1 January 2001. Several administrative clauses were added to the revised regulations, including the requirement of a person who proposes to import or export from Canada a controlled substance for the purpose of transit to notify Environment Canada at least fifteen days in advance.

Significant changes to this agreement include the immediate ban in the trade of bromochlormethane with countries that are not parties to the Montreal Protocol effective 1 January 2001 and a similar prohibition in the trade in HCFCs as of 1 January 2004. According to Canada's Environment Minister, David Anderson, 'Canadians can be proud of Canada's prominent role in the development and implementation of the 1987 Montreal Protocol. We have supported and adopted all previous amendments at the earliest opportunity to protect the ozone layer.'[97]

Climate Change and Human Health

Climate change is the quintessential global issue demanding action at every level of society—individually and collectively. Education and learning are necessary starting points for mobilizing action.[98]

Elizabeth Dowdeswell, United Nations Under-Secretary-General
and Executive Director of the United Nations
Environment Programme.

One of the difficulties in predicting the health consequences of climate change is that scientists are not totally certain or consistent in their estimates of the extent of actual climate change. The most recent report of the Intergovernmental Panel on Climate Change (IPCC), released on 22 January 2001—warns that the average temperature could rise between 1.4 and 5.8 degrees Celsius over the next hundred years. Only five years earlier, this same panel estimated that the maximum rise in temperature would be just 3.5 degrees.[99] This increase in the upper limit is significant because change of that magnitude is comparable to that which prompted the Ice Age 20,000 years ago. This estimate constitutes the strongest warning about climate change ever issued by an international body.[100]

The terms 'global warming', 'enhanced greenhouse effect', and 'thinning of the ozone layer' are often used interchangeably. However, the truth of the matter is that all of these contribute to a larger phenomenon called climate change. Climate change is not totally attributable to human activities. There have always been normal fluctuations in climate, such as those caused by El Niño. As defined by the United Nations Framework Convention, climate change is 'a change in climate which is attributed directly or indirectly to human activity that alters the composition of the global atmosphere and which is, in addition to natural climate variability, observed over comparable time periods.'[101] Often, climate variability is mistaken for climate change. In the summer of 2000, Canadians witnessed ninety-one tornadoes on the Prairies, more than double the normal number, and the storms in December 2000 were the worst seen in years. Moreover, flash flooding in Saskatchewan was the worst ever recorded on the Prairies. All of these events are examples of extreme variability of the weather which, according to Canadian climatologists, is 'one of the hallmarks of climate change.'[102]

Global warming refers generally to the natural warming trends that Earth has experienced through much of its history. The *enhanced greenhouse effect* is an intensification of the *natural* greenhouse effect caused by a concentration of greenhouse gases trapped in the atmosphere. This concentration has largely been caused by the burning of fossil fuels and the clearing of forests. Because the greenhouse effect absorbs most of the energy (by retaining it in the lower atmosphere) it is possible for life to survive. Without the natural greenhouse effect, the temperatures on Earth would be some 33°C colder than they are now.[103] Climate change, on the other hand, refers to changes in all the interconnected weather elements of the Earth (temperature, precipitation, and wind patterns).[104] Even though global warming and ozone depletion are interrelated atmospheric phenomena, they are not the same thing. Although changing levels of ozone can alter the climate system, the primary cause of climate change is the increase in atmospheric concentration of carbon dioxide, methane, nitrous oxide, and other greenhouse gases.[105]

Mitigating Measures versus Adaptation Strategies

In some cases, climate change will be beneficial for it will result in longer growing seasons and less harsh winters in certain regions of the world. For those states that have the capability and ingenuity, there *may* be economic advantages. Other areas—particularly tropical and subtropical countries—will be thrown into conditions of drought or flooding. While some government reports speak to the economic opportunities that might present themselves as a result of climate change, others talk about things that individuals and governments can do to alter the trajectory of climate change. Such attempts to change human behaviours and industrial practices are referred to as mitigating measures. They include targets agreed to at international Conferences such as Kyoto and targets established in federal-provincial undertakings. Recently, because many of these targets are not considered to be achievable and governments appear reluctant to force their countries to comply with them, an alternative to mitigation has been advanced. This strategy accepts the fact that there will be climate change and suggests that research should be concentrated on finding ways to adapt to these changes. This strategic shift to adaptation will require huge investments in infrastructure such as dikes to control rising sea levels.[106] There will also be stresses on water distribution and sewer systems as sea levels rise. Moreover, because extreme events are more likely, hydro lines, bridge piers, and dams are all highly vulnerable.[107] Environmental groups and most scientists believe that mitigation is the only strategy that governments should be entertaining. Some industrial groups, however, believe that the adaptation strategy offers considerable potential. If nation-states and industries are not prepared to commit themselves to mitigation targets, it may well be that adaptation will become our only choice, by default.

Greenhouse Gases (GHGs)

Many of the international and national initiatives that have been undertaken to address climate change involve reducing emission of greenhouse gases (GHG). Of these gases, carbon dioxide alone is said to account for 55 to 60 per cent of the warming effect.

> Like water and nitrogen, carbon has its own vast natural cycles. Some 39,000 billion tonnes are stored in the oceans. Another 1,550 billion tonnes are closeted in soils. Land plants stock 560 billion tonnes—445 billion tonnes of that locked up in forest and woodland. Soil and plants give out and reabsorb around 100 million tonnes per year.[108]

Although man-made carbon dioxide accounts for only a relatively small portion of the total, it is nevertheless compounding the problem. It has been estimated that the burning of fossil fuel emits around 5.4 billion tonnes of carbon each year. Tropical deforestation contributes perhaps 1.6 billion tonnes. Oceans and vegetation between them absorb just over half of our output.[109]

In the 1980s, CFCs were responsible for an estimated quarter of the man-made greenhouse effect and man-made methane accounted for an estimated 15 per cent of global warming. Methane (like carbon dioxide) is also part of the natural cycle. Some 170 million tonnes a year are produced by wetlands, termites, oceans, and fresh water. But the man-made output, running at 360 million tonnes a year, is now double that of natural sources.

Natural emissions of nitrous oxide total around 6 billion tonnes; human output is only a quarter of that. The chemical breakdown of fertilizers is thought to be responsible for four-fifths of the man-made emissions.

It has been concluded that greenhouse-gas-induced climate change will be felt particularly in nighttime temperatures,

> as the heat trapping effect of the greenhouse gases (GHGs) prevents radiative nighttime cooling of the earth. This climate change effect will also be exacerbated in cities by the 'urban heat island effect,' which involves the nighttime release of heat stored during the day in cement and metal urban materials.[110]

Global Climate Change

According to data from ice cores and other sources, the 1980s and 1990s were the warmest decades of the past hundred years, and temperature records reveal that the Earth has warmed by an average of 0.6°C over the past 100 years.[111] In order to cope with the environmental, social, and economic consequences of climate change, governments and scientists around the world are studying the problem. It has been difficult to predict just what the effects of climate change will be on people, animals, nature, and resources. The study *Human Health & Global Climate Change*, sponsored by the PEW Center on Global Climate Change, concludes that there will be both direct and indirect effects. Among the direct effects are those that cause physiological stress (for example, high temperatures) or bodily injury (such as storms and floods, for example). Indirect effects, on the other hand, refer to phenomena such as a decline in food supplies and the spread of certain diseases.[112] The direct effects in North America will include hotter summers and possibly colder winters. The United States has already witnessed considerable death tolls as a result of heat waves, in 1995, 1998, and 1999. This points to a connection between warmer temperatures and human health, particularly among the elderly and the poor.[113] For less vulnerable groups, continued exposure to warm temperatures leads to acclimatization, described as 'a physiologic change in the body that allows it to adapt to the increased warmth'.[114] Because of uncertainties about future climate variability and future trends in social and technological factors that may have mitigating effects, it is difficult to predict what heat-wave mortality rates might be in the years ahead.[115] Conflicting results have been obtained for studies of wintertime mortality: some conclude that lower temperatures will have a negligible effect on infectious diseases that peak in the winter (for example, influenza); others suggest there will be higher mortality rates.[116] It is also uncertain whether climate change will increase the frequency of severe events such as hurricanes and flooding, which can cause deaths, particularly in coastal areas and on flood plains.

Researchers are more certain about the indirect health effects of climate change. They know, for example, that warmer temperatures lead to higher levels of air pollutants and greater dispersion of fungal spores and pollen, which may increase allergic reactions and asthma.[117] It is also likely that tropical diseases will move northward into areas where there is little or no immunity.

Climate Change in Canada

> Canada really is the canary in a coal mine; we're likely to see the impacts of climate change first among countries. We're already at the point where it won't just affect your children or your grandchildren. This will have implications for you.[118]

In Canada, the federal government has undertaken an intensive study in attempting to educate Canadians about the implications of climate change for their own lives. In this sense, many of the findings are anthropocentric. This discussion will confine itself to an overview of the ways in which climate change may affect human and non-human health.

As the twenty-first century begins, the planet is 0.6 degrees Celsius warmer on average than it was at the beginning of the last century, according to Canadian climatologists. In Canada, temperatures are, on average, 1.1 degrees Celsius warmer and in Canada's northwest, the increase in temperature has been 1.5 or 1.6 degrees—nearly three times the global average increase.[119] This means that climate change has already started. As one scientist says: 'The train has left the station.'[120] Scientists have predicted that over the next century, Canada's average temperature may rise anywhere between 4.5 and 9 degrees Celsius, depending on location and season.[121]

For Canada's northern Native peoples, climate change will be catastrophic. It is expected that the permafrost could slowly melt, turning the Arctic tundra into a 'messy quagmire', which would not be traversable. It is also likely that there will be severe spring flooding along northern rivers, with implications for migration routes of northern wildlife. About the *specific* effects that global change may have on Canada, we cannot be certain. However, there are some general patterns that are known. For example, mid-latitude forests will be vulnerable to fires. It has also been predicted that, in areas now experiencing water shortages, this problem will worsen. This will lead to further loss of wildlife habitat and the disappearance of some wetlands. While Canada will likely be spared massive damage of the sort described earlier, it is likely that our coastal areas, forests, and agricultural lands located in warmer climates may be adversely affected by greater loss of soil moisture through evaporation, which would lead to crop failure.[122] The recent adverse effect on crops on the Prairies of a warm winter in 2000 and considerable wet weather in the spring and summer points to the potential impact of climate change. Many Prairie crops were infested with bacteria, fungi, and viruses—all of which might become more widespread as greenhouse gases heat up the planet.[123] It is expected that the greatest adverse effects will be

> on the developed coastlines and deltas, like the Vancouver region, Prince Edward Island, Halifax, and St John's. In these coastal areas, there may be more high tides and storm surges caused when storm winds dash large amounts of rising water against shorelines. Increased precipitation could lead to heavy spring flooding along many rivers in both Arctic and sub-Arctic areas of Canada's North.[124]

As for wildlife, it is likely that adaptable species will be able to fill new niches or expand their present habitats. However, it is also certain that a number of species may see their migration routes interrupted and find themselves stranded. The drying up of Prairie wetlands will devastate migrating and nesting waterfowl. In the Arctic, a loss of sea ice will likely cause massive problems for marine mammals, including seals, walruses, polar bears, and fish that are dependent on ice cover and cold water.[125]

UN Framework Convention on Climate Change (UNFCC), 1994, and the Kyoto Protocol, 1997

The Intergovernmental Panel on Climate Change (IPCC) was established in 1988 by the World Meteorological Organization and the United Nations Environment Programme out of growing concerns that the greenhouse effect would result in a warming of the Earth's surface. In December 1990, the UN General Assembly established the Intergovernmental Committee for a Framework Convention on

Climate Change. The result of the committee's negotiations was the Framework Convention on Climate Change that was presented at the United Nations Conference on Environment and Development in Rio de Janeiro in June 1992. Over 150 countries (including Canada) signed the agreement, which came into force on 21 March 1994. In December 1997, an international conference on greenhouse gases was held in Kyoto, Japan. After two days of talks, a global treaty to limit the production of greenhouse gases was negotiated.[126] Only thirty-eight developed nations and the countries in transition in central and eastern Europe were asked to make commitments at Kyoto; individual nations have different targets, but the overall reduction in greenhouse gases from 1990 levels is 5.2 per cent. Instead of establishing a specific target date, it was agreed that countries would be allowed to average their emissions over a five-year period (2008–2012).[127] The Kyoto Protocol addresses the six main types of greenhouse-gases: carbon dioxide (CO_2), methane (CH), nitrous oxide (NO), hydrofluorocarbons (HFCs), perfluorocarbons (PFCs), and sulphur hexafluoride (SF).

In particular, the Kyoto Protocol is concerned about the first three of these listed greenhouse gases because they are produced primarily by human activities. Currently, 175 countries have ratified the UNFCC, which includes measures such as binding commitments, targets and timetables for the reduction of carbon dioxide emissions, financial mechanisms, technology transfer, and responsibilities of developed and developing countries. However, there continue to be a number of stumbling blocks. The largest is that the reduction targets are voluntary. Although the treaty is legally binding for countries that ratify it, there are no penalties if the targets are not achieved. There is no incentive for some countries to become aggressive in meeting targets (such as imposing carbon taxes, for example) if others are allowed to continue with the status quo. In other words, reductions on carbon emissions suffer from the free-rider problem. This is a critical problem because no supranational organization has the authority to force compliance. Another problem is related to several provisions of Kyoto that are flexible, namely, emissions trading and credits for carbon sinks. While there is agreement that both of these ideas have merit and should be allowed, the details of these provisions have yet to be spelled out. A number of developed countries, including the United States, Japan, New Zealand, Australia, and Canada (known as the Umbrella group) would like—their critics argue—to maximize the provisions for trading emissions, allow emissions trading with developing countries, and include an excessive amount of carbon sinks in their emission calculations.

The term carbon sinks refers to the effect that protected forests and new forests have in absorbing carbon dioxide, which is the chief culprit in global warming. Proponents argue that carbon sinks would allow countries to establish less rigid emissions reductions. By the same token, the inclusion of carbon sinks in the calculation will, proponents argue, encourage good and sustainable forestry practices. While the flexibility provisions of the Kyoto Protocol do provide for the claiming of 'credits' for investing in tree planting or other activities that take carbon out of the atmosphere, finding a satisfactory method for calculating these credits has been contentious. At the most recent meeting in The Hague at the end of 2000, no resolution to the issues of trading emissions and carbon sinks was made.[128]

The Umbrella Group also believes that the targets arrived at in the Kyoto Protocol have been calculated by a formula that benefits members of the European Union while disadvantaging other industrialized countries. Critics of the EU targets (which propose a reduction of 15 per cent from 1990 levels by 2010, with an interim target of 7.5 per cent by 2005)[129] argue that the European strategy of 'sharing the pain' when it comes to cutting emissions, known as the European bubble, puts them at a distinct advantage over countries like Canada and the United States. The European bubble works in the following way. Germany and Denmark have promised cuts of 25 per cent, Britain has agreed to 10 per cent, and France will remain even. This allows Portugal to raise its emissions by 40 per cent, Greece by 30 per cent and Spain by 17 per cent.[130]

In the end, thirty-eight industrial countries agreed to reduce their greenhouse-gas emissions from 1990 levels. Developing countries, including major emitters of greenhouse gases, such as China and India, were asked to set voluntary reduction targets.[131] The Kyoto Protocol will take effect only when it has been ratified by fifty-five countries representing 55 per cent of 1990 carbon-dioxide emissions. It is legally binding on individual countries only when their governments have ratified it.[132]

The future of the Kyoto Protocol experienced a major setback on 28 March 2001, when Christie Todd Whitman, head of the US Environmental Protection Agency, confirmed that the country would not implement the treaty. This statement came just two days after the European Union wrote to President George W. Bush seeking his commitment to the Kyoto Protocol. This was the latest policy reversal by the president on the issue of emissions. On 13 March 2001, he reversed his pledge to legislate limits on carbon dioxide emissions from US power plants, saying rising energy prices would make those measures too costly.[133] The Global Climate Coalition, which is based in Washington, DC, praised the decision, claiming that more time invested in trying to 'fix' the fundamentally flawed treaty would 'simply be a waste of valuable resources that are critically needed in other areas to develop far more promising approaches to effectively address the important climate issue.'[134] Other groups were far more critical. The director of government relations with the Union of Concerned Scientists stated: 'This is the most anti-environmental act by an American president in modern history.'[135] The fifteen countries of the European Union have announced that they will ratify the Kyoto Protocol by 2002 with or without American participation. An announcement by the European environment ministers stated: 'The Kyoto Protocol is still alive—no individual country has the right to declare a multilateral agreement as dead.'[136] After the Bush announcement the Canadian environment minister, David Anderson, said Kyoto was all but dead without American support.

Canada's National Action Program on Climate Change, 1995

In December 1992, Canada became the eighth country to ratify the Framework Convention on Climate Change. In 1994, a task force consisting of business leaders, environmentalists, academics, and federal officials was established to examine economic measures that could encourage various economic sectors to limit their greenhouse-gas emissions voluntarily.[137] This task force was established in response to the UN Framework Convention on Climate Change, which charged the industrialized countries to develop a number of economic instruments to achieve the objectives of the Convention. Among the measures considered were registered retired savings plans for energy retrofits, enhanced financing for retrofits, and tax exemptions for bus passes.[138] At the Kyoto conference, Canada committed itself to cut greenhouse-gas emissions by 6 per cent from 1990 levels by 2012. (This compares to the European Union's reduction of 15 per cent from 1990 levels by 2010, with an interim target of 7.5 per cent by 2005.[139]) In real terms, the Canadian target means a reduction of 26 per cent because of the rise of emissions since 1990.[140] Table 5.3 illustrates emission levels for the year 1995 for 8 selected countries.

The commitment made by the Government of Canada at Kyoto in December 1997 went further than what had been agreed to by nine provinces at a meeting in Regina the previous month. (Quebec had sought overall emission reductions from 1990 levels.) The provinces agreed that it 'made sense to stabilize greenhouse gas emissions, mostly carbon dioxide, to 1990 levels by 2010.'[141] This agreement in principle became known as the *stabilization strategy*, and most provinces and

Table 5.3 Carbon Emissions from Burning of Fossil Fuels, Selected Countries, 1995

Country	Total Emissions (million tonnes)	Share of World Carbon Emissions (per cent)	Emissions per Capita (tonnes)	Emissions Growth 1990–95 (per cent)
United States	1,394	22.9	5.3	6.2
Russia	437	7.2	2.9	−27.7
Japan	302	5.0	2.4	8.7
Germany	234	3.8	2.9	−10.2
China	806	13.3	0.7	27.5
India	229	3.8	0.3	27.7
Indonesia	56	0.9	0.3	38.8
Brazil	62	1.0	0.4	19.8
TOTAL	3,521	57.9	15.2	—

Source: State of the World, 1997, as seen in *The Globe and Mail*, November 29, 1997, A20.

companies working with these targets in mind believed that this would be the Canadian target agreed to at Kyoto. Given that emissions had increased by as much as 13 per cent since 1990, federal officials claimed that this was a commitment of enormous significance. The emission 'target' agreed to by the federal environment minister at the time was criticized by activists as not going far enough. At the same time, the commitment made by the federal government was assailed as unfair by the provinces, which had not been consulted. The western oil-producing provinces saw this as yet one more attempt by central Canada to attack its energy sector. Manufacturers argued that these targets would weaken Ontario's economy 'because manufacturing will be hard hit as a result of anti-pollution requirements, leading to increased energy costs, and the transportation industry will suffer because of higher fuel bills.'[142] Business interest groups, including the Business Council on National Issues, argued that the more appropriate policy would have been simply to hold to 1990 levels (the stabilization strategy) because industries had developed business plans on the basis of these targets. In the years following Kyoto, there have been criticisms by environmentalists that the Kyoto target set by the federal government in 1997 is unlikely to be achieved. Most observers agree that changes in Canadian domestic policy alone will not be sufficient and that the only chance of Canada's meeting its Kyoto target is if it is allowed to buy emission credits from developing countries.[143]

Can Canada Meet Its Kyoto Targets?
Despite all the accolades that flowed to the Liberal government for its commitment made at Kyoto in 1997, the government's record since that time has been disappointing. Figure 5.1 shows Canada's Kyoto target for GHG emissions reductions. As indicated in this chart, if no substantive actions are taken, and it is 'business as usual', Canada will be 21 per cent above its Kyoto commitment by 2010. This shortfall is commonly referred to as the Kyoto gap. Environmentalists claim that Canada's target was nothing short of grandstanding, of paying lip service to the notion of being seen as 'greener' by Canadians. According to a Greenpeace climate-change specialist, not one federal measure has been put into place to fight greenhouse gases.[144]

Some scientists have been critical of the government for putting up some of the strongest resistance to the implementation of the Kyoto Protocol (namely, arguing that increased emissions reading and carbon sinks should be used in emissions calculations). The impasse in the negotiations at the December 2000 meetings in The Hague points to the continuing failure of the parties to set up a way to implement it. This intransigence is apparent not just on the international scene. Although the federal government has pledged $500 million to combat climate change, many of the provinces, including Alberta, Ontario, and Saskatchewan, have refused to participate. It is small wonder that environmental groups and climate change experts are frustrated by government ambivalence and inaction on climate change.

Figure 5.1. Canada's Kyoto Target and the Kyoto Gap

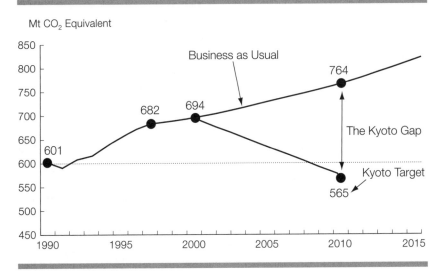

Source: Analysis and Modelling Group, *Canada's Emissions Outlook: An Update*, December, 1999.

Returning to the question of whether or not Canada's Kyoto target can be achieved, the answer is yes, it can. However, this will require an act of will by governments and business. This will require creative policies and difficult decisions. For example, if governments were prepared to reinvest in mass public transit, introduce taxes to discourage the use of the cars, and offer incentives to change from internal combustion engines to fuel-cell technologies, we would have a serious chance of reaching this target. However, as some are quick to point out, because Canada does not have a domestically owned automobile industry, we have little influence on the next generation of automotive engineering.[145] Such a policy would also have large numbers of critics, ranging from the oil and natural gas sector to the automobile industry. Clearly, meeting the Kyoto targets will require a significant restructuring of the Canadian energy sector as well as major changes in the transportation used by Canadians.

Government of Canada Action Plan 2000 on Climate Change

Since the Kyoto convention in 1997, the federal Liberal government has given mixed signals about its commitment to the targets. According to the *Globe and Mail*, a secret memorandum was presented to cabinet by Environment Minister David Anderson and Natural Resources Minister Ralph Goodale in November 1999, describing global warming as 'the most profound *economic* challenge facing the country since the Second World War with the scale of change to the Canadian economy . . . far greater than the oil shocks of the 1970s or free trade.'[146]

At the same time, the memorandum noted that 'dealing with global warming will create economic opportunities if the government acts now'[147] (although it is silent as to what these opportunities might be). With the release of the *Government of Canada Action Plan 2000 on Climate Change*, the Climate Change Action Fund, which was established in 1998, was extended. The fund initially consisted of $50 million a year. In addition, the 2000 budget committed a further $60 million for various energy-efficiency and renewable-energy programs.

Action Plan 2000 was the culmination of an initiative launched in 1998 at the direction of Canada's first ministers. More than 450 experts from industry, academia, and non-governmental organizations, together with officials from the federal, provincial, territorial, and municipal governments joined in a two-year consultation process to arrive at solutions to climate change.[148] Recognizing that most stakeholders in both the public and private sectors must be convinced that any solutions will not undermine their economic stability, the provinces and territories, along with the Government of Canada, have put forward a series of actions that will form the First National Climate Change Business Plan. This plan calls for the federal government to invest up to $500 million on specific actions that will reduce greenhouse-gas emissions. Action Plan 2000 targets the economic sectors that are most responsible for greenhouse gas emissions and, when fully implemented, it will take Canada one third of the way to achieving the target established in the Kyoto Protocol. It will reduce Canada's GHG emissions by about 65 megatonnes per year during the commitment period of 2008–2012. Further the Plan claims that the remainder of Canada's Kyoto target will be addressed by actions in future plans.[149] It should be noted that Ontario did not sign this plan as it believed a number of the measures in it would threaten economic development in the province.

Figure 5.2 illustrates the percentage of greenhouse-gas emissions by sector. As illustrated in this figure, the transportation, oil and gas, industry, and electricity sectors are the sectors that emit the most greenhouse gases.

Figure 5.2 also shows projected emissions of GHGs in the year 2010 unless control measures are implemented. Most of the measures contained in Action 2000 are voluntary and use language such as 'educate', 'promote best practices', 'encourage', and 'the Government of Canada will work with provinces, territories and partners in pursuing these initiatives'. At the same time, the federal government has reduced GHGs from its own buildings and operations by 19 per cent and intends to reduce them by a further 12 per cent by 2010,[150] through building retrofits, better management of government vehicles, the purchase of environmentally friendly products, and the downsizing of operations. In so doing, it hopes to help create a market for certain new technologies on the verge of becoming viable.[151]

Conclusions on Climate Change

To conclude, there are massive costs for both the mitigation and adaptability strategies related to climate change. The Kyoto Protocol, while seen as a necessity by health-care specialists and environmental groups, is viewed as a bad deal

Figure 5.2. Greenhouse Gas Emissions by Sector, to 2020, Megatonnes
CO₂ Equivalent

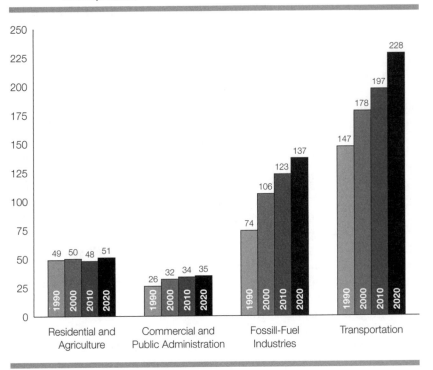

Source: Annex C, 'National Energy and Emissions Results', *Canada's Emissions Outlook: An Update*
(Ottawa: National Resources Canada, 1997).

by many Canadian businesses. The dilemma faced by policy makers is clearly articulated in the statement by the president of the Canadian Association of Petroleum Producers in 1998: 'The real issue is how the government will reconcile the targets agreed to at Kyoto and its commitment to no punitive taxes, more jobs, and continued economic growth for Canada.'[152]

Municipal Solid-Waste Management

This section will be limited to a discussion of waste that comes from Canadian households, institutions, businesses, and light industry—commonly described as municipal solid waste. It will not consider the management of liquid, radioactive, or hazardous wastes—three very different environmental problems in their own right. The problem of waste management and the generation and disposal of waste has been described as 'probably the most immediate in terms of direct impact on the everyday lives of Canadians.'[153] Canada produces more waste per capita than any other country in the world (1.7 kilograms per person per day), followed closely by the United States and Australia.[154] More recent figures (from 1995) reveal that Canadians generate 30 million tonnes of solid waste each year, about one-fifth more than the average of other OECD nations.[155] At the beginning of the 1990s, 82 per cent of Canadian municipal solid waste was disposed of in landfills, about 7 per cent was incinerated, and only 11 per cent was recycled.[156] There is little reason to think that Canadians improved their wasteful ways in the late 1990s; in fact, the generation of waste continues to be a huge policy and management issue. In practical terms, almost any measures pertaining to the management of wastes is sure to draw the ire of the public. Ronald Poland points out that this results in a social paradox:

> On one hand the public demands the convenience and services responsible for generating much of the waste which is found objectionable; on the other hand, communities are unwilling to tolerate development of facilities which deal with waste materials. All the while, the underlying need for protection of public health through sound management of waste materials must be satisfied.[157]

Waste management has emerged as a critical issue as we move into the twenty-first century. Not only is the land available for new landfills scarcer than it once was, but many sites are approaching capacity. As a result of the growing toxicity of landfills caused by years of dumping synthetic organic substances such as pesticides, paint removers, and degreasers, municipalities are increasingly facing difficulties in both finding new sites and gaining public acceptance of alternative measures. This problem was seen in 2000, in a heated debate about the decision by Toronto to send its garbage to Kirkland Lake to be buried in an abandoned mine. The Town of Kirkland Lake, crippled by mine closures and high unemployment, saw the Adams Mine proposal as an opportunity to become a leader in waste-management technology and was a welcoming 'host' for the Toronto's garbage. In the short run, the project was expected to generate thirty jobs for local people. The City of Toronto, having been told several years earlier by the Province that the last remaining landfill site in the Greater Toronto Area was to be closed by 2002, had been involved in negotiations with a private contractor for several years. The City argued that shipping the garbage north was its only solution, and it entered into an agreement with a private company—Rail Cycle North—to do just that. Despite a series of environmental and hydrological studies by consultants showing that the project was safe and environmentally sound, Toronto's plan became highly controversial. Environmentalists and Native groups made presentations to City Council arguing that the Adams Mine proposal was an environmental disaster-in-waiting with the potential to cause widespread water contamination. They also believed that the proposal should be forced to undergo an environmental assessment under the Canadian Environmental Assessment Act. (It had undergone a provincial assessment, but was exempted from a federal assessment.) Many Toronto residents believed that a problem made in Toronto should be solved in Toronto. Why had Toronto not embarked on an innovative program to deal with this problem, as Edmonton and Guelph had?

Forced to make a final decision before the municipal elections in November 2000, the City Council voted to proceed with the deal. Rail Cycle North subsequently withdrew from the deal because of changes in the language of the contract relating to liability. Early in 2001, however, there were some indications that discussions between the City and Rail Cycle North had begun again. The Adams Mine project points to a growing problem for many municipalities in Canada and elsewhere—landfills are reaching the end of their lives, and cities have been left with few options in the disposal of their solid waste. The following sections will examine the 'greener' alternatives to landfills, the reasons why they have failed to take root, and the relationship between waste management and health and well-being.

Jurisdictional Authority for Solid-Waste Management

Under Canadian environmental law, solid waste is distinguished from hazardous waste; in particular, it is not in liquid form and tends to be less toxic.[158] Until the 1960s and early 1970s, waste sites and their management were either unregulated or were regulated by municipal by-laws. By the mid-1970s, however, environmental regulations were put into effect and responsibility for solid waste regulation shifted from the municipal to the provincial level.[159] Municipalities and private contractors are now subject to provincial laws and regulations governing solid-waste management. Currently, municipalities or private waste companies wishing to build either a landfill or an incinerator must obtain a licence under the basic environmental assessment law of that province. If the site in question has to be rezoned, necessary approvals must also be received under the relevant planning legislation.[160]

Methods of Waste Management

Because of the growing toxicity of landfills, public criticism relating to the location of new facilities, and a recognition that other waste methods should be pursued, attention has been increasingly focused on what is known as integrated waste management, which combines several methods of waste disposal. Integrated waste management is now being used in most North American cities. Most jurisdictions are now required, by law, to have mandatory recycling programs and goals for waste reduction. For example, in 1989 Ontario established a goal of reducing its waste by 50 per cent by 2000 compared to the base year of 1987.[161] These same objectives were also adopted by the other provinces and the federal government as an initiative of the Canadian Council of Ministers of the Environment later that year.[162] This kind of strategy involves the 'three Rs': reduction, reuse, and recycling. Incineration, when accompanied by the 'capture of heat energy for generation of electricity, district heating, or other purposes', is sometimes referred to as the fourth 'r'—recovery.[163] Although the technologies for these processes are available and are being used in some places, one of the things that has delayed their widespread use has been the high cost. Alternative methods, including incinerators and recycling facilities, require complex machinery and processes.[164] For cash-strapped municipalities, these kinds of expenditures have been determined not to be feasible. In addition, the public has grown suspicious of new types of facilities—particularly if they are to be near their residential neighbourhoods.

Landfills

For most of our history, landfills (or garbage dumps, as they were once called) have been the disposal method of choice for most Canadian communities. In the past, they were handy and accessible, and land was readily available. Landfills continue to be widely used because of their relatively low costs and the low technology required. However, as household products became more hazardous, many of these landfill dumps became highly toxic. Over time, municipal solid-waste landfills, through the process of decomposition and percolation of moisture through the waste, generated leachate.[165]

An investigation of a recycling and composting centre in Guelph, Ontario—a city of about 95,000—by Hans Tammemagi has found that the cost of the centre was $27 million. This included the cost of pilot studies, permits, the truck fleet, and land costs. By the time full capacity is reached, the annual operating cost will be $3.7 million, although it has been estimated that the sales of recyclables will yield revenues of $4.4 million a year, for a yearly operating profit of $700,000.[166] More details of the Guelph experiment will be described later in this section. The cost of establishing these kinds of centres for much larger municipalities explains why landfills continue to be popular. However, they must be monitored for many years even after they are no longer being used. This perpetual-care cost must be kept in mind when municipalities are evaluating methods for waste disposal. On the other hand, once incinerators and recycling centres have outlived their useful lifetimes, they can be dismantled, and the land sold.[167]

In spite of compelling economic arguments about the disadvantages of landfills, most scientists believe they will continue to be used in North America because of population increases. Tammemagi concludes that alternatives to landfill and the three 'Rs' are necessary if we are to make a significant dent in total waste volume. In his view, the only technology now available that offers real hope for significant reduction is incineration—a controversial technology. Moreover, changes in people's habits must accompany any new technologies if waste reduction is to be achieved. In some cases, these changes may have to be legislated. For example, in Denmark nonrefillable beverage containers have been banned. Moreover, in Finland and Germany, 95 per cent and 73 per cent, respectively, of containers for soft drink, beer, wine, and spirits are refillable. This compares to approximately 7 per cent in the United States (in 1993).[168] Japan is commonly seen as one of the most advanced jurisdictions that best exemplifies the conserver society. Because of a land shortage, they have a well-developed recycling program, complemented by incineration. By 1987, Japan had 1,900 incinerators.[169] Table 5.4 shows the percentage of waste that is disposed of by various methods in Japan, the United States, and Canada.

Recycling

Recycling is the major form of waste diversion to date. Studies have shown that voluntary recycling is not as effective as mandatory recycling.[170] Municipalities must educate their residents about such programs and the details related to the types of materials that should be recycled. It is critical that landlords of rental complexes and commercial enterprises also participate in these types of programs despite some logistical barriers. For example, apartments have little space for storing waste and commercial operations are usually serviced by private waste contractors.[171] Once the recyclables have been picked up at the curb, they are taken to materials-recovery facilities, 'where the various metal, glass, paper, and plastic components are separated, packaged (usually in bales), and stored until they can be shipped.'[172]

Composting

Composting is nature's way of recycling—it decomposes and transforms such materials as food scraps, leaves and yard trimmings, paper, wood, manure, and the remains of agricultural crops into a soil-like product called humus. It has been estimated that 50 per cent of all total waste could be composted.[173] Composting is a specialized component of the recycling process. Some municipalities offer free backyard composters to residents while others are experimenting with collecting organic wastes separately. Larger composting facilities will be needed for apartment buildings, businesses, and neighbourhoods.[174] In cases where waste-management companies are used, this will require an investment in composting facilities.

Incineration

Incineration as a method of waste disposal has been more widespread in Europe than in North America.[175] It is popular because it reduces the volume of the waste. Although one by-product of this process is heat, there are also some dangerous

Table 5.4 Comparison of US, Japanese, and Canadian Municipal Waste Management

	United States (1995)	Japan (1987)	Canada (1995)
Recycled	21%	50%	21%
Incinerated	20	34	4
Landfilled	59	16	75

Source: Hans Tammemagi, *The Waste Crisis* (Toronto: Oxford University Press, 1999), 43.

by-products, including air pollution and ash.[176] Because of these toxic by-products, the public are usually opposed to new incinerators near residential neighbourhoods. Although manufacturers of incinerators have been working to develop new scrubber technologies that will capture the contaminants before they are released, these innovations have not solved the problem of how to dispose of the hazardous waste contaminants that are captured. In the late 1980s, Ontario banned incineration (it was the only jurisdiction in North America to do so); however, this ban was reversed by the Harris government when it came to power in 1995.[177]

Guelph—A Success Story

Guelph is a mid-sized Ontario city that has exceeded the province's 50 per cent diversion objective. In fact, in its first year of operation (1996), its Wet-Dry Centre was already achieving 54 per cent diversion from landfills. This centre has two main parts—a large building that receives and processes dry waste, and two attached buildings that receive and compost wet waste.[178] The wet-dry system differs significantly from the blue-box method of recycling used by most other North American cities in that it requires residents to separate their wet and dry waste. Compostable (i.e., wet) waste is placed in semi-transparent green plastic bags and dry waste (i.e., non-recyclable and non-compostable waste) is placed in transparent bags or labelled containers.[179] The City has a fleet of specially designed garbage trucks in which wet and dry garbage are placed in separate compartments. All waste is unloaded and processed indoors in order to minimize odours and avoid attracting birds—an important consideration since an airport is located nearby.[180]

The Ontario Ministry of the Environment requires compost to be maintained for at least three days at 55 degrees C or higher in order to destroy pathogens and weed seeds. Tammemagi describes the next process used in Guelph:

> The compost spends 4 weeks in the channels being progressively turned—rolled down the channel—by special machines which run on rails set on top of the concrete channel walls. . . . The compost is then placed for 4 weeks in two long windows inside the back part of the building for secondary composting. The compost is aerated from below during this stage and is turned by a front-end loader about once a week. Fresh water is added for moisture. . . . The finished compost is screened and cured outside on a paved storage area for six months. After this aging, it is sold in bulk for landscaping and site-restoration uses.[181]

The City is currently seeking additional waste from the commercial and industrial sectors within its boundaries (much of this continues to go to private landfills). An innovative feature of the Guelph system is that efforts are being made to seek out niche markets that may be interested in some of the waste. For example, industrial plastic film that is separated in the dry process has been supplied to a local cottage industry that makes pillows.[182] Manual labour for the facility is provided by a placement agency that finds work for people with disabilities.

In 1999, a custom-designed anaerobic digester began operation. Not only does this digester generate methane, which, in turn, generates electrical power, but it can also decompose plastics, leather, rubber, and other materials currently being sent to landfills.[183]

Policy Instruments Available to Governments
There are two difficult tasks related to municipal solid waste facing our governments. First, since it will serve no useful purpose if materials such as newspapers or glass bottles are stored indefinitely in warehouses,[184] it is up to governments to ensure that there is a market for recyclables. This may require municipalities to enter into partnerships with private agencies or to become a partner in a not-for-profit organization charged with finding buyers for recycled goods. The second task, which is no less formidable, is to encourage recycling and conservation by commercial and industrial enterprises as well as by individuals. And in fact there have been several programs—mostly voluntary—introduced by governments. For example, in the early 1990s, the federal government established the Environmental Choice Programme, which encouraged industries to use recycled materials in their production processes. If approved by the program, the manufacturer could display the Environmental Choice logo on the product. Critics of the program argued that it did little to distinguish between the amounts of recycled goods that went into the manufactured good. In other words, how much of a product needed to be from recycled materials in order to qualify for a logo? Similarly, in 1990 the National Packaging Protocol was developed jointly by a number of interested parties, including federal and provincial environment departments, packaging industries, and environmentalists, with the objective of diverting packaging wastes from disposal by 50 per cent by 2000.[185] Governments in Canada have resisted the use of laws and regulations to require recycling but have used the threat of such regulations to induce voluntary action by industry.[186]

Traditionally, solid-waste management has been paid for exclusively through municipal property taxes. Critics argue that this may be one of the biggest obstacles to persuading citizens, businesses, and industries to become less wasteful. For example, funding recycling through property taxes sends no direct signal to industry to use products and packaging that are environmentally friendly. Some observers have suggested the use of garbage user fees, the logic being that if households must pay for every bag of garbage they put out for collection, they will have more incentive to both reduce and reuse.[187] These kinds of programs (which do exist in Europe and elsewhere) entail certain administrative costs. For example, it is necessary to establish procedures for distributing garbage bags or tags and to set up a garbage-user-fee system.

To conclude, as was seen in the discussion of Guelph's Wet-Dry facility, new and innovative methods for solid waste management require a large financial investment, committed citizens and businesses, and a collective will to practise conservation. It appears that for large cities such as Toronto, there is much more work ahead to resolve the problem of municipal solid waste. Substantial financial help from both the provinces and the federal government will likely be necessary before we will see a large-scale diversion of garbage away from landfills.

As far as health is concerned, the biggest threat is that some current and old landfill sites are not being properly managed and monitored. The direct effects on health and well-being consist of the risks from run-off, incineration, and the handling of biological wastes.[188] As was evident in the arguments made by delegations opposing the Adams Mine proposal, one of the greatest dangers of landfills is that they may contaminate the surface and groundwater running off the sites. In addition, studies have found high levels of lead in landfill sites. We now know that lead levels in soil are the principal determinant of lead levels in the blood of children living in cities.

Conclusions on the Health Imperative

A growing number of studies have drawn strong correlations between environmental contaminants and health and well-being. Not only do these point to threats to young children but also to others who may be particularly vulnerable to poor air and water quality as well as to air-borne contaminates. All of this evidence should persuade policy makers to take steps to control these sources of contaminants and toxins in the environment. Not only are human health and well-being adversely affected, but so, too, is the health and well-being of animal and plant life.

Climate change also has important implications for health and well-being. Should human ingenuity not be able to slow down the rate of climate change, many parts of the world, their inhabitants, wildlife, and vegetative life will be adversely affected. Although the effects will not be immediate, the environmental health of today's children and their children is at stake.

The Security Imperative

Thomas F. Homer-Dixon has predicted that a scarcity of crop land, fresh water, and forests, may have dire social consequences for the developing world, including insurrections, ethnic clashes, urban unrest, and other forms of civil violence.[189] Although this thesis is not a particularly novel one, what makes Homer-Dixon's findings compelling are the examples he provides to show that these consequences have already been realized. Moreover, the existence of this acute violence helps to refute the argument advanced by Pollyannas and cornucopians that there are no limits to human population growth and wealth. While Homer-Dixon is more optimistic than contemporary doomsday thinkers, he does caution that the developed world should not ignore the scarcity scenario. Moreover, his prediction that there may be local conflicts over resource scarcities has a particular resonance in Canada, where skirmishes have become commonplace between Aboriginal and non-Aboriginal fishers and loggers, and western Canadians and oil and gas companies.

Local Conflict

In the case of the fish resource, Homer-Dixon's typology of environmental scarcity would be classified as a supply-induced scarcity because the fish resource has become depleted in quantity. Additionally, he would argue that the fish resource creates rivalry because its use by one group (Aboriginals) reduces its availability for others.[190]

Chapter 4 of this book chronicled the policies of the federal government in its attempts to restore the fishery on both the eastern and western coasts. These efforts have been undermined by foreign fishing, disputes between American and Canadian fishers over jurisdiction, failures of fishers to comply with quota limits, and a lack of scientific data. More recently, since the decision by the Supreme Court of Canada in the Marshall case, some Aboriginal fishers believe that their treaty rights to fish supersede federal quotas and fishing regulations. This has led to local conflict with non-Aboriginal fishers, who now argue that they are being forced out of the fishery altogether. The result has been heightened tensions.

A different kind of dispute involves civil disobedience by individuals against corporations. The most prominent of these involved Wiebo Ludwig and members of his family and immediate community near Rocky Mountain House, Alberta. Ludwig, a farmer, and other members of his commune community were charged with vandalism after sour-gas wells were sabotaged. Ludwig, who was frustrated with the proliferation of gas drilling and worried that these activities were harming the health of his family, friends, and animals, is alleged to have embarked on a campaign of vandalism. (At the time of writing, this case is before the courts.) Ludwig's reaction to harassment by other local residents who were afraid that the continued vandalism might threaten their livelihoods, culminated in the shooting death of a local teenager who had trespassed on Ludwig's farm in June 1999. As of January 2001, no arrests had been made in this case.

Ludwig was not the only local resident concerned about sour gas. Other farmers and ranchers as well as local veterinarians had expressed fears about this continued practice. A veterinarian, Cheryl Waldner, told CBC News, 'We did find a consistent association between increased risk of stillbirth and exposure to flared sour gas.'[191] Although there have been no deaths from a blowout in seventeen years, sour gas contains hydrogen sulfide, which can kill within seconds and is found in about 10 per cent of Alberta's gas wells.[192] The oil companies point to the tight regulation of these wells by the Alberta Energy and Utilities Board, but cuts to the board have caused the number of inspections per year to be reduced from 2,000 to about 400.[193] Of particular concern is the practice of 'flaring', which is a routine procedure for burning off waste gas. It is estimated that there are more than 5,000 flares in Alberta, mostly in rural areas.[194] Environmentalists have reported that the Rocky Mountain House conflict is not isolated and that there have been confrontations in at least half a dozen other communities in Alberta.

North-South Conflict

The other type of conflict having important implications for Canada is north-south conflicts, which Homer-Dixon describes as 'conflicts between the developed and developing worlds over mitigation of, adaptation to, and compensation for global environmental problems like global warming, ozone depletion, threats to biodiversity, and decreases in fish stocks.'[195] Although he believes that there will not be open warfare between the North and South, he does foresee ethnic clashes and civil strife. By civil strife he means 'insurgency, banditry, and coups d'état caused by environmental scarcity that affects economic productivity and, in turn, people's livelihoods, the behavior of élite groups, and the ability of states to meet these changing demands.'[196] Homer-Dixon is convinced that the constant debate among neo-Malthusians, economic optimists, and 'share-the-wealth' distributionists does little to advance solutions to these looming conflicts. He himself proposes that the sharing of technologies, skills, and knowledge—what he calls human ingenuity—will be necessary, particularly in the developing world.

Conclusions on the Health and Security Imperatives

Most Canadians believe instinctively that a polluted and contaminated environment will be harmful to their health. However, it is the toxins that we do not see and are not aware of that constitute the real threat. Similarly, because climate change is so slow, many Canadians consider it to be no immediate threat. Yet the ultimate effects may be devastating to many Canadians and to plant and animal life in this country. All of these factors indicate that there are new and emergent health imperatives that warrant a response by us all. Over and above the health-related issues associated with the current state of our environment, lies the ever present challenge that future conflicts and wars may be waged over resource scarcities, such as food and water. With the conflict at Burnt Church, New Brunswick, we have witnessed first-hand how resource issues can become violent.

Suggestions for Further Reading

Canadian Environmental Law Association and the Ontario College of Family Physicians, *The Children's Health Project: Environmental Standard Setting and Children's Health* (Toronto: Canadian Environmental Law Association, 2000) < http//www.cela.org >

Steingraber, Sandra, *Living Downstream* (New York: Addison-Wesley, 1997).

Tammemagi, Hans, *The Waste Crisis* (Toronto: Oxford University Press, 1999).

Suggestions for Small-Group Discussion

1. To what degree have environmentalists succeeded in casting the environment as an important health issue? What more should they do?
2. Should provinces require that municipalities be responsible for disposing of their waste within their own boundaries?
3. What is your home town doing about recycling? About waste management?
4. In July 2001, Canada agreed to pursue its objectives for reducing greenhouse gases in accordance with the terms of the Kyoto Protocol. Does it have the tools in place to achieve these targets?
5. In terms of the potential of north–south conflicts over resources, where do you believe that conflict may be inevitable? Why?

Multilateral Environmental Agreements, Trade Liberalization, and the Environment

This chapter discusses a number of multilateral environmental agreements (MEAs) and international trade agreements that Canada has been party to since the early 1980s. In the 1988 federal general election, only 43 per cent of all voters supported the Progressive Conservative Party, which was the only party that supported free trade. Yet five years later, the Liberal Party, which had taken an anti-free-trade position in 1988, signed Canada on as one of three parties to the North American Free Trade Agreement (NAFTA). Canada is also a member of the World Trade Organization. We now appear to be well on the road to trade liberalization—a road that we cannot leave. As parties to a number of MEAs and international trade agreements, many concerned groups have advanced the argument that trade harmonization will ultimately mean a loss of Canadian sovereignty, that is, our ability to control our own domestic policies in a variety of key policy areas ranging from culture to social programs such as health care and, perhaps most important, the environment.

Multilateral Environmental Agreements and Canadian Sovereignty

By the end of 1999, Canada had signed or endorsed more than thirty international agreements. Nevertheless, it has failed to live up to many of the terms of these agreements, as was noted in connection with GHGs in the preceding chapter. This failure does not necessarily mean that Canada's policy makers and politicians are dishonest; in fact this kind of failure has been endemic among many other parties to these agreements. Unsuccessful implementation can be attributed to a variety of factors, including changes in political priorities or changes in public opinion. More important, the failure to implement the measures set out in protocols reflects the political dilemma posed by the concept of sovereignty.

As it is traditionally understood, sovereignty takes two forms. The first pertains to the formal recognition of sources of international authority in joint decision making. That is, in their *external* affairs, states have formal juridical authority. The second form of sovereignty refers to states' discretion over *internal* policy in which they are also seen as having autonomy. In the Canadian case, this authority is complicated by the division of powers as set out in the Constitution. Many contemporary 'realist' and 'neo-realist' scholars argue that until these two areas of jurisdiction and sovereignty are transformed, 'no effective collective environmental protection will be possible through traditional treaty making.'[1]

At the present time, the absence of enforceable international law means that the global environment can be protected only through collective agreements, arrived at by the time-consuming and cumbersome processes of diplomacy, or by granting some powers to international institutions that are guaranteed limited authority.[2]

International Environmental Agreements Prior to Stockholm (1972)

Historically, the primary purpose of international agreements among nations has been for security through military alliances, such as the North Atlantic Treaty Organization (NATO). But since the second half of the twentieth century, there have been agreements that address non-military issues, such as international trade and environmental protection. As far as the environment is concerned, there have been a number of international agreements, including a treaty on fisheries management and the environment (the 1909 Boundary Waters Treaty between the United States and Canada); the Migratory Birds Convention signed by the two countries in 1917; the International Convention on Whaling of the 1940s; and the Nordic Convention of the 1960s that provided for common action by the Scandinavian countries to protect their shared environment.[3] Before the UN Conference on the Human Environment (UNCHE) in Stockholm in 1972, other agreements having important implications for the environment included 'a treaty governing Antarctica (1959), a partial nuclear-test-ban treaty (1963), a treaty governing the exploration and use of outer space (1967), and several international agreements on such ocean-related matters as whaling, the use of marine resources, and ocean pollution.'[4]

The Stockholm Conference of 1972

Despite the existence of these earlier international initiatives, the Stockholm conference was the first international effort to evaluate and discuss the environment in a comprehensive matter. It was a watershed event in internationalizing and legitimizing the environmental movement, 'both in terms of its formal output and in terms of its informal impact on environmentalism'.[5] It served to redefine international environmental issues by focusing on all humans in both the developed and developing world and by recognizing that pollution and natural-resource management needed an international approach. This conference helped to establish the pattern that followed in the next two decades, including a wide-ranging number of international diplomatic missions and debates, international efforts to build new institutions, and global movements for social change.[6]

An underlying theme at Stockholm embraced by many of the participants attending the conference—and particularly those from the North—was that environmental problems are the by-product of an affluent, industrialized way of life. The 'times' were an important consideration, as well. Stockholm took place in the shadow of the Cold War; in fact the Conference was boycotted by the governments of Eastern Europe and the Soviet Union after a dispute over the representation of the divided Germany. For the most part, many of the discussions taking place at Stockholm were contentious. One of the few points on which governments could agree was 'the primacy of state sovereignty'.[7]

Some environmentalists were disappointed with a number of the twenty-six principles that were enshrined in the Declaration of the Stockholm Conference, which failed to abandon the ideal of industrial development in its new buzz phrase 'sustainable development'. The Conference gave this term the following definition: 'a process of change in which the exploitation of resources, the direction of investment, the orientation of technological development, and institutional change are all in harmony and enhance both current and future potential to meet human needs and aspirations.'[8] The Declaration's definition of sustainable development did not challenge the right of states to exploit their own resources (with the provision that no environmental damage would occur beyond their borders), and it had a strong anthropocentric tone. Wildlife, forests, wetlands, and other important components of the earth's ecosystems were all but forgotten in this definition. While there was some sympathy for the notion that the developing world should have its chance to reap the economic benefits of northern-style industrial development, many environmentalists were disappointed with this rather traditional and antiquated view of development. Nevertheless, some positive things did flow from the Stockholm Conference, including the creation of the United Nations Environment Programme (UNEP) and a spirit of co-operation in which nations were called upon to work together to develop international laws on liability and compensation for environmental damage.[9]

After Stockholm

A series of other important agreements were negotiated after Stockholm: the Convention on International Trade in Endangered Species (CITES) in 1973, the Convention on the Prevention of Marine Pollution by Dumping of Wastes and Other Matter in 1979, and the Economic Commission for Europe Convention on Long-Range Transboundary Air Pollution, also in 1979. Another important conference followed in 1987—the World Commission on Environment and Development (the Brundtland Commission), which gave rise to a series of other agreements, including the Global Convention on the Control of Transboundary Movements of Hazardous Wastes (in 1989) and the Kyoto Protocol (discussed in Chapter 5).[10] These agreements—and those coming before them—called for collective action, usually consisting of two stages: (1) the identification of the problem by the scientific community; and (2) the negotiation of a plan for collective action. While the collective will of the representatives attending these conferences was almost always in favour of the goals and ideals of these agreements, which were usually signed by the diplomatic representatives of the nations involved, this was simply the first step. The more difficult hurdle in the process has always been the ratification by the government of each nation. Assuming that the ratification process was successful, domestic laws then had to be drafted to reach the reduction limit for the particular nation stipulated by the agreement.[11] As in the case of Kyoto, implementation of objectives and ratification have remained elusive for many member states. The effectiveness of these international agreements has also been called into question given the voluntarist principles underlying international law and organization.

The Rio Earth Summit

In June 1992 the United Nations Conference on Environment and Development (the Earth Summit) convened in Rio de Janeiro with nearly 10,000 official delegates from 150 nations. A parallel Global Forum bringing together thousands of activists and concerned citizens met at another location in Rio. The discussions held at both conferences were covered by an estimated 8,000 journalists.[12] There was considerable enthusiasm about this meeting because it was the largest international conference ever held on the environment. Activists believed that it demonstrated 'the world's growing consensus on the importance of ecological problems'.[13] There were several important differences between the nature and organization of the Stockholm and Rio meetings. These reflected many of the underlying changes that had taken place in the world during the intervening two decades. For example, the Rio meeting, in contrast to the one held in Stockholm, took place in the 'relatively optimistic afterglow of the end of the Cold War, amidst a general sense of new opportunities for global cooperation.'[14] In the two decades between the conferences, however, the notion that there was both a 'pollution of affluence' and a 'pollution of poverty' had gained much broader acceptance. It became evident for the first time that environmental concerns were not the exclusive property of the affluent or of the industrialized countries.[15] Another significant difference between these two meetings was the scope of their respective agendas. Rio had a far broader and more complex agenda. Moreover, scientific improvements during the years after Stockholm had improved the ability of scientists to measure, monitor, and model the complex processes of environmental change.[16] In other words, climate change was no longer some abstract concept; data were now available to demonstrate the extent of the problem and its implications for agricultural capacities, water supplies, and wetlands, among other resources. A third significant change pertained to the ability of participating countries to monitor environmental problems and issues at the nation-state level. Nearly all of the governments converging on Rio de Janeiro had some form of national environmental bureaucracy; at the time of the Stockholm Conference, almost none did.[17]

Rio represented a new consensual approach to addressing environmental problems and for that reason generated enthusiasm among environmental groups and activists, but did it have any tangible results? Canada joined other countries in committing that by 2002—ten years after the summit—there would be measurable progress toward sustainable development. As we enter the new century, it has been asked whether there has been any quantifiable improvement as a result of this commitment. In the view of the Commissioner of the Environment and Sustainable Development, 'Canada [has] failed to meet its commitments flowing from the Earth Summit. . . . In these and other areas, the federal government needed to pay more attention to the management side of the sustainable development equation.'[18] This report was particularly critical of Canada's international commitments to the North, which accounts for 40 per cent of our land mass and two-thirds of our coastline. According to the report, pesticides, industrial chemicals, and heavy metals constitute major threats to the environmental quality of the Arctic. This contamination 'accumulate[s] in the fatty tissues of fish and wildlife and attack[s] a fundamental aspect of Aboriginal culture in the North— its reliance on traditional or "country" foods'.[19]

The Status of Ongoing Conventions

Although a number of environmental agreements have been reached in principle (estimated to total more than 900) and signed at these environmental conferences, in the years following major conferences of that kind, there is a long period of bargaining and international diplomacy in the pursuit of ratification. The low levels of implementation have frustrated many environmentalists and have resulted in criticism of the international environmental regime. One of the difficulties encountered in the bargaining process is the 'logic of collective action', which suggests that individual countries will not co-operate if their sovereignty is seriously challenged and if they fear that their own costly actions will not be reciprocated. They will not participate if they suspect that the lack of action by other countries will not be observed, or even if they are not sure that other parties' actions can be effectively monitored.[20] The important question is what effect these international agreements and meetings have on environmental policy making in Canada. Cynics might suggest that Canada's participation in these forums makes for good public relations but has little effect. Others, including Robert Boardman, suggest that there are some benefits; in particular, he suggests that the international level is 'a germination area for environmental policy ideas.'[21] Some of these ideas, he argues, have set the themes of national environmental debates. And, on occasion, cross-national comparisons on issues such as waste have provided ammunition for the politics of shaming.[22] Hundreds of agreements and protocols have been agreed to but for which ratification and negotiation continue. The following discussion considers one of the more controversial protocols pertaining to the international environment.

Convention on Biological Diversity

The Convention on Biological Diversity defines biological diversity as 'the variability among living organisms from all sources including terrestrial, marine, and other aquatic ecosystems and the ecological complexes of which they are part; this includes diversity within species, between species, and between ecosystems.'

> As of December 1994, the number of states that signed or acceded to the convention had risen to 168, of which 106 have so far ratified the agreement. Progress on this convention was stalled because the problems to be tackled were so wide-ranging and complex. As a result, it took two and a half years to prepare the ground for the first major working meeting at the ministerial level.[23]

This meeting was held in Nassau in the Bahamas. After some tough negotiations, Sweden managed to persuade the conference that the annual themes of the work program should be the earth's major ecosystems. The idea was to give the discussions on biodiversity a more practical focus by dealing with one important ecosystem at a time and trying to implement the convention in relation to specific problems within that ecosystem in different countries.[24] In 1995, the theme was marine and coastal ecosystems; in 1996, agricultural ecosystems; and in 1997, forests. Although Sweden called for forests to be included in the work plan, Brazil firmly blocked this move. At the Nassau conference, NGOs were highly critical of the fact that forestry issues were omitted as a result of Brazil's opposition.[25] The progress of this convention has been crippled by problems caused by funding shortfalls. Since Rio, the Global Environment Facility (GEF), which is subject to the authority of the convention, has been the target of much criticism by the Group of 77 (the developing countries and China). They believe that the GEF has too close links with the World Bank, and they have proposed that an independent and separate fund be set up under the Convention.[26]

The United States was the last country to sign the convention, and it did so on the very last day possible. It has been suggested that the US reluctance to sign this agreement was largely due to pressure from industry, which was afraid of losing its freedom to exploit developing countries. The United States is one of the sixty-two countries that have still to ratify the agreement, and the Republican-dominated Congress of Clinton's second administration appeared less than enthusiastic about ratification.[27] Under the new Bush administration, ratification is unlikely.

Aside from those political difficulties that imperil the ratification of the Biodiversity Convention, serious differences emerged in Nassau on the subject of biotechnology and its safety—'biosafety'. Sweden's view was that international controls on the ecological risks of biotechnology products must be put in place under the convention. The United States and Germany would prefer that the issue be kept out of the convention altogether. The ultimate decisions and discussions surrounding this biosafety protocol held in Montreal in 2000 were discussed earlier in the section on GM foods and the agricultural resource in Canada.

The Role of International Institutions

Since the creation of the United Nations in 1945, there has been a rapid increase in the number of international organizations. A number of international organizations are relatively new and promote international co-operation by coaxing and coercing governments into signing international agreements. These organizations, which vary widely in type and nature, range from the United Nations and its agencies, such as the United Nations Environmental Program (UNEP) and the World Meteorological Organization, to organizations representing multinational business corporations doing business in a number of nations. They also include professional organizations in each of the various sciences, which provide a means for both transmitting information on new discoveries throughout the world and bringing its members together for regular face-to-face discussion, as well as international environmental pressure groups, such as Greenpeace and Friends of the Earth. All of these organizations are made up of members from many different nations, and all have some autonomy. It has been traditionally understood that these organizations are not the instrument of any one nation-state, although this is a hotly debated topic. This discussion will primarily focus on those international organizations that are important in the area of the environment.

After its creation in 1945, the United Nations spawned a wide array of NGOs in a wide variety of areas. In 1948 the International Union for the Conservation of Nature and Natural Resources was established, with a mandate for collaborative scientific research. This led to the founding in 1961 of the World Wildlife Fund (WWF). Another important organization of the UN is the United Nations Environment Programme (UNEP), which was considered to be largely the product of the 1972 Stockholm Conference. These organizations attempt to co-ordinate environmental agreements among the myriad actors involved in the international environmental arena. For the most part, two kinds of environmental problems are addressed by these organizations:

> All international environmental treaties deal with one of two types of environmental problems: (1) protection of physical commons *outside* national control, like the oceans or the atmosphere, and (2) protection of assets or resources that exist *within* a country's territorial control, although the effect of that country's decisions may be felt elsewhere, such as in transboundary pollution problems or the protection of a migratory species. Both types of problems affect industrialized and developing countries.[28]

As far as domestic issues are concerned, Principle 21 of the Declaration of the United Nations Conference on the Human Environment reads: 'States have . . . the sovereign right to exploit their own resources pursuant to their own environmental policies, and the responsibility to ensure that activities within their jurisdiction or control do not cause damage to the environment of other States or of areas beyond the limits of national jurisdiction.'

Although the objectives of the United Nations and its organizations are admired by many of its member states, its credibility as the 'voice' of nations has been overshadowed in the past ten years by the emergence of large and powerful trading organizations, such as the World Trade Organization, and agreements such as the General Agreement of Tariffs and Trade (GATT) and the North American Free Trade Agreement (NAFTA). These agreements will be discussed below as they pertain to the relationship between trade and the environment.

Trade and the Environment

It is not surprising that environmentalists have seen both trade and globalization as enemies that were undermining many environmental goals. While trade, particularly free trade, implies a withdrawal from markets by government, environmental measures often call for increased state intervention. In addition, trade tends to be supported by powerful corporate and multinational interests while environmental goals tend to be supported by relatively less powerful nonprofit organizations and citizen groups. As trade deals have become more public, the antipathy of environmentalists to these discussions has become more vocal as was demonstrated at recent meetings held in Seattle (in 1999), The Hague (in 2000), and Quebec City (in April 2001). Trade agreements and economic integration are thought to undermine the ability of governments to take action to protect the environment, resulting in a downward harmonization of regulatory standards. Environmentalists also describe this trend as the 'race to the bottom' because governments may be induced to relax their regulations in order to create a competitive advantage for domestic businesses.[29] Environmentalists also have other criticisms, including the emphasis on economic growth which they believe will only create an increased demand for natural resources. They are also convinced that dispute-settlement panels are biased against the use of import bans as instruments for influencing the environmental practices of other countries.[30] Furthermore, environmentalists contend that WTO procedures give only limited access to environmental NGOs. The following pages discuss the theory of free trade; the evolution of GATT and its successor, the WTO, and how these agreements affect the environment; and, finally, some of the contentious points of the North America Free Trade Agreement (NAFTA).

The Theory and Rationale for Free Trade

The justification for free trade is largely premised on five theoretical principles. First, there is the theory of 'comparative advantage'. According to this principle, some countries are more suited to doing some things than others.[31] Many economists claim that all nations benefit from trade because of the principle of 'comparative advantage':

> Each country specializes in what it can produce most cheaply and has an advantage in. As producers vie with each other to improve production and sell their goods, they become more efficient. Efficiency and competition thrive off each other. . . . Japan has made its wealth on manufactured goods, despite being poor in natural

resources and energy. But for poor countries, as their economies now stand, free trade would mean condemning them to continue their role as low cost producers of primary goods for Western consumption.[32]

The second principle of free trade is that the private sector is always better than the state sector, because the dead hand of bureaucracy quickly stifles initiative and wastes money. Therefore, argues the free trader, get the state off the backs of people and industry. The third principle of free trade is that living standards rise under free trade. Even though there may be inequalities in wealth as a result of entrepreneurial activity, some wealth will trickle down to the poorest, so even they ultimately benefit. Fourth, free trade, it is argued, gives consumers more choice and more information to enable them to make choices. And lastly, free trade promotes the most efficient use of resources, people, and capital.[33]

The difficulty with many of these principles is that they do not hold true in practice. The 'comparative-advantage' principle, for example, holds that there will be some balance. The theory runs into difficulty when one country can produce products more cheaply than others and has no incentive to trade, or when a country has little or no comparative advantage in anything.[34] In cases where a certain balance does not exist, countries are compelled to introduce protectionist measures—such as tariffs, embargoes, quotas, and exclusionary specifications or regulations. Yet, these are the measures, free-traders argue, that reduce the internal specialization of labour and decrease global wealth.[35] As for criticisms that free trade perpetuates environmentally unfriendly practices and the unequal distribution of wealth, free-trade proponents argue that only when the economy is back in good shape through 'growth' will there be enough wealth and political opportunity to address the environment and world equity.[36] In other words, free-trade advocates argue that the expansion of domestic economies will alleviate poverty and will provide citizens and their governments with greater resources to spend on protecting the environment. Simply stated, the vast majority of free-trade advocates embrace the ideal of continued economic growth.[37]

The Environmental Critique of Free Trade

Free trade runs counter to many of the arguments made by greens in favour of decentralization, sustainability, and reduced consumption. Moreover, considerable environmental costs result from free trade. For example, increases in international trade mean that more materials and goods are transported around the globe with a resulting increase in energy use and increased pollution. The transport involved in international trade is estimated to account for one-eighth of the world's oil consumption.[38] Moreover, greens point to a series of oil spills as evidence of other environmental costs of this kind of trade. Greens also argue that the gearing of entire economies to raw-material exports for international trade has damaging environmental consequences at the point of extraction or production, particularly in developing countries. Although the horror stories of mineral extraction are many, perhaps the best-publicized case concerns tropical timber. While part of the environmental damage is the actual destruction of sizable tracts of rainforest for export, equally devastating are the roads built for commercial logging, which, in their wake, bring farmers, miners, and those seeking fuelwood.[39]

Critics of free trade believe that a more accurate definition would be the freedom enjoyed by global corporations to be independent of local and global regulation and to have no responsibility for human rights, environmental protection, or economic fairness.

> Multinational corporations are 'free' to flee from countries with strong and worthy regulations for protecting human health, worker safety, and the environment to countries with less stringent—and less stringently enforced—regulations. They are 'free' to relocate plants and production to parts of the globe where the going manufacturing wage is $1.85 an hour. They are 'free' to produce and sell chemicals that were banned from use in one country to farmers in a less developed country and produce food for export to the country that banned the chemical in the first place. Multinationals are 'free' to export food products even if it means that those who grow the food go hungry.'[40]

To be fair, there are probably some light greens who support limited free trade and who believe that improvements in green technologies may provide some solutions to certain environmental problems, including the thorny questions about resource use and waste disposal.[41] However, for the most part, it is safe to say that greens, as a group, do not support large-scale trade liberalization. Though they have been described as 'globaphobic', there is evidence that the environment has not come out of these major trade agreements as a winner. The following sections discuss the actual practice of free trade as embodied in GATT, WTO, and NAFTA.

General Agreement of Tariffs and Trade (GATT) and the World Trade Organization (WTO)

> The GATT agreement was the offspring of a much more ambitious attempt in the late 1940s to establish an international trade organization (ITO) with more substantial powers. This organization, based on the Havana Charter, was to be the third pillar of the Bretton Woods institutions along with the IMF and the World Bank, but the implementing bill failed to be passed by the United States Senate. The GATT itself was in fact only a treaty or agreement, as its name implies, serviced by a secretariat. It was not a full-blown international organization in the traditional sense.[42]

Most trade experts concede that GATT was the brainchild of the United States and that it formed an important part of American strategy to extend the US economic system to the rest of the world, particularly to those countries whose industrial economies were gravely wounded after the Second World War.[43] As initially conceived by the United States, it was thought that an international trade organization (ITO) would be ideally situated within the UN system in order to complement the International Monetary Fund (IMF) and the World Bank. Generally speaking, the IMF was involved in financing the projects of sovereign states while the World Bank financed international projects.[44]

The twenty-three participating countries negotiated trade agreements worth an estimated US$10 billion in the opening round of GATT held in Geneva in 1947. There were eight rounds in all with the last meetings (called the Uruguay Round) running from 1986 to 1994. Collectively, the value of trade covered by these rounds is estimated at US$500 billion. By the final round, the scope and extent of this international trade had expanded nearly fivefold and 117 countries were involved.[45] GATT established the multilateral framework for dealing with trade barriers that not only impeded trade and growth but 'contributed to economic downturns in the post-war years.'[46] This framework has continued to be used and was adapted for NAFTA.

GATT was based on two principles: non-descrimination and reciprocity.

Non-discrimination

If a 'contracting party' to GATT wanted to impose a duty on its imports from one country, it had to apply the same duties to all other sources (the only exceptions were customs unions and free-trade areas, whose members were allowed to enjoy preference over external trade areas).[47] Article I ('Most Favoured Nation') prevents countries from treating an imported product (for example, French wine) any differently from the same product from another country (such as Australian wine).[48] Article III ('National Treatment') requires countries to treat imports (for example, California wine) no less favourably than they treat domestically produced goods and services (such as Canadian wine).

Reciprocity

If one country lowered its tariffs on another's exports, it could expect the other to lower its tariff in return. The other GATT members were required to make the same concessions, thus creating a 'virtuous circle' of liberalization.[49] Article II ('Tariff Reduction') is considered to be GATT's most fundamental principle because the elimination of tariffs ensures full access to markets. In the past twenty years, countries have been creative in indirectly restricting access to domestic markets by erecting non-trade barriers (NTBs). An example (provided by Audley) illustrates how NTBs work. Assume that a country passes a regulation calling for metal edges on skis—which only domestic ski manufacturers use—on the justification that the snow in that particular country 'requires' a particular kind of metal for effective performance.[50] Clearly, the country's intent is to protect the domestic ski manufacturers from cheaper imports from elsewhere. Knowing that protection (through the imposition of a tariff) will be a violation of Article II, nation-states find another way (regulation) that effectively serves the same purpose.

Before the Uruguay Round (held in Punta del Este, Uruguay in 1976) GATT was concerned only with the trade in goods; the agreement did not apply to services.

What made this last round of talks so revolutionary was that it represented an extraordinary extension of trade liberalization.[51] It was significantly different from previous rounds in this respect and was, by far, the most complicated of any postwar multilateral agreement. Its reach went far beyond just tariff cutting to incorporate new areas such as agriculture, services, foreign investments, and intellectual property into the GATT framework.[52] It was estimated that GATT applied to an estimated 90 per cent of world trade. What must be understood about this agreement, however, was that it was strictly that. Because it was not an organization, it did not have formal standing in the way that a sovereign nation does.[53]

It should not, however, be assumed that the principles of GATT were universally embraced by nation-states around the world. Indeed, there was considerable opposition to this agreement. In India, for example, there was much hostility to GATT's proposals on intellectual property rights. As an expression of deep concern, over 250 eminent Indians signed a statement calling GATT an extreme threat to the 1970 Indian Patents Act.[54] Other developing countries were critical of GATT on the grounds that it had failed to eliminate what was perceived as old-style Northern protectionism. Of particular concern were textiles.

Yet another criticism was launched by environmentalists who argued that environmental standards imposed by a country could be construed as some sort of hidden tariff designed to protect domestic industries. In order for the participating countries to remain competitive, GATT contained a number of disincentives for countries to develop effective environmental regulations:

> In theory, a government wishing to do this [i.e., develop environmental regulations] can establish import tariffs to offset pollution control costs, so that domestic producers will not be at a disadvantage when competing with imports from countries without similar environmental regulations. Or, a country could subsidize the costs of environmental protection with general revenues by underwriting pollution control costs. Neither of these options is likely to find favour under GATT, since it limits the right of governments to implement tariffs and subsidies. Any nation that decides to do so may face retaliation for creating a 'restraint on trade'. Under the proposed new rules, much of the authority to protect the environment or food or jobs or small businesses will be taken away from national and local governments and the community and transferred to trade ministers, TNCs [transnational corporations] and the MTO (now WTO).[55]

The World Trade Organization and the Environment

The Uruguay Round gave birth to the World Trade Organization, which, unlike its predecessor, was created as a multilateral trade *organization*. As it was conceived, it was to be more universal in its obligations and membership. Moreover, its proponents claimed that it would be more effective than GATT largely because the dispute-settlement provisions were seen as decidedly superior to those of its predecessor.[56] Because GATT was an agreement only, the resolution of trade disputes had been a matter for negotiation and compromise. Although trade panels could pass judgement assigning fault, compliance 'ultimately depended on the willing-ness of each member to accept the rulings of trade panels.'[57] GATT did allow coun-tries to impose retaliatory trade sanctions, but they could do so only with the offending country's consent. The WTO no longer requires this consent, and it ren-ders rulings on cases referred to it within a year. Retaliatory trade sanctions are considered to be one of the most potent remedies under international law.[58] Sup-porters of the WTO claimed that it will be more politicized through more frequent ministerial attendance, and will have a more visible presence and clout in eco-nomic policy than the Bretton Woods institutions.[59] The organization of the WTO allows for the possibility of majority voting. In the eyes of its supporters, this means that the WTO will have real life and independence.[60]

Membership in the WTO is contingent on accepting all the results of the Uruguay Round, including the agreements on goods and services, and intellec-tual property. Previous waivers and exceptions have been abolished.[61] In the past, countries were not obliged to accept and adopt all the various non-trade barrier agreements. This option is no longer available. To be a member of the WTO, a country is to be bound by all the agreements on goods and services, and most of the agreements on non-trade barriers, though 'there is still room to mod-ulate participation in some agreements by means of limited exemptions (for example services) though a full opt out is not allowed.'[62]

The hostility of environmentalists in Canada and the United States to GATT and WTO grew in the early 1990s in the wake of several decisions made by the impar-tial GATT Dispute Settlement Panel. Indeed, 'in all of the environment-related dis-pute settlements WTO panels have adjudicated, the panels have ruled in favour of the country challenging the domestic regulation.'[63] That said, Hoberg argues that the limitations that trade agreements place on domestic regulations have been highly overdrawn and that the texts of the decisions do contain room for environ-mental measures.[64] Table 6.1 lists the eight cases that have arisen under the WTO involving regulations having implications for health or the environment. In seven of these cases, the dispute panels overturned domestic regulations.[65] Brief sum-maries of three of these cases follows.

Canadian Export Ban on Unprocessed Fish (1988)

The Canadian government imposed an export ban on unprocessed, west-coast herring and salmon in 1987. These restrictions were introduced to enable local fishers to continue to earn a living while limiting fishing. GATT ruled that the measure was not allowable since it was designed to protect Canadian processors and employment and that therefore the primary goal of the policy was not to protect fish.[66]

The Tuna-Dolphin Case (1991)

In 1991, the dispute panel ruled in favour of Mexico in a dispute with the United States over the welfare of dolphins. This was the first important environmental

Table 6.1 Resolution of WTO Cases Related to the Environment, 1988–1999

Case	Year	Outcome
Canada—export ban on unprocessed fish	1988	overturned
Thailand—cigarette ban	1990	overturned
US tuna-import ban	1991	overturned
US auto standards	1994	upheld
US refinery standard	1996	overturned
US shrimp-import ban	1998	overturned
EU beef-import ban	1998	overturned
Australian salmon-import ban	1999	overturned

Source: George Hoberg, 'Trade, Harmonization, and Domestic Autonomy in Environmental Policy' (Vancouver: University of British Columbia, 2000), http://www.policy.ca.

case decided under GATT rules, and environmentalists considered it to be a serious blow. The timing of the decision, however, was critical, coming as it did just a few months before the 1992 Rio Conference. The American Marine Mammal Protection Act (MMPA) had been amended in 1988 by the United States to set conditions for the harvesting of tuna. This Act, which had been in effect since 1972, was intended to protect dolphins from the worst excesses of tuna fishing in the east Pacific, where dolphins and tuna often swam together.[67] In response to complaints about Mexican fisheries practices, the United States placed an embargo on the import of Mexican tuna on the grounds that the fish 'had been caught in purse-seine nets, which kill dolphins cruelly and in greater numbers than US law permits.'[68] Mexico challenged the law as 'unfair trade rules', and a three-person panel upheld its objection. The panel deemed the MMPA illegal, setting a precedent that threatened a country's right to use trade measures as a way to protect the environment.[69] The United States attempted to justify the ban under the environmental exceptions in Article XX; however, the panel ruled that the measure must be applied within US jurisdiction and must be 'necessary' to protect the resource of concern. The panel also concluded that one country could not use trade measures to influence the environmental practices of another country.[70] By establishing this 'extra-territoriality' standard, the ruling had important environmental implications for subsequent fisheries-management schemes.

European Union Ban on North American Beef Treated with Growth Hormones (1989)

One of the most controversial WTO decisions concerned the EU's ban on American and Canadian beef treated with growth hormones. The United States and Canada's case revolved around their position that the ban was inconsistent with Article 3.1, which requires that there be 'scientific justification' for a ban.[71]

In other words, because it could not be scientifically proved that growth hormones in beef harmed human health, the panel overruled the EU ban, effectively saying that the burden of proof to demonstrate this link rested with the EU. The decision provoked considerable rancour because it threatened the viability of the precautionary principle in international trade.

These decisions made by GATT and its successor organization, the WTO, have alarmed environmentalists, who fear that they have set a precedent that may threaten international agreements for protecting the environment. At the same time, policy analysts such as George Hoberg argue that the jurisprudence surrounding the WTO rules that were relevant to domestic environmental regulations 'is quite immature and poorly developed'.[72] For example, countries that do not comply with the regulations set forth in the Montreal Protocol could claim GATT protection on the basis that these provisions hinder trade. Environmentalists have charged that the main beneficiaries of GATT reforms will be international corporations and the main losers will be the environment and the world's poor.[73]

The Millennial Round

In November and December 1999, ministers from the 134 WTO member countries met in Seattle to discuss a new round of trade negotiations which were dubbed 'the Millennial Round'. Ostensibly, the meetings had been intended as an opportunity to draw up an agenda for a new round of global trade talks, which were scheduled to last about three years. The issues considered as the most pressing included European farm subsidies and whether or not to tax sales on the Internet.[74] Rather than leading to a consensus among the member countries, the talks were viewed mostly as a disaster because they were derailed by thousands of protesters, who insisted that 'globalization [had] become another word for capitulation to the worst excesses of capitalism, a cover for eliminating hard-won protections for the environment and workers' rights.'[75] The Millennial Round of trade talks is more likely to be remembered as the 'Battle of Seattle'.

The protesters came from a wide variety of interests and countries, although there is little question that trade unions, in particular, had a strong organizing presence. According to Larry Dohrs, an activist with the Seattle chapter of the Free Burma Coalition: 'Strong majorities of American voters support basic labor rights and environmental provisions in trade agreements. It's that simple.'[76]

As noted by Richard Lacayo, protesters at the Seattle meetings championed a variety of causes, ranging from farm subsidies to intellectual-property rights. In certain respects, the diversity of the opposition to the WTO has made it difficult for the public to focus on any one area. There is no question, however, that environmentalists had a strong agenda with two key issues. First, many greens believed that the WTO should use its muscle to demand that developing countries be forced to comply with more rigid environmental standards. This would force international companies from the developed world to be more responsible for their activities in the developing world. And second, unless developing countries were compelled to raise their standards as a pre-condition of trading with the developed world, their domestic environments would continue to deteriorate.

Environmentalists argue that the WTO facilitates environmental damage in that increased and liberalized trade has been 'perceived as enabling some firms to transfer their environmental problems elsewhere. Countries with lower environmental standards often allow them to despoil natural resources such as forests, to run polluting factories or dump waste in a manner forbidden at home.'[77] Supporters of the WTO have made the counter-argument that trade agreements could require countries wishing to export to adopt environmental standards that are similar to those in countries with tighter regulations. These could result in increased environmental protection.[78] Moreover, increased economic development in poorer countries will, in the long run, lead to increased environmental protection. In other words, environmental standards could be expected to rise only after a developing country had experienced some economic growth. Environmentalists, not convinced by this argument, point to previous decisions on disputes that have undermined domestic conservation programs. They remain convinced that the developed countries are unlikely to work towards more rigid environmental programs as long the WTO is silent about environmental standards in the developing world. Although Article XX allows countries to impose restrictions relating to conservation, it has been interpreted very narrowly. The WTO also allows subsidies for environmental purposes, and there are provisions in other agreements that allow for some environmental control, for example, refusal to grant a patent when a product is likely to damage the environment.

The bottom line for greens is that the WTO has not been receptive to banning manufacturing practices that are seen as penalizing exporting practices, because this type of action is seen as an attempt to impose an extraterritorial exercise of jurisdiction: 'While a product that is polluting in itself may be refused entry, what is not allowed is banning a product because the production process used in the exporting country does not meet the environmental standards of the importing country.'[79] In other words, the WTO does not allow differing environmental standards to be used as a barrier to trade. A country is free to adopt whatever environmental laws it pleases inside its territory provided the objective and means are legitimate and it applies the same rules to its own firms. A country can forbid the importation only of goods that are defective and banned domestically; it cannot impose a barrier on the grounds of production methods.[80] This position was adopted mainly to ensure that developing countries are not penalized for having lower environmental standards. The trade-first, environment-second approach taken by the WTO continues to be condemned by many greens, but the WTO seems committed to maintaining it.

Case Study—*Trade and the Environment: Bovine Growth Hormone*

A growth hormone, BST, developed by Eli Lilly, a subsidiary of Monsanto, was hailed as a tool for increasing yields of milk in cows. Early estimates were that it could increase yields by up to 25 per cent. Almost immediately, the hormone pro-voked debate that pitted dairy farmers, citizens' groups, and environmentalists against a huge pharmaceutical company. As well as pointing out that there was already a glut of milk on the market, opponents argued that the hormone could be unsafe for cows and humans and cause infections in cattle. Lilly responded by retaining the services of Burson-Marsteller (B-M) and Hill and Knowlton (H & K), the two largest public relations firms in the world, to lead the pro-growth-hor-mone fight.[81]

This dispute began on 1 January 1989, when the European Union imposed a ban on beef raised with growth hormones, forcing US meat producers to seek alternative markets, primarily in Japan, Mexico, and Egypt. This ban was the cul-mination of a mass movement against hormones led by consumer activists in Germany and Italy who argued that the hormones were carcinogenic.[82] Although the scientific data on that point were not conclusive in the minds of US meat pro-ducers, there was agreement that there was a desexing, calming effect on animals that led to unnaturally quick growth, especially when the hormones were over-used. In financial terms, it has been estimated that a single $1 hormone can save $20 in quick-fattening costs.[83] In retaliation for the EU ban, the United States imposed 11 per cent tariffs on many EU products, including tomatoes, tomato sauce, boneless beef, instant coffee, certain alcoholic drinks, fresh and concen-trated juices, pet food, and certain pork products.[84] Canada expressed similar objections. The EU countered with tariffs on American walnuts, dried prunes, peaches, papayas, and apricots. This dispute between North America and the EU raised fears of an all-out trade war.

B-M and H & K together built a grassroots network of 'business executives and lobbyists; biotech company executives; farmers; veterinarians; university profes-sors; high school teachers; Chambers of Commerce; and elected and appointed officials.'[85] Members of this network were encouraged to promote the acceptance of the hormone by lobbying their legislators, writing op-ed pieces for news-papers, sending letters to the editor, circulating petitions, and so on. By the end of 1999, BST was still legal in the United States and Canada.

The bovine growth hormone was not the first hormone controversy—which helps to explain why the EU imposed the ban. Some seven years earlier, the syn-thetic hormone estrogen diethylstilbestrol (DES)—also used in the beef indus-try—was detected in baby food in Italy, Germany, and Holland. It had the effect of causing babies of both sexes to develop breasts. In addition, medical studies revealed that children of women treated with DES had a predisposition to uterine and ovarian cancer. After that, Australia, Argentina, Brazil, New Zealand, and various other meat-producing countries agreed to ship only hormone-free meat to Europe.

Although the outbreak of foot-and-mouth disease (FMD) is different from the dispute about bovine growth hormone, it does demonstrate the relationship between trading blocs and domestic policy (see Box 6.1).

Box 6.1 Foot-and-Mouth Disease

Foot-and-mouth disease, (also known as hoof-and-mouth disease) was first identified in 1897. It is caused by a virus and is a highly contagious disease almost exclusive to cattle, sheep, swine, goats, and other cloven-hoofed animals.[1] Since that time there have been a number of outbreaks, including one in Saskatchewan in 1952. With the increase in globalized trade and larger livestock operations, there have been a number of recent serious outbreaks of the disease, including one in South Africa (2000–1) and in Macedonia and Albania in 1996. Until recently, the worst outbreak of the virus occurred in 1967 in the United Kingdom, which resulted in the slaughtering of 430,000 animals. On 19 February 2001, the British government announced that thirty-six cases of the livestock virus had been detected—all of which could be traced to a single farm in Northumberland in northern England. It has been estimated that up to 1,000,000 animals will eventually be slaughtered. The detection of FMD in UK livestock sent shock waves through the European Union and in countries that had imported British livestock and food products. Immediately, the EU countries ordered the slaughter of thousands of sheep, cows, and deer brought from Britain before the outbreak was discovered, including the slaughter of 20,000 sheep by France.

One of the difficulties associated with foot-and-mouth disease is that not all livestock get the virus and, for the most part, it is not fatal except in very young animals which may die without showing any symptoms. There is no cure, and the virus usually runs its course in two or three weeks, after which the great majority of animals recover naturally.[2] Nevertheless, once the disease is detected, farmers cannot move their animals and cannot earn income. As of May 2001, FMD cases had been found in France, the Netherlands, Germany, Saudi Arabia, Norway, and Argentina, among other countries. In terms of containment strategies, these countries have been forced to choose between the two options of slaughtering or mass vaccination or a combination of the two. Although the outright slaughter of massive numbers of livestock has been heavily criticized by some animal rights groups, others, including the Scotland Farmers' Union have said that it is the only solution given that the tests used in confirming the virus are not always accurate.[3] Indeed, so great is the fear of contagion that the animals' bodies are burned to ash and then buried in deep pits.[4] On 12 March 2001, the British Government announced plans to slaughter any sheep or pig found within an approximate five-kilometre radius of any confirmed outbreak in the northeastern county of Cumbria and southern Scotland.

Since the virus can be carried on clothing, uninfected animals, or vehicles, countries where the disease has yet to be discovered took extreme precautions. The Canadian Food Inspection Agency took the lead in developing Canada's policy, which was established in a lengthy document entitled *Foot and Mouth Disease Strategy*. Among its many provisions, this document set out disinfection routines for vehicles and people working in infected zones. It also established a surveillance zone at least ten kilometres wide around infected zones. Moreover, any movement of animals could only be done through licence. In the event that FMD was detected, all stockyards, auction markets, sales, fairs, zoos, and other livestock concentration points would be closed. The feeding of swill to pigs—long thought to be a source of FMD—would immediately be prohibited.

As for the strategy of slaughter or mass vaccination, the policy paper is ambiguous. Because pigs are the biggest amplifiers of the disease (one pig can produce as much virus as 1,000 to 3,000 cattle), the document does state that 'it is important that decision for pre-emptive slaughter be made without delay'. In the event that crops have been treated with manure from an infected source, these, too, must be destroyed. Further complicating the prevention and containment strategy is the fact that insects, rodents, and birds are potential mechanical carriers of the virus.

In addition to the measures set out in the *Foot and Mouth Disease Strategy*, the Canadian government immediately implemented a number of other measures:

- Travellers from countries affected by foot-and-mouth disease were subject to special border checks.
- Warning messages were shown on television and videos on airplanes.[5]
- Customs officials were given the authority to refuse entry of goods from an infected country. (A British ship loaded with military equipment was refused entry into Canada in April 2001.)
- Troops from other countries were not allowed into the country if they had been in an area affected by foot-and-mouth within the previous fourteen days (twenty-eight days in the case of British military personnel).
- The government encouraged farmers not to allow visitors from countries with foot-and-mouth disease.
- Sniffer dogs were used by customs officers at airports to root out meat products.
- Passengers arriving on international flights were required to step through mats of disinfectant to remove any traces of the virus from their shoes.
- Canadian cattle farmers embarked on plans to ear-tag all cattle leaving their farms with individual identification numbers so that any outbreak could be traced and contained.

As of 15 April 2001, no new cases have been reported in continental Europe. No cases of the disease have been reported in Canada or the United States. For the time being, the immediate crisis appears to be over and the threat to the Canadian agricultural industry appears to have dissipated. However, what the FMD crisis of 2001 has done is remind us of how quickly an epidemic in one country can spread to others as a result of globalized trade and how trade and its importance dictates policy choices. For example, because countries having FMD are banned in trading their products until the epidemic has disappeared, farmers have opted for the quick slaughter rather than pursuing a vaccination strategy. Moreover, because inoculated animals bear the same foot-and-mouth antibodies as infected animals, there is concern among farmers that consumers may be reluctant to buy animal products where vaccinations have been used.

Notes

1. This highly contagious disease causes blisters in the mouth and nose and on the teats and feet of cloven-hoofed animals. The discharge from the blisters is heavily infected with the virus, as are saliva, milk, urine, and other secretions. Thus, the disease is readily spread by contact; by contaminated food, water, soil, or other materials; or through the air. Humans, who seldom contract the disease, may be carriers, as may rats, dogs, birds, wild animals, and frozen meats.
2. Amina Ali, 'Foot-and-Mouth Disease', Mar. 2001, < http://www.cbc.ca >.
3. 'British Farmers Divided over Latest Foot-and-Mouth Measures', 19 Mar. 2001 < http://www.cbc.ca >.
4. Laura King, 'English Hoof-and-Mouth Disease Spreading', 26 Feb. 2001, < http://www.purefood.org >.
5. 4 April 2000, < http://www.cbc.ca >.

NAFTA and the Environment

On 12 August 1992, the United States, Canada, and Mexico agreed on a plan for free trade that would gradually eliminate tariffs over fifteen years and stimulate trade and investment. While protecting the 1988 free trade agreement between the United States and Canada, this new agreement created the world's largest common market in total production, with 370 million consumers. The rationale behind the agreement was that it would make American and Canadian industries more competitive by using low-cost Mexican labour, advanced US technology, and rich Canadian resources.[86]

One of the criticisms launched by Canadian greens was that NAFTA would result in the downward harmonization of environmental standards. The concern was that, rather than Mexico becoming more 'green', the United States and Canada would become more grey. Unless upward harmonization of environmental regulations took place, it was argued, pressure from uncompetitive businesses at home would force domestic standards down and factories would be encouraged to move to the country where environmental standards are the lowest.[87]

It is difficult to know for sure what NAFTA has meant for the Canadian economy or the environment. In terms of jobs, the net effects of NAFTA are negligible. The government claims that about 30,000 jobs have been created but that the same number have been eliminated since the beginning of 1994. In terms of the environment, there are some disturbing trends. The international body responsible for setting international pesticide standards, called the Codex Alimentarius, has set standards ten to fifty times more lax that the American standards. The 'Codex allows fifty times the amount of DDT residue on bananas as does [the American] Food and Drug Administration.'[88] Critics alleged that at the meetings leading up to the adoption of these standards, which were held largely behind closed doors, representatives of the agrochemical conglomerates were very much in evidence.

Like GATT, NAFTA adopted the principle of national treatment: 'Each Party shall accord to investors of another party treatment no less favourable than it accords, in like circumstances, to its own investors with respect to the establishment, acquisition, expansion, management, conduct, operation, and sale of other disposition of investments.' Moreover, with respect to provincial or state practices, national treatment means treatment no worse than that accorded to a good coming from a province or state within the same country.[89] NAFTA also recognizes that a state may be compelled to protect various industries, environmental goods, or cultural products and allows for this through an exemption clause. This 'national treatment' can be given to goods listed as exceptions in an escape clause. Canadian lumber as well as Canadian beer are listed in this clause. On the other hand, Canadian water and other resources are not listed. In many ways, the environmental provisions of NAFTA are similar to those spelled out by the WTO, including the requirement that the burden of proof be placed on the party that challenges an environmental regulation as a barrier to trade. There are, however, two provisions that do make NAFTA distinct—the side-agreement on the environment (NAAEC) and Chapter 11 (Article 1110), which 'allows corporations to sue member governments for compensation for expropriating or reducing the value of their investment.'[90]

North American Agreement on Environmental Co-operation

At the time NAFTA was being debated, there were widespread concerns among ENGOs and the public that a commercial trade agreement would prevent the three countries from developing continental environmental standards or labour standards.[91] Knowing the fragility of NAFTA and the continuing discontent with it, the political leaders of all three countries concluded that under no circumstances would the agreement itself be re-opened. Therefore, the environmental side-agreement would have to stand on its own.[92] In other words, the supplemental NAAEC could have a 'greening' effect on NAFTA only from the outside, not the inside.[93] To say the least, this did not assuage the concerns of ENGOs that the environmental considerations would be given short shrift in trade negotiations. Moreover, the difficult history of the issue of acid rain and bilateral co-operation to combat it (discussed in the previous chapter) did not give much comfort to ENGOs in any of the three countries that such co-operation would be forthcoming. Although President George Bush gave environmental guarantees in May 1991, the environment ministers of the three countries did not sign the final legal text of NAAEC until September 1993.[94] This delay was the result of a change in government in the United States as well as American insistence that the side-agreements be enforced by trade sanctions and that 'permanent secretariats [be established] to support the labour and environmental parallel agreements.'[95]

The NAAEC called for the creation of a North American Commission on Environmental Cooperation (CEC), which would determine the ecological effects of liberalized trade. In addition, the side agreement established a dispute-settlement mechanism that 'seeks to address complaints by one party about the quality of the domestic administration and enforcement of environmental protection schemes of another party.'[96] It is important to note that this provision only addresses the enforcement of a country's own laws and cannot be used to seek changes to those laws.[97] Although a party to NAAEC may theoretically withdraw from its provisions and still retain its membership in NAFTA, such an action would likely create a political crisis given how contentious the environmental guarantees were during the negotiations. In fact, it has been said that such an action would probably endanger the existence of NAFTA itself.[98]

Although there was guarded optimism at the time the NAAEC was instituted, the question that arises is whether or not it has been effective in safeguarding environmental standards related to trade issues. The difficulty of the procedure that one country must follow to impose sanctions on a country that fails to enforce its own laws is evident. As of May 2000, no sanctions have resulted, even though twenty-seven submissions have been received by the Commission.[99] Of only eleven cases that have been concluded, ten have been terminated, withdrawn, or dismissed. Although one resulted in a published factual record, no action was taken.[100] A number of cases are still under review, but the record to date indicates that the time-consuming process and a less than aggressive stance taken by the NAAEC have not had the results that optimists had hoped for. In fact, the executive director for the NAAEC was relieved of his duties in 1999 when it appeared he was interested in taking a harder stand.

Chapter 11 of NAFTA

Chapter 11 of the North American Free Trade Agreement, which has been described as the investment chapter, allows companies to sue countries if the expected returns on their investment are reduced by government actions—what the chapter calls 'expropriation'. Canadian courts have long recognized that land-use regulation is not expropriation; thus, it has been an established tradition that legislatures may legitimately regulate property use in the public interest without having to pay compensation. The difficulty with Chapter 11 of NAFTA is that its concept of expropriation is so broad 'that a governmental regulatory action which reduces the potential for generating profits may apparently generate a claim for compensation.'[101] To date, there have only been several Chapter 11 cases involving Canadian interests.

The Ethyl and Methanex cases

Two cases, one recent and one that is under way, that have environmental implications involve additives to gasoline. In the first case an American company, Ethyl Corporation, filed a claim against the Canadian government for $350 million (Canadian) for its decision to ban the use of MMT, a neuro-toxin, in gasoline. It has also been alleged that MMT may damage modern emission-control equipment in cars.[102] What is interesting about the MMT case is that the US Environmental Protection Agency has banned the use of this additive for a number of years; however, Ethyl successfully defended its use before the American courts, which required the EPA to approve its use.[103] The resolution of the NAFTA case was complicated. When Parliament passed an Act banning the interprovincial trade and importation of MMT in 1997, it did so on the grounds that the additive damaged emission-control devices and not on the grounds that it was a toxic substance. If the government had had the evidence to justify the ban on the basis of public health, the resolution of the case might have been different. In the end, the government decided not to ban MMT and agreed to a settlement of US $13 million with Ethyl.[104]

Although the government was accused of following the wrong strategy in calling for the ban of MMT by choosing a trade ban rather than an environmental measure, the implications of this case are of concern to a number of ENGOs. The Canadian Environmental Law Association concluded that 'the right of the Parliament of Canada to pass an environmental and health protection law can now give rise to a claim from the polluter for a huge amount of compensation.'[105] This conclusion has been questioned by George Hoberg. He believes that the issue of regulatory success by a NAFTA government before a dispute-settlement panel, using the precautionary principle, with uncertain scientific data, has not been tested.[106] However, given the recent decision in the Metalclad case (described below), Hoberg's cautious optimism may be overdrawn.

A more recent case revolves around a dispute that has been simmering since 1996, when the US government ordered that pollution-reducing additives such as methyl tertiary butyl ether (MTBE) had to be used in gasoline in parts of the country where smog was particularly heavy. After MTBE had been in use for several years, however, several studies done in California linked it to cancer. The US government argued that state governments should not have to pay compensation to corporations when they enact health and environment laws.[107] Methanex, a Vancouver company and the world's largest producer of methanol, has claimed that the California government violated a fundamental provision of NAFTA when it banned MTBE because of 'unproven' concerns about its effect on the environment. The California government said it banned MTBE because it was 'appearing in 10,000 groundwater wells in the state and [was suspected] of causing health problems.'[108] This case has been described as a 'US $1 billion battle between a giant methanol producer and the world's most powerful government.'[109] Methanex Corporation's defence is that there is nothing wrong with MTBE and that 'there is no epidemiological evidence to support the notion that MTBE has a causal link to cancer.'[110] This case has not yet been resolved but has generated considerable controversy on both sides of the border: 'It is one thing for American firms to challenge Canadian or Mexican laws, but when a Canadian firm uses the same provisions to challenge US law, US trade officials take notice.'[111]

Metalclad Corp. versus Mexico

Another Chapter 11 case that has environmental implications is the Metalclad case. The case involved an American company, Metalclad, that purchased a Mexican firm known as Coterin in September 1993 after it had received all required federal permits, including the land-use permit. The permit allowed for the construction of a hazardous-waste landfill in a sparsely populated valley in the state of San Luis Potosi, some 70 kilometres from the city of Guadalcazur. Immediately, intense opposition arose in the local community. After obtaining an eighteen-month extension of its construction permit from Mexico's National Ecological Institute (INE), Metalclad began construction of the landfill. Two separate engineering reports concluded that, with proper engineering, the site would be suitable for hazardous wastes. However, local protesters (allegedly with help from state troopers)[112] caused a delay in the opening of the facility. Metalclad agreed to a number of concessions regarding the protection of native species and even agreed to provide free medical services to the Guadalcazar community.

City officials remained resolute in their opposition to the hazardous waste facility and denied Metalclad's construction permit. Guadalcazar also obtained an injunction in challenging the agreement entered into by Metalclad with INE and the independent federal office for environmental protection. Just as his term was expiring, the Governor of San Luis Potosi established a protected natural area that included the landfill site.[113] Although the site had been inspected and approved by both the state and federal governments, the City of Guadalcazur ordered a halt to the construction in October 1994 on the grounds that the company had failed to obtain a municipal permit (the company said that the INE had told it that it was optional). The City had also received the results of a geological audit performed by environmental impact analysts from the University of San Luis Potosi, who deemed the plan to be an environmental hazard to surrounding communities because the landfill was on an alluvial stream that had the potential to contaminate the local water supply. The City ordered the landfill to be closed.[114]

On 2 January 1997, Metalclad demanded arbitration under Chapter 11 claiming that San Luis Potosi and Guadalcazar (and Mexico itself by virtue of its authority for the conduct of its political subdivisions) had violated ss.1105 and 1110 of

NAFTA (concerning free and equal treatment of investments, directly or indirectly expropriating investments, or taking any measure 'tantamount' to expropriation). More than three years later, the arbitrators found that Mexico had violated both of these provisions and awarded Metalclad $16.7 million. It had been seeking $90 million (US). Undeterred, Mexico used a third-party appeal mechanism, and decided to challenge the decision before the BC Supreme Court.

There were a number of troubling factors associated with the arbitrators' decision. First, the hearings were closed, which many observers felt was in violation of the transparency obligations of NAFTA. Second, there were concerns that the panel's overly broad language and 'its apparent downgrading of "environmental concerns" that conflict with investors' expectations'[115] could be used in future to justify compensation even if an investor has some economic use of his or her property. Michelle Swenarchuk points to yet another problem. It has been alleged that the Mexican federal government (unofficially) encouraged Metalclad's NAFTA lawsuit 'so that it [could] deflect the political fall-out of forcing the state to open the facility. If Metalclad's claims are indeed accurate, this case raises the disturbing possibility that investors can use their rights to collude with governments to force unwanted or even dangerous investments on unwilling populations.'[116] However, the greatest implication of the Metalclad decision is that municipalities and provinces may be rendered defenceless if agreements are signed between the federal government and other parties. After the first Metalclad ruling, for example, Vancouver City Council passed a resolution petitioning 'the federal government to refuse to sign any new trade and investment agreements such as . . . the Free Trade Area of the Americas, that include investor-state provisions similar to the ones included in NAFTA.'[117] On 20 February 2001, Mr Justice Tysoe of the BC Supreme Court, in a bold move, allowed a grassroots Internet media group to film and broadcast Mexico's appeal of NAFTA's decision. If this decision holds up, it may address some of the concerns about the secrecy of NAFTA arbitrations. In his 48-page opinion that was filed on 2 May 2001, Justice Tysoe upheld the ruling by the NAFTA dispute panel ordering the government of Mexico to pay damages to Metalclad Corporation. This represented the first ruling in an investor-to-state lawsuit under NAFTA in which a corporation has won. In the aftermath of this decision, there was a sense that although Metalclad had won, the general impact of the decision upon the claims of other NAFTA investors was still unclear.

All of the participating countries have expressed concern about Chapter 11 and how unfavourable decisions hamper them in passing laws related to the environment and health. Canada has proposed that a clarifying note be added to NAFTA, setting out the conditions under which a corporation may use the investor-stake mechanism. However, there is a certain reluctance to open it to renegotiation for fear that it will precipitate an open season on other parts of the agreement. A number of bodies, including some governments, ENGOs, and environmental groups would like to see the secretive process of review opened up, although the governments of Mexico, the United States, and Canada have been less than enthusiastic.

Proportional-Sharing Provision

The proportional-sharing provision of NAFTA has far-reaching implications for North American energy development. This rule entitles the United States to a proportional share of Canadian energy resources in perpetuity or until the resources are totally exhausted.[118] The Canadian government is powerless to impose export controls and the United States can lay claim to the amount of Canadian exports used at the time when the market does impose constraints. This clause is unique for there is no equivalent to it in any WTO agreements. Moreover, this sharing clause does not apply between the United States and Mexico.[119] Another unique characteristic of NAFTA as it pertains to oil and gas is that it exempts government subsidies for oil and gas development from trade challenge.[120]

Conclusions

Optimists claim things are changing and there is compelling evidence that population growth and resource consumption is slowing in the North. In the developing countries, however, population and consumption are growing. Moreover, many Third World countries are industrializing and polluting at Western levels. All of this does not bode well for a greener world. 'In terms of the global commons, the poor in developed countries probably do little more damage than the average person in developing countries. Rich Southerners, meanwhile, do just as much damage as the average Northerner.'[121]

As the world continues to become more interconnected by the trading of goods and services, there is considerable concern that sovereign nation-states may encounter obstacles to new legislation in the areas of health and the environment. Environmental groups continue to be vigilant in their efforts to ensure that international economic agreements do not threaten domestic environmental policies and practices. Although an environmental side agreement was eventually attached to NAFTA and was hailed as a victory for the environment, its success has been limited. Indeed, there is growing concern that countries may be reluctant to pass new environmental measures for fear they will be overturned. Countries are in a no-win situation. If they have their regulations overturned, it reduces the legitimacy of the dispute-settlement mechanism, incites opposition towards governments, and creates dissent among civil society groups. If they simply choose not to regulate, they earn the scorn of ENGOs but probably the support of business. There is already persuasive evidence that a regulatory chill has set in, and the new Bush administration in Washington does little to allay these fears. Similarly, the Chrétien government that was elected in the fall of 2000 has said little about its environmental plans for the next few years. Therefore, the political will to launch challenges and sanctions against our trading partners appears to be at a low ebb as we enter the twenty-first century.

This pessimism should, however, not be overstated. Some victories have been scored by environmental groups—the defeat of the MAI and protests at Seattle and The Hague. It is clear that the financial stakes surrounding these trading agreements are huge. At the same time, the environmental and health costs of trade liberalization are unknown. It will take courage, resolve, and leadership by the participating countries and their ENGOs to demonstrate that the health and environment of their citizens are more important than the profits of corporations.

Suggested Further Reading

Audley, John J., Green *Politics and Global Trade: NAFTA and the Future of Environmental Politics* (Washington, DC: Georgetown University Press, 1997).

Hoberg, George, 'Trade, Harmonization, and Domestic Autonomy in Environmental Policy' (01 July 2000) < www.policy.ca >

Jackson, Andrew, and Matthew Sanger, eds, *Dismantling Democracy* (Ottawa: Canadian Centre for Policy Alternatives and James Lorimer, 1998).

Johnson, Pierre Marc, and André Beaulieu, *The Environment and NAFTA* (Washington, DC: Island Press, 1996).

Shrybman, Steven, *A Citizen's Guide to the World Trade Organization* (Ottawa: Canadian Centre for Policy Alternatives and James Lorimer, 1999).

Suggestions for Small-Group Discussion

1. Beginning in Seattle and continuing in Davos, Quebec City, and Genoa, disparate groups of citizens are mobilizing around the issue of globalization. For some, the key issue is human rights, for others, the power of corporations. Many others believe that globalization and trade are bad for the environment. Expand on this critique. To what evidence do activists point to support their position?

2. Do any cases currently before the World Trade Organization involve challenges to trade practices considered to be environmentally unfriendly?

3. What is the current status of Bovine Growth Hormone (BST)?

4. Assess the decision reached by the North American Agreement on Environmental Co-operation (NAAEC) on the Metalclad case.

5. Are there any current Chapter 11 cases that have environmental implications?

Epilogue

Over the past eighteen months, it has been almost a part-time job staying abreast of domestic and international developments relating to the environment. From following the proceedings of the Walkerton Inquiry to the meetings in Beijing and The Hague on climate change as well as the provincial election campaign in British Columbia, it has been a busy time. Moreover, the outbreak of cryptosporidium in North Battleford, Saskatchewan, in the spring of 2001 is a stark reminder that environmental problems of the past have a way of recurring. All of these issues and extensive international summitry are evidence that few environmental problems of the twentieth century have been solved and that many challenges remain in addressing the degraded nature of our Earth—our global commons—as we enter the twenty-first century. This is not to suggest that there have not been some successes. The Montreal Protocol on Substances That Deplete the Ozone Layer has been relatively effective in reducing levels of depletion. A number of leading scientists believe that it might be possible to restore the ozone layer by the middle of the twenty-first century. Similarly, the agreement reached between the United States and Canada on acid rain was a success story which shows that bilateral co-operation can work if there is the political will and public support. Both of these agreements demonstrate that through co-operation and collective action we do have the capacity to be innovative and long-term in our attitude to the environment.

Storm clouds, however, continue to hover over the global environmental problems of POPs and climate change, among others. Blocs of countries have mobilized, charging each other with underhanded efforts to find loopholes in the wording of international agreements and framework conventions. To compound the problem, there is no supranational organization that has the authority to ensure that targets are reached by the participating countries. What we are left with—in both the domestic and international spheres—is a litany of well-intentioned agreements with voluntary targets and objectives that are dependent on political and corporate good will.

As for resource issues in this country—the quality of drinking water, the bulk sale of water, genetically modified foods, continuing evidence that our offshore fisheries have a long way to go to recovering—all point to the need to be more green in our policy making and decision making. While new types of policy instruments that have emerged in the 1980s and 1990s have enjoyed some success, governments in this country have seemingly become less willing to exercise leadership on the environmental front. Indeed, scientists have concluded that, rather than meeting the targets agreed to at Kyoto, the Government of Canada continues to take a business-as-usual approach, fearful that anything more will alienate business and inhibit industrial development. There is also the sense that any form of regulation in the resource area will be construed by organizations such as the World Trade Organization and NAFTA as barriers to trade. This has led to a climate that is characterized more by a regulatory chill than an activist blueprint for change. Canada's proximity to the United States, its increasing economic integration into the American economy, and its membership in NAFTA all point to a continuing follow-the-leader strategy by Canadian governments. The fact that President Bush has been considered an enemy of the environment by many US green groups, coupled with his appointment of a 'wise use' advocate as Secretary of the Interior does not bode well for a greening of public policy south of our border, particularly in the area of climate change.

In the aftermath of Walkerton and the 2000 election, the environment continues not to resonate with many Canadians as a critical issue. Chapter Five has put forward the view that environmentalists and other greens need to re-frame the environment as an issue that is connected to the policy of health and security. As a stand-alone public-policy issue, the environment has been too easily dismissed by policy makers, business, governments, and the public. Issues such as health, education, and economic growth will continue to squeeze out the environment from the key political debates in this country unless there is a fundamental strategic change in direction by green activists and organizations and a growing awareness among our citizens that we may be running out of time.

There are many unanswered questions as we begin the twenty-first century. Will we see the environment emerge as a critical political issue that is related to health care and domestic and international security? Will environmental groups continue to attempt to influence decision makers, even though governments will probably continue to be pro-business and pro-economic growth? Under what circumstances might this activism be manifested in widespread civil disobedience? Will new technologies provide new and safe ways to dispose of waste? And, most important, will we Canadians become more vocal in articulating our concerns about the state of our environment—our commons?

Notes

Introduction

1. Garrett Hardin, 'The Tragedy of the Commons', *Science* 162 (1968): 1243–8.
2. David Feeny, Fikret Berkes, Bonnie J. McCay, and James Acheson, 'The Tragedy of the Commons: Twenty-two Years Later', in Ken Conca, Michael Alberty, and Geoffrey D. Dabelko, eds, *Green Planet Blues: Environmental Politics from Stockholm to Rio* (Boulder, Colo.: Westview Press, 1995), 53.
3. Feeny et al., 'The Tragedy of the Commons: Twenty-two Years Later', 61.
4. Susan Jane Buck Cox, 'No Tragedy of the Commons', *Green Planet Blues*, 47.
5. Cox, 'No Tragedy of the Commons', 52.
6. Cox, 'No Tragedy of the Commons', 52.
7. Feeny et al., 'The Tragedy of the Commons: Twenty-two Years Later', 54.
8. Elinor Ostrom, *Governing the Commons* (Cambridge: Cambridge University Press, 1990), 14.
9. As quoted in Paul Harrison, *The Third Revolution* (London: I.B. Tauris, 1992), 264.
10. Harrison, *The Third Revolution*, 264.
11. Feeny et al. 'The Tragedy of the Commons: Twenty-two Years Later', 61.

Chapter One

1. J. Ronald Engel, 'Liberal Democracy and the Fate of the Earth', in Steven C. Rockefeller and John C. Elder, eds, *Spirit and Nature* (Boston: Beacon Press, 1992), 70.
2. Garrett Hardin, 'Cassandra's Role in the Population Wrangle', in Paul R. Ehrlick and John P. Holden, eds, *The Cassandra Conference* (College Station, Tex: Texas A & M University Press, 1988), 15.
3. Robert Paehlke, 'Democracy and Environmentalism', in Robert Paehlke and Douglas Torgerson, eds, *Managing Leviathan* (Peterborough: Broadview Press, 1990), 36.
4. Some examples of violations of political freedoms include section 98 of the Criminal Code prohibiting 'unlawful associations', which was introduced after the Winnipeg General Strike in 1919. This section was not repealed until 1936. Another case was the internment and or deportation of Japanese Canadians during the Second World War. A third example is the invocation in 1970 of the War Measures Act, which was used to imprison over 400 Quebec separatists who had no association with the radical separatist cell, the FLQ.
5. Matthew Alan Cahn, *Environmental Deceptions* (New York: State University of New York Press, 1995), 4.
6. Roger Gibbins and Loleen Youngman, *Mindscapes* (Toronto: McGraw-Hill Ryerson, 1996), 29.
7. Gibbins and Youngman, *Mindscapes*, 29.
8. Cahn, *Environmental Deceptions*, 1.
9. Alan S. Miller, *Gaia Connections* (Boston: Beacon Press, 1991), 18.
10. Marcel Wissenburg, *Green Liberalism* (London: University College London, 1998), 53.
11. Wissenberg, *Green Liberalism*, 53.
12. Ibid., 19.

13. Paul R. Ehrlich and John P. Holdren, eds, *The Cassandra Conference* (College Station: Texas A & M University Press, 1988), ix.

14. Robert Paehlke, *Environmentalism and the Future of Progressive Politics* (Peterborough, Ont.: Broadview Press, 1990), 3–5.

15. See Robin Eckersley, *Environmentalism and Political Theory* (New York: State University of New York Press, 1992), 35–47.

16. Ibid., 34.

17. Ibid., 39.

18. Murray Bookchin, 'Ecology and Revolutionary Thought', in R. Roelofs, J. Crowley, and D. Hardest, eds, *Environment and Society* (Englewood Heights, N.J.: Prentice Hall 1980), 187–94.

19. Timothy Doyle and Doug McEachern, *Environment and Politics* (London: Routledge, 1998), 47.

20. Ibid., 49.

21. Robin Eckersley, *Environmentalism and Political Theory* (New York: State University of New York Press 1992), 1.

22. Wissenburg, *Green Liberalism*, 73.

23. Tim Hayward, *Ecological Thought: An Introduction* (Cambridge: Polity Press, 1994), 131.

24. Wissenburg, *Green Liberalism*, 74.

25. Susan M. Leeson, 'Philosophical Implications of the Ecological Crisis: The Authoritarian Challenge to Liberalism', *Polity* 11 (1979): 306.

26. Doug Macdonald, *The Politics of Pollution* (Toronto: McClelland & Stewart, 1991), 83.

27. Ibid., 83.

28. Hayward, *Ecological Thought: An Introduction*, 31.

29. Macdonald, *The Politics of Pollution*, 83.

30. Ibid., 81.

31. Ibid., 81.

32. Cahn, *Environmental Deceptions*, 8.

33. Engel, 'Liberal Democracy and the Fate of the Earth', 70.

34. Cahn, *Environmental Deceptions*, 5.

35. Ibid., 5.

36. John Opie, *Nature's Nation* (Orlando: Harcourt Brace, 1998), 137.

37. Hayward, *Ecological Thought*, 104.

38. Opie, *Nature's Nation*, 467.

39. Cahn, *Environmental Deceptions*, 13.

40. Ibid., 14.

41. Ibid., 187.

42. Ken Conca and Geoffrey D. Dabelko, eds, *Green Planet Blues*, 2nd edn (Boulder, Colo.: Westview Press, 1998), 11.

43. David Harvey, *The Condition of Postmodernity* (Oxford: Blackwell, 1989), 294, 296.

44. Timothy W. Luke, *Capitalism, Democracy, and Ecology* (Urbana, Illo: University of Illinois Press, 1999), 218.

45. Engel, 'Liberal Democracy and the Fate of the Earth', 68.

46. William Clark, as quoted in Scott Allen, 'Then Again, Earth May Take a Turn for the Better', *Boston Globe*, 16 Dec. 1999.

47. James Hansen, director of NASA's Goddard Institute for Space, as quoted in Scott Allen, 'Then Again, Earth May Take a Turn for the Better', *Boston Globe*, 16 Dec. 1999.

48. Greg Easterbrook as quoted in Doyle and McEachern, *Environment and Politics*, 4.

49. Wissenburg, *Green Liberalism*, 213.

50. Eckersley, *Environmentalism and Political Theory*, 49.
51. Hayward, *Ecological Thought*, 437–8.
52. George Sessions and Arne Naess as quoted in Doyle and MacEachern, *Environment and Politics*, 38–9.
53. Eckersley, *Environmentalism and Political Theory*, 51.
54. Barbara Noske, *Humans and Other Animals* (London: Pluto, 1989), 160.
55. Mark Dowie, *Losing Ground* (Cambridge, Mass.: MIT Press, 1996), 235.
56. Dowie, *Losing Ground*, 235.
57. World Commission on Environment and Development (WCED), *Our Common Future* (New York: Oxford University Press, 1987).
58. Miller, *Gaia Connections*, 4.
59. Marcia Nozick, *No Place like Home* (Ottawa: Canadian Council on Social Development, 1992), 12.
60. C. Goodland, 'The Case That the World Has Reached Limits', in R. Goodland, H.E. Daly and S.E. Serafy, eds, *Population, Technology, and Lifestyle* (Washington, DC: Island Press, 1992), 3–22.
61. Herman E. Daly, 'Sustainable Growth: An Impossibility Theorem', in Herman E. Daly and Kenneth N. Townsend, eds, *Valuing the Earth: Economics, Ecology, Ethics* (Cambridge, Mass: MIT Press, 1993), 267.
62. Cahn, *Environmental Deceptions*, 127
63. Dobson, *Green Political Thought*, 17.
64. Brian Tokar, *The Green Alternative* (San Pedro: R. & E. Miles, Calif., 1992), 64.
65. Tokar, *The Green Alternative*, 3.
66. See Graham Lyons, Evonne Moore, and Joseph Wayne Smith, *Is the End Nigh? Internationalism, Global Chaos and the Destruction of the Earth* (Sydney: Avebury, 1995).
67. C. Glendinning, 'Notes Toward a Neo-Luddite Manifesto', *Utne Reader*, March/April, 1990.
68. Tokar, *The Green Alternative*, 27.
69. Ibid., 27.
70. Hayward, *Ecological Thought: An Introduction*, 107.
71. Tokar, *The Green Alternative*, 31.
72. Dowie, *Losing Ground*, 229.
73. Edward Goldsmith et al., 'A Blueprint for Survival', in Andrew Dobson, ed., *The Green Reader* (New York: Mercury House, 1991), 73.
74. Goldsmith et al., 'A Blueprint for Survival', 75.
75. E.F. Schumacher, *Small Is Beautiful* (London: Abacus, 1974), 62.
76. Stephen C. Rockefeller, 'Faith and Community in an Ecological Age', in Steven C. Rockefeller and John C. Elder, eds, *Spirit and Nature* (Boston: Beacon Press, 1992), 143.
77. Rockefeller, 'Faith and Community in an Ecological Age', 143–4.
78. Tokar, *The Green Alternative*, 4.
79. According to Paul Harrison, this system supplemented labourers' wages whenever they fell below the bare subsistence level, calculated according to the price of a gallon loaf and the size of the family. Its net effect was to allow employers to cut wages below the subsistence level, and therefore leave the poor no better off than before. See *The Third Revolution* (London: I.B. Tauris, 1992), 12.
80. Harrison, *The Third Revolution*, 12.
81. Ibid., 12.
82. Paul Ehrlich and Anne Ehrlich, *The Population Bomb* (New York: Ballantine, 1969), 35.

83. Paul Ehrlich and Anne Ehrlich, 'Population, Resources, Environment', *New Scientist* 36 (1970): 652.

84. Hayward, *Ecological Thought: An Introduction*, 147.

85. Harrison, *The Third Revolution*, 16.

86. Ibid., 18.

87. Garrett Hardin, 'Cassandra's Role in the Population Wrangle', in Paul R. Ehrlich and John P. Holdren, eds, *The Cassandra Conference* (College Station, Texas A & M University Press, 1988), 14.

88. As quoted in Dobson, *Green Political Theory*, 45.

89. J.E. Lovelock, *Gaia: A New Look at Life on Earth* (Oxford: Oxford University Press, 1979), 8.

90. Ibid., 46.

91. Miller, *Gaia Connections*, 2.

92. D.H. Meadows, D.L. Meadows, J. Randers, and W.W. Behrens III, *The Limits to Growth* (Washington, DC: Potomac Associates, 1972), as excerpted in 'The Limits to Growth', in Ken Conca, Michael Alberty, and Geoffrey D. Dabelko, eds, *Green Planet Blues* (Boulder, Colo.: Westview Press, 1995), 28.

93. Meadows et al., *Green Planet Blues*, 29.

94. Dobson, *Green Political Theory*, 74.

95. Harrison, *The Third Revolution*, 17.

96. Opie, *Nature's Nation*, 194.

97. Ibid., 193.

98. Henry David Thoreau, Walden (1859), Chapter 6, note 1. All of Thoreau's writings can be found at this site.

99. Opie, *Nature's Nation*, 194.

100. Ibid., 196.

101. Ibid., 198.

102. Ibid., 204.

103. Thomas Berry, 'The Viable Human', in George Sessions, ed., *Deep Ecology for the Twenty-first Century* (Boston: Shambhala, 1995), 12.

104. Ibid., 12.

105. Rod Preece, *Animals and Nature: Cultural Myths, Cultural Realities* (Vancouver, UBC Press, 1999), 158.

106. Ibid., 159.

107. Peter Knudtson and David Suzuki, *Wisdom of the Elders* (Toronto: Stoddart, 1992), 3–4.

108. Ibid., 15.

109. Ibid., 15.

110. J. Donald Hughes, 'American Indian Ecology', in Roger S. Gottlieb, ed., *This Sacred Earth* (New York: Routledge, 1996), 138.

111. Ibid., 131.

112. Ibid., 135.

113. W.C. Vanderwerth, ed., *Indian Oratory: Famous Speeches by Noted Indian Chieftains* (Norman, Okla.: University of Oklahoma Press, 1971), 121.

114. Hughes, 'American Indian Ecology', 143.

115. As quoted in T.C. McLuhan, *Touch the Earth* (Toronto: New Press, 1971), 110.

116. T.C. McLuhan, *The Way of the Earth* (New York: Simon & Schuster, 1994), 378.

117. As quoted in McLuhan, *The Way of the Earth*, 386–7.

118. Mary José Hobday, as quoted in McLuhan, *The Way of the Earth*, 387–8.

119. Knudtson and Sukuki, *Wisdom of the Elders*, 121.
120. Ibid., 122.
121. Ibid., 13.
122. Ibid., 84.
123. Menno Boldt, *Surviving as Indians* (Toronto: University of Toronto Press, 1993), 170.
124. Knudtson and Suzuki, *Wisdom of the Elders*, 83.
125. O.P. Dwivedi, 'Satyagraha for Conservation: Awakening the Spirit of Hinduism', in Roger S. Gottlieb, ed., *This Sacred Earth*, 151.
126. Ibid., 151–2.
127. David Kingsley, 'Christianity as Ecologically Harmful' and 'Christianity as Ecologically Responsible', in Roger S. Gottlieb, ed., *This Sacred Earth*, 107.
128. Rockefeller, 'Faith and Community in an Ecology Area', *Spirit and Nature*, 147–8.
129. Rockefeller, 'Faith and Community in an Ecology Area', 148.
130. Lynn White, 'The Historical Roots of Our Ecological Crisis', in Gottlieb, ed., *This Sacred Earth*, 189.
131. Ibid.
132. Ibid.
133. Chatsumarn Kabilsingh, 'Early Buddhist Views on Nature', in Gottlieb, ed., *This Sacred Earth*, 149.
134. Ibid.
135. Ibid., 149–50.
136. Ibid., 155.
137. Ibid., 161.
138. Ibid.
139. Miller, *Gaia Connections*, 12.
140. Ibid., 5.
141. Rockefeller, 'Faith and Community in an Ecology Area', 143.
142. Aldo Leopold, 'A Sand County Almanac', in Gottlieb, ed., *This Sacred Earth*, 30.
143. Leopold, 'A Sand County Almanac', 30.
144. Ibid., 31.
145. Rockefeller, 'Faith and Community in an Ecology Area', 166.
146. William Leiss, *The Domination of Nature* (New York: George Braziller, 1972), 83.
147. Marx, Karl, *Capital: A Critique of Political Economy* (New York: International, Vol. I, 177.
148. Leiss, *The Domination of Nature*, 83.
149. Luke Martell, *Ecology and Society* (Cambridge: Polity Press, 1994), 149.
150. Ibid., 150.
151. Ibid., 152.
152. Eckersley, *Environmentalism and Political Theory*, 94.
153. Doyle and MacEachern, *Environment and Politics*, 40.
154. Ibid., 41.
155. Murray Bookchin, as quoted in *Defending the Earth: A Debate between Murray Bookchin and Dave Foreman* (Montreal: Black Rose, 1991), 31–2.
156. Bookchin, *Ecological Society*, 69.
157. Ibid.
158. Luke, *Capitalism, Democracy, and Ecology*, 201.
159. Ibid., 199.

160. Carolyn Merchant, *Earthcare: Women and the Environment* (New York: Routledge, 1995), 5.
161. Ibid.
162. Ibid., 11.
163. Ibid., 5.
164. Eckersley, *Environmentalism and Political Theory*, 64.
165. Judith Plant, 'Women and Nature', in Andrew Dobson, ed., *The Green Reader*, 100.
166. Miller, *Gaia Connections*, 22.
167. Karen J. Warren, 'Feminism and Ecology: Making Connections', *Environmental Ethics* 11 (Spring 1989): 17.
168. Warren, 'Toward an Ecofeminist Ethic', *Studies in the Humanities*, Dec. 1988, 151.
169. Ibid., 103.
170. Eckersley, *Environmentalism and Political Theory*, 67.
171. Merchant, *Earthcare: Women and the Environment*, 157. See also Lois Marie Gibbs, *The Love Canal: The Story Continues* (Gabriola Island, BC: New Society, 1998).
172. See Vandana Shiva and Maria Mies, *Ecofeminism* (Halifax, Fernwood: 1993).
173. Macdonald, *The Politics of Pollution*, 73.
174. Peter Singer, *Animal Liberation* (New York: Avon, 1975), 3; emphasis in original.
175. Miller, *The Gaia Connection*, 257.
176. Jeremy Bentham, 'Introduction to the Principles of Morals and Legislation', *Library of Classics*, vol. 6 (Indianapolis, Ind.: Hafner, 1948).
177. Miller, *Gaia Connections*, 254.
178. Ibid., 157–8.

Chapter Two

1. Mark Dowie, *Losing Ground: American Environmentalism at the Close of the Twentieth Century*, (Cambridge: MIT Press, 1995), 223.
2. Ibid., 223.
3. Manuel Castells, *The Information Age: Economy, Society and Culture. Volume II: The Power of Identity* (Oxford: Blackwell, 1997), 110.
4. Ibid., 113.
5. Ibid., 122.
6. Ibid., 70.
7. Ibid., 70.
8. Ibid., 11.
9. Timothy Doyle and Doug McEachern, *Environment and Politics* (London: Routledge, 1998), 55.
10. Ibid., 55.
11. Ibid., 56.
12. Ibid., 59–60.
13. Ibid., 55.
14. Robert Paehlke, 'Green Politics and the Rise of the Environmental Movement', in Thomas Fleming, ed., *The Environment and Canadian Society* (Scarborough: ITP Nelson, 1997), 53.
15. John McCormick, *Reclaiming Paradise* (Indianapolis, Ind.: Indiana University Press, 1989), 47.
16. Among the Group of Ten were the National Parks and Conservation Association, the National Wildlife Association, The Natural Resources Defense Council, Izaak Walton

League, Environmental Defense Fund, and the Environmental Policy Institute, Defenders of Wildlife. See Castells, *The Information Age*, 114.

17. Paehlke, 'Green Politics and the Rise of the Environmental Movement', 254.

18. Gerald Killan and George Warecki, 'The Algonquin Wildlands League and the Emergence of Environmental Politics in Ontario, 1965–1974', *Environmental History Review* 16, no. 4 (Winter 1992): 2.

19. Castells, *The Information Age*, 115.

20. For more information on the Love Canal and the chronology of events, from the citizens'-group perspective, see Lois Marie Gibbs, *The Love Canal: The Continuing Story* (Gabriola Island, BC: New Society Press, 1998).

21. Castells, *The Information Age*, 116.

22. Ibid., 116.

23. Dowie, *Losing Ground*, 243.

24. McCormick, *Reclaiming Paradise*, 49.

25. Castells, *The Information Age*, 119.

26. John Opie, *Nature's Nation* (Orlando, Fla.: Harcourt Brace, 1998), 386.

27. Ibid., 388.

28. Christopher Manes, *Green Rage* (Boston: Little Brown, 1990), 56.

29. Killan and Warecki, 'The Algonquin Wildlands League', 3.

30. Doug Macdonald, *The Politics of Pollution* (Toronto: McClelland & Stewart, 1991), 85.

31. Ulf Hjelmar, *The Political Practice of Environmental Organizations* (Aldershot: Ashgate, 1996), 125.

32. Ibid., 125–6.

33. McCormick, *Reclaiming Paradise*, 50.

34. Eckersley, *Environmentalism and Political Theory*, 10.

35. Manes, *Green Rage*, 50.

36. Tokar, *The Green Alternative*, 35.

37. Killan and Warecki, 'The Algonquin Wildlands', 3.

38. Ibid., 5.

39. Opie, *Nature's Nation*, 415.

40. Jacqueline Vaughan Switzer, *Green Backlash* (Boulder, Colo.: Lynne Rienner, 1997), 9.

41. Manes, *Green Rage*, 45.

42. Switzer, *Green Backlash*, 9.

43. Dowie, *Losing Ground*, 105–6.

44. Ibid., 106.

45. Ibid., 109.

46. See SmartWood *Program Description*, < http://www.smartwood.org. >

47. Karen Burshtein, 'Good Wood', *Globe and Mail*, 12 Aug. 2000.

48. Ibid.

49. Wendy Stueck, 'BC Forestry Firms Slam US Chain's Wood Ban', *Globe and Mail*, 9 Aug. 2000.

50. 'Joint Statement by Companies and ENGOs', < http://www.trees2k.org/news > (29 May 2000).

51. Greenpeace Canada/Sierra Club of BC, 'Greenpeace: Interfor, West Fraser Become Markets Targets in Japan', < http://www.trees2k.org/news > 20 July 2000.

52. ForestEthics, 'Press Release: Largest Rainforest Conservation Measure in North American History', 4 April 2001.

53. Ibid.

54. ForestEthics, 'Questions and Answers about the Agreement Reached in British Columbia', < ForestEthics.org > (4 April 2001).

55. Ibid.

56. 'Risky Plan for Ontario's North', editorial, *Toronto Star*, 24 May 1999.

57. Ibid.

58. Sheldon Lipsey, 'Deal Betrays Grassroots Effort', letter to the Editor, *Toronto Star*, 9 Aug. 1999.

59. 'Lands for Life Keeps Getting Worse', letter to the Editor, *Toronto Star*, 25 July 1999.

60. 'Forest Accord Hands the North to Loggers', editorial, *Toronto Star*, 25 Apr. 1999.

61. Dowie, *Losing Ground*, 115.

62. Ibid., 207.

63. See G. Bruce Doern and Thomas Conway, *The Greening of Canada* (Toronto: University of Toronto Press, 1994).

64. Doyle and McEachern, *Environment and Politics*, 81.

65. Ibid.

66. Ibid., 102.

67. Ibid., 101.

68. Third-party advertising refers to advertising for a political party by some other organization. This kind of advertising was used extensively in Canada during the 1988 election, which was waged primarily on the issue of free trade. Several years later, legislation was passed that imposed strong limitations on this kind of spending. This legislation was challenged successfully on the grounds that it violated freedom of expression under the *Charter of Rights and Freedoms*. A subsequent amendment to the *Canada Elections Act* that received royal assent in June 2000 allows third parties to spend up to $150,000 in federal general elections. It will not come into effect until January 2001. However, no more than $3,000 of this amount can be spent in any one federal riding. It is expected that this amendment will also be challenged.

69. Hjelmar, *The Political Practice of Environmental Organizations*, 110.

70. Sierra Legal Defence Fund web site. (< http://www.sierralegal.org >).

71. Ibid.

72. Hjelmar, *The Political Practice of Environmental Organizations*, 111.

73. Christopher J. Bosso, 'After the Movement: Environmental Activism in the 1990s', in Michael E. Kraft and Norman J. Vig, eds, *Environmental Policy in the 1990s: Towards a New Agenda* (Washington, DC: Congressional Quarterly Press, 1995), 39.

74. Ibid., 40.

75. Ibid., 41.

76. MiningWatch Canada 1999–2000, < http://www.miningwatch.ca. >

77. MiningWatch Canada, 'Balancing the Books: The Hidden Costs of Mining', < http://www.miningwatch.ca/publications > .

78. As quoted in Mineral Policy Centre, Mining Watch Canada and Minewatch UK, Joint Press Release, 'One of World's Worst Mine Disasters Gets Worse'. 11 Aug. 1999.

79. Geoff Evans, director of Mineral Policy Institute, as quoted in MiningWatch Canada, 'One of World's Worst Mine Disasters Gets Worse'.

80. MiningWatch Canada, Press Release, 'Canadian Gold Mining Interests Involved in Police Shootings in Ghana, West Africa', 22 Dec. 1999.

81. Paul Wapner, 'In Defense of Banner Hangers: The Dark Green Politics of Greenpeace', in Bron Raymond Taylor, ed., *Ecological Resistance Movements* (Albany, NY: State University of New York, 1995), 300.

82. Ibid.

83. As quoted in Christopher Manes, *Green Rage*, 57.

84. Stewart Bell, 'Greenpeace Serves "No Public Benefit"', *National Post*, 5 June 1999.

85. Wapner, 'In Defense of Banner Hangers', 307.

86. Steven Yearley, *The Green Case* (London: HarperCollinsAcademic, 1991), 70.

87. Ibid.

88. CBC Newsworld, 'BC women bare all in fight over island's forest', < http://www. cbc.ca/news/2000/08/27 > (28 Aug. 2000).

89. Brian McAndrew, 'Showdown at the Oak Ridges Moraine', *Toronto Star*, 12 Feb. 2000.

90. 'Scientists Rally for Oak Ridges Moraine', *Toronto Star*, < http://www.thestar.com/ editorial/updates/gta > (1 Feb. 2000).

91. McAndrew, 'Showdown at the Oak Ridges Moraine'.

92. Canadian Environmental Law Association, June 1998, *Homepage*, < http://www. web.net/cela > (25 Feb. 2000).

93. Canadian Environmental Law Association, June 1998. 'About CELA', < http://www. web.net.cela/about > (18 Mar. 2000).

94. Ibid.

95. Ibid.

96. Ibid.

97. Ibid.

98. Dowie, *Losing Ground*, 241.

99. Mike Robinson, *The Greening of British Party Politics* (Manchester: Manchester University Press, 1992), 206.

100. Dowie, *Losing Ground*, 242.

101. Petra Kelly and Gert Bastian were two of the six founding members of Die Grünen. The others were Roland Vogt, Joseph Beuys, the Czech exile Milan Horaček, and the expelled East German economist Rudolf Bahro.

102. Under the *Canada Elections Act*, to register as a political party, a party must nominate candidates in at least fifty electoral districts at least sixty days before the election is called. In 1997, fourteen parties were registered; however, only nine had their registrations confirmed and five lost their registration. Only registered parties are entitled to reimbursement of certain election expenses and to paid and free broadcasting time.

103. 'BC Green Leader Loses Control of Party', *Toronto Star*, 20 Mar. 2000.

104. Dan Hauka, 'Dosanjh Admits Defeat as Greens Pull Ahead', *Calgary Herald*, 9 May 2001.

105. Sasha Nagy, 'BC Voters Head to the Polls', *Globe and Mail*, 16 May 2001.

106. Often referred to as the Cairns thesis. In 1968, Alan Cairns put forward the argument that there were a number of distortions caused by Canada's single-member-plurality electoral system. See Alan C. Cairns, 'The Electoral System and the Party System in Canada, 1921–1965', *Canadian Journal of Political Science* 1, no. 1 (March 1968): 55–80.

107. Manuel Castells, *The Power of Identity*, 110.

108. See Paul R. Abramson and Ronald Inglehart, *Value Change in Global Perspective* (Ann Arbour, Mich.: University of Michigan Press, 1995).

109. Sharon Beder, *Global Spin: The Corporate Assault on Environmentalism* (Tornes, Devon: Green Books, 1997), 16.

110. Abramson and Inglehart, *Value Change in Global Perspective*, 97.

111. Ronald Inglehart, 'Public Support for Environmental Protection: Objective Problems and Subjective Values in 43 Societies', *Political Science and Politics*, March 1995, 65.

112. The PDI is calculated by subtracting the percentage of materialists from the percentage of post-materialists. See Abramson and Inglehart, *Value Change in Global Perspective*, 91.

113. Abramson and Inglehart, *Value Change in Global Perspective*, 135.

114. Ibid., 267–8.

115. Ibid., 96.

116. Ibid.

117. Inglehart, 'Public Support for Environmental Protection', 70.

118. Harold D. Clarke and Marianne C. Stewart, 'Green Words and Public Deeds: Environmental Hazards and Citizen Response in Canada and the United States', in Jon Pammett and Alan Frizzell, eds, *Shades of Green* (Ottawa: Carleton University Press, 1998), 77.

119. Donald E. Blake, Neil Guppy, and Peter Urmetzer, 'Being Green in BC', *The British Columbian Quarterly*, no. 112 (Winter 1996–97), 42.

120. Blake, Guppy, and Urmetzer, 'Being Green in BC', 44.

121. Ibid., 47.

122. Ibid., 50–1.

123. Ibid., 59–60.

124. Harold D. Clarke, Jane Jenson, Lawrence LeDuc, and Jon H. Pammett, *Political Choice in Canada* (Toronto: McGraw-Hill Ryerson, 1979), 243–4.

125. Clarke et al., *Political Choice in Canada*, 244.

126. H.D. Clarke et al., *Absent Mandate*, 3rd edn (Toronto: Gage Educational, 1996), 4.

127. Robert C. Paehlke, *Environmentalism and the Future of Progressive Politics* (New Haven, Conn.: Yale University Press, 1989), 232.

128. Beder, *Global Spin*, 18.

129. Ibid., 21.

130. Brian Tokar as quoted in Joyce Nelson, 'Great Global Greenwash: Burson-Marsteller, Pax Trilateral and the Brundtland Gang vs. the Environment', *CovertAction* 44 (1993): 27.

131. Beder, *Global Spin*, 32.

132. Ibid., 47.

133. Ibid., 53.

134. Eloy Casagrande Junior and Richard Welford, 'The Big Brothers: Transnational Corporations, Trade Organizations and Multilateral Financial Institutions', in Richard Welford, ed., *Hijacking Environmentalism* (London: Earthscan, 1997), 138.

135. Ibid., 139.

136. Ibid., 140.

137. Ibid., 141.

138. Robert A. Hackett and Richard Gruneau, *The Missing News: Filters and Blind Spots in Canada's Press* (Ottawa: Centre for Policy Alternatives, 2000), 169.

139. Ibid.

140. Ibid., 170.

141. Ibid.

142. Mark Evans, 'Canada Second in Internet Use', *Globe and Mail*, 22 Mar. 2000.

143. See Kevin A. Hall and John E. Hughes, *Cyberpolitics: Citizen Activism in the Age of the Internet* (Lanham: Rowman & Littlefield, 1998).

144. E-mail correspondence with Rex Turgano, 31 Aug. 2000.

145. Matthew Mendelsohn and Robert Wolfe, *Probing the Aftermyth of Seattle: Canadian Public Opinion on International Trade, 1980–2000*, Working Paper 12, Queen's University, School of Policy Studies, Dec. 2000, 3.

Chapter Three

1. George Hoberg, 'Environmental Policy: Alternative Styles', in Michael M. Atkinson, ed., *Governing Canada* (Toronto: Harcourt Brace Jovanovich, 1993), 311.

2. Melody Hessing and Michael Howlett, *Canadian Natural Resource and Environmental Policy* (Vancouver: UBC Press, 1997), 5.

3. David Vanderzwaag and Linda Duncan, 'Canada and Environmental Protection', in Robert Boardman, ed., *Canadian Environmental Policy: Ecosystems, Politics, and Process* (Toronto: Oxford University Press, 1992), 22.

4. Hessing and Howlett, *Canadian Natural Resource and Environmental Policy*, 7.

5. Doug Macdonald, *The Politics of Pollution* (Toronto: McClelland & Stewart, 1991), 51.

6. Hessing and Howlett, *Canadian Natural Resource and Environmental Policy*, 5.

7. Ibid., 7.

8. For a discussion of agreements reached in these disputes, see Leo Barry, 'Offshore Petroleum Agreements: An Analysis of the Nova Scotian and Newfoundland Experience', in J.O. Saunders, ed., *Managing Natural Resources in a Federal State* (Calgary: Carswell, 1986).

9. Macdonald, *The Politics of Pollution*, 51.

10. Hessing and Howlett, *Canadian Natural Resource and Environmental Policy*, 50.

11. Macdonald, *The Politics of Pollution*, 51–2.

12. Ibid., 52.

13. Vanderzwaag and Duncan, 'Canada and Environmental Protection', 5.

14. Ibid., 6.

15. M. Paul Brown, 'Organizational Design as Policy Instrument', in Robert Boardman, ed., *Canadian Environmental Policy: Ecosystems, Politics and Process*, 24.

16. George Hoberg, 'North American Environmental Regulation', in G. Bruce Doern and Stephen Wilks, eds, *Changing Regulatory Institutions in Britain and North America* (Toronto, University of Toronto Press, 1998), 309.

17. Ibid.

18. Hoberg, 'Environmental Policy', 315.

19. Hoberg, 'North American Environmental Regulation', 310.

20. Hoberg, 'Environmental Policy', 334.

21. Hoberg, 'North American Environmental Regulation', 311.

22. Ibid.

23. Ibid., 313.

24. Joseph L. Castrilli, *Environmental Control of the Mining Industry in Canada and Chile* (Toronto: Canadian Environmental Law Association, 1998), 30.

25. Grace Skogstad and Paul Kopas, 'Environmental Policy in a Federal System', in Robert Boardman, ed., *Canadian Environmental Policy: Ecosystems, Politics, and Process* (Toronto: Oxford University Press, 1992), 51.

26. Hoberg, 'Environmental Policy', 323.

27. James E. Alt, Margaret Levi, and Elinor Ostrom, eds, *Competition and Cooperation* (New York: Russell Sage, 1999), xv.

28. Kathryn Harrison, 'Retreat from Regulation: The Evolution of the Canadian Regulatory Regime', in G. Bruce Doern et al., eds, *Changing the Rules: Canadian Regulatory Regimes and Institutions* (Toronto: University of Toronto Press, 1999), 123–4.

29. Hoberg, 'North American Environmental Regulation', 314.

30. Kathryn Harrison, 'Voluntarism and Environmental Governance', Apr. 1999, 2, <http://www.policy.ca> (20 Jan. 2001).

31. Ibid., 3.

32. Ibid., 9.

33. John Moffet and François Bregha, 'Responsible Care', in Robert B. Gibson, ed., *Voluntary Initiatives and the New Politics of Corporate Greening* (Peterborough, Ont.: Broadview Press, 1999), 69.

34. Ibid.
35. Ibid., 71.
36. Ibid., 74, 78.
37. Ibid., 85.
38. Debora L. VanNijnatten, 'The ARET Challenge', in Robert B. Gibson, ed., *Voluntary Initiatives and the New Politics of Corporate Greening*, 93.
39. Ibid., 93–4.
40. Ibid., 98.
41. Ibid.
42. Harrison, 'Voluntarism and Environmental Governance', 11.
43. See Chapter 7, 'Deregulation, Industry Self-Regulation and the Certification Scam', in Elizabeth May, *At the Cutting Edge* (Toronto: Key Porter, 1998), 57–61.
44. Brown, 'Organizational Design as a Policy Instrument', 27.
45. Ibid., 30.
46. Herman Bakvis and Neil Nevitte, 'The Greening of the Canadian Electorate: Environmentalism, Ideology and Partisanship'. Paper presented to the Annual Meeting of the Canadian Political Science Association, University of Victoria, Victoria, BC, 28 May 1990, 2.
47. Brown, 'Organizational Development as a Policy Instrument', 32.
48. Ibid., 37.
49. Hoberg, 'North American Environmental Regulation', 316.
50. Ibid.
51. Vanderzwaag and Duncan, 'Canada and Environmental Protection', 4.
52. Skogstad and Kopas, 'Environmental Policy in a Federal System', 45.
53. Vanderzwaag and Duncan, 'Canada and Environmental Protection', 8.
54. Mark Winfield, 'The Ultimate Horizontal Issue: The Environmental Policy Experiences of Alberta and Ontario, 1971–1993', *Canadian Journal of Political Science* 27 (1994).
55. Anita Krajnk, 'Neo-Conservatism and the Decline of the Environment Ministry', *Canadian Public Policy* 26, no. 1 (2000): 112.
56. Ibid., 114.
57. Ibid., 115.
58. Ibid., 123.
59. Ibid.
60. Ibid., 124.
61. Canadian Environmental Assessment Agency, *Review of the Canadian Environmental Assessment Act: A Discussion Paper for Public Consultation*, Dec. 1999, <http://199.212.18.103/discussion_e.htm> (8 Jan. 2001).
62. Ibid.
63. Ibid.
64. Canadian Institute for Environmental Law and Policy, *Mining's Many Faces* (Toronto: The Institute, 2000), 35.
65. George Hoberg, 'Sleeping with an Elephant', *Journal of Public Policy* 11, no. 1 (1991): 108.
66. Ibid., 110.
67. Ibid., 111.
68. Environment Canada, *Canada's Plan for Protecting Species at Risk—Habitat Measures*, <www.ec.gc.ca/sara/report/report11.htm> (16 Jan. 2000).
69. See COSEWIC's website. <http://www.COSEWIC.org>.

70. See 'What Is RENEW?' < http://www.cws-scf.ec.gc.ca/es/renew/RENEW97_98 > .

71. Bill Freedman, Lindsay Roger, Peter Ewins, and David M. Green, 'Species at Risk in Canada', in *Politics of the Wild*, edited by Karen Beasely and Robert Boardman (Toronto: Oxford University Press), 27.

72. Fraser Institute, 'Crying Wolf: Does Canada Have an Endangered Species Crisis?' *Public Policy Sources* 1 (1999) < http://www.fraserinstitute.ca/publications > (18 Nov. 2000).

73. From a statement by Pierre Gratton, Proceedings of the Standing Committee on Environment and Sustainable Development, Parliament of Canada, 17 Oct. 2000.

74. Canadian Wildlife Association, 'Comments on the Canada Endangered Species Protection Act' (Ottawa: The Association, 1997), 4.

75. Ibid., 5.

76. Ibid., 18.

77. Environment Canada, *Canada's Plan for protecting Species at Risk—Habitat Measures*, < http://www.ec.gc.ca/sara/report/report11.htm > (16 Jan. 2000).

78. Ibid.

79. The Fraser Institute, 'Crying Wolf—Conclusion'.

80. Environment Canada, *Canada's Plan for Protecting Species at Risk-Compensation*, < http://www.ec.gc.ca/sara/report/report12.htm > (16 Jan. 2000).

81. Environment Canada, *Canada's Plan for Protecting Species at Risk—Compliance and Enforcement*, < http://www.ec.gc.ca/sara/report/report13.htm > (16 Jan. 2000).

82. On 1 February 2001, the terms of a cash deal that might settle a lawsuit over the *E. coli* water disaster was presented to the residents of Walkerton, Ontario. At least $2,000 would be paid by the Ontario government to every resident of Walkerton. The deal would allow individual cases to be evaluated separately, particularly when there had been deaths and serious illness, with no pre-set limits. Moreover, anyone whose business suffered as a result of the contamination or who suffered real estate losses would also be able to apply for additional compensation, again with no pre-set limits. Under the agreement, insurers for the defendants (including the municipality, the utilities commission, and the area health unit) would pay the first $17 million of compensation and another $5 million in legal fees. The Province of Ontario would be responsible for the remainder of the claim. In the event that the offer is accepted by the residents and approved by a court, the provincial government will not admit that it did anything wrong in the contamination tragedy. The plaintiffs had been seeking $250 million in general and punitive damages.

Chapter 4

1. H.A. Innis, *The Cod Fisheries: The History of an International Economy*. Rev. edn (Toronto: University of Toronto Press, 1954), 492.

2. Ibid., 495.

3. Patricia Marchak, *Green Gold* (Vancouver: University of British Columbia Press, 1983), xiii.

4. See 'A Plea for Time' in H.A. Innis, *The Bias of Communication* (Toronto: University of Toronto Press, 1951), 61–91.

5. David Ralph Matthews, *Controlling Common Property* (Toronto: University of Toronto Press, 1993), 41.

6. Ibid., 74.

7. Usufruct property is property over which users have the right to exclude non-users.

8. Matthews, *Controlling Common Property*, 74.

9. Gordon H. Scott, 'The Economic Theory of a Common-Property Resource: The Fishery', *Journal of Political Economy* 62, no. 2 (1954): 124–42.

10. Matthews, *Controlling Common Property*, 41.
11. Garrett Hardin, 'The Tragedy of the Commons', *Science* 162 (1968): 1244.
12. Matthews, *Controlling Common Property*, 76–7.
13. James E. Alt, Margaret Levi, and Elinor Ostrom, *Competition and Cooperation* (New York: Russell Sage Foundation, 1999), xviii.
14. Elinor Ostrom, *Governing the Commons* (Cambridge: Cambridge University Press, 1990), 22.
15. Marchak, *Green Gold*, 12.
16. Ken Johnstone, *The Vanishing Harvest* (Montreal: Montreal Star, 1972), 49–50.
17. Ibid., 50.
18. Ibid., 56.
19. Paul Harrison, *The Third Revolution* (London: I.B. Tauris, 1992), 49.
20. Johnstone, *The Vanishing Harvest*, 55.
21. Ragnar Arnason and Lawrence Felt, eds, *The North Atlantic Fisheries: Successes, Failures and Challenges*, vol. 3 (Charlottetown: Institute of Island Studies, 1995), 17–19.
22. Anthony Davis, *Dire Straits: The Dilemmas of a Fishery* (St John's, Nfld.: Institute of Social and Economic Research, 1991), 71.
23. Arnason and Felt, *The North Atlantic Fisheries*, 19.
24. Davis, *Dire Straits*, 73.
25. Ibid., 75.
26. Johnstone, *The Vanishing Harvest*, 20–1.
27. Ibid., 21.
28. Ibid., 55.
29. Canada, Department of Fisheries and Oceans, *Northern Cod—A Fisheries Success Story* (Ottawa: Minister of Supply and Services, 1980).
30. Davis, *Dire Straits*, 76.
31. Matthews, *Controlling Common Property*, 48–9.
32. Ibid., 49.
33. Davis, *Dire Straits*, 80.
34. Ibid.
35. Ibid., 89–90.
36. Craig Palmer and Peter Sinclair, *When the Fish Are Gone* (Halifax: Fernwood, 1997), 41.
37. Ibid., 40.
38. Ibid., 42.
39. Ibid., 44–5.
40. Ibid., 42.
41. Lawrence Felt and R. Locke, 'It Were Well to Live Mainly off Fish', in Arnason and Felt, *The North Atlantic Fisheries: Successes, Failures, and Challenges*, vol. 3 (Charlottetown: Institute of Island Studies, 1995), 217.
42. Matthews, *Controlling Common Property*, 48–9.
43. Department of Fisheries and Oceans, *Newsrelease* 5 Aug. 1999, 1.
44. Felt and Locke, 'It Were Well to Live Mainly off Fish', 211.
45. Palmer and Sinclair, *When the Fish Are Gone*, 46–7.
46. Ibid.
47. Northern Cod Review Panel, *Independent Review of the State of the Northern Cod Final Report* (Ottawa: Minister of Supply and Services Canada, 1990) 129.
48. Felt and Locke, 'It Were Well to Live Mainly off Fish', 218.

49. Ibid.
50. Northern Cod Review Panel, *Independent Review of the State of the Northern Cod*, 13.
51. Palmer and Sinclair, *When the Fish Are Gone*, 83–4.
52. Ibid., 63.
53. Jeffrey A. Hutchings and Ransom A. Myers, 'The Biological Collapse of Atlantic Cod off Newfoundland and Labrador', in Ragnar Arnason and Lawrence Felt, eds, *The North Atlantic Fisheries—Successes, Failures and Challenges* (Charlottetown: Institute of Island Studies, 1995), 76.
54. Felt and Locke, 'It Were Well to Live Mainly off Fish', 220–1.
55. Ibid.
56. Ibid., 212.
57. Palmer and Sinclair, *When the Fish Are Gone*, 47.
58. Ibid., 47.
59. Ibid., 74–5.
60. Ibid., 75.
61. Felt and Locke, 'It Were Well to Live Mainly off Fish', 219.
62. Ibid., 221.
63. Ibid., 223.
64. Ibid., 223–4.
65. Rick Maclean, 'Fishing Fury', CBC *News Online*, 17 Nov. 1999, 3, < http://cbc.ca/news/indepth/fishingfury/index.html >.
66. Maclean, 'Fishing Fury', 6.
67. R. v. Marshall, 17 Sept. 1999, < http://www.sc-gc.ca >.
68. Ibid.
69. Maclean, 'Fishing Fury', 2.
70. Allison Dunfield, 'First Nations Grand Chief Slams Fisheries', *Globe and Mail*, 17 Aug. 2000.
71. 'Burnt Church Mi'kmaq, DFO Set for Lobster Showdown', CBC *News*, 11 Aug. 2000, < http://www.cbc.ca >.
72. Anne McIlroy and Heather Scoffield, 'Big Buyout of Atlantic Fishermen Proposed', *Globe and Mail*, 27 Nov. 1999.
73. Arnason and Felt, *The North Atlantic Fisheries*, 294.
74. Felt and Locke, 'It Were Well to Live Mainly off Fish', 224.
75. Department of Fisheries and Oceans, *The Atlantic Fisheries Review—Discussion Paper*, 2000 < www.dfo-mpo.gc.ca > (11 May 2001).
76. Arnason and Felt, *The North Atlantic Fisheries*, 25.
77. Ibid., 26.
78. Worldwatch Institute, 'Atlantic Salmon Face Poisonous Waters', 30 Dec. 1998.
79. Ibid.
80. Ibid.
81. David Suzuki Foundation, News Release, 'Study Identifies Serious Environmental Damage from Netcage Aquaculture', < www.davidsuzuki.org > (17 Apr. 2001).
82. Terry Glavin, *Dead Reckoning* (Vancouver: Douglas & McIntyre, 1996), 15.
83. Johnstone, *The Vanishing Harvest*, 32.
84. Glavin, *Dead Reckoning*, 16.
85. Ibid., 3–4.
86. Johnstone, *The Vanishing Harvest*, n.p.

87. Glavin, *Dead Reckoning*, 13.
88. Ibid., 5.
89. Ibid., 7.
90. Ibid., 7.
91. Ibid., 39.
92. Ibid., 38.
93. Peter O'Neil, 'Taking Stock of the Salmon Treaty', *Vancouver Sun*, 5 July 1999, < www.vancouversun.com >.
94. Robert Matas, 'Good Hauls Not Enough to End Ban on BC Coho, Ottawa Says', *Globe and Mail*, 29 July 1999.
95. Robert Matas and Barrie McKenna, 'Deal Aims to End Annual Salmon Wars', *Globe and Mail*, 4 June 1999.
96. Ibid.
97. Peter McCluskey, 'The Salmon War', *CBC News Online*, 5 Aug. 1999.
98. O'Neil, 'Taking Stock of the Salmon Treaty', 1.
99. Matas, 'Good Hauls Not Enough'.
100. Davis, *Dire Straits*, 87–8.
101. Palmer and Sinclair, *When the Fish Are Gone*, 38.
102. Ibid.
103. Canadian Institute for Environmental Law and Policy, *Mining's Many Faces*, 2000, 58.
104. Mary Louise McAllister and Cynthia Jacqueline Alexander, *A Stake in the Future: Redefining the Canadian Mineral Industry* (Vancouver: UBC Press, 1997), 21.
105. Ibid.
106. Ibid., 32.
107. Harrison, *The Third Revolution*, 39.
108. Ibid.
109. Ibid., 40.
110. Ibid.
111. Ibid., 41.
112. McAllister and Alexander, *A Stake in the Future*, 5.
113. Canadian Institute for Environmental Law and Policy, *Mining's Many Faces* (Toronto: The Institute, 2000), 14.
114. Ibid.
115. Ibid.
116. Ibid., 15.
117. Ibid., 11.
118. Ibid., 12.
119. Ibid., 16.
120. McAllister and Alexander, *A Stake in the Future*, 3.
121. Canadian Environmental Law Association (CELA), 'MiningWatch Canada: Our Eye on the Industry', 7.
122. Ibid., 8.
123. Ibid.
124. CIELP, *Mining's Many Faces*, 26.
125. Ibid., 32.
126. Chetwynd Environmental Society, 'Mining and Land Use Planning in British Columbia—Time for Change', Paper presented to the May 2000 Minerals North Conference, < http://www.miningwatch.org/emcbc/library >.

127. Environmental Mining Council of British Columbia, *A Modest Proposal? Limiting Liability and Waste Management Regulations for Mining*, 29 Mar. 2000, < http://www.miningwatch.org/emcbc/news >.

128. T. Speers, 'Clean-up Will Need $3 Billion and 20 Years', *Ottawa Citizen*, 25 Oct. 1990.

129. CIELP, *Mining's Many Faces*, 42.

130. Ibid., 44.

131. Ibid., 43.

132. Ibid., 37.

133. Ibid., 42.

134. John D. Wirth, *Smelter Smoke in North America: The Politics of Transborder Pollution* (Lawrence, Ka.: University of Kansas Press, 2000), 1.

135. Wirth, *Smelter Smoke in North America*, 208.

136. Ian MacQuarrie, 'Agriculture and Ecology', in Thomas Fleming, ed., *The Environment and Canadian Society* (Scarborough: ITP Nelson, 1997), 55.

137. It has been estimated that 40 per cent of the world's people do not receive adequate and balanced nutrients to meet their basic dietary requirements. Also, a growing number of people have diets that are deficient in micronutrients such as vitamin A, iodine, iron, selenium, and zinc. The consequences of micronutrient malnutrition, or 'hidden hunger', are enormous in terms of a nation's healthcare costs, lost productivity, and sluggish development. For example, deficiencies of iron, iodine, and zinc lead to increased mortality and morbidity rates, decreased cognitive abilities in children born to deficient mothers, reduced family livelihood, and immense suffering among those afflicted.

138. MacQuarrie, 'Agriculture and Ecology', 47.

139. Ibid., 50.

140. Ibid.

141. Ibid., 49.

142. Gord Surgeoner, 'Measuring Risk Reduction in Pesticide Use', *Agrifood Research in Ontario*, 21, no. 3 (1998–9): 2.

143. Surgeoner, 'Measuring Risk Reduction in Pesticide Use', 2.

144. MacQuarrie, 'Agriculture and Ecology', 49.

145. Ibid.

146. Wayne Bennett and Gordon Surgeoner, 'Fly Control in Swine Barns', *Agrifood Research in Ontario* 19, no. 3 (1996): 9.

147. Bennett and Surgeoner, 'Fly Control in Swine Barns', 9.

148. Heather Scoffield, 'Honey, There's a Gene in My Soup', *Globe and Mail*, 21 Aug. 1999.

149. Ibid.

150. Ibid.

151. 'Food at the Crossroads', *The World at Six*, CBC Radio, 12 Oct. 1998.

152. 'Food at the Crossroads'.

153. Dr Ann Clark as quoted in 'Food at the Crossroads'.

154. Dr Philip Regal as quoted in 'Food at the Crossroads'.

155. 'Environmentalists Warn New Bill Easy on Biotech Companies', *CBC Newsworld Online*, 30 Aug. 1999.

156. 'Food at the Crossroads'.

157. Alan S. Miller, *Gaia Connections* (Savage, Md.: Rowman & Littlefield, 1991), 260.

158. 'Food at the Crossroads'.

159. See Campaign for Food Safety web page < http://www.purefood.org >.

160. See Campaign for Food Safety web page < http://www.purefood.org >.

161. 'Food at the Crossroads'.

162. Ann MacMillan, 'Genetically Modified Foods: The British Debate', CBC *Television News Online*, Nov. 1999, < http://www.cbc.ca/news/viewpoint/correspondents/ macmillan_gmf.html > (30 Mar. 2000).

163. Ibid.

164. Debora MacKenzie, 'Unpalatable Truths', *New Scientist*, 17 Apr. 1999. < http://www. newscientist.com/nsplus/insight/gmworld/gmfood/gmfood.html > , (29 Mar. 2000).

165. MacKenzie, 'Unpalatable truths'.

166. Office of Biotechnology, Canadian Food Inspection Agency, *Backgrounder*, 'Food Derived from Biotechnology', 1, < http://www.cfia-acia.agr.ca/english/ppc/biotech/ food.html > .

167. Ibid.

168. 'Environmentalists Warn New Bill Easy on Biotech Companies', 30 Aug. 1999, CBC *Newsworld Online*, < http://www.newsworld.cbc.ca > .

169. Memorandum to the Honourable Allan Rock, Minister of Health, Health Canada from Staff, Food Directorate Health Protection Branch, Re: 'Threats to public health', 30 Sept. 1999. Canadian Health Coalition web site, < http://www.healthcoalition.ca/ sciencepetition.html > (30 Mar. 2000).

170. Leanne Hachey, 'The Food Fight', CBC *News Online*, 29 Jan. 2000 < http://www.cbc. ca/news/indepth/foodfight/index.html > .

171. Council of Canadians, 'Independent Group of Scientists Releases Study Disputing Federal Claims That Genetically Engineered Foods Are Safe', 18 Jan. 2000, < http://www.canadians.org/campaigns/ > .

172. Ann E. Clark, 'Food Safety of GM Crops in Canada: Toxicity and Allergenicity', 2000, < http://www.councilcanadians.ca > .

173. Ibid., 2.

174. Scoffield, 'Honey, There's a Gene in My Soup', 2.

175. Ibid., 3.

176. Ibid., 4.

177. Kim Honey, 'Divisions Remain on Biosafety Protocol', *Globe and Mail*, 29 Jan. 2000.

178. 'Agreement Reached in Biosafety Talks'. 29 Jan. 2000, < http://www.cbc.ca > .

179. 'Frankenfoods and Politics', Editorial, *Globe and Mail*. 27 Jan. 2000.

180. Honey, 'Divisions Remain on Biosafety Protocol'.

181. Alan McHughen, *Pandora's Picnic Basket* (Oxford: Oxford University Press, 2000), 3.

182. Ann Macey, '1999 Organic Statistics', *Eco-Farm & Garden*, Winter 2001, 38.

183. Canadian Organic Growers, *Down to Earth Newsletter*, Feb./March/Apr. 2000, 6.

184. Canadian Organic Growers, 'Bio-Diversity: A Matter of Survival', Feb./March/Apr. 2000.

185. Ross M. Welch, 'Toward a Greener Revolution: Creating More Healthful Food Systems', *Agricultural Research* (May 1999), 2.

186. Union of Concerned Scientists, *Briefing: Industrial Agriculture: Features and Policy*, < http://www.ucsusa.org/agriculture > (10 June 2000).

187. Ontario Ministry of Agriculture, Food and Rural Affairs, *Discussion Paper on Intensive Agricultural Operations in Rural Ontario*, 1, < http://www.gov.on.ca/OMAFRA > . (accessed 15 Aug. 2000.)

188. Canadian Environmental Law Association, Brief No. 384, *Submission by the Canadian Environmental Law Association to the Ministries of Agriculture, Food, and Rural Affairs and Environment on the Discussion Paper on Intensive Agricultural Operations in Ontario*, 15 Feb. 2000.

189. Andrew Nikiforuk, 'Giant Hog Operation Rejected by Community', *Globe and Mail*, 13 July 2000.

190. Ibid.
191. Centre for Policy Alternatives, 'Large-Scale Hog Production and Processing: Concerns for Manitobans', (Ottawa: The Centre, 1999), 1.
192. Ibid., 22.
193. Ontario Ministry of Agriculture, Food and Rural Affairs, News Release, *Backgrounder: Task Force on Intensive Agricultural Operations in Rural Ontario Consultation*, July 2000.
194. CELA, *Submission to the Ministries of Agriculture, Food, and Rural Affairs and Environment*, 3.
195. Ibid., 5.
196. Douglas Powell, 'Don't Blame Industrial Farms for E. coli', *National Post*, 3 June 2000.
197. Harrison, *The Third Revolution*, 46.
198. Ibid., 47–8.
199. See Science Council of Canada, *Sustainable Agriculture: The Research Challenge* (Ottawa: The Council, 1992).
200. Jamie Swift, *Cut and Run* (Toronto: Between the Lines, 1983), 35.
201. Ibid.
202. Ibid., 42.
203. Jeremy Wilson, *Talk and Log* (Vancouver: University of British Columbia Press, 1998), 3.
204. See Jeremy Wilson, *Talk and Log* (Vancouver: UBC Press, 1998); Ben Cashore, *Governing Forestry: Environmental Group Influence in British Columbia and the US Pacific Northwest*, PhD thesis, University of Toronto 1997; and George Hoberg, *Regulating Forestry: A Comparison of Institutions and Policies in British Columbia and the US Pacific Northwest* (Vancouver: FEPA 1993).
205. Larry Pratt and Ian Urquhart, *The Last Great Forest* (Edmonton: NuWest Press, 1994), 1.
206. Pratt and Urquhart, *The Last Great Forest*, 15.
207. Ben Cashore, 'What should Canada do when the softwood lumber agreement expires?' 20 April 2001. This analysis was posted on Policy.ca—a non-partisan resource for the public analysis of Canadian policy issues.
208. Swift, *Cut and Run*, 24.
209. Ibid.
210. Ibid., 25.
211. Ibid., 23–4.
212. Ibid., 23.
213. E.T. Allen, as quoted in Richard Allan Rajala, *Clearcutting the Pacific Rain Forest* (Vancouver: UBC Press, 1998), 92–3.
214. Ibid., 93.
215. Ibid., 99.
216. Ibid., 89.
217. Marchak, *Green Gold*, 353.
218. Rajala, *Clearcutting the Pacific Rain Forest*, 168–9.
219. Marchak, *Green Gold*, 36.
220. Wilson, *Talk and Log: Wilderness Politics in British Columbia*, 13.
221. Wilson, *Talk and Log*, 13.
222. Wilson, *Talk and Log*, 13.
223. Rajala, *Clearcutting the Pacific Rain Forest*, 167.
224. Wilson, *Talk and Log*, 80.
225. Ibid.

226. Ibid., 91.
227. Ibid., 14.
228. Ibid.
229. Ibid., 63.
230. Ibid., 15.
231. Ibid.
232. M. Patricia Marchak, Scott L. Aycock, and Deborah M. Herbert, *Falldown—Forest Policy in British Columbia* (Vancouver: David Suzuki Foundation and Ecotrust Canada, 1999), 14.
233. Ibid., 18.
234. Ibid., 17.
235. Ibid.
236. Ibid., 18.
237. Ibid., 66.
238. Wilson, *Talk and Log*, 21.
239. Ibid.
240. Ibid.
241. Ibid., 23.
242. As reported in Richard Schwindt and Terry Heaps, *Chopping Up the Money Tree: Distributing the Wealth from British Columbia's Forests* (Vancouver: David Suzuki Foundation, 1996), 47–9.
243. Wilson, *Talk and Log*, 36.
244. Ibid., 37.
245. Ibid.
246. Ibid.
247. Ibid., 42.
248. Marchak, *Green Gold*, 30.
249. Pratt and Urquhart, *The Last Great Forest*, 95.
250. Wilson, *Talk and Log*, 28.
251. Ibid., 43.
252. Ibid., 46.
253. Ibid., 49–50.
254. Ibid., 53.
255. Ibid., 55.
256. Ibid., 60.
257. Ibid., 63.
258. Marchak, *Green Gold*, 372.
259. Ibid.
260. Marchak et al., *Falldown*, 13.
261. Ibid., 14.
262. Pratt and Urquhart, *The Last Great Forest*, 111.
263. Ibid., 117.
264. Ibid., 120.
265. Forest Action Network, 'Canadian Companies to Stop Buying Ancient Forest Products', 31 May 2000.
266. Forest Action Network, 'History of FAN', < http://www.fanweb.org/history > (26 Aug. 2000).

267. Martin O'Malley and Angela Mulholland, 'Canada's Water', *CBC News Online*, 4 July 1999, 3, < http://www.cbcnews.cbc.ca/news/indepth/water/ >.

268. Isobel W. Heathcote, 'Canadian Water Resources and Management', in Thomas Fleming, ed., *The Environment and Canadian Society* (Scarborough: ITP Nelson, 1997), 60.

269. Andrew Nikiforuk, 'National Water Crisis Forecast', *Globe and Mail*, 7 June 2000.

270. Ibid.

271. Ibid.

272. Population Action International, as quoted in Marq de Villiers, *Water* (Toronto: Stoddart, 1999), 19.

273. de Villiers, *Water*, 19.

274. Ibid., 20.

275. Heathcote, 'Canadian Resources and Management', 60.

276. Ibid.

277. Ibid., 61.

278. Ibid., 49.

279. Ibid., 50.

280. Ibid.

281. Ibid., 185.

282. Martin Mittelstaedt, 'Water Bottler's Permit Upheld by Appeal Panel', *Globe and Mail*, 21 Dec. 1999.

283. *CBC Newsworld Online*, 'Newfoundland Bails on Water Sales', 20 Oct. 1999.

284. O'Malley and Mulholland, 'Canada's Water', 5-6.

285. de Villiers, *Water*, 282.

286. Ibid., 81-2.

287. O'Malley and Mulholland, 'Canada's Water', 8.

288. de Villiers, *Water*, 281.

289. Ibid., 265.

290. (editorial), *Globe and Mail*, 23 May 1998.

291. O'Malley and Mulholland, 'Canada's Water', 7.

292. de Villiers, *Water*, 276.

293. O'Malley and Mulholland, 'Canada's Water', 4.

294. de Villiers, *Water*, 278.

295. Steven Shrybman, 'A Legal Opinion Concerning Water Export Controls and Canadian Obligations under NAFTA and the WTO', *West Coast Environmental Law*, 15 Sept. 1999, 1.

296. Ibid.

297. Gil Yaron, 'The Final Frontier: A Working Paper on the Big 10 Global Water Corporations and the Privatization and Corporatization of the World's Last Public Resource' (Ottawa: Polaris Institute and the Council of Canadians), 8.

298. Ibid.

299. Harrison, *The Third Revolution*, 51.

300. Ibid., 52.

301. Kathleen Cooper, 'A Sustainable Water Policy for Ontario', *Intervenor* 24, no. 1 (Jan.–Mar. 1999): 6.

302. Ibid.

303. Martin Mittelstaedt, 'Bottlers Free to Drain off Groundwater', *Globe and Mail*, 3 July 1999.

304. Ibid.

305. de Villiers, *Water*, 235.

306. Ibid., 113.

307. Ibid., 113, 279.

308. Ibid., 126.

309. CBC News, 'Indepth Backgrounder: Cryptosporidium', *CBC News Online*, May 2001, < http://www.cbc.ca > .

310. John Barber, 'Walkerton's Woes Continue a Year Later', *Globe and Mail*, 5 May 2001.

311. Thomas Walkom, 'Fatal Outbreak Exposes Something Rotten in the State of Farming', *Toronto Star*, 27 May 2000.

312. E. Oziewicz, 'Bacterial Outbreak Kills Four in Ontario', *Globe and Mail*, 25 May 2000.

313. Ken Kilpatrick, 'Concern Grows about Pollution from Megafarms', *Globe and Mail*, 30 May 2000.

314. Susan Bourette, 'Harris Ignored Walkerton's Pleas in '98', *Globe and Mail*, 15 June 2000.

315. Terence Corcoran, 'When Nature Kills', *National Post*, 27 May 2000.

316. *Maclean's*, 'The Mail', 26 June 2000, 4.

317. Environment Canada, 'Clean Water—Life Depends on It!' *Freshwater Series* A-3, (Ottawa: Minister of Supply and Services Canada, 1992).

318. Ontario Clean Water Agency web site, < http://www.ocwa.com/corpprof.htm > .

319. Richard Foot, 'Ontario May Be Only Place Where Towns Solely Accountable for Water', *National Post*, 2 June 2000.

320. Susan Bourette and Richard Mackie, 'Utility Not Legally Required to Test Water', *Globe and Mail*, 1 June 2000.

321. Ibid.

322. Kilpatrick, 'Concern Grows about Pollution from Megafarms'.

323. Tom Blackwell, 'Water-safety Checks Halved under Harris', *National Post*, 19 June 2000.

324. Bourette, 'Harris Ignored Walkerton's Pleas'.

325. Richard Mackie, 'Environment Ministry Memos Warned of Water Crisis', *Globe and Mail*, 13 June 2000.

326. Ibid.

327. de Villiers, *Water*, 333.

328. Ibid., 341.

329. Frederick W. Frey, 'The Political Context of Conflict and Cooperation over International River Basins', *Water International* 18, no. 1 (1993).

330. de Villiers, *Water*, 363.

331. Ibid., 354.

332. Ibid., 354–5.

Chapter 5

1. Dr Samuel Epstein, as quoted in Martin Mittelstaedt, 'Environmental Factors for Higher Cancer Rates', *Globe and Mail*, 27 Mar. 1999.

2. Margaret Munro, 'Pesticides Discovered in Amniotic Fluid', *National Post*, 15 June 1999.

3. Steve Kroll-Smith and H. Hugh Lloyd, *Bodies in Protest* (New York: New York University Press, 1997), 1.

4. In the early nineteenth century, the air of European cities was thought to be the source of infection and disease. The word miasma, which entered popular conversation, meant dangerous, deathlike air. Noxious exhalations from open sewers and industrial effluents were thought to be the culprit.

5. Daniel S. Blumenthal and A. James Ruttenber, eds, *Introduction to Environmental Health*, 2nd edn (New York: Springer, 1995), 5.

6. Sandra Steingraber, *Everyday Carcinogens: Acting for Prevention in the Face of Scientific Uncertainty*, transcription of keynote address McMaster University, Hamilton, Ont., 27 Mar. 1999.

7. Children's Health Project, *Environmental Standard Setting and Children's Health* (Toronto: Canadian Environmental Law Association and Ontario College of Family Physicians, 2000), 75.

8. Ibid.

9. Robert N. Proctor, 'The Politics of Cancer', in Jennifer Chesworth, ed., *The Ecology of Health* (Thousand Oaks, Calif.: Sage, 1996), 134.

10. *Everyday Carcinogens: Stopping Cancer Before It Starts* (Study released as part of a workshop on cancer prevention at McMaster University, 27 Mar. 1999).

11. Proctor, 'The Politics of Cancer', 134.

12. Canadian Institute of Child Health, *What on Earth?* (proceedings of the National Symposium on Environmental Contaminants and the Implications for Child Health), May 1997 (Ottawa: The Institute, 1977).

13. 'Our Children and the Environment', *Environmental Health Perspectives* 106, no. 6 (June 1998): A263.

14. Steingraber, *Everyday Carcinogens*, 6.

15. Martin Mittelstaedt, 'Environmental Factors Blamed for Higher Cancer Rates', *Globe and Mail*, 27 Mar. 1999.

16. Sandra Steingraber, *Living Downstream* (New York: Addison-Wesley, 1997), 259.

17. Ibid., 260.

18. Ibid., 262.

19. Ibid.

20. Children's Health Project, *Environmental Standard Setting*, 61.

21. Wayne Miller and Garry B. Hill, 'Child Asthma', *Health Reports* (Winter 1998): 9–21.

22. Children's Health Project, *Environmental Standard Setting*, 74.

23. André Picard, 'Toxic Soup May Be Choking Our Kids, Study Finds', *Globe and Mail*, 22 Aug. 2000.

24. Children's Health Project, *Environmental Standard Setting*, 66.

25. Ibid., 71.

26. Ibid., 68.

27. Ibid., 69.

28. World Wildlife Fund Canada, < http://www.wwfcanada.org/navframe.html > 31 Dec. 2000.

29. Picard, 'Toxic Soup May Be Choking Our Kids'.

30. Ibid.

31. Ibid.

32. The entire study is available on the Ontario Medical Association's web site. < http://www.oma.org >.

33. Brian McAndrew, 'Smog Costs to Top $1 Million, Doctors Warn', *Toronto Star*, 28 June 2000.

34. Paul Harrison, *The Third Revolution* (London: I.B. Tauris, 1992), 207.

35. Donald T. Wells, *Environmental Policy* (Saddle River, NJ: Prentice Hall, 1996), 55.

36. John Harte, 'Acid Rain', in Paul H. Ehrlich and John P. Holden, eds, *The Cassandra Conference* (College Station: Texas A&M University Press, 1988), 141.

37. Harte, 'Acid Rain', 142.

38. Harrison, *The Third Revolution*, 205.
39. Don Munton and Geoffrey Castle, 'The Continental Dimension', in Robert Boardman, ed., *Canadian Environmental Policy: Ecosystems, Politics, and Process* (Toronto: Oxford University Press, 1992), 213.
40. Harrison, *The Third Revolution*, 206.
41. Munton and Castle, 'The Continental Dimension', 212.
42. Ibid., 214.
43. Ibid.
44. Ibid., 215.
45. Wells, *Environmental Policy*, 53.
46. Munton and Castle, 'The Continental Dimension', 218.
47. Ibid.
48. Wells, *Environmental Policy*, 54.
49. Environment Canada, *1997 Canadian Acid Rain Assessment, vol. 1, Summary of Results* (Ottawa, 1998), 1.
50. Ibid.
51. Ibid.
52. Ibid., 2.
53. Campbell, 'Our Cities, Our Air, Our Health: Perspectives on Urban Air Quality and Human Health', in Thomas Fleming, ed., *The Environment and Canadian Society* (Scarborough: ITP Nelson, 1997), 111.
54. Campbell, 'Our Cities, Our Air, Our Health', 112.
55. Ibid.
56. Ibid., 113.
57. *CBC News Online*, 'Canada, US Sign Clean Air Deal', 8 Dec. 2000. < www.cbc.ca >.
58. Colin Freeze and Martin Mittelstaedt, 'Ottawa Targets Smog Levels with $120 Million in Funds', *Globe and Mail*, 20 Feb. 2001.
59. Children's Health Project, *Environmental Standard Setting*, 50.
60. Ibid., 51.
61. See M. Haines et al., 'Dioxins and Furans', in *Persistent Environmental Contaminants and the Great Lakes Basin Population: An Exposure Assessment* (Ottawa: Health Canada, 1998).
62. World Wildlife Federation, *'What Are POPs?'*, < http://www.wwf.ca/pops/index.html > (31 Dec. 2000).
63. Children's Health Project, *Environmental Standard Setting*, 51.
64. Ibid., 53.
65. Environment Canada, 'Canada to Sign and Ratify the United Nations Convention on Persistent Organic Pollutants (POPs)' (News release), 9 May 2001.
66. Canadian Environmental Network Toxins Caucus, *Towards the Development of a Global Treaty on Persistent Organic Pollutants*, (Toronto: Canadian Environmental Law Association), 10 Nov. 2000.
67. Ibid.
68. Eli Neidert and Glenn Havelock, *Report of the Canadian Food Inspection Agency* (Ottawa: Supply and Services Canada, 6 November 1998).
69. Ibid.
70. Ibid.
71. As quoted in Alanna Mitchell, 'Pesticide Residues on Canadian Produce Double', *Globe and Mail*, 24 May 1999.
72. Munro, 'Pesticides Discovered in Amniotic Fluid'.

73. Ibid.

74. Children's Health Project, *Environmental Standard*, 155.

75. Ibid., 158.

76. Ibid., 154.

77. Barrie McKenna, 'Ontario's Pollution Second Only to Texas on List of Offenders', *Globe and Mail*, 10 Aug. 1999.

78. Ibid.

79. Ibid.

80. T.C. McLuhan, *The Way of the Earth* (New York: Simon & Schuster, 1994), 394.

81. NASA Facts on Line, 'Ozone: What Is It, and Why Do We Care about It?'. < http://pao.gsfc.nasa.gov/gsfc/service/gallery/fact_sheets/earthsci/ozone.htm > (31 Dec. 2000).

82. Ibid.

83. Ibid.

84. Ibid.

85. Mario J. Molina and F.S. Rowland, 'Stratospheric Sink for Chlorofluoromethanes: Chlorine Atom-catalysed Destruction of Ozone', *Nature* 248 (28 June 1974): 811.

86. Harrison, The Third Revolution, 209.

87. Ibid., 208.

88. Ibid., 209.

89. Ibid.

90. Ozone Secretariat, 'Home Page', < http://www.unep.ch/ozone/treaties.htm > (1 Jan. 2000).

91. Sebastian Oberthür, *Linkages between the Montreal and Kyoto Protocols*, paper prepared for Inter-Linkages, International Conference on Synergies and Coordination between Multilateral Environmental Agreements, 14, 15, and 16 July 1999, 1.

92. See articles 2A-E of the *Montreal Protocol on Substances That Deplete the Ozone Layer*. The full Protocol as amended can be accessed on the home page of the Ozone Secretariat, < http://www.unep.org/ozone/mont_t.htm > (1 Jan. 2000).

93. UNEP, 'There Is No Room for Complacency', news release, 16 Sept. 1999.

94. UNEP, '$440 Million Agreed for Phasing Out Developing Country CFCs', press release, 3 Dec. 2000.

95. Ibid.

96. Ibid.

97. Environment Canada, 'Canada Shows Continued Leadership on Protecting the Ozone Layer', news release, 18 Dec. 2000.

98. As quoted in Environment Canada, *A Primer on Climate Change—The Atmospheric Environment*, < http://www.ec.gc.ca/primer > .

99. Mitchell, Alanna. 'Scientists Raise Alarm of Climate Catastrophe', *Globe and Mail*, 22 Jan. 2001.

100. Ibid.

101. Environment Canada, 'What Is Climate Change?' < http://www.ec.gc.ca/climate/whatis/index.html > (15 Sept. 2000).

102. Alanna Mitchell, '2000 Weather Hints at Climate Change', *Globe and Mail*, 2 Jan. 2000.

103. Environment Canada, *A Primer On Climate Change*, 6.

104. Ibid., 2.

105. Ibid.

106. International Institute for Sustainable Development, *A Guide to Kyoto: Climate Change and What It Means to Canadians* (Ottawa: The Institute, 1998), 8.

107. Ibid.
108. Harrison, *The Third Revolution*, 210.
109. John M. Balbus and Mark L. Wilson, *Human Health and Global Climate Change: A Review of Potential Impacts in the United States* (PEW Center on Global Climate Change, 2000), 10.
110. Balbus and Wilson, *Human Health and Global Climate Change*, 12.
111. Environment Canada, *Climate Trends*. Environment Canada Web site, < http://www.ec.gc.ca/climate > (20 Sept. 2000).
112. Balbus and Wilson, *Human Health and Global Climate Change*, 10.
113. Ibid., 12.
114. Ibid.
115. Ibid.
116. Ibid., 13.
117. Ibid., 15.
118. Robert Hornung, Director of the Climate Change Program, Pembina Institute, Ottawa, as quoted in Alanna Mitchell, '2000 Weather Hints at Climate Change'.
119. Alanna Mitchell, '2000 Weather Hints at Climate Change'.
120. As quoted in Alanna Mitchell, '2000 Weather Hints at Climate Change'.
121. Ibid.
122. Environment Canada, *A Primer on Climate Change*, 4.
123. Mitchell, '2000 Weather Hints at Climate Change'.
124. Environment Canada, *A Primer on Climate Change*, 9.
125. Ibid.
126. International Institute for Sustainable Development, *A Guide to Kyoto*, 1.
127. Ibid., 2.
128. Anne McIlroy and Mark MacKinnon, 'Cabinet Okays Plan to Fight Global Warming', *Globe and Mail*, 15 Dec. 1999.
129. Alan Freeman, 'Europe Opts to Share Gas Pains', *Globe and Mail*, 1 Dec. 1997.
130. Freeman, 'Europe Opts to Share Gas Pains'.
131. Edward Greenspon, 'Officials Give Kyoto Deal Positive Spin', *Globe and Mail*, 12 Dec. 1997.
132. Ibid.
133. 'US Pulls Out of Kyoto Protocol', *Environmental News Service*, 28 March 2001, < www.ens.lycos.com >.
134. Glenn Kelly, executive director of Global Climate Coalition, as quoted in 'US Pulls Out of Kyoto Protocol'.
135. Alden Meyer as quoted in 'US Pulls Out of Kyoto Protocol'.
136. 'Europe will Ratify Kyoto Protocol Without the USA', *Environmental News Service*, 2 April 2001. < www.ens.lycos.com >.
137. Environment Canada, *Canada's National Action Program on Climate Change 1995*, < http://www.ec.gc.ca/climate/resource/cnapcc/c3part03.html > (6 Jan. 2000).
138. Ibid.
139. Freeman, 'Europe Opts to Share Gas Pains'.
140. McIlroy and MacKinnon, 'Cabinet Okays Plan to Fight Global Warming'.
141. Brent Jang, 'Ottawa's Greenhouse Gas Target Draws Fire', *Globe and Mail*, 2 Dec. 1997.
142. Ibid.
143. McIlroy and MacKinnon, 'Cabinet Okays Plan to Fight Global Warming'.
144. Steven Guilbeault, as quoted in ibid.

145. International Institute for Sustainable Development, *A Guide to Kyoto*, 12.

146. McIlroy and MacKinnon, 'Cabinet Okays Plan to Fight Global Warming'.

147. Ibid.

148. Environment Canada, *Government of Canada Action Plan 2000 on Climate Change*, 1.

149. Ibid., 2.

150. Ibid., 11.

151. Ibid.

152. International Institute for Sustainable Development, *A Guide to Kyoto*, 9.

153. Kim Shikaze, 'Solid Waste Management: Issues, Priorities and Progress' in Murray E. Haight, ed., *Municipal Solid Waste Management* (Waterloo, Ont.: University of Waterloo Press, 1991), 3.

154. Ibid.

155. Douglas Macdonald, 'The Solid Waste Issue', in Thomas Fleming, ed., *The Environment and Canadian Society* (Scarborough, Ont.: ITP Nelson, 1997), 203.

156. Shikaze, 'Solid Waste Management', 4.

157. Ronald J. Poland, 'The Role of Sanitary Landfill in Future Waste Disposal Strategies', in Murray E. Haight, ed., *Municipal Solid Waste Management*, 95.

158. Macdonald, 'The Solid Waste Issue', 203.

159. Ibid., 204.

160. Ibid., 208.

161. Hans Tammemagi, *The Waste Crisis* (Toronto: Oxford University Press, 1999), 33.

162. Macdonald, 'The Solid Waste Issue', 205.

163. Tammemagi, *The Waste Crisis*, 34.

164. Ibid., 37.

165. Peter Kmet, 'Controlling Landfill Leachate Migration', in Murray E. Haight, ed., *Municipal Solid Waste Management*, 55.

166. Tammemagi, *The Waste Crisis*, 36–7.

167. Ibid., 37.

168. Ibid., 41.

169. Ibid., 42.

170. Ibid., 46.

171. Ibid., 48.

172. Ibid.

173. The Composting Council of Canada, 'Home Page', < http://www.compost.org/natural.html > (2 Jan. 2000).

174. Tammemagi, *The Waste Crisis*, 55.

175. Macdonald, 'The Solid Waste Issue', 210.

176. Ibid., 209.

177. Ibid., 210.

178. Tammemagi, *The Waste Crisis*, 181.

179. Ibid., 180.

180. Ibid., 183.

181. Ibid., 189–90.

182. Ibid., 191.

183. Ibid., 192.

184. Macdonald, 'The Solid Waste Issue', 210.

185. Ibid., 212.

186. Ibid.
187. Ibid., 213.
188. Hertzman, 'Confronting Health Issues in Solid Waste Management', in Murray E. Haight, ed., *Municipal Solid Waste Management*, 43.
189. Thomas Homer-Dixon, *Environment, Scarcity and Violence* (Princeton: Princeton University Press, 1999).
190. Homer-Dixon, Environment, *Scarcity and Violence*, 48.
191. As quoted in 'Tension in the Oil Patch', 5 Sept. 1999, < http://radio.cbc.ca/news/tension > .
192. _____. 'Tension in the Oil Patch', 5 Sept. 1999. < http://radio.cbc.ca/news/tension > .
193. Ibid.
194. Ibid.
195. Homer-Dixon, *Environment, Scarcity and Violence*, 5.
196. Ibid.

Chapter Six

1. Peter M. Haas and Jan Sundgren, 'Evolving International Environmental Law', in Nazli Choucri, ed., *Global Accord* (Cambridge, Mass.: MIT Press, 1993), 402.
2. Doug Macdonald, The Politics of Pollution (Toronto: McClelland & Stewart, 1991), 58–9.
3. Ken Conca and Geoffrey D. Dabelko, eds, *Green Planet Blues*, 2nd edn (Boulder, Colo.: Westview Press, 1998), 19.
4. Ibid.
5. John J. Audley, *Green Politics and Global Trade: NAFTA and the Future of Environmental Politics* (Washington, DC: Georgetown University Press, 1997), 31.
6. Conca and Dabelko, *Green Planet Blues*, 19.
7. Ibid., 75.
8. World Commission on Environment and Development, *Our Common Future* (New York: United Nations, 1987), 46.
9. Audley, *Green Politics and Global Trade*, 31.
10. Macdonald, *The Politics of Pollution*, 59.
11. Ibid., 59–60.
12. Conca and Dabelko, *Green Planet Blues*, 161.
13. Michael E. Kraft and Norman J. Vig, eds, *Environment Policy in the 1990s: Toward a New Agenda*, 2nd edn (Washington, D.C.: Congressional Quarterly Press, 1994) 3.
14. Ken Conca, Michael Alberty, and Geoffrey D. Dabelko, *Green Planet Blues* (Boulder, Colo.: Westview Press, 1995) 6.
15. Ibid., 7.
16. Ibid.
17. Ibid., 8.
18. Report of the Commissioner of the Environment and Sustainable Development to the House of Commons (Ottawa: Department of Public Works and Government Services, 25 May 1999) 7.
19. Ibid., 11.
20. Ibid., 403.
21. Robert Boardman, 'The Multilateral Dimension', in Robert Boardman, ed., *Canadian Environmental Policy: Ecosystems, Politics, and Process* (Toronto: Oxford University Press, 1992), 226.
22. Boardman, 'The Multilateral Dimension', 226.

23. Hanneberg, Peter, 'First Meeting of Parties to Biodiversity Convention', *Enviro* 19 (June 1995): 2-4.

24. Ibid., 4.

25. Ibid.

26. Ibid.

27. Ibid.

28. Report of the Commissioner of the Environment and Sustainable Development to the House of Commons, 405.

29. George Hoberg, 'Trade, Harmonization, and Domestic Autonomy in Environmental Policy', 2, < http://www.policy.ca > (1 July 2000).

30. Ibid., 3.

31. Lang and Hines, *The New Protectionism* (New York: New Press, 1993), 20.

32. Ibid., 20-1.

33. Ibid., 20.

34. Ibid., 21.

35. Ibid., 20.

36. Ibid., 9.

37. Audley, *Green Politics and Global Trade*, 35.

38. Lang and Hines, *The New Protectionism*, 61.

39. Ibid., 63.

40. Ibid., viii.

41. Audley, *Green Politics and Global Trade*, 33.

42. Brian McDonald, *The World Trading System* (New York: St Martin's Press, 1998), 41.

43. Lang and Hines, *The New Protectionism*, 46.

44. Ibid.

45. McDonald, *The World Trading System*, 32.

46. Ibid., 33.

47. Lang and Hines, *The New Protectionism*, 47.

48. Audley, *Green Politics and Global Trade*, 31.

49. Lang and Hines, *The New Protectionism*, 47.

50. Audley, *Green Politics and Global Trade*, 23.

51. Lang and Hines, *The New Protectionism*, 11.

52. Ibid., 46.

53. Ibid., 47.

54. Ibid., 51.

55. Ibid., 51-2.

56. McDonald, *The World Trading System*, 41.

57. Steven Shrybman, *A Citizen's Guide to the World Trade Organization* (Ottawa: Canadian Centre for Policy Alternatives and James Lorimer, 1999), 17.

58. Shrybman, *A Citizen's Guide to the World Trade Organization*, 17.

59. McDonald, *The World Trading System*, 41.

60. Ibid.

61. Ibid., 41-2.

62. Ibid., 42.

63. Hoberg, 'Trade, Harmonization, and Domestic Autonomy in Environment Policy', 12.

64. Ibid.

65. Ibid.

66. Lang and Hines, *The New Protectionism*, 63.
67. Ibid., 65.
68. Bhagwati, Jagdish, 'The Case for Free Trade', in Conca et al., eds, *Green Planet Blues*, 173.
69. Lang and Hines, *The New Protectionism*, ix.
70. Hoberg, 'Trade, Harmonization, and Domestic Autonomy', 14.
71. Ibid., 22.
72. Ibid., 27.
73. Lang and Hines, *The New Protectionism*, 52.
74. Lacayo, Richard, 'Rage against the Machine', *Time* (Canadian edn), 13 Dec. 1999, 25.
75. Ibid., 24.
76. Ibid.
77. McDonald, *The World Trading System*, 257
78. Ibid., 258.
79. Ibid., 264.
80. Ibid., 265.
81. Rowell, *Green Backlash*, 113.
82. Nicholas V. Gianaris, *The North American Free Trade Agreement and the European Union* (Westport, Conn.: Praeger 1998), 139.
83. Ibid., 139.
84. Ibid.
85. Rowell, *Green Backlash*, 113.
86. Gianaris, *The North American Free Trade Agreement*, 17.
87. Bhagwati, 'The Case for Free Trade', 174–5.
88. Lang and Hines, *The New Protectionism*, viii.
89. West Coast Environmental Law, *Legal Opinion re: Water Export Controls and Canadian International Trade Obligations* (Vancouver: West Coast Environmental Law, 17 Aug. 1999) 6.
90. Hoberg, George, 'Trade, Harmonization, and Domestic Autonomy' 30. (paper accessed 1 Jan. 2001).
91. Pierre Marc Johnson, and André Beaulieu, *The Environment and NAFTA* (Washington, DC: Island Press, 1996), 121.
92. Ibid., 123.
93. Ibid., 124.
94. Ibid., 123.
95. Ibid.
96. Ibid., 126.
97. Hoberg, 'Trade, Harmonization, and Domestic Autonomy', 30.
98. Johnson and Beaulieu, *The Environment and NAFTA*, 127.
99. Hoberg, 'Trade, Harmonization, and Domestic Autonomy', 31.
100. Ibid.
101. Canadian Environmental Law Association, *Stomping on the Earth: Trade, Trade Law, and Canada's Ecological Footprints* (Toronto: CELA, 1999), 5.
102. Hoberg, 'Trade, Harmonization, and Domestic Autonomy', 32.
103. Ibid.
104. Ibid.
105. Canadian Environmental Law Association, *Stomping on the Earth*, 5.
106. Hoberg, 'Trade, Harmonization, and Domestic Autonomy', 34.

107. Peter Morton, '$1B Methanol Battle Fires Up This Week', *National Post*, 5 Sept. 2000.

108. Ibid.

109. Ibid.

110. Ibid.

111. Hoberg, 'Trade, Harmonization, and Domestic Autonomy', 35.

112. Steven L. Kass and Jean M. McCarroll, 'The "Metalclad" Decision under NAFTA's Chapter 11', *New York Law Journal*, 27 Oct. 2000, < http://www.clm.com/pubs/pub-990359_1.html > (19 Feb. 2001).

113. Kass and McCarroll, 'The "Metalclad" Decision'.

114. Michelle Swenarchuk, 'The MAI and the Environment', in Andrew Jackson and Matthew Sanger, eds, *Dismantling Democracy* (Ottawa: Canadian Centre for Policy Alternatives and James Lorimer, 1998), 125.

115. Kass and McCarroll, 'The "Metalclad" Decision'.

116. Swenarchuk, 'The MAI and the Environment', 127.

117. As quoted in Naomi Klein, 'Democracy, When You Least Expect It', *Globe and Mail*, 28 Feb. 2001.

118. Shrybman, *A Citizen's Guide to the World Trade Organization*, 73.

119. Ibid.

120. Ibid., 74.

121. Harrison, *The Third Revolution*, 258.

References

Abramson, Paul R., and Ronald Inglehart. 1995. *Value Change in Global Perspective*. Ann Arbor: University of Michigan Press.

'Agreement Reached in Biosafety Talks'. 2000. *CBC News*, 29 Jan.

'Agreement Reached in Biosafety Talks'. 2000. Canadian Broadcasting Corporation News Online. < http://www.cbc.ca > (29 Jan. 2000).

Ali, Amina, 2000. 'Foot-and-Mouth disease'. < http://www.cbc.ca > (March 2001).

Allen, Scott. 'Then Again, Earth May Take a Turn for the Better'. *Boston Globe*. 16 Dec. 1999.

Alt, James E., Margaret Levi, and Elinor Ostrom, eds. 1999. *Competition and Cooperation*. New York: Russell Sage Foundation.

Appleton, Barry. 1994. *Navigating NAFTA*. Toronto: Carswell.

Arnason, Ragnar, and Lawrence Felt, eds. 1995. *The North Atlantic Fisheries: Successes, Failures and Challenges*. Charlottetown: Institute of Island Studies. Vol. 3.

Audley, John J. 1997. *Green Politics and Global Trade: NAFTA and the Future of Environmental Politics*. Washington, DC: Georgetown University Press.

Bakvis, Herman, and Neil Nevitte. 1990. 'The Greening of the Canadian Electorate: Environmentalism, Ideology and Partisanship'. Paper presented to the Annual Meeting of the Canadian Political Science Association, University of Victoria, British Columbia.

Balbus, John M., and Mark L. Wilson. 2000. *Human Health and Global Climate Change— A Review of Potential Impacts in the United States*. New York: PEW Center on Global Change.

Barber, John. 2001. 'Walkerton's Woes Continue a Year Later'. < http://www.globeandmail.com > (12 May 2001).

Beazley, Karen, and Robert Boardman, eds. 2001. *Politics of the Wild*. Toronto: Oxford University Press.

Beder, Sharon. 1997. *Global Spin: The Corporate Assault on Environmentalism*. UK: Green Books.

Bell, Stewart. 1999. 'Greenpeace serves "No Public Benefit"', *National Post*. 5 June.

Bennett, Wayne, and Gordon Surgeoner. 1996. 'Fly Control in Swine Barns'. *Agri-food Research in Ontario* 19, 3.

Berry, Thomas. 1995. 'The Viable Human'. In *Deep Ecology for the Twenty-First Century*, edited by George Sessions. Boston: Shambhala.

Bhagwati, Jagdish. 1995. 'The Case for Free Trade'. *Green Planet Blues*. Edited by Ken Conca, Michael Alberty, and Geoffrey D. Dabelko. Boulder, Colo.: Westview Press.

Blackwell, Tom. 2000. 'Water-Safety Checks Halved under Harris'. *National Post*, 19 June.

Blake, Donald E., Neil Guppy, and Peter Urmetzer. 1996/97. 'Being Green in BC'. *BC Studies*, Winter.

Blumenthal, Daniel S., and A. James Ruttenber, eds. 1995. *Introduction to Environmental Health*. 2nd ed. New York: Springer.

Boardman, Robert, ed. 1992. *Canadian Environmental Policy: Ecosystems, Politics, and Process*. Toronto: Oxford University Press.

Boldt, Menno. 1993. *Surviving as Indians*. Toronto: University of Toronto Press.

Bookchin, M. 1980. 'Ecology and Revolutionary Thought'. In *Environment and Society*. Edited by R. Roelofs, J. Crowley, and D. Hardest. Englewood Hights, N.J.: Prentice-Hall.

Bookchin, Murray. 1982. *The Ecology of Freedom: The Emergence and Dissolution of Freedom.* Palo Alto, Calif.: Cheshire Books.

Bourette, Susan, and Richard Mackie. 2000. 'Walkerton Inquiry to Focus on Province'. < http://www.torontostar.com > (6 Mar. 2001).

Bosso, Christopher J. 1994. 'After the Movement: Environmental Activism in the 1990s'. In *Environmental Policy in the 1990s: Towards a New Agenda.* Edited by Michael Kraft and Norman J. Vig. Washington, DC: Congressional Quarterly Press.

Bourette, Susan. 2000. 'Harris Ignored Walkerton's Pleas in '98'. *Globe and Mail.* 15 June.

Bourette, Susan, and Richard Mackie. 2000. 'Utility Not Legally Required to Test Water'. *Globe and Mail,* 1 June.

'British Farmers Divided over Latest Foot-and-Mouth Measures'. 2001. Canadian Broadcasting Corporation News Online. < http://www.cbc.ca > (19 Mar. 2001).

'B.C. Women Bare All in Fight over Island's Forest'. 2000. Canadian Broadcasting Corporation Newsworld, < http://www.cbc.ca/news > (27 Aug. 2000).

Brown, M. Paul. 1992. 'Organizational Design as Policy Instrument'. In *Canadian Environmental Policy: Ecosystems, Politics, and Process.* Edited by Robert Boardman. Toronto: Oxford University Press.

Burshtein, Karen. 2000. 'Good Wood'. *Globe and Mail,* 12 Aug.

Cahn, Matthew Alan. 1995. *Environmental Deceptions.* New York: State University of New York Press.

Campbell, Monica. 1997. 'Our Cities, Our Air, Our Health: Perspectives on Urban Air Quality and Human Health'. In *The Environment and Canadian Society.* Edited by Thomas Fleming. Scarborough: ITP Nelson.

Canada. Commissioner of the Environment and Sustainable Development 1999. *Report to the House of Commons,* 25 May. Ottawa: Department of Public Works and Government Services.

Canada. Department of Fisheries and Oceans. 1999. *Newsrelease.* 5 Aug.

———. 1980. *Northern Cod—A Fisheries Success Story.* Ottawa: Minister of Supply and Services.

Canadian Centre for Policy Alternatives. 2000. 'Large-Scale Hog Production and Processing: Concerns for Manitobans'. < http://www.policyalternatives.ca > (20 Jan. 2000).

Canadian Environmental Law Association. *Homepage.* < http://www.web.net/cela > .

———. 1999. 'MiningWatch Canada: Our Eye on the Industry'. *Intervenor* 24, no. 3.

———. 'Environmentalists Attack Legality and Politics of Plutonium Airlift'. < http://www. web.net/cela > (18 Mar. 2000).

———. 2000. 'Canadian Environmental Law Association to Represent Concerned Walkerton Citizens'. Media Release. 2 Aug.

———. 2000. Brief No. 383. *Submission by the Canadian Environmental Law Association to the Ministries of Agriculture, Food, and Rural Affairs and Environment on the Discussion Paper on Intensive Agricultural Operations in Ontario.* 15 Feb. Toronto: The Association.

———. 1999. *Stamping on the Earth: Trade, Trade Law, and Canada's Ecological Footprints.* Toronto: The Association.

———. 2000. *Submission by the Canadian Environmental Law Association to the Ministries of Agriculture, Food and Rural Affairs and Environment on the Discussion Paper on Intensive Agriculture Operations in Ontario.* < http://www.cela.org > (15 Feb. 2000).

Canadian Environmental Law Association, the Canadian Union of Public Employees, and the Council of Canadians. 1998. 'Our Water Is Not for Sale'. Joint Press Release. < http://www.cela.ca > (7 Dec. 1998).

Canadian Environmental Network Toxins Caucus. 2000. *Towards the Development of a Global Treaty on Persistent Organic Pollutants.* Toronto: Canadian Environmental Law Association.

Canadian Environmental Law Association and the Ontario College of Family Physicians. 2000. Children's Health Project. *Environmental Standard Setting and Children's Health.* Toronto: Canadian Environmental Law Association.

Canadian Environmental Network Toxins Caucus. 2000. *Towards the Development of a Global Treaty on Persistent Organic Pollutants.* Toronto: Canadian Environmental Law Association. 10 Nov.

Canadian Food Inspection Agency. Office of Biotechnology. 1999. 'Food Derived from Biotechnology'. < http://www.cfia-acia.agr.ca/english/ppc/biotech/food.html > (Nov. 1999).

Canadian Food Inspection Agency. 2001. *Foot and Mouth Disease Strategy.* Ottawa: The Agency. < http://www.inspection.gc.ca > (17 May 2001).

Canadian Food Inspection Agency. 2001. 'Extra Measures Announced for Foot-and-Mouth Disease'. News Release. < http://www.inspection.gc.ca > (3 Apr. 2001).

Canadian Health Coalition. 2000. 'Threats to Public Health'. < http://www.canadahealth.org > (30 Mar. 2000).

Canadian Institute for Environmental Law and Policy. 2000. *Mining's Many Faces.* Toronto: The Institute.

Canadian Institute of Child Health. 1997. *What on Earth? Proceedings of National Symposium on Environmental Contaminants and the Implications for Child Health.* Ottawa: The Institute.

Canadian Organic Growers. 2000. 'Bio-Diversity: A Matter of Survival'. *Down to Earth Newsletter.* Feb/March/April.

Canadian Organic Growers. 2000. *Down to Earth Newsletter,* (February/March/April 2000).

Canadian Wildlife Federation. 1997. 'Comments on the Canada Endangered Species Protection Act'. < http://www.cwf.org > .

Capra, Fritjof. 1995. 'Deep Ecology: A New Paradigm'. In *Deep Ecology for the Twenty-First Century.* Edited by George Sessions. Boston: Shambhala.

Capra, Fritjof, and Charlene Spretnak in collaboration with Wulf-Rüdiger Lutz. 1984. *Green Politics.* New York: E.P. Dutton.

Casagrande, Eloy Jr, and Richard Welford. 1997. 'The Big Brothers: Transnational Corporations, Trade Organizations and Multilateral Financial Institutions'. In *Hijacking Environmentalism.* Edited by Richard Welford. London: Earthscan.

Cashore, Ben. 2001. 'The Canada-U.S. Softwood Lumber Dispute. Now What Should Canada Do?' < http://www.policy.ca > (20 Apr. 2001).

———. 2001. 'What Should Canada Do When the Softwood Lumber Agreement Expires?' < http://www.policy.ca > (27 Mar. 2001).

Castrilli, Joseph L. 1998. *Environmental Control of the Mining Industry in Canada and Chile.* Toronto, Canadian.

Castells, Manuel. 1997. *The Information Age—Economy, Society and Culture.* Vol. II. *The Power of Identity.* Oxford: Blackwell.

Centre for Policy Alternatives. 1999. 'Large-Scale Hog Production and Processing: Concerns for Manitobans'. Ottawa: Centre for Policy Alternatives.

Chetwynd Environmental Society. 2000. 'Mining and Land Use Planning in British Columbia —Time for Change'. Paper presented to the May 2000 Minerals North Conference.

Children's Health Project. 2000. Environmental Standard Setting and Children's Health. Toronto: Canadian Environmental Law Association and the Ontario College of Family Physicians.

Clark, E. Ann. 2000. 'Food Safety of GM Crops in Canada: Toxicity and Allergenicity', < http://www.councilcanadian.ca > .

Clarke, Harold D., and Marianne C. Stewart. 1997. 'Green Words and Public Deeds: Environmental Hazards and Citizen Response in Canada and the United States'. In *Shades of Green.* Edited by Alan Frizzell and Jon Pammett. Ottawa: Carleton University Press.

Clarke, Harold D., Jane Jenson, Lawrence LeDuc, and Jon H. Pammett. 1979. *Political Choice in Canada*. Toronto: McGraw-Hill Ryerson.

———. 1996. *Absent Mandate*. 3rd edn. Toronto: Gage.

Conca, Ken, Michael Alberty, and Geoffrey D. Dabelko, eds. 1995. *Green Planet Blues*. Boulder, Colo.: Westview Press.

———. 1998. *Green Planet Blues*. Second edn. Boulder, Colo.: Westview Press.

Cooper, Kathleen. 1999. 'A Sustainable Water Policy for Ontario'. *Intervenor* 24 (Jan.–Mar).

Corcoran, Terence. 2000. 'When Nature Kills'. *National Post*. 27 May.

Council of Canadians. 2000. 'Independent Group of Scientists Releases Study Disputing Federal Claims That Genetically Engineered Foods are Safe'. 18 Jan.

Daly, Herman E. 1993. 'Sustainable Growth: An Impossibility Theorem'. In *Valuing the Earth: Economics, Ecology, Ethics*. Edited by Herman E. Daly and Kenneth Townsend. Cambridge: Cambridge University Press.

Davis, Anthony. 1991. *Dire Straits: The Dilemmas of a Fishery*. St John's: Institute of Social and Economic Research.

Department of Fisheries and Oceans. 2001. *Atlantic Fisheries Review*. Ottawa: Department of Supply and Services. < http://www.dfo.mpo.gc.ca > (11 May).

De Villiers, Marq. 1999. *Water*. Toronto: Stoddart.

Dobson, Andrew. 1990. *Green Political Thought*. 2nd edn. London: Routledge.

———. 1991. *The Green Reader*. London: Mercury House.

Doern, G. Bruce, and Thomas Conway. 1995. *The Greening of Canada*. Toronto: University of Toronto Press.

Dowie, Mark. 1996. *Losing Ground*. Cambridge, Mass.: MIT Press.

Doyle, Timothy, and Doug MacEachern. 1998. *Environment and Politics*. London: Routledge.

Dunfield, Allison. 2000. 'First Nations Grand Chief Slams Fisheries'. *Globe and Mail*, 17 Aug.

Dwivedi, O.P. 1996. 'Satyagraha for Conservation: Awakening the Spirit of Hinduism'. In *This Sacred Earth*. Edited by Roger S. Gottlieb. New York: Routledge.

Eckersley, Robin. 1992. *Environmentalism and Political Theory*. New York: State University of New York Press.

Ehrlich, Paul, and Anne Ehrlich. 1970. 'Population, Resources, Environment'. *New Scientist* 36.

Ehrlich, Paul R., and John P. Holdren, eds. 1988. *The Cassandra Conference*. College Station, Tex.: Texas A&M University Press.

Ehrlich, Paul, and Anne Ehrlich. 1969. *The Population Bomb*. New York: Ballantine.

Engel, J. Ronald. 1992. 'Liberal Democracy and the Fate of the Earth'. In *Spirit and Nature*. Edited by Steven C. Rockefeller and John C. Elder. Boston: Beacon Press.

Environment Canada. 2000. 'Canada Shows Continued Leadership on Protecting the Ozone Layer'. *News Release*. 18 Dec.

———. 2000. Canada's Plan for Protecting Species at Risk. 16 Jan. < www.ec.gc.ca/sara/report11.htm > .

———. 2000. 'What is Climate Change?' < http://www.ec.gc.ca/climate/whatis/index.html > (15 Sept. 2000).

———. 2000. *Government of Canada Action Plan 2000 on Climate Change*.

———. 1997. *A Primer on Climate Change—The Atmospheric Environment*. < http://www.ec.gc.ca/primer > .

———. 1995. *Canada's National Action Program on Climate Change*. < http://www.ec.gc.ca/climate/resource/cncpcc/c3part03.html > (6 Jan. 2001).

———. 1992. *Clean Water—Life Depends on It!* Freshwater Series A-3. Ottawa: Minister of Supply and Services Canada.

————. 2001. 'Canada to Sign and Ratify Global Agreement to Protect Human Health from Dangerous Pollutants'. News Release. < http://www.ec.gc.ca > (9 May 2001).

————. 1998. *1997 Canadian Acid Rain Assessment*. Vol. 1, Summary of the Results. Ottawa: Ministry of Supply and Services.

Environmental Mining Council of British Columbia. 2000. *A Modest Proposal? Limiting Liability and Waste Management Regulations for Mining*. 29 Mar.

'Environmentalists Warn New Bill Easy on Biotech Companies'. 1999. *CBC Newsworld Online*. 30 Aug. < http://www.newsworld.cbc.ca >.

Epstein, Samuel. 1999. 'Everyday Carcinogens: Stopping Cancer Before It Starts'. Paper presented at conference at McMaster University, 27 Mar.

'Europe Will Ratify Kyoto Protocol without the USA'. 2001. Environment News Service. < http://www.ens.lycos.com > (13 May 2001).

Evans, Mark. 2000. 'Canada Second in Internet Use'. *Globe and Mail*. 22 Mar.

Felt, Lawrence et al. 1995. 'It Were Well to Live Mainly off Fish'. In *The North Atlantic Fisheries: Successes, Failures and Challenges*. Edited by Ragnar Arnason and Lawrence Felt. Charlottetown: Institute of Island Studies. Vol. 3.

Fleming, Thomas, ed. 1997. *The Environment and Canadian Society*. Scarborough, Ont.: ITP Nelson.

'Food at the Crossroads'. 1998. *The World at Six*. CBC Radio, 12 Oct.

Foot, Richard. 2000. 'Ontario May Be Only Place Where Towns Solely Accountable for Water'. *National Post*. 2 June.

'Foot-and-Mouth under Control, UK Study Says'. 2001. < http://www.torontostar.com > (11 May).

'Foot-and-Mouth Terror Threat Worries Food Agency'. 2001. Canadian Broadcasting Corporation News Online. < http://www.cbc.ca > (6 Apr. 2001).

'Forest Accord Hands the North to Loggers'. 1999. Editorial, *Toronto Star*, 25 Apr.

Forest Action Network. 2000. 'Canadian Companies to Stop Buying Ancient Forest Products'. < http://www.fanweb.org > (31 May 2000).

ForestEthics. 2001. 'Questions and Answers about the Agreement Reached in British Columbia'. < http://www.forestethics.org > (10 May 2001).

————. 2000. 'History of FAN'. < http://www.fanweb.org > (26 Aug. 2000).

ForestEthics. 2001. 'Largest Rainforest Conservation Measure in North American History'. Press Release < http://www.forestethics.org > (11 May 2001).

Foulkes, Amy. 2001. 'Mad Cow: The Science and the Story—A Crisis for Britain'. < http://www.cbc.ca > (12 Jan. 2001).

'France Struggles with Mad Cow Crisis'. 2001. Canadian Broadcasting Corporation News Online. < http://www.cbc.ca > (12 Jan. 2001).

'Frankenfoods and Politics'. 2000. *Globe and Mail*, 27 Jan.

Fraser Institute. 1999. 'Crying Wolf: Does Canada Have an Endangered Species Crisis?' < http://www.fraserinstitute.ca/publications >.

Fraser Institute. 1999. 'Myths and Facts about NAFTA and the FTA'. *Public Policy Sources*, no. 11, < http://www.fraserinstitute.org >.

Freeman, Alan. 1997. 'Europe Opts to Share Gas Pains'. *Globe and Mail*. 1 Dec.

Freeze, Colin, and Martin Mittelstaedt. 2000. 'Ottawa Targets Smog Levels with $120 Million in Funds'. *Globe and Mail*, 20 Feb.

Frey, Frederick W. 1993. 'The Political Context of Conflict and Cooperation over International River Basins'. *Water International* 18, no. 1.

Frome, Michael. 1996. *Chronicling the West: Thirty Years of Environmental Writing*. Seattle: The Mountaineers.

Gianaris, Nicholas V. 1998. *The North American Free Trade Agreement and the European Union*. Westport, Conn.: Praeger.

Gibbons, Roger, and Loleen Youngman. 1998. *Mindscapes*. Toronto: McGraw-Hill Ryerson.

Gibbs, Lois Marie. 1998. *Love Canal—The Story Continues*. Gabriola Island, BC: New Society Publishers.

Glavin, Terry. 1996. *Dead Reckoning*. Vancouver: Douglas & McIntyre.

Glendinning, C. 1990. 'Notes toward a Neo-Luddite Manifesto'. *Utne Reader*. March/April.

Goldsmith, Edward et al. 1991. 'A Blueprint for Survival'. In *The Green Reader*. Edited by Andrew Dobson. New York: Mercury House.

Goodland, C. 1992. 'The Case That the World Has Reached Limits'. In *Population, Technology, and Lifestyle*. Edited by R. Goodland, H.E. Daly, and S.E. Serafy. Washington, DC: Island Press.

Gottlieb, Roger S., ed. 1996. *This Sacred Earth*. New York: Routledge.

Greenfield, Gerard. 2001. 'The NAFTA ruling on Metalclad vs. Mexico'. < http://www.wto action.org > (5 May 2001).

———. 2001. 'The Ties That Bind: A Brief Note on NAFTA Chapter 11-type Rules in Canada's Bilateral Agreements'. < http://www.wtoaction.org > (5 May 2001).

Greenspon, Edward. 1997. 'Officials Give Kyoto Deal Positive Spin'. *Globe and Mail*. 12 Dec.

Greer, Jed, and Kenny Bruno. 1996. *Greenwash—The Reality behind Corporate Environmentalism*. New York: Apex Press.

Haas, Peter M., and Jan Sundgren. 1993. 'Evolving International Environmental Law'. In *Global Accord*. Edited by Nazli Choucri. Cambridge, Mass.: MIT Press.

Hachey, Leanne. 2000. 'The Food Fight'. *CBC News Online*, 29 Jan.

Hackett, Robert A., and Richard Gruneau. 2000. *The Missing News: Filters and Blind Spots in Canada's Press*. Ottawa: Centre for Policy Alternatives.

Haight, Murray E., ed. 1991. *Municipal Solid Waste Management*. Waterloo. Ont.: University of Waterloo Press.

Haines, M., et al. 1998. 'Dioxins and Furans'. In *Persistent Environmental Contaminants and the Great Lakes Basin Population: An Exposure Assessment*. Ottawa: Health Canada.

Hall, Keven A., and John E. Hughes. 1998. *Cyberpolitics: Citizen Activism in the Age of the Internet*. Lanham: Rowman and Littlefield.

Hanneberg, Peter. 1995. 'First Meeting of Parties to Biodiversity Convention'. *Enviro* 19 (June).

Hardin, Garrett. 1968. 'The Tragedy of the Commons'. *Science* 162.

———. 1988. 'Cassandra's Role in the Population Wrangle'. In *The Cassandra Conference*. Edited by Paul R. Ehrlich and John P. Holdren. College Station, Tex.: Texas A & M University Press.

Harrison, Kathryn. 1996. *Passing the Buck*. Vancouver: UBC Press.

———. 1990. 'Voluntarism and Environmental Governance'. April. < http://www.policy.ca >.

———. 1999. 'Retreat from Regulation: The Evolution of the Canadian Regulatory Regime'. In *Changing the Rules: Canadian Regulatory Regimes and Institutions*. Edited by G. Bruce Doern et al. Toronto: University of Toronto Press.

Harrison, Paul. 1992. *The Third Revolution*. London: I.B. Tauris.

Harte, John. 1988. 'Acid Rain'. In *The Cassandra Conference*. Edited by Paul H. Ehrlich and John P. Holden. College Station, Tex.: Texas A & M University Press.

Hauka, Dan. 2001, 'Dosanjh Admits Defeat As Greens Pull Ahead'. *Calgary Herald*, 9 May.

Harvey, David. 1989. *The Condition of Postmodernity*. Oxford: Blackwell.

Hayward, Tim. 1994. *Ecological Thought—An Introduction*. Cambridge: Polity Press.

Heathcoate, Isobel W. 1997. 'Canadian Water Resources and Management'. In *The Environment and Canadian Society*. Edited by Thomas Fleming. Scarborough, Ont.: ITP Nelson.

Hertzman, R. 1991. 'Confronting Health Issues in Solid Waste Management'. *Municipal Solid Waste Management*. Edited by Murray E. Haight. Waterloo: University of Waterloo Press.

Hessing, Melody, and Michael Howlett. 1997. *Canadian Natural Resource and Environmental Policy*. Vancouver: UBC Press.

Hjelmar, Ulf. 1996. *The Political Practice of Environmental Organizations*. Aldershot, UK: Ashgate.

Hoberg, George. 1991. 'Sleeping with an Elephant'. *Journal of Public Policy* 11, no. 1.

———. 1993. 'Environmental Policy: Alternative Styles'. In *Governing Canada*. Edited by Michael M. Atkinson. Toronto: Harcourt Brace Jovanovich.

———. 1998. 'North American Environmental Regulation'. In *Changing Regulatory Institutions in Britain and North America*. Edited by G. Bruce Doern and Stephen Wilks. Toronto: University of Toronto Press.

———. 2000. 'Trade, Harmonization, and Domestic Autonomy in Environmental Policy, 1 July. < http://www.policy.ca >.

Homer-Dixon, Thomas. 1993. 'Physical Dimensions of Global Change'. In *GlobalAccord*. Edited by Nazli Choucri. Cambridge, Mass.: MIT Press.

———. 1999. *Environment, Scarcity, and Violence*. Princeton, N.J.: Princeton University Press.

Honey, Kim. 2000. 'Divisions Remain on Biosafety Protocol'. *Globe and Mail*, 29 Jan.

Hughes, J. Donald. 1996. 'American Indian Ecology'. In *This Sacred Earth*. Edited by Roger S. Gottlieb. New York: Routledge.

'Indepth Backgrounder: Cryptosporidium'. 2001. Canadian Broadcasting Corporation News Online. < http://wwcbc.ca > (8 May 2001).

'Indepth: Mad Cow: The Science and the Story'. 2000. Canadian Broadcasting Corporation News Online. < http://www.cbc.ca > (12 Jan. 2001).

Inglehart, Ronald. 1995. 'Public Support for Environmental Protection: Objective Problems and Subjective Values in Forty-three Societies'. *Political Science and Politics*. Mar.

Innis, Harold A. 1951. 'A Plea for Time'. In *The Bias of Communication*. Toronto: University of Toronto Press.

———. 1954. *The Cod Fisheries: The History of an International Economy*. Rev. edn. Toronto: University of Toronto Press.

International Institute for Sustainable Development. 1998. *A Guide to Kyoto: Climate Change and What It Means to Canada*, < http.//www.iisd.ca >.

Jackson, John. 2000. *A Citizen's Guide to the National Pollutant Release Inventory*. Toronto: Canadian Institute for Environmental Law and Policy.

Jang, Brent. 1997. 'Ottawa's Greenhouse Gas Target Draws Fire'. *Globe and Mail*, 2 Dec.

Johnson, Pierre Marc, and André Beaulieu. 1996. *The Environment and NAFTA*. Washington, DC: Island Press.

Johnstone, Ken. 1972. *The Vanishing Harvest*. Montreal: Montreal Star.

Kabilsingh, Chatsumarn. 1996. 'Early Buddhist Views on Nature'. In *This Sacred Earth*. Edited by Roger S. Gottlieb. New York: Routledge.

Kass, Steven L. and Jean M. McCarroll. 2001. 'The "Metalclad" Decision under NAFTA's Chapter 11'. *New York Law Journal*. < http://www.clm.com > (19 Feb. 2001).

Killan, Gerald, and George Warecki. 1992. 'The Algonquin Wildlands League and the Emergence of Environmental Politics in Ontario, 1965–1974'. *Environmental History Review* 16, no. 4.

Kilpatrick, Ken. 2000. 'Concern Grows about Pollution from Megafarms'. *Globe and Mail*, 30 May.

King, Laura. 2001. 'English Hoof-and-Mouth Disease Spreading'. < http://www.purefood.org > (26 Feb. 2001).

Kingsley, David. 1996. 'Christianity as Ecologically Harmful' and 'Christianity as Ecologically Responsible'. In *This Sacred Earth*. Edited by Roger S. Gottlieb. New York: Routledge.

Klein, Naomi. 2001. 'Democracy, When You Least Expect It'. *Globe and Mail*, 28 Feb.

Knudtson, Peter, and David Suzuki. 1992. *Wisdom of the Elders*. Toronto: Stoddart.

Kraft, Michael E., and Norman J. Vig, eds. *Environmental Policy in the 1990s: Towards a New Agenda*. Washington, DC: Congressional Quarterly Press.

Krajnk, Anita. 2000. 'Neo-Conservatism and the Decline of the Environmental Ministry'. *Canadian Public Policy* 26.

Kroll-Smith, Steve, and H. Hugh Lloyd. 1997. *Bodies in Protest*. New York: New York University Press.

Lacayo, Richard. 1999. 'Rage against the Machine'. *Time*. Canadian edn. 13 Dec.

'Lands for Life Keeps Getting Worse'. 1999. Editorial. *Toronto Star*, 25 July.

Lang, Tim, and Colin Hines. 1993. *The New Protectionism*. New York: New Press.

Lee, Martha F. 1995. *Earth First! Environmental Apocalypse*. Syracuse, NY: Syracuse University Press.

Leiss, William. 1972. *The Domination of Nature*. New York: George Braziller.

Lipschutz, Ronnie D. 1996. *Global Civil Society and Global Environmental Governance*. Albany, NY: State University of New York Press.

Lipsey, Sheldon. 1999. 'Deal Betrays Grassroots Effort'. Letter to the Editor. *Toronto Star*, 9 Aug.

Lovelock, J.E. 1979. *Gaia: A New Look at Life on Earth*. Oxford: Oxford University Press.

Luke, Timothy W. 1999. *Capitalism, Democracy, and Ecology*. Urbana and Chicago: University of Illinois Press.

Lyons, Graham, Evonne Moore, and Joseph Waynes Smith. 1995. *Is the End Nigh? Internationalism, Global Chaos and the Destruction of the Earth*. Sydney: Avebury.

McAllister, Mary Louise, and Cynthia Jacqueline Alexander. 1997. *A Stake in the Future*. Vancouver: UBC Press.

McAndrew, Brian. 1999. 'Ontario's Pollution Second Only to Texas on List of Offenders'. *Toronto Star*, 10 Aug.

————. 2000. 'Showdown at the Oak Ridges Moraine'. *Toronto Star*, 12 Feb.

————. 2000. 'Smog Cost to Top $1 Million, Doctors Warn'. *Toronto Star*, 28 June.

Macdonald, Doug. 1991. *The Politics of Pollution*. Toronto: McClelland & Stewart Inc.

Macdonald, Douglas. 1997. 'The Solid Waste Issue'. *The Environment and Canadian Society*. Edited by Thomas Fleming. Scarborough: ITP Nelson.

Maclean's. 2000. 'The Mail'. 26 June.

McCluskey, Peter. 1999. 'The Salmon War'. *CBC News Online*, 5 Aug.

McCormick, John. 1989. *Reclaiming Paradise*. Indianapolis and Bloomington: Indiana University Press.

McDonald, Brian. 1998. *The World Trading System*. New York: St Martin's Press.

MacKenzie, Debora. 1999, 'Unpalatable Truths'. *New Scientist*. < http://www.newscientist.com> (17 Apr. 1999).

Mackie, Richard. 2000. 'Environmental Ministry Memos Warned of Water Crisis'. *Globe and Mail*, 13 June.

McHughen, Alan. 2000. *Pandora's Picnic Basket*. Oxford: Oxford University Press.

McIlroy, Anne. 1997. 'Canada Pushing Greenhouse Loophole'. *Globe and Mail*, 6 Dec.

————. 1999. 'Ottawa Blasted over Greenhouse Gas'. *Globe and Mail*, 15 June.

McIlroy, Anne, and Mark MacKinnon. 1999. 'Cabinet Okays Plan to Fight Global Warming'. *Globe and Mail*, 15 Dec.

McIlroy, Anne, and Heather Scofield. 1999. 'Big Buyout of Atlantic Fishermen Proposed'. *Globe and Mail*, 27 Nov.

McKenna, Barrie. 1999. 'Ontario's Pollution Second Only to Texas on List of Offenders'. *Globe and Mail*, 10 Aug. < http://www.globeandmail.com > .

Maclean, Rick. 1999. 'Fishing Fury'. *CBC News Online*. 17 Nov. < http://www.cbc.ca/news/indepth/fishingfury/index.html > .

McLuhan, T.C. 1971. *Touch the Earth*. Toronto: New Press.

———. 1994. *The Way of the Earth*. New York: Simon & Schuster.

MacMillan, Anne. 1999. 'Genetically Modified Foods: The British Debate'. *CBC News Online*. Nov.

Macquarrie, Ian. 1997. 'Agriculture and Ecology'. In *The Environment and Canadian Society*. Edited by Thomas Fleming. Scarborough: ITP Nelson.

Macey, Ann. 2001. '1999 Organic Statistics', *Eco-Farm: Garden* (Winter).

'Mad Cow Disease and Humans'. 2000. *Rachel's Environment and Health Weekly*. < http://www.rachel.org > (20 Jan.).

Manes, Christopher. 1990. *Green Rage*. Boston: Little Brown.

Marchak, M. Patricia, Scott L. Aycock, and Deborah M. Herbert. 1999. *Falldown—Forest Policy in British Columbia*. Vancouver: David Suzuki Foundation and Ecotrust Canada.

Marchak, Patricia. 1983. *Green Gold*. Vancouver: University of British Columbia Press.

Martell, Luke. 1994. *Ecology and Society*. Cambridge: Polity Press.

Marx, Karl. 1967. *Capital: A Critique of Political Economy*. Edited by Frederick Engels. New York: International.

Matas, Robert, and Barrie McKenna. 1999. 'Deal Aims to End Annual Salmon Wars'. *Globe and Mail*. 4 June.

Matas, Robert. 1999. 'Good Hauls Not Enough to End Ban on BC Coho, Ottawa Says'. *Globe and Mail*, 29 July. < http://www.globeandmail.com > .

Matthews, David Ralph. 1993. *Controlling Common Property*. Toronto: University of Toronto Press.

May, Elizabeth. 1998. *At the Cutting Edge*. Toronto: Key Porter.

Meadows, D.H., D.L. Meadows, J. Randers, and W.W. Behrens III. 1972. 'The Limits to Growth'. As excerpted in *Green Planet Blues*. Edited by Ken Conca, Michael Alberty, and Geoffrey D. Dabelko. Boulder, Colo.: Westview Press, 1995.

Mendelsohn, Matthew, and Robert Wolfe. 2000. *Probing the Aftermyth of Seattle—Canadian Public Opinion on International Trade, 1980–2000*. Working Paper 12. Queen's University, School of Policy Studies. December.

Merchant, Carolyn. 1995. *Earthcare: Women and the Environment*. New York: Routledge.

Mertyl, Steve. 2001. 'BC Court Ruling Upholds Most of NAFTA Arbitration Award to Metalclad'. < http://www.canada.com/news > (14 May 2001).

Miller, Alan S. 1991. *Gaia Connections*. Savage, MD.: Rowman and Littlefield.

Miller, Wayne, and Gary B. Hill. 1998. 'Child Asthma'. *Health Reports*, Winter.

MiningWatch Canada. 1999. 'One of World's Worst Mine Disasters Gets Worse'. Ottawa: MiningWatch Canada, 11 Aug.

———. 1999. 'Canadian Gold Mine Interest Involved in Police Shootings in Ghana, West Africa'. Ottawa: MiningWatch Canada, 22 Dec.

———. 1999. *Balancing the Books: The Hidden Costs of Mining*. Ottawa: MiningWatch, Canada.

Mitchell, Alanna. 1999. 'Pesticide Residues on Canadian Produce Doubles: Report'. *Globe and Mail*, 24 May. < http://www.globeandmail.com > .

———. 2000. '2000 Weather Hints at Climate Change'. *Globe and Mail*, 2 Jan.

———. 2001. 'Scientists Raise Alarm of Climate Catastrophe'. *Globe and Mail*, 22 Jan.

Mittelstaedt, Martin. 1999. 'Environmental Factors Blamed for Higher Cancer Rates'. *Globe and Mail*, 27 Mar. < http://www.globeandmail.com > .

———. 1999. 'Toronto Pollution Levels Pose Increasing Health Threat'. *Globe and Mail*, 12 June.

————. 1999. 'Bottlers Free to Drain Off Groundwater'. *Globe and Mail*, 3 July.

————. 1999. 'Water Bottler's Permit Upheld by Appeal Panel'. *Globe and Mail*, 21 Dec.

Moffett, John, and François Bregha. 1999. 'Responsible Care'. In *Voluntary Initiatives and the New Politics of Corporate Greening*. Edited by Robert B. Gibson. Peterborough, Ont.: Broadview Press.

Molina, Mario J., and F.S. Rowland. 1974. 'Stratospheric Sink for Chlorofluoromethanes: Chlorine Atom-Catalysed Destruction of Ozone'. *Nature* 248 (28 June).

Montpetit, Éric, and William D. Coleman. 1999. 'Policy Communities and Policy Convergence'. *Canadian Journal of Political Science* 32, no. 4.

Morton, Peter. 2000. '$1B Methanol Battle Fires Up This Week'. *National Post*, 5 Sept.

Muldoon, Paul. 2000. 'The Case against Water Exports'. *Opinion*. Toronto: Canadian Environmental Law Association. < http://www.cela.ca > (Mar.).

Munro, Margaret. 1999. 'Pesticides Discovered in Amniotic Fluid'. *National Post*, 15 June.

Munton, Don, and Geoffrey Castle. 1992. 'The Continental Dimension'. In *Canadian Environmental Policy: Ecosystems, Politics, and Process*. Edited by Robert Boardman. Toronto: Oxford University Press.

Nagy, Sasha. 2001. 'BC Voters Head to the Polls'. *Globe and Mail*, 16 May.

NASA. 2000. 'Ozone: What Is It and Why Do We Care about It?' < http://www.pao.gsfc. nasa.gov/gsfc/service/gallery/fact_sheets/earthsci/ozone.htm > (31 Dec.).

Neidert, Eli, and Glenn Havelock. 1998. *Report of the Canadian Food Inspection Agency*. Ottawa, 6 Nov.

Nelson, Joyce. 1993. 'Great Global Greenwash: Burson-Marsteller, Pax Trilateral and the Brundtland Gang vs. the Environment'. *CovertAction*.

'Newfoundland Bails on Water Sales'. 1999. *CBC Newsworld Online*. 20 Oct.

Nikiforuk, Andrew. 2000. 'National Water Crisis Forecast'. *Globe and Mail*, 7 June.

————. 2000. 'Giant Hog Operation Rejected by Community'. *Globe and Mail*, 13 July.

Noske, Barbara. 1989. *Humans and Other Animals*. London: Pluto.

Nozick, Marcia. 1992. *No Place like Home*. Ottawa: Canadian Council on Social Development.

Oberthür, Sebastien. 1999. *Linkages between the Montreal and Kyoto Protocols*. Paper prepared for Inter-Linkages Conference on Synergies and Coordination between Multilateral Environmental Agreements, 14–16 July.

O'Malley, Martin, and Angela Mulholland. 1999. 'Canada's Water'. *CBC News Online*, 4 July. < http://www.cbcnews.ca/news/indepth/water > .

O'Neil, Peter. 1999. 'Taking Stock of the Salmon Treaty'. *Vancouver Sun*, 5 July. < www. vancouversun.com > .

Ontario Ministry of Agriculture, Food, and Rural Affairs. 2000. *Discussion Paper on Intensive Agricultural Operations in Rural Ontario*. Toronto: The Ministry.

Ontario. Ministry of Agriculture, Food and Rural Affairs. 2000. *Discussion Paper on Intensive Agricultural Operations in Rural Ontario*. < http://www.gov.on/OMAFRA > (15 Aug. 2000).

Ontario. Ministry of the Environment. 2000. *Protecting Drinking Water for Small Waterworks in Ontario*. Discussion Paper. Toronto: The Ministry.

Ontario Pork. 2001. 'Foot and Mouth Outbreak Confirmed in United Kingdom'. < http://www. ontariopork.on.ca > (17 Mar.).

Opie, John. 1998. *Nature's Nation*. Orlando, Fla.: Harcourt Brace.

'Our Children and the Environment'. 1998. *Environmental Health Perspectives*. Vol. 106, 6.

Ostrom, Elinor. 1990. *Governing the Commons*. Cambridge: Cambridge University Press.

Oziewicz, Estanislao. 2000. 'Bacterial Outbreak Kills Four in Ontario'. *Globe and Mail*, 25 May.

Ozone Secretariat Home Page < http://www.unep.ch/ozone/treaties.htm > (1 Jan. 2001).

Paehlke, Robert C. 1989. *Environmentalism and the Future of Progressive Politics*. New Haven, Conn.: Yale University Press.

Paehlke, Robert. 1997. 'Green Politics and the Rise of the Environmental Movement'. In *The Environment and Canadian Society*. Edited by Thomas Fleming. Scarborough, Ont.: ITP Nelson.

Paehlke, Robert, and Douglas Torgerson, eds. 1990. *Managing Leviathan*. Peterborough, Ont.: Broadview Press.

Palmer, Craig, and Peter Sinclair. 1997. *When the Fish Are Gone*. Halifax: Fernwood.

'Parasite Still in Saskatchewan Town's Water'. 2001. < http://www.torontostar.com > (4 May 2001).

Picard, André. 2000. 'Toxic Soup May Be Choking our Kids'. *Globe and Mail*, 22 Aug.

Plant, Judith. 1991. 'Women and Nature'. In *The Green Reader*. Edited by Andrew Dobson. London: Mercury House.

Poland, Ronald J. 1991. 'The Role of Sanitary Landfill in Future Waste Disposal Strategies'. *Municipal Solid Waste Management*. Edited by Murray E. Haight. Waterloo: University of Waterloo Press.

'Potentially Deadly Parasite Found in Town's Water'. 2001. < http://www.globeandmail.com > (4 May 2001).

Powell, Douglas. 2000. 'Don't Blame Industrial Farms for E.coli'. *National Post*, 3 June.

Pratt, Larry, and Ian Urquhart. 1994. *The Last Great Forest*. Edmonton: NeWest Press.

Preece, Rod. 1999. *Animals and Nature: Cultural Myths, Cultural Realities*. Vancouver: UBC Press.

Proctor, Robert N. 1996. 'The Politics of Cancer'. In *The Ecology of Health*. Edited by Jennifer Chesworth. Thousand Oaks, Calf.: Sage.

R. v. Marshall. September 17, 1999. < http://www.sc.gc.ca > .

Rajala, Richard Allan. 1998. *Clearcutting the Pacific Rain Forest*. Vancouver: University of British Columbia Press.

Rich, Bruce. 1995. 'The World Bank and Environmental Reform'. In *Green Planet Blues*. Edited by Ken Conca, Michael Alberty, and Geoffrey D. Dabelko. Boulder, Colo.: Westview Press.

Richardson, Sarah. 1992. 'Sustaining Canada's Prosperity'. In *Trade, Environment and Competitiveness*. Edited by John Kirton and Sarah Richardson. Ottawa: National Round Table on the Environment and the Economy.

'Risky Plan for Ontario's North'. 1999. *Toronto Star*. 24 May.

Robinson, Mike. 1992. *The Greening of British Politics*. Manchester: Manchester University Press.

Rockefeller, Steven C. 1992. 'Faith and Community in an Ecological Age'. In *Spirit and Nature*. Edited by Steven C. Rockefeller and John C. Elder. Boston: Beacon Press.

Rowell, Andrew. 1996. *Green Backlash*. New York: Routledge.

Schwindt, Richard, and Terry Heaps. 1996. *Chopping Up the Money Tree: Distributing the Wealth from British Columbia's Forests*. Vancouver: David Suzuki Foundation.

Schumacher, E.F. 1974. *Small is Beautiful*. London: Abacus.

Science Council of Canada. 1992. *Sustainable Agriculture: The Research Challenge*.

'Scientists Rally for Oak Ridges Moraine'. 2000. *Toronto Star*, 1 Feb.

Scoffield, Heather. 1999. 'Honey, there's a gene in my soup'. *Globe and Mail*. 21 Aug.

Scott, Gordon H. 1954. 'The Economic Theory of a Common-Property Resource: The Fishery'. *Journal of Political Economy* 62:2.

Shikaze, Kim. 1991. 'Solid Waste Management—Issues, Priorities and Progress'. *Municipal Solid Waste Management*. Edited by Murray E. Haight. Waterloo: University of Waterloo Press.

Shiva, Vandana, and Maria Mies. 1993. *Ecofeminism*. Halifax: Fernwood Press.

'Should Canada Worry?' 2001. Canadian Broadcasting Corporation News Online. < http://www.cbc.ca > (12 Jan. 2001).

Shrybman, Steven. 1999. *A Citizen's Guide to the World Trade Organization*. Ottawa: Canadian Centre for Policy Alternatives and James Lorimer and Company.

———. 1999. *A Legal Opinion Concerning Water Export Controls and Canadian Obligations under NAFTA and the WTO*. Vancouver: West Coast Environmental Law Association.

Singer, Peter. 1975. *Animal Liberation*. New York: Avon Books.

Skogstad, Grace and Paul Kopas. 1992. 'Environmental Policy in a Federal System'. In *Environmental Policy: Ecosystems, Politics, and Process*. Edited by Robert Boardman. Toronto: Oxford University Press.

'Slaughter on Suspicion in Britain'. 2001. *Globe and Mail*, 21 Mar.

Speers, T. 1990. 'Clean-up will need $3 billion and 20 years'. *Ottawa Citizen*, 25 Oct.

Steingraber, Sandra. 1999. *Keynote Address*. 'Everyday Carcinogens: Acting for Prevention in the Face of Scientific Uncertainty'. McMaster University, Hamilton, Ontario. 27 March. Transcribed text. < http://www.stopcancer.org/steingraber_transcript.shtml > .

———. 1997. *Living Downstream*. New York: Addison-Wesley.

'Study Identifies Serious Environmental Damage from Netcage Aquaculture'. 2001. < http://www.davidsuzuki.org > (17 Apr. 2001).

Stueck, Wendy. 2000. 'BC forestry firms slams US chain's wood ban'. *Globe and Mail*. 9 Aug.

Sundquist, Bruce. 2001. 'Fishery Degradation—A Global Perspective'. *Edition* 5. < http://www.factoryfarm.org > (11 May).

Surgeoner, Gord. 1998–99. 'Measuring Risk Reduction in Pesticide Use'. *Agri-food research in Ontario*. Vol. 21 No. 3.

Swenarchuk, Michelle. 1998. 'The MAI and the Environment'. In *Dismantling Democracy*. Edited by Andrew Jackson and Matthew Sanger. Ottawa: Canadian Centre for Policy Alternatives and James Lorimer & Company Ltd.

Swift, Jamie. 1983. *Cut and Run*. Toronto: Between the Lines.

Switzer, Jacqueline Vaughan. 1997. *Green Backlash*. Boulder: Lynne Rienner Publishers, Inc.

Tammemagi, Hans. 1999. *The Waste Crisis*. Toronto: Oxford University Press.

'The Mail'. 2000. *Maclean's*, 26 June.

Thoreau, Henry David. 2001. *Walden*. < http://www.walden.org > (12 May).

Tokar, Brian. 1992. *The Green Alternative*. San Pedro: R. & E. Miles.

Torgerson, Douglas. 1999. *The Promise of Green Politics*. Durham: Duke University Press.

UNEP Press Release. 2000. '$440 million agreed for phasing out developing country CFCs'. 3 Dec.

UNEP Press Release. 1999. 'There is no room for complacency'. 16 Sept.

UNEP. 1998. *Policy Effectiveness and Multilateral Environmental Agreements*. Environment and Trade 17.

'UN Says Foot-and-Mouth a Global Threat'. 2001. Canadian Broadcasting Corporation News Online. < http://www.cbc.ca > (15 Mar. 2001).

'U.S. Pulls Out of Kyoto Protocol'. 2001. Environment News Service. < http://www.ens.lycos.com > (13 May 2001).

Urquhart, Ian. 1999. 'Lands Deal May Not Last a Lifetime after All'. *Toronto Star*, 4 Aug.

Vanderwerth, W.C., ed. 1971. *Indian Oratory: Famous Speeches by Noted Indian Chieftains*. Norman: University of Oklahoma Press.

Vanderzwaag, David and Linda Duncan. 1992. 'Canada and Environmental Protection'. In *Canadian Environmental Policy: Ecosystems, Politics, and Process*. Edited by Robert Boardman. Toronto: Oxford University Press.

VanNijnatten, Debora L. 1999. 'The ARET Challenge'. In *Voluntary Initiatives and the New Politics of Corporate Greening*. Edited by Robert B. Gibson. Peterborough: Broadview Press.

Wapner, Paul. 1995. 'In Defense of Banner Hangers: The Dark Green Politics of Greenpeace'. In *Ecological Resistance Movements*. Edited by Bron Raymond Taylor. Albany: The State University of New York Press.

Warren, Karen J. 1989. 'Feminism and Ecology: Making Connections'. *Environmental Ethics* 11.

————., ed. 1997. *Ecofeminism*. Bloomington and Indianapolis: Indiana University Press.

Welch, Ross M. 1999. 'Toward a Greener Revolution: Creating More Healthful Food Systems'. *Agricultural Research* (May).

Wells, Donald T. 1996. *Environmental Policy*. Saddle River, N.J.: Prentice-Hall.

White, Lynn. 1994. 'The Historical Roots of Our Ecological Crisis'. In *This Sacred Earth*. Edited by Roger S. Gottlieb. New York: Routledge.

Wilson, Jeremy. 1998. *Talk and Log: Wilderness Politics in British Columbia*. Vancouver: UBC Press.

Windfield, Mark. 1994. 'The Ultimate Horizontal Issue: The Environmental Policy Experiences of Alberta and Ontario, 1971–1993'. *Canadian Journal of Political Science* 27.

Wirth, John D. 2000. *Smelter Smoke in North America: The Politics of Transborder Pollution*. Lawrence, Kans.: University of Kansas Press.

Wissenberg, Marcel. 1998. *Green Liberalism*. London: UCL Press.

World Commission on Environment and Development. 1987. *Our Common Future*. New York: United Nations.

World Wildlife Federation. 2000. *What Are POPs?* < http://www.wwf.ca > (31 Dec.).

Yaron, Gil. 2000. *The Final Frontier. A Working Paper on the Big 10 Global Water Corporations and the Privatization and Corporatization of the World's Last Public Resource*. Ottawa: Polaris Institute and the Council of Canadians.

Yearley, Steven. 1991. *The Green Case*. London: HarperCollinsAcademic.

2000. 'Burnt Church Mi'kmaq, DFO Set for Lobster Showdown'. *CBC News*. 11 Aug.

Index

9450

OCT 1 7 2003